Excel

SCIENCE
STUDY GUIDE

Year 10

Get the Results You Want!

Jim Stamell & Geoffrey Thickett

PASCAL
PRESS

Contents

CHAPTER 4

Motion, force and energy .. 137

CHAPTER 5

Investigations and problem solving............ 174

How to use this book

The Australian Curriculum

This study guide covers the complete course of the Year 10 Science Australian Curriculum including:

- all core knowledge
- all required problem-solving skills
- all aspects of the scientific method.

The book is divided into sections based on the Australian Curriculum's three learning strands and substrands. The three learning strands in the Australian Curriculum are:

- Science Understandings (Biological Sciences; Chemical Sciences, Earth and Space Sciences; Physical Sciences)
- Science as a Human Endeavour
- Science Inquiry Skills.

The Science as a Human Endeavour strand is covered in Chapters 1 to 4, plus each substrand of the Science Understandings strand is treated as follows:

- Chapter 1—Biological Sciences
- Chapter 2—Chemical Sciences
- Chapter 3—Earth and Space Sciences
- Chapter 4—Physical Sciences.

Chapter 5 covers the Science Inquiry Skills strand.

Tips for tests and examinations

Preparation

In order to prepare for your school exams, you will need to examine the Contents section at the front of the book and then identify the relevant sections of this book before you begin to revise and practise exam-style questions.

Each topic in your school programs for Year 10 may have integrated content from more than one of these different areas of study. It is unlikely that you will have studied the content in this order.

You need to allow sufficient time for this thorough revision—at least one week for a class test and at least three weeks for a major examination. Revise the content of the chapter or section and attempt all questions. Use the supplied answers to determine which areas you need further work in.

Test/exam questions

Multiple-choice questions

In order to answer these sorts of questions, make sure that you do the following.

- Read the stem of the question thoroughly.
- Look carefully at any diagrams, flow charts or tables, and interpret them thoroughly.
- Choose the letter of the best response and not just a correct independent statement; if you don't know the answer, make the most logical choice you can.

Free-response questions

In order to answer this type of question effectively, follow the guidelines below.

- Highlight the verbs and key words in the question and respond accordingly.
- Don't waste time by restating the question; keep your answers concise.
- Label any diagrams that you draw with a pencil and ruler.
- Line graphs should occupy more than 80% of the available grid space.
- All graphs must have a title and the axes should have linear scales and be appropriately labelled with titles and units.
- Any experimental methods must be written as a series of numbered sentences in the present or past tense.
- Repeating the experiment at least five times or more can improve the reliability of experimental results.
- For questions involving the scientific method, ensure that you state the dependent and independent variables, the variables you controlled (kept the same) and the experiment that you used as a control.
- When drawing a table of data, ensure that the table is fully bounded by lines to create columns and rows. The column headings and units should occupy the first row.

Features of this book

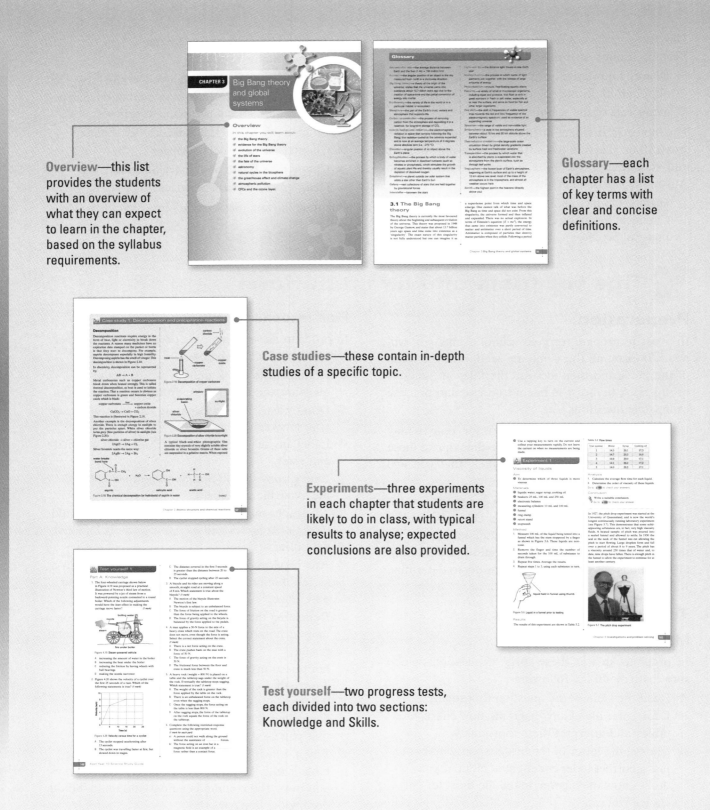

Overview—this list provides the students with an overview of what they can expect to learn in the chapter, based on the syllabus requirements.

Glossary—each chapter has a list of key terms with clear and concise definitions.

Case studies—these contain in-depth studies of a specific topic.

Experiments—three experiments in each chapter that students are likely to do in class, with typical results to analyse; expected conclusions are also provided.

Test yourself—two progress tests, each divided into two sections: Knowledge and Skills.

You will be thoroughly prepared for examinations and tests when you use this study guide. This guide is an effective revision and study program for exams and class tests in Year 10.

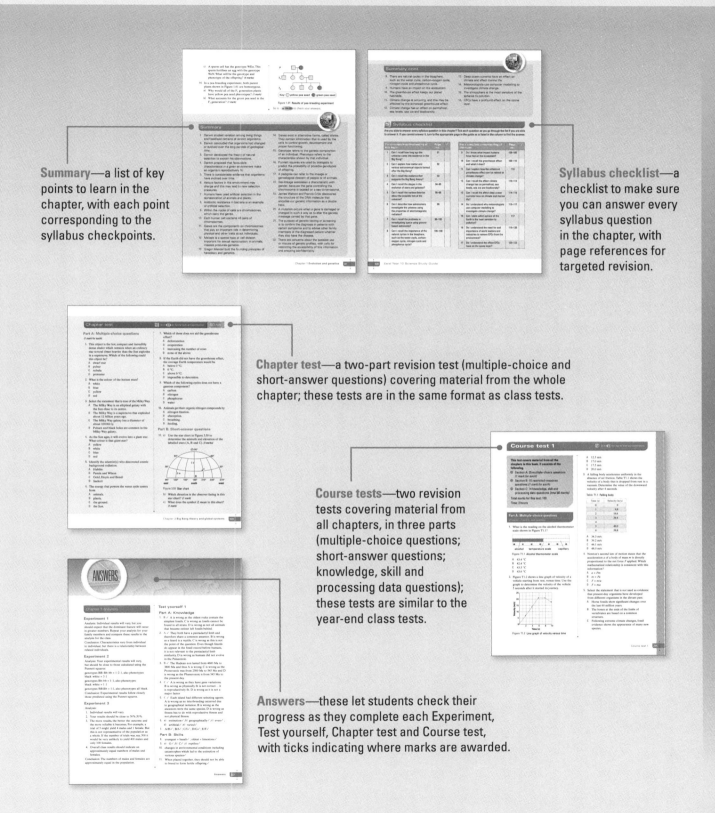

Summary—a list of key points to learn in the chapter, with each point corresponding to the syllabus checkpoints.

Syllabus checklist—a checklist to make sure you can answer every syllabus question in the chapter, with page references for targeted revision.

Chapter test—a two-part revision test (multiple-choice and short-answer questions) covering material from the whole chapter; these tests are in the same format as class tests.

Course tests—two revision tests covering material from all chapters, in three parts (multiple-choice questions; short-answer questions; knowledge, skill and processing data questions); these tests are similar to the year-end class tests.

Answers—these let students check their progress as they complete each Experiment, Test yourself, Chapter test and Course test, with ticks indicating where marks are awarded.

CHAPTER 1

Evolution and genetics

Overview

In this chapter you will learn about:

- Charles Darwin and the theory of evolution
- evidence for evolution by natural selection
- the geological time scale
- Darwin's tree of life
- environmental selection pressures
- artificial selection
- antibiotic- and pesticide-resistant strains of pathogens
- chromosomes and genes
- meiosis and fertilisation
- Gregor Mendel and his pea experiments
- dominant and recessive genes
- genotypes and phenotypes
- genetic crosses, pedigrees and sex-linked genes
- Watson and Crick's model of DNA
- DNA mutation
- genetic technologies.

Glossary

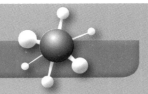

Allele—an alternative form of a gene (one member of a pair) that is located at a specific position on a specific chromosome

Anaemia—a deficiency in the number of red blood cells or in their haemoglobin content. There is a reduced ability of blood to transfer oxygen to different tissues. This results in pallor, shortness of breath and lack of energy.

Antibiotic resistance—the presence of antibiotics in the environment of bacteria can act as a selecting agent and promote the growth of resistant strains

Artificial selection—selective breeding of plants and animals to produce desirable qualities

Autosome—a chromosome other than a sex chromosome

Carrier—an organism possessing a recessive gene whose effect is masked by a dominant allele; the associated trait is not apparent but can be passed on to offspring

Comparative anatomy—the science of comparing similar structures in the bodies of animals or plants

Cross-pollinate—the transfer of pollen from the anthers of one flower to the stigma of another flower such as by the action of wind or insects

Diploid—a cell or organism consisting of two sets of chromosomes: usually, one set from each parent

DNA—acronym for **d**eoxyribo**n**ucleic **a**cid, a long linear polymer found in the nucleus of a cell, shaped like a double helix

Eon—the largest division of the geological time scale

Evolution—the genetic change in organisms that leads to the production of new species

Extinction—the permanent disappearance of a species

Gene—a molecular unit of heredity of a living organism; a segment of DNA, occupying a specific place on a chromosome

Genetics—the study of the patterns of inheritance of specific traits; a branch of biology dealing with heredity

Genome—all of the genetic information (all of the hereditary material) possessed by an organism

Geographic isolation—habitats can be isolated from one another by geographical features such as oceans, rivers, cliffs, deserts and so on

Haploid—an organism or cell having only one complete set of chromosomes, ordinarily half the normal diploid number

Karyotype—the chromosomes of a cell, usually shown as an arrangement of chromosome pairs in descending order of size

Mutation—a change in the code sequence of a DNA molecule

Natural selection—the process in which species naturally reproduce and pass on to their offspring characteristics that make them more suited to their environment; this process is affected by the environment

Nucleotides—the basic components that make up a DNA molecule

Progeny—a genetic descendant or offspring

Punnett square—a diagrammatic representation of a particular cross in genetics used to calculate the frequencies of the different genotypes and phenotypes among the offspring; first used in 1942

Pure-breeding—identical individuals that are bred for many generations from members of the same strain and always produce offspring with the same physical features when self-pollinated or cross-pollinated with other identical individuals

Radiometric dating—a process of measuring the age of a rock, mineral or fossil by measuring the activity of various radioisotopes in the sample

Replication—the process by which the DNA molecule makes a copy of itself

Self-pollinate—the transfer of pollen from the anthers to the stigma of the same flower or of another flower on the same plant

Species—a group of organisms that can naturally breed to produce fertile offspring

Survival of the fittest—those organisms that have been selected by the environment and survive to reproduce

Trait—a distinguishing characteristic or quality; the expression of genes in an observable way such as eye colour, blood type or nose size

Triplet code—a sequence of three nucleobases (nitrogen bases)

Variation—differences in characteristics in a population

1.1 Darwin and evolution by natural selection

In the 1830s a young 23-year-old graduate called Charles Darwin joined a scientific expedition as a naturalist on the naval ship *HMS Beagle* that set out to survey the coast of South America. During the 5-year voyage that took the *Beagle* around the world, Darwin collected specimens of plants and animals and studied the geology of each region he visited. He sent rocks, fossils and information about the geology of South America back to England. During the voyage of the *Beagle*, Darwin started to think about the evidence for the theory of the great catastrophes in the Earth's past. This theory proposed that the forces that operate on the Earth today also operated in the past and that catastrophes were not necessary to explain the changes in the Earth and its life forms over time.

On his return to England, Darwin began to organise his collected specimens and fossils. During the voyage, he had noticed the wide variety of life forms and the great variations within each species. On the islands of the Galapagos in the Pacific Ocean, for instance, he had observed many different species of finches and giant tortoises. Each species seemed to occupy its own island. Darwin started to think that the population of finches on each island had originated from birds that had arrived from the mainland. He reasoned that the different conditions on each island had led to gradual changes until the finches eventually became different from each other. Some finches had become adapted to feeding on insects and lived mainly in the trees. Others lived in the low shrubs on the ground and had different-shaped beaks as their diets were different (see Figure 1.1).

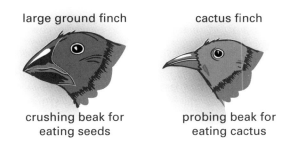

large ground finch

cactus finch

crushing beak for eating seeds

probing beak for eating cactus

Figure 1.1 Darwin's finches

For 20 years, Darwin studied and collected more information on variation among living species and the fossilised remains of extinct organisms. He also experimented with selective breeding to understand how some characteristics could be selected and how this might apply in natural examples. He came to the conclusion that over the long period of Earth's history, species had gradually changed or evolved.

Darwin proposed the theory of natural selection to explain his observations. Here are the major points of Darwin's theory.

1. There is a natural variation in characteristics within the population of any species. For example, humans have different hair colour, eye colour, height, blood type and many other characteristics. In kookaburras there is a natural variation in beak length, flight muscle strength and claw length.

2. In nature, organisms struggle to survive. A herbivore such as an antelope must eat sufficient grass each day to remain healthy. It must be fast enough to escape from hunting lions. Slow runners may be more readily captured. In times of drought, the weaker individuals may die from starvation. This struggle for survival also keeps the population numbers in check. A rapid population rise leads to less grass for each individual. The rise in population also leads to more food for carnivores and they then begin to bring the population of antelopes under control. Disease also keeps a population in check.

3. Organisms with favourable characteristics in a given environment will survive to reproduce. An organism that fails to reproduce is said to be 'reproductively unfit'. The organisms with the favourable characteristics have a better chance in competing for available food and water. Reproductive fitness does not necessarily correlate with physical fitness.

4. The population of future generations of a species will therefore contain a greater proportion of individuals who have inherited these favourable characteristics.

5. Gradually, the preservation of favourable characteristics leads to a change in the characteristics of the natural population. As long as the environment does not change, the species becomes better adapted to its environment. The environment has effectively selected certain characteristics for survival. This is also called survival of the fittest.

Darwin used his theory of natural selection to explain why the finches on the separate islands of the

Galapagos had become different species. He argued that certain variations in the natural populations were favoured on one island, but different characteristics were favoured on another. Thus, natural selection led to the populations of each island becoming different over time. Their geographic isolation ensured that the populations on different islands rarely interbred and so different species evolved on each island.

1.2 Evidence for evolution by natural selection

There is considerable evidence that present-day organisms have developed from different organisms in the distant past. Let's examine some of this evidence.

Earth is extremely old

The primitive Earth formed about 4600 million years ago as matter condensed from the spinning disk of a newly formed planetary nebula. The hot Earth then cooled and the landmasses, oceans and atmosphere formed.

Using the technique of radiometric dating, scientists have determined the absolute age of various rocks and minerals. This technique is based on measuring the relative quantities of radioactive elements and their decay products. With this information and a knowledge of the half-lives of radioisotopes such as uranium-238, rubidium-87 and potassium-40, scientists can measure the age of the rock sample.

Example: Zircons

These minerals contain potassium-40 and its decay product (argon-40). The half-life of potassium-40 is 1300 million years which means that it takes 1300 million years for half the original potassium-40 present in the zircon to decay into argon-40. The oldest zircons (dated by radiometric analysis) were formed 4200 million years ago. Radiometric measurements of Earth rocks and Moon rocks (from the Apollo missions) give ages between 3300 and 4000 million years.

The great age of Earth has allowed sufficient time for the processes of evolutionary change to occur.

Sedimentary strata and the law of superposition

Comparisons of rock sequences and sedimentary strata around the world led to the idea that the surface rock layers were younger than the deeper layers. William Smith (1769–1839) expressed this observation in the law of superposition (see Figure 1.2).

In a sequence of sedimentary strata, the layers are increasingly older with increasing depth from the surface.

Radiometric measurements have since confirmed this law.

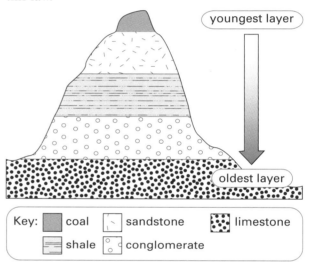

Figure 1.2 Law of superposition

The fossil record over geological time

Fossil record

Fossils are the remains or record of ancient life. The geologist Adam Sedgwick (1785–1873) was one of the first scientists to establish the great age of Cambrian fossils in Wales and Scotland. His work led to the idea that many fossils represented species that had become extinct in an ancient period of Earth's history.

Figure 1.3 shows an example of a trilobite fossil. These fossils became important in unravelling Earth's history because they evolved so rapidly, allowing geologists to date the rocks in which the trilobites are found. These widespread marine organisms spanned a number of geological time periods, and certain kinds of trilobites only appeared for a short geological period. Hence, finding these fossils can instantly tell geologits the age of the rock layer it is in.

Figure 1.3 Trilobite fossil

As more fossils were collected and analysed from various strata, it soon became apparent that the fossils in deeper sedimentary strata were less complex in body structure than fossils in higher strata. Radiometric measurements showed that these lower layers and fossils were much older than fossils in strata closer to the surface. Thus the fossils of the most primitive fish are found in much deeper (and older) layers than the earliest mammal fossils. The oldest fossil layers contain impressions or traces of simple single-celled organisms. Stromatolite fossils (a type of cyanobacteria) found in the Pilbara region in Western Australia have been dated at 3500 million years old.

The following points should be carefully noted.

> The fossil evidence therefore supports the view that the earliest life forms were very simple and that they changed into more complex organisms over geological time.
> Fossils reveal that the appearance of new life forms did not occur at an even rate over geological time.
> The fossil record has shown that more than one new species sometimes developed from a pre-existing species.
> The fossil record is incomplete since not all organisms become fossilised after death.

Geological time scale

The geological time scale divides the time between Earth's formation and the present into divisions and smaller subdivisions according to major events and the types of life forms that appeared or became extinct in Earth's history. As scientists gain more knowledge about these events, the placement of the divisions on the time scale is changed. The time scale shown in Figure 1.4 is an average of the current range of published data.

Note: you do not need to remember all the details shown in this time scale but you will be expected to process data based on it.

Some of the major features of the geological time scale include the following.

> The 4.6 billion years is divided into four eons of varying length.
> There is no fossil evidence of life forms in the Hadean eon (4.6 to 3.8 billion years ago).
> Simple life forms (bacteria) appeared in the Archaean eon (3.8 to 2.5 billion years ago).
> The fossil record shows increasing complexity of life forms in the Proterozoic eon (2.5 billion to 545 million years ago). Protozoans, aquatic plants and hard-shelled invertebrates (e.g. corals) had appeared by the end of this eon.
> The current eon is called Phanerozoic (545 million years ago to the present day) and shows the continued evolution of animals, including vertebrates, and land plants. The Phanerozoic eon is further divided into three eras. (The time before the Phanerozoic is often referred to as the Precambrian.) Some of the important events in these eras include the following.
>   • Palaeozoic era (545 to 248 million years ago). This era began with a period of rapid evolution; fish are the dominant vertebrates; amphibians and then reptiles evolve; land plants (mosses, ferns and the earliest conifers) appear; largest mass extinction of marine invertebrates ends the era.
>   • Mesozoic era (248 to 65 million years ago). Reptiles continue to evolve; dinosaurs appear and become extinct by the end of the Mesozoic; birds appear and the earliest mammals appear near the end of the era; large land plants such as conifers appear; flowering plants start to appear.
>   • Cainozoic (or Cenozoic) era (65 to 0 million years ago). Modern mammals appear; flowering plants dominate the land; humans appear about 2 million years ago.

These eras are further subdivided into small subunits called periods. The Cainozoic is now divided into seven epochs rather than two periods.

Eon	Era	Period	Fauna	Flora
Phanerozoic	Cenozoic (Cainozoic) 0 — 65	time is divided into 7 epochs 0 — 65	• humans appear 2 million years ago • mammals increase in size • mammals diversify • birds diversify	• modern flora • forests develop • grasslands • flowering plants diversify
	Mesozoic 248	Cretaceous 146	• dinosaurs flourish • major extinctions at end of Cretaceous (including dinosaurs)	• first flowering plants (magnolias/palms)
		Jurassic 208	• dinosaurs dominate • first birds	• conifers and ferns dominate
		Triassic 248	• many reptiles • first dinosaurs • first mammals	• conifers • cycads
	Palaeozoic	Permian 280	• amphibians and reptiles are dominant	• cone trees dominant
		Carboniferous 360	• giant insects • amphibians • early reptiles	• large tree ferns • increasing cone plants
		Devonian 408	• fish flourish • insects	• first ferns • first seed-bearing plants
		Silurian 438	• jawed fish • freshwater fish	• first vascular plants
		Ordovician 500	• primitive fish • molluscs • corals	• red/green algae • first land plants (mosses)
		Cambrian 545	• many marine invertebrates • trilobites and arthropods	• algae • no land plants
Proterozoic 2500	Precambrian	—	• soft-bodied invertebrates (jellyfish, worms) • algae in the oceans	
Archaean 3800		—	• life forms appear in the fossil record • simple cellular organisms including archaea, bacteria, cyanobacteria	
Hadean 4600		—	• no life—Earth too hot	

Figure 1.4 Geological time scale; dates are in Ma (millions of years ago)

Darwin's tree of life

Darwin likened the sequence of life forms over geologic time to the trunk and branches of a tree, as shown in Figure 1.5. The base of the trunk represented the simplest, primitive forms of life. Moving up the trunk, which is equivalent to moving through time, shows that some of the early life forms evolve into more complex organisms. Some evolutionary events lead to branches from the main trunk. The organism at a branching point becomes the common ancestor of several evolutionary lines. The common ancestor becomes extinct at the time of this divergence. Not all these branches survive over time, and so their evolutionary line becomes extinct. Other branches lead to the formation of the major kingdoms of living things. From these major branches spring smaller branches which form the major families, genera and species of each kingdom. An accurate tree of life cannot be drawn, because our knowledge is incomplete.

Evidence from horse fossils

The evolution of the modern horse (*Equus*) has been firmly established from fossils dating back to 60 million years ago. The ancient ancestor of the horse (*Eohippus*) had four toes (compared with

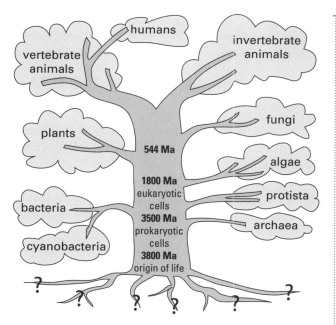

Figure 1.5 Darwin's tree of life; Ma = million years ago

one toe in *Equus*) and was as small as a dog. The sequence of fossil forms thus shows that the modern horse developed from a different organism in the distant past.

Fossil evidence describing the development of the horse supports evolution because it shows that organisms change over a long time.

Catastrophes and extinction events

The fossil record shows many examples of sudden mass extinctions where all members of a species disappear from the fossil record. These mass extinctions (which usually accounted for at least 75% of species alive at the time) seem to be related to worldwide catastrophes. The extinction of the dinosaurs at the end of the Mesozoic era (65 million years ago) is a well-known example of a catastrophic event. Over 99.9% of all species that have existed on Earth are now extinct. Scientists have collected evidence of catastrophic events that may be related to extreme climate change, sea level changes and collisions of comets/meteorites with Earth.

The fossil record shows that following each mass extinction, many new species appear.

The abundance of life forms has varied throughout geological time. This information can be displayed using a graph such as Figure 1.6. Abundance is shown

by the thickness of the band for each organism. The thicker the band, the more abundant is the organism. When the thickness drops to zero, the organism has become extinct.

Example: Trilobites

Trilobites are invertebrates (crawling and swimming arthropods) that thrived in shallow seas in the Palaeozoic era. They first appeared in the fossil record about 545 million years ago and became extinct about 245 million years ago as shown in Figure 1.6. Their appearance in the fossil record is often used to signal the start of the Palaeozoic era. Their period of greatest abundance was in the first 40 million years of the Palaeozoic era. Their numbers then declined and they became extinct near the close of the Palaeozoic era.

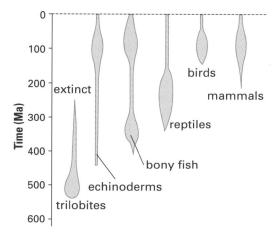

Figure 1.6 Extinctions and new species

Evidence from comparative anatomy

Georges Cuvier (1769–1832) compared the anatomy of fossils and related living organisms. He showed that these fossils were different from those of living species. Since then, comparative anatomy has shown that the bones at the ends of the forelimbs of many different vertebrates (including humans) are based on a common pattern or structure. Figure 1.7 compares the forelimbs of three different species.

The comparative anatomy data is used as evidence of evolution from a common ancestor in the distant past.

Evidence from geographic distribution of living things

The theory of plate tectonics explains that the continents of Earth are in constant motion. In the

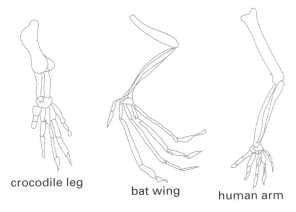

crocodile leg

bat wing

human arm

Figure 1.7 Comparison of the forelimbs of vertebrates

distant past the continents were joined and animals and plants were not geographically isolated as they are today. They were able to disperse across vast areas of land. As the giant continent (Pangaea) split up (about 225 million years ago) and the smaller landmasses moved to different latitudes, animals and plants became geographically isolated. Under these new environmental conditions, the animals and plants evolved to produce new species which were quite different to the common ancestral species, since the environments were so different. The east coast of South America and the west coast of Africa were formerly joined in a large continental mass called Gondwana. Australia, India and Antarctica were also part of this land mass. It began to break apart 100 million years ago as shown in Figure 1.8.

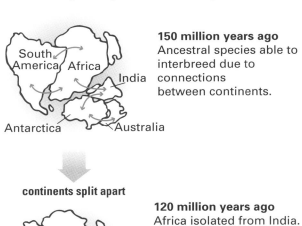

150 million years ago
Ancestral species able to interbreed due to connections between continents.

continents split apart

120 million years ago
Africa isolated from India. Interbreeding between populations in Africa and India ceases; populations evolve independently due to geographical isolation.

Figure 1.8 Continental drift

Comparisons of various fern and reptile fossils from along the margins of these separated continents show that many modern species shared a common ancestor.

Evidence from biochemistry and DNA analysis

Chimpanzees and humans share identical amino acid sequences in several enzymes (proteins) found in their respiratory systems. This shows that the DNA genetic code for these proteins is the same in both species. Overall, humans and chimpanzees have 98.4% of DNA in common. This and other DNA evidence suggests that humans and chimpanzees shared a common ancestor about 4 to 5 million years ago. This common (extinct) ancestor was quite different from both modern humans and chimpanzees. Biologists have established evolutionary trees of organisms based on DNA sequences. These evolutionary sequences show the importance of DNA mutations in the process of evolutionary change. It is important to remember that humans did not evolve from chimpanzees or apes. These animals are just as modern as we are; we just had a common ancestor in the long-distant past.

The great similarities of some enzymes and DNA of chimpanzees and humans support evolution, as they point to a recent common ancestor that gave rise to humans and chimpanzees.

1.3 Environmental selection pressures

Environmental selection pressures affect the survival of species over a short term (e.g. months and years) or a long term (e.g. millions of years). Various factors in the environment may change and this may lead to new selection pressures. Selection pressures need to affect reproduction and survival to have any effect on evolution. For example, if a new predator in an area only eats old prey that are past reproductive age then this will not have any effect on the prey's evolution. However, if another predator only eats immature prey then the loss of genetic variation in these pre-reproductive individuals will have a great effect on the survival and evolution of the prey.

Let's look at some examples.

> Climate change. Consider an example where the original local environment was temperate with

good rainfall and over time the climate changed so it became more arid with very little rainfall. Plants would initially be affected and plants that have high water requirements will struggle to survive and may gradually die out. This will allow other plants that are tolerant to drying out to survive and then reproduce and colonise the area. This in turn will affect the population of animals that depend on these plants. Over time the living organisms in this local environment will change.

> Disease. If a new virus is introduced into a natural population of monkeys, it can spread quickly if most monkeys are not immune. Many deaths may occur but those that have natural immunity due to variations in their genes will survive and reproduce and so over time the proportion of naturally immune individuals will increase.

> Gene mutation. Genes can change over time and these changes are called mutations. While most mutations are harmful, some are beneficial and lead to changes in a population. Consider two species of moth (white and brown) in a grassy woodland. The caterpillars of these moths eat the grasses and compete for this food resource. If a beneficial mutation occurs in the brown moths that leads to stronger mouthparts and larger bodies, which may allow these brown caterpillars to eat grass at a faster rate than the white caterpillars, then the gene mutation has created a selection pressure. White moth caterpillars can no longer compete for food as well as the brown moth caterpillars and so fewer survive to reproduce.

There are two well-known examples of mutations in humans that produce resistance to infection by malarial parasites. In North Africa, some of the population have a blood group called Duffy. There are three types: Duffy A, Duffy B and Duffy negative. The few that have the Duffy negative blood are less likely to be infected with malaria. This gene mutation has produced a protein that works in a similar way to the old protein, but with additional functions that assist in preventing infection.

Sickle-cell anaemia is another example of a mutation that can be sometimes beneficial and sometimes harmful. The sickle-cell allele causes the normally round red blood cell to have a sickle shape. Two copies of the gene is fatal, but one copy leads to sickle-cell anaemia. In general this is a harmful mutation because the sickle cells are less efficient at absorbing oxygen than normal

red blood cells. In certain areas of Africa where malaria is prevalent, the mutation is favourable because people with sickle-shaped blood cells are less likely to become infected with malaria. They survive while those with normal blood cells die. There is a relative advantage in having the mutant gene in that environment (see Figure 1.9).

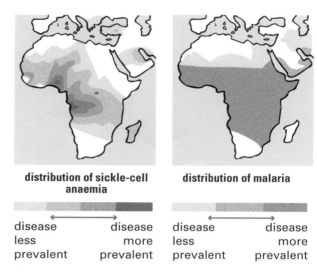

distribution of sickle-cell anaemia

distribution of malaria

disease less prevalent ⟷ disease more prevalent

disease less prevalent ⟷ disease more prevalent

Figure 1.9 Distribution of sickle-cell anaemia and malaria in Africa

> Geographical isolation. Geographical isolation can prevent interbreeding in a population. Consider Figure 1.10 in which the natural population of an organism consists of dark and light individuals that normally can interbreed. If an event occurs that leads to geographical isolation then the new environments may result in survival advantages of each group. Over time the proportion of the dark and light individuals in each new environment changes. If further changes (e.g. mutations) occur over time then the populations can become so different that they can no longer interbreed if individuals are brought back together (e.g. in a zoo). The variations in the finches on the Galapagos islands occurred over time because of geographical isolation.

1.4 Artificial selection

Humans have used artificial selection in the domestication of animals and plants. Various animals and plants have been selectively bred to produce desirable qualities. People (rather than nature) select the animals and plants that will reproduce. Selective breeding leads to a decrease in genetic diversity. This

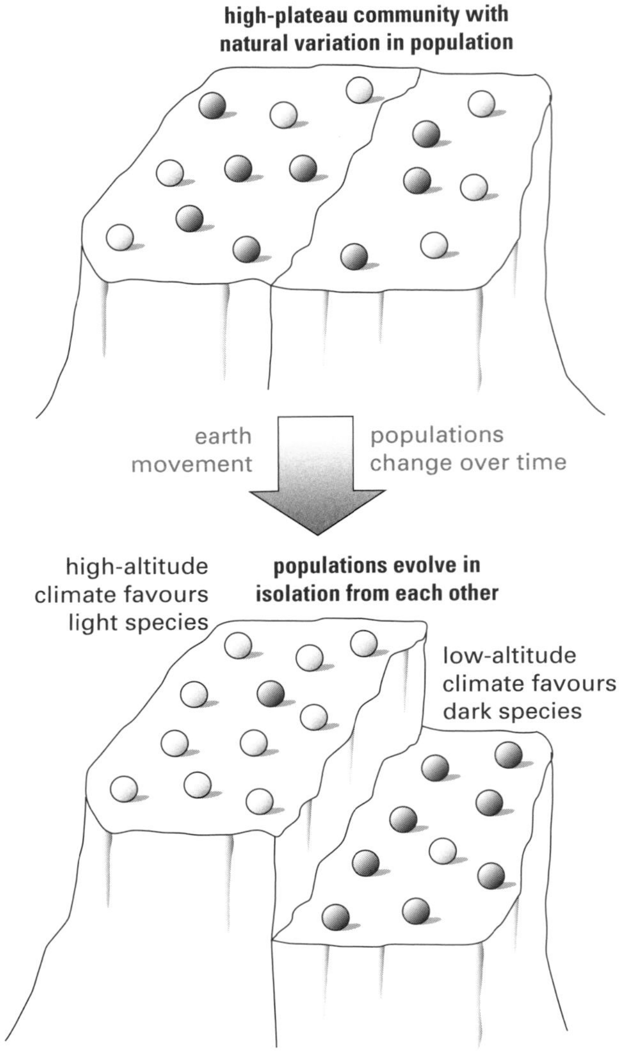

high-plateau community with natural variation in population

earth movement

populations change over time

high-altitude climate favours light species

populations evolve in isolation from each other

low-altitude climate favours dark species

Figure 1.10 Geographic isolation

can lead to serious consequences as it eliminates the natural variation required for natural selection to work. The following are some examples of artificial selection.

- Broccoli, cauliflower and cabbage. All these vegetables are the result of selective breeding from variants of wild mustard. Wild mustards typically produce yellow flowers but due to natural variation there are some mutants in which the flower never properly develops. By selectively breeding these mutants over many years, farmers have developed the modern broccoli.

- Corn. Wild corn had kernels that fell off the cob and this method allowed the seeds to be dispersed. A mutant variety of wild corn had kernels that did not fall off. This mutant variety was effectively sterile as it could not disperse its seeds. Humans selectively bred this mutant and so after many generations it became the dominant variety of corn despite the fact that it could not reproduce in the wild.

- Granny Smith apple. The Granny Smith apple originated in Eastwood (Sydney), New South Wales, in 1868 from a chance seedling propagated by Maria Ann Smith. The tree is thought to be a hybrid of *Malus sylvestris*, the European wild apple, pollinated with the domestic apple *M. domestica*. Granny Smith apples are light green in colour. They are eaten raw and commonly used in pie baking, and are popular around the world.

- Chickens. Over thousands of years, chickens (*Gallus gallus domesticus*) have been selectively bred to lay lots of eggs. The wild fowls of South-East Asia and India were the ancestors of these chickens. Some of these ancestral chickens were selected as they laid more eggs than the average. Laying hens in their prime may produce as many as 300 eggs a year. By continually breeding the best egg-laying chickens, more chicks are born with these favourable genes. Other chickens were bred for their meat; they can put on a lot of mass in a short period of time. Meat chickens from commercial intensive farming generally live for 6 weeks before slaughter while a free-range, or organic-meat, chicken will usually be slaughtered at around 14 weeks.

- Dogs. There are over 150 breeds of dogs. They are all descended from wolves. Using artificial selection, dogs of all different sizes, features and behaviours have been bred with desirable characteristics. These desirable characteristics are then maintained by ensuring that only dogs of the same breed are allowed to mate. It is important to remember that all the different breeds of dog are still the same species (*Canis familiaris*).

- Pigeons. Charles Darwin observed that there were many variants in a pigeon population. These variations help the pigeons to survive and reproduce. In 1855 Darwin set up a pigeon house to closely study this variation. His research showed that the many breeds of pigeons all derive from one ancestral pigeon called the rock pigeon (*Columba livia*). Over hundreds of years, breeders had been able to select for a variety of minor traits present in the natural pigeon population.

1.5 Antibiotic- and pesticide-resistant strains of pathogens

Since World War II, antibiotics have been used to cure bacterial diseases. The first antibiotic developed was penicillin which was extracted from a fungus called *Penicillium*. Since then many different types of antibiotics have been developed. Scientists have observed that over time, an antibiotic loses its ability to kill particular bacteria. This is known as antibiotic resistance and it is an example of artificial selection. A natural population of bacteria has variation due to natural mutations. Some of these strains or variants are not killed when exposed to antibiotics and so over time the presence of antibiotics in their environment acts as a selecting agent and the population of antibiotic-resistant strains rises. It is important to remember that these resistant strains always existed in the natural population in small numbers but the change in the environment produced by the presence of the antibiotic (the selecting agent) has led to the resistant strains becoming dominant.

Staphylococcus aureus is a pathogenic bacteria that is found on the skin and mucous membranes of at least a third of the world's population. Within 4 years of the mass production of penicillin, resistant strains of this bacteria (commonly called staph) had developed. One of the major causes of the development of resistant strains is the failure to take a sufficient dose of the antibiotic. If a patient does not take the full course of antibiotic then the frequency of resistant strains increases and this genetic resistance to an antibiotic can be transferred to other bacteria.

Methicillin-resistant *Staphylococcus aureus* (MRSA) is a bacterium responsible for several difficult-to-treat infections in humans. (Methicillin is a semi-synthetic antibiotic related to penicillin. While it is rarely prescribed now, the term is still used to describe strains resistant to all penicillins.) This resistance does make MRSA infection more difficult to treat with standard antibiotics and hence more dangerous. MRSA is especially a problem in hospitals and nursing homes where patients with open wounds, invasive devices inserted and weakened immune systems are at greater risk of infection than the general public.

The number of drug-resistant microbes is rising and their increase is linked to the use of antibiotics in livestock such as pigs and poultry. Resistance develops when some microbes survive the drug treatment (see Figure 1.11). Avoparcin is an antibiotic drug which has been regularly used by pig and poultry farmers as a growth promoter. It prevents the growth of undesirable bacteria in the intestines of these animals and helps in the uptake of protein in the animals' diet. Vancomycin is an antibiotic used in humans to treat infections that do not respond to other antibiotics. Vancomycin and avoparcin have

1. Antibiotic avoparcin is fed to pigs and poultry to promote growth.

2. Animals' enterococci bacteria become resistant to avoparcin—and incidentally to vancomycin, a similar human antibiotic.

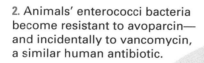

3. Hundreds of millions of resistant organisms are excreted in each gram of faeces.

4. Resistant pig bacteria may be transferred via piggery waste to humans working with the animals.

5. Chicken bacteria can spread through the carcass when processing often bursts intestines.

6. Humans can be infected during meat preparation or by eating improperly cooked meals.

Figure 1.11 Antibiotics used in farming pigs and chickens

many chemical similarities. Microbes that cause diseases such as tuberculosis and bacterial infections are developing strains that are resistant to antibiotic treatments, including vancomycin.

Agriculture has been plagued for thousands of years by pests that eat crops. Farmers have used selective breeding practices to create varieties of fruits, grains and vegetables that are naturally more resistant to plant pathogens. These plant pathogens include caterpillars, spiders, grasshoppers, beetles, bacteria and fungi. In the 20th century, chemical companies developed pesticide sprays that killed the pests without killing the crops. Over time, pesticide resistance developed in a similar way to antibiotic resistance. Continued use of pesticides led to an increase in pesticide-resistant strains of these pathogens as shown in Figure 1.12. Continued use of streptomycin pesticides that are used to control a bacterial disease of apples called 'fire blight' have led to streptomycin-resistant bacteria. The pesticides are acting as selecting agents which promote change in the natural population.

Monoculture is an agricultural practice of growing one single crop, with very little genetic variation, over a wide area. It is commonly used in modern industrial agriculture allowing for large harvests requiring minimal labour. However, monocultures can lead to the quicker spread of diseases, where a uniform crop is susceptible to a pathogen. Modern agriculturists have selected crops for high yields and high palatability, making them more susceptible to pests as they sacrifice natural resistance for productivity. These genetically homogenous monocultures do not possess the necessary ecological defence mechanisms to tolerate the impact of potential pest populations. Despite the substantial increase in the use of pesticides (currently about 500000 t annually of active ingredient worldwide), the loss of yields due to pests in many crops can reach 20 to 30%.

 Test yourself 1

Part A: Knowledge

1. Which statement is true concerning the fossil record? *(1 mark)*
   - **A** The oldest rocks contain the most complex fossil forms.
   - **B** Amphibians occur in the fossil record before birds.
   - **C** Fossils can be found in all rock strata from each geological period since the beginning of the world.
   - **D** Fossils of extinct animals and plants can be found in the rock strata of the Earth.

2. Figure 1.13 shows the bones of the limb of a lizard. They are similar to the bones found in a human's forearm. This similarity is used to support which one of the following ideas? *(1 mark)*

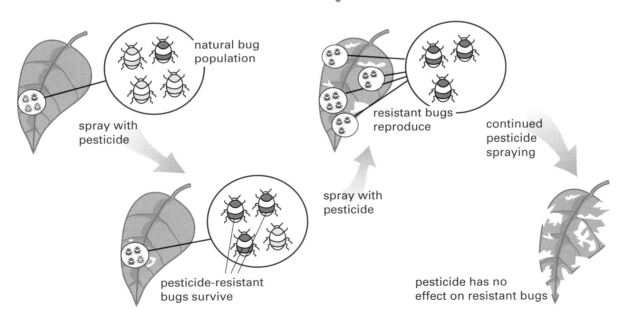

Figure 1.12 Pesticide resistance

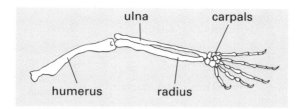

Figure 1.13 Limb bones of a lizard

A Lizards and humans have evolved from a common ancestor in the distant past.

B Both animals are mammals.

C Lizards appeared in the fossil record before humans.

D Both animals evolved in the Palaeozoic era.

3. Fossils of ancient bacteria have been found in Australian rocks that date back to 3.2 billion years ago. In which eon of time did these bacteria live? *(1 mark)*

A Hadean

B Archaean

C Proterozoic

D Phanerozoic

4. A major point in Darwin's theory of natural selection is that *(1 mark)*

A all members in a natural population of a species have identical genetic characteristics.

B only the physically fit organisms survive to reproduce.

C living things with favourable characteristics in a given environment survive long enough to reproduce.

D disease is the major factor in an organism's struggle for existence.

5. Darwin studied the various species of finch on the Galapagos Islands in the Pacific Ocean. He concluded from this study that *(1 mark)*

A the finches on each island had interbred with finches from other islands for millions of years.

B the ancestors of the finches from different islands were different species.

C different environmental-selecting agents on each island had led to the finches evolving into separate species.

D geographic isolation had led to new species only when the physically fit finches could fly between different islands.

6. Complete the following restricted-response questions using the appropriate word.
   (1 mark for each part)

   a) The extinction of the dinosaurs was an .... event that occurred at the end of the Mesozoic Era (65 million years ago).

   b) Evolution occurs when members of a species become .... isolated.

   c) Fossils reveal that evolution of new species did not occur at an .... rate over geological time.

   d) Antibiotic resistance is an example of .... selection.

   e) The abundance of life forms has .... throughout geological time.

7. Use the code letters to match the terms or phrases in each column. *(1 mark for each part)*

Column 1		Column 2	
A	Charles Darwin	F	age of strata increases with depth
B	favourable characteristics	G	incomplete
C	environment	H	Galapagos Islands
D	fossil record	I	selecting agent
E	law of superposition	J	reproductively fit

Part B: Skills

8. Figure 1.14 shows a sequence of rock layers in a cutting. Name the youngest and oldest layers.
   (2 marks)

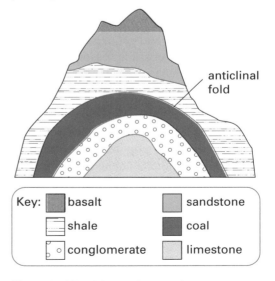

Figure 1.14 Rock layers in a cutting

9. According to Darwin's theory of evolution, different species share a common ancestor sometime in the geological past. The tree of life shows the location of this common ancestor by the point where two separate branches meet. Look at the section of an evolutionary tree in Figure 1.15 and answer the following questions.

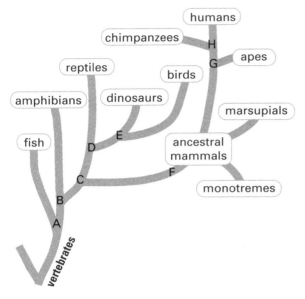

Figure 1.15 Branches of an evolutionary tree

a) Which letter represents the common ancestor of humans and apes? *(1 mark)*

b) Which letter represents the common ancestor of birds and mammals? *(1 mark)*

c) Which modern vertebrate class shares a common ancestor with the extinct dinosaurs? *(1 mark)*

10. Some organisms existed for quite long periods of geological time and yet eventually became extinct. Suggest a possible reason for the extinction of organisms. *(1 mark)*

11. For sexually reproducing organisms, the term *species* is defined as 'a population of organisms that are capable of interbreeding'. How could you prove that each population of finches on the islands of the Galapagos are separate species? *(1 mark)*

12. The bones in the forelimbs of various vertebrate animals have been used as an argument for the proposal that organisms evolve from a common ancestor. Figure 1.16 shows the forelimb bones of various vertebrates and, as a comparison, a human forearm.

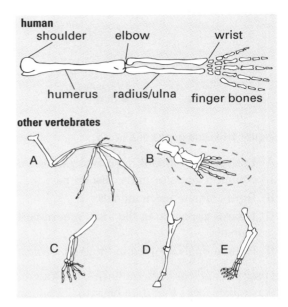

Figure 1.16 Forearms of vertebrates

a) Which forelimbs correspond with the following animals?
   i) lion *(1 mark)*
   ii) bat *(1 mark)*
   iii) whale *(1 mark)*
   iv) frog *(1 mark)*
   v) horse *(1 mark)*

b) Explain how these forelimb bones could be used to argue a case for a common ancestor. *(2 marks)*

13. Figure 1.17 shows a portion of the tree of life showing the evolution of the plant kingdom. Study the tree and answer the following questions.

a) Flowering plants (angiosperms) can be classified into two groups called monocotyledons and dicotyledons.
   i) How far back in time did these two groups diverge from a common ancestor? *(1 mark)*
   ii) Name a modern member of each of these groups. *(2 marks)*

b) i) How long ago did the first land plants appear? *(1 mark)*
   ii) What group of land plants appeared first in the fossil record? *(1 mark)*

c) What group are the ancestors of the angiosperms? *(1 mark)*

d) i) Which group appears first in the fossil record: the angiosperms or the gymnosperms? *(1 mark)*

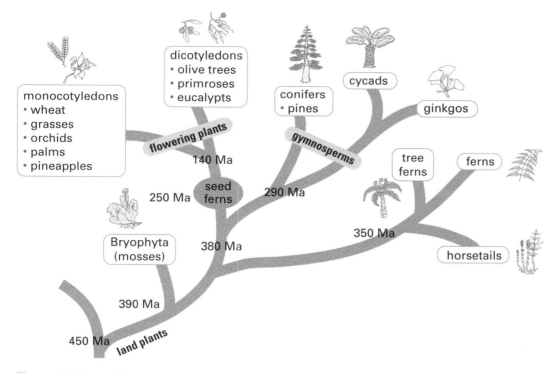

Figure 1.17 Tree of life for the plant kingdom

ii) Name some modern members of the gymnosperms. *(2 marks)*

iii) Gymnosperms evolved from ferns. Is this statement true or false? *(1 mark)*

e) Which two of the following plants are most closely related: pines, grass, olive tree, tree fern, palms? *(1 mark)*

14. Of all the species that have ever lived on Earth, 99.9% are now extinct. Five times in the last 500 million years the global ecosystem has collapsed and over 75% of life forms on the planet at each time suddenly went extinct.

The five great extinction events occurred at the following times:

E_1 = 440 Ma

E_2 = 365 Ma

E_3 = 251 Ma

E_4 = 205 Ma

E_5 = 65 Ma.

a) The largest of these events was 251 Ma, when 96% of species became extinct. In what geological era and period did this extinction event occur? *(2 marks)*

b) One of these events signalled the end of the dinosaurs. When did this occur? *(1 mark)*

c) Figure 1.18 shows a graph of the change in sea level over the last 500 million years.

One extinction event led to 75% of marine species disappearing. Which extinction event do you think this might be? *(1 mark)*

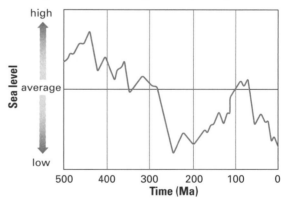

Figure 1.18 Sea level changes

Go to **pp. 227–228** to check your answers.

1.6 Chromosomes and genes

Cells are the basic building blocks of all living things. We as humans, for example, are made up of trillions of cells. They provide structure for the body, take in nutrients from food, convert those nutrients into energy, allow us to grow, and carry out all the specialised functions that make us who we are. Cells also contain our body's hereditary material and can make copies of themselves.

DNA, or deoxyribonucleic acid, is the hereditary material in almost all organisms including humans. Nearly every cell has the same DNA, with most of it being located in the cell nucleus. A small amount of DNA is also found in mitochondria.

Chromosomes

Hidden from normal view in the nucleus of each cell, the DNA molecule is packaged into thread-like structures called chromosomes. Each chromosome is made up of DNA that makes many tight coils around supporting proteins as shown in Figure 1.19.

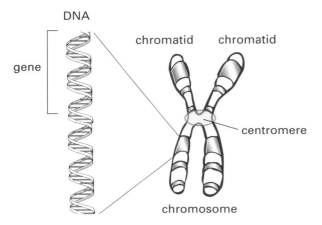

Figure 1.19 Structure of a chromosome

When the cell is not dividing, chromosomes are not visible in the cell's nucleus. But they do become visible under a microscope when the cell begins to divide. Most of what we know about chromosomes was found by observing chromosomes during cell division.

Each chromosome has a centromere, a constriction point, dividing the chromosome into two parts, or 'arms'. Each of these two identical parts of the chromosome (the left and right parts in Figure 1.19) is referred to as a chromatid. Where the centromere is located on each chromosome gives the chromosome its characteristic shape, and helps to locate specific genes.

When chromosomes are coiled and condensed, it is possible to take a photograph of the entire set of chromosomes using a microscope. In higher plants and animals, chromosomes from body cells can be matched up in pairs as shown in Figure 1.20. These pairs are known as homologous chromosomes, as they look alike. The chromosomes can be arranged in a diagram called a karyotype. In a karyotype the chromosomes are paired and arranged from largest to smallest, and numbered.

Notice the following about Figure 1.20.

> Humans normally possess 46 chromosomes: 22 pairs + 1 pair of sex chromosomes

> Males possess one X and one Y chromosome; females possess two X chromosomes.

> Except for the different sex chromosomes, which determine gender, the other chromosomes are identical in males and females.

The number of chromosomes in each cell of an organism has nothing to do with its size or

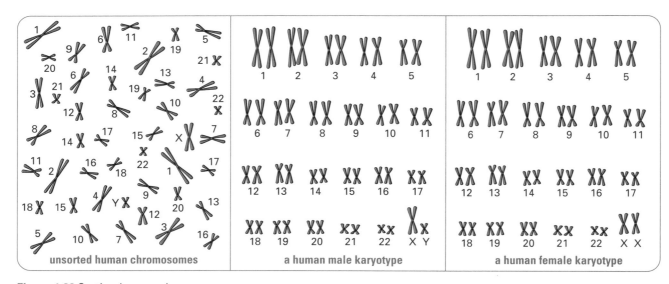

Figure 1.20 Sorting human chromosomes

intelligence. For example, the female of the jack jumper ant (*Myrmecia pilosula*), a species of bull ant that is native to Australia, has only two chromosomes. On the other hand, the adders tongue fern (genus *Ophioglossales*) has the highest chromosome count (1262) of any known living organism. Most other organisms, plant or animal, have less than 100 chromosomes.

Genes

Genes are the components on chromosomes that play an important role in determining physical and other traits about individuals (see Figure 1.21). They carry information that helps make you who you are: light or dark skin, curly or straight hair, tall or short, eye colour, the shape of your nose, blood type, and so on are all passed through the generations of your family in genes. A gene is a segment of DNA that issues instructions to the cells using chemically coded 'messages' to produce specific proteins that the cells can use.

Suppose the coils on a chromosome were stretched out. We can imagine beads to be located at various lengths along this coil. Each of these 'beads' is a gene, which is a piece of genetic information with one particular function. There are thousands of genes on each chromosome with about 23 000 genes making up the human genome. And every gene consists of thousands, even hundreds of thousands, of chemical units.

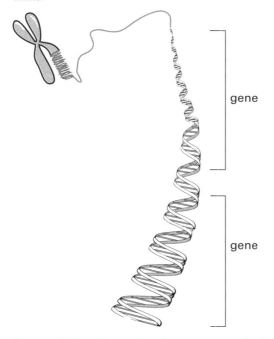

Figure 1.21 A region on the chromosome codes for a gene

Each gene is located at a specific point on the chromosome. Since chromosomes come in pairs, there are two copies of each gene. The exception applies to the genes carried on the sex chromosomes: the X and Y. Since men have only one copy of the X chromosome, they have only one copy of all the genes carried on the X chromosome.

Our bodies are composed of many different types of cells such as those in the skin, muscle, liver and brain performing different functions. All of these different cell types contain the same genes, and each cell requires particular proteins to function correctly. So different genes become active in different cells to produce the necessary specific proteins. This means that not all the genes in the cell are 'switched on' or active in every cell. For example, the genes that are needed in a kidney cell are different from the genes that are active in a lung cell.

The Human Genome Project, begun in 1990 and completed in 2003, had a primary goal to identify and map the genes of the human genome. Although the exact number of genes is still uncertain, work will be continuing for several more years to obtain a reliable measure. The reason for this uncertainty is that predictions are obtained from different computational methods and gene-finding programs.

1.7 Meiosis and fertilisation

In normal cell division (mitosis), two identical cells are formed from one original cell. These two new cells are called daughter cells and the original cell is called the parent cell. The daughter cells are identical to one another and to the original parent cell. In sexual reproduction, a different type of cell division called meiosis occurs.

But first, some definitions.

- Gamete: a cell that fuses with another cell during fertilisation (conception) in sexually reproducing organisms. A female gamete is called an ovum (or egg), while a male gamete is a sperm. In humans the ovum is about 20 times larger than the human sperm cell.
- Diploid cell: a cell that contains two sets of chromosomes, one set of chromosomes coming from each parent. For example, humans have two sets of 23 chromosomes (for a total of 46 chromosomes) in each of their body cells. This

is often abbreviated to $2n$, where n refers the number of pairs of chromosomes. For humans this equation would be $2n = 46$.

> Haploid cell: a cell that contains only one of each of the pairs of chromosomes. Gametes are haploid cells that are produced by meiosis. The haploid number refers to the number of chromosomes within the nucleus of a cell that comprises one complete chromosomal set. For humans this can be written as $n = 23$. The difference between haploid and diploid cells is shown in Figure 1.22.

> Fertilisation: the union of two sex cells, each with only a haploid number of chromosomes, resulting in a diploid zygote (the initial cell formed when two gamete cells are joined by means of sexual reproduction). For example, a human male sperm ($n = 23$) fuses with a human female egg ($n = 23$) to produce a fertilised egg, or zygote, where $2n = 46$. The entire process of development of new individuals is known as reproduction.

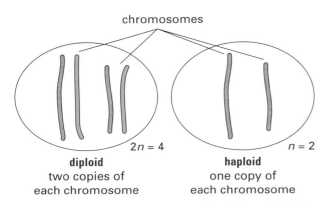

chromosomes

$2n = 4$
diploid
two copies of each chromosome

$n = 2$
haploid
one copy of each chromosome

Figure 1.22 The difference between haploid and diploid

Meiosis

Meiosis is a special type of cell division important for sexual reproduction. In animals, meiosis produces gametes (sperm and egg cells), while in some other organisms, such as bacteria, plants, algae and fungi, it generates spores.

While meiosis is similar to the cell division process of mitosis, there are two important differences.

> Chromosomes in meiosis recombine and this shuffles the genes around producing a different genetic combination in each gamete. This is called crossing-over.

> Meiosis gives rise to four genetically unique haploid cells, whereas mitosis produces two genetically identical diploid cells.

Figure 1.23 shows the steps in meiosis.

Variation in chromosomes occurs during crossing over. This is an exchange of genetic material between homologous chromosomes. It occurs in meiosis but not in mitosis. Crossover often occurs when matching regions on matching chromosomes break and then reconnect to the other chromosome as shown in Figure 1.24. This gives rise to a huge variety of combinations so no two eggs or sperms are identical.

Fertilisation

There are two components to reproduction:

> producing haploid gametes, such as sperm and ova, through the nuclear division called meiosis (see Figure 1.25)

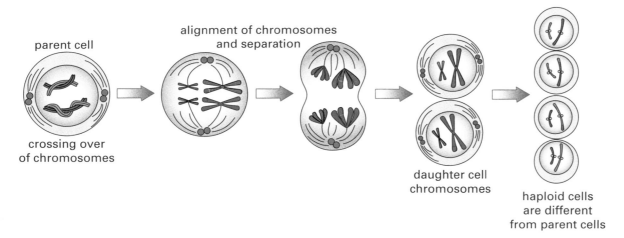

parent cell

crossing over of chromosomes

alignment of chromosomes and separation

daughter cell chromosomes

haploid cells are different from parent cells

Figure 1.23 Steps in meiosis

> fusing the two gametes during fertilisation, resulting in the diploid number of chromosomes of the organism being restored.

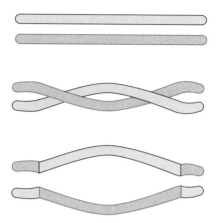

Figure 1.24 Illustrating crossing over

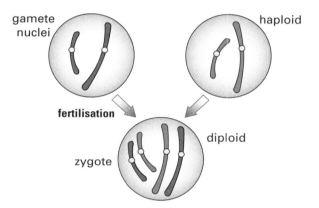

Figure 1.25 The components of reproduction

It is important that the chromosome number be halved during meiosis. If this did not occur, then the resulting zygote would have twice the diploid number and the chromosome number would double in each subsequent generation. For example, we are diploid organisms. That means each cell of our bodies contains 23 pairs ($2n = 46$) chromosomes. When we produce gametes (sperm or egg) the chromosome number is halved to 23. During fertilisation:

23 chromosomes from sperm + 23 chromosomes from egg = 23 pairs of chromosomes in the new individual

And so the original number, 46 (= 23 pairs), is re-established.

Each sample of human semen contains between 200 and 300 million sperm. The sperm ($n = 23$) travels through the female's cervix to eventually meet an egg ($n = 23$). If the sperm manages to enter the egg,

it becomes fertilised ($2n = 46$) and a new life can begin. It takes only one sperm to fertilise the egg (see Figure 1.26).

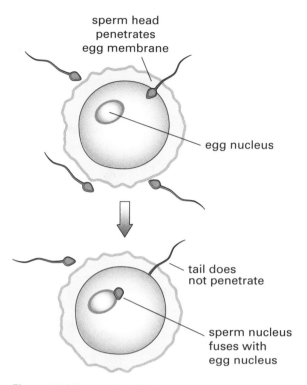

Figure 1.26 Human fertilisation

1.8 Mendel and dominant and recessive genes

Over 150 years ago, in a monastery garden in Austria, the monk Gregor Mendel (1822–1884) conducted breeding experiments with garden peas, thus building the founding principles of hereditary and genetics. In all, he used some 28 000 pea plants over a period of 8 years.

Peas (*Pisum sativum*) are easily cultivated, have a natural variation in their observable characteristics (traits) and Mendel could control their pollination. His first step was to produce a supply of genes that always breeds true. This means that when these plants were allowed to self-pollinate, or were pollinated by plants of the same trait, they only ever produced plants with the same trait, generation after generation. Table 1.1 and Figure 1.27 show some of the traits of pea plants.

Table 1.1 Characteristics of garden peas

Characteristics (traits)	Contrasting appearances
seed colour	green and yellow
seed shape	round and wrinkled
pod colour	green and yellow
stem length	long and short
flower position	terminal (top) and axial (side)

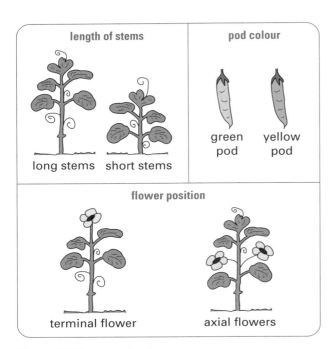

Figure 1.27 Some traits of peas

Once he had produced a stock of pure-breeding plants, he could conduct experiments where he cross-pollinated plants with different characteristics and observed the traits of their progeny (offspring). This technique is called hybridising. By conducting many experiments, he was able to make valid conclusions that were less influenced by chance alone.

Crossing pure-bred parents

Table 1.2 shows some typical results from various mating experiments. The process of mating is also called crossing (and is shown by ×). In each experiment, the pure-breeding parent generation is labelled P, while the first generation of offspring is labelled F_1. (F_1 stands for filial 1.)

These experiments showed Mendel that one characteristic seemed to dominate the other. For seed colour, yellow dominated the green so that no green progeny appeared in the first generation (see

Figure 1.28). Mendel used the term dominant to describe the characteristics that only appear in the F_1 generation when pure-bred stocks were crossed.

Table 1.2 Results of crossing pure-bred parents

Trait	Parents (P)	First generation (F_1)
seed colour	green × yellow	all yellow
seed shape	round × wrinkled	all round
pod colour	green × yellow	all green
stem length	long × short	all long
flower position	terminal × axial	all axial

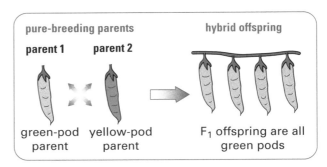

Figure 1.28 Simple crossing experiment

Crossing the F_1 generation

Mendel's next step was to cross the F_1 generation with one another and examine the characteristics that appeared in the second generation (F_2) as shown in Figure 1.29. Table 1.3 shows some typical results. In the F_2 generation most plants showed the dominant characteristic, but the second characteristic reappeared. Mendel termed this characteristic 'recessive', meaning 'hidden'. A ratio dominant to recessive of 3:1 always occurred.

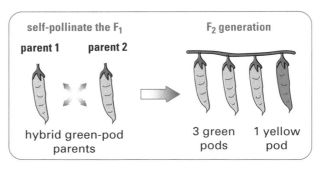

Figure 1.29 Crossing the F_1 generation

Of course, he didn't get this ratio exactly, since chance comes into play. For example, suppose in one experiment he obtained 5574 green pods and 1849 yellow pods, then the ratio 5574:1849 is very close to 3:1. The predicted or expected ratio does not tell us the actual ratio of green to yellow pods in a particular pea plant, but rather the most probable ratio.

Table 1.3 Results of crossing the F₁ generation

Trait	F₁ generation	F₂ generation ratio
seed colour	yellow × yellow	3:1 (yellow:green)
seed shape	round × round	3:1 (round:wrinkled)
pod colour	green × green	3:1 (green:yellow)
stem length	long × long	3:1 (long:short)
flower position	axial × axial	3:1 (axial:terminal)

Mendel's conclusions

Mendel's contribution to the study of what was later to be known as genetics was unique because of his methodical approach to a definite problem, and his use of clear-cut variables and application of mathematics (in particular, statistics) to the problem.

Mendel's experiments showed the following.

- Each parent contributes one hereditary factor for each trait shown in the offspring.
- Two members of each pair of factors segregate from each other during the formation of gametes.
- Males and females contribute equally to the traits in their progeny.
- The blending theory of inheritance was proved wrong. (This theory held that tall plants × short plants give intermediate height plants, or that a black-furred animal mating with a white-furred animal should always produce grey progeny.)
- Acquired traits are not inherited. (An acquired trait is a trait obtained during one's lifetime. So chopping off the tails from rats does not produce a following generation of tail-less rats; a weightlifter's muscle mass is not passed on to his children.)

While he published his results in 1865, they were overly statistical and biologists of his day usually had little grounding in mathematics, so they didn't appreciate its implications. Soon afterwards he became abbot of the monastery and his experiments ceased.

1.9 Genotypes and phenotypes

It wasn't until 1900 that Mendel's work was re-discovered by a new generation of scientists. From 1909 his hereditary factors were known as genes, and the science of hereditary as genetics. Various terms were coined to explain his observations.

- Genes exist in alternative forms, called alleles. For seed colour in peas, for example, the alleles are yellow and green.
- The dominant gene is represented by a capital letter and the recessive gene is represented by a lower-case letter. For example, for seed colour in peas, 'Y' represents the dominant yellow gene, while 'y' represents the recessive green gene.
- Genes come in pairs. During sex cell formation, 50% of the gametes receive one gene and the remainder the other gene. At fertilisation one allele is inherited from the male parent and one from the female parent.
- Individuals that have inherited identical genes are called homozygous, or pure breeders. Individual with different alleles are called heterozygous or hybrids. In peas, for example, YY or yy represent homozygous individuals and Yy represents heterozygous individuals.
- Further, YY can be referred to as homozygous dominant, as both dominant alleles are present; yy can be referred to as homozygous recessive, as both recessive alleles are present.
- Genotype is a term referring to the genetic composition of the individual for a particular trait. A true breeding pea plant that produces yellow seeds has the YY genotype.
- Phenotype is a term referring to the characteristic shown by an individual. The phenotype for both YY or Yy individuals in pea seeds is yellow. The phenotype of yy is green. (See Figure 1.30.)

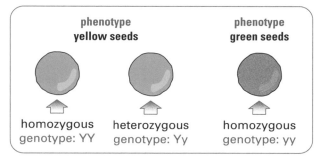

Figure 1.30 Genotype and phenotype for pea seed colour

We know chromosomes come in pairs, so genes come in pairs. Since genes occupy the same loci (same position on homologous, or paired, chromosomes), the genes must be referring to the same trait. For example, at a particular point (locus) on homologous chromosomes there will be one of two alleles for the gene that expresses yellow or green colour for pea seeds (see Figure 1.31).

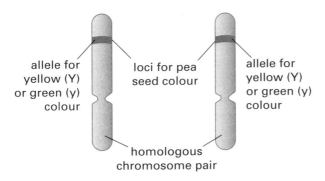

Figure 1.31 Gene for pea seed colour on homologous chromosomes

There will be two alleles from one parent, and two from the other parent, a total of four. The two copies of a gene separate into different gametes in equal numbers. So if in peas one parent has the genotype YY for pea colour then its gametes can only contain the allele Y (see Figure 1.32). If the other parent has the genotype Yy for pea colour then its gametes can either contain the allele Y or y (see Figure 1.33). There will be four possible ways that these alleles could be paired in the offspring, and some or all of them could be repeated.

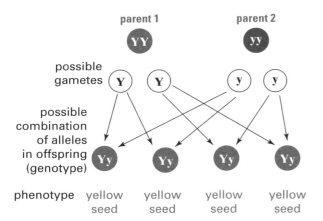

Figure 1.32 A genetic diagram showing how pure-breeding pea plants can cross

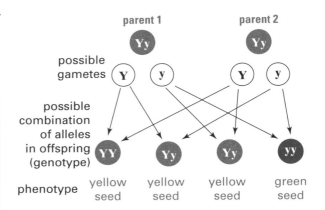

Figure 1.33 A genetic diagram showing how heterozygous pea plants can cross

1.10 Genetic crosses, pedigrees and sex-linked genes

The British geneticist Professor Reginald Punnett (1875–1967) is probably best remembered today as the creator of the Punnett square, a tool still used by biologists to predict the probability of possible genotypes of offspring.

For example, the cross Yy × Yy can be shown in a Punnett square as seen in Figure 1.34.

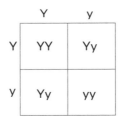

Figure 1.34 Punnett square

The alleles from each parent are written across the top and down the left-hand side. It does not matter which position the male or female occupies. As before, Y represents the dominant allele for yellow seed colour and y the recessive allele for green seed colour.

Immediately obvious from the square is the ratio of genotypes YY:Yy:yy = 1:2:1, while the ratio of phenotypes for the seeds is yellow:green = 3:1.

Example: Galactosaemia

There are over 4000 human diseases caused by single gene defects, which can be inherited (or passed down) through families; for example, sickle-cell anaemia, cystic fibrosis and galactosaemia.

Galactosaemia is a rare genetic metabolic disorder (1 in every 60 000 births) that affects an individual's ability to break down the sugar galactose properly. Lactose found in foods such as dairy products is broken down by an enzyme into glucose and galactose. In people with galactosaemia, the enzymes needed to further break down galactose are missing entirely or are in very low concentrations. This leads to toxic levels of waste products that can be fatal without treatment.

For a child to show the disorder, he or she must inherit one defective recessive gene from each parent. Let G represent the normal condition without the disorder and g represent the recessive gene for the disorder. Figure 1.35 shows how this gene is inherited. There is a 25% chance that a child born will not inherit the defective gene. They will be normal (unaffected) and can't pass on this condition. There is a 50% chance they will be carriers. Carriers inherit one normal gene and one defective gene but show no symptoms of galactosaemia. There is a 25% chance that the child born will be affected and will therefore need medical treatment.

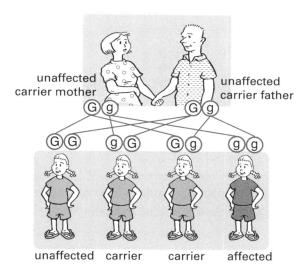

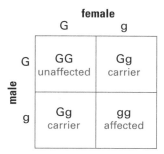

Figure 1.35 Genetic diagram and Punnett square for galactosaemia

Recessive genes have a habit of 'skipping a generation' or more. As this example shows, for an individual to exhibit the condition they must inherit both recessive alleles. If a condition is very harmful then the recessive allele will not be too frequently found in the population and so it may be several generations before the condition again expresses itself. But there had to be a first person with the condition at some point. In other words, in the distant past, someone had a DNA change in his or her gene so it became a galactosaemia version.

Of course, many traits are not controlled by just one gene, but by a number of genes. Think about hair colour or height or skin colour. This can complicate the study of genetics.

Pedigrees

A pedigree can refer to the lineage or genealogical descent of people or of animals. They do not need to be purebred or descend just from royalty. Doctors often ask whether particular conditions run in families or whether a relative displayed certain symptoms in the past. It can be used to show a family history of some diseases. This gives them an insight into treatment.

Figure 1.36 shows a pedigree for a hypothetical family that displays a certain condition. This condition does not necessarily need to be a disease. Children are given from left to right in order of birth. So, for example, the couple shown in generation I had five children in order: girl, girl, girl, boy, boy. Two of the girls and one boy showed symptoms of the condition. Also, three of the five children married and had children of their own.

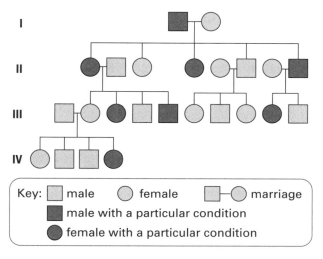

Figure 1.36 Pedigree chart showing four generations of a hypothetical family

A problem with a chart like this is that it can become cluttered and unwieldy after several generations.

Sex-linked genes

Tortoiseshell is a fur colouring found mostly in female cats. Cats of this colour are mottled, with patches of orange or cream and chocolate, black or blue. Why frequently found in female cats? Because some genes for coat colours in cats are located on the X sex chromosome, and this is known as sex linkage.

In mammals, the female carries two X chromosomes (XX) while the male has one X and one Y chromosome (XY). Genes carried on the X or Y chromosome are called sex-linked genes.

There are over 1000 human X-linked genes while the much smaller Y chromosome carries only about 26 genes. Many of the non-sex-determining X-linked genes are responsible for abnormal conditions such as haemophilia, Duchene muscular dystrophy, fragile-X syndrome, some high blood pressure, congenital night blindness and the most common red–green colour blindness.

Haemophilia is a rare bleeding disorder where the blood doesn't clot normally. People born with haemophilia have little or no clotting factor. This is a protein needed for normal blood clotting. There are several types of clotting factors and they work with platelets to help the blood clot. Sufferers are often prescribed coagulating medications taken orally or intravenously to lessen the bleeding.

Haemophilia in humans is caused by an X-linked recessive allele. It is more common in males than in females because males carry only one copy of the gene in each of their cells. Hence, they express the trait when they inherit one recessive allele (1 in every 5000 male births). On the other hand, a female must inherit two of these alleles, which is a less likely event. Tsarevitch Alexei of Russia (1904–1918, heir to the Russian throne) was the most famous sufferer of X-linked haemophilia.

Figure 1.37 shows the likely offspring of a haemophiliac father and a normal female. (Normal in this context means the person does not carry the allele of the gene for haemophilia.) All of the daughters inherit an X chromosome with the mutation (recessive haemophiliac gene) from their father, and will be carriers. All the sons inherit a normal X from the mother, and so will not display the disease.

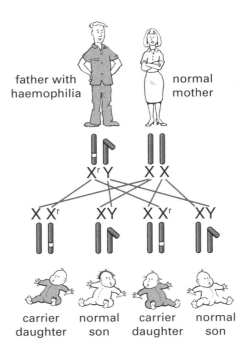

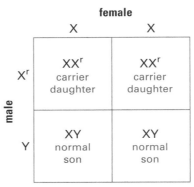

Figure 1.37 Haemophiliac father × normal mother (X^r indicates X chromosome carries recessive haemophilia gene)

Figure 1.38 shows another cross, this time a normal father and a carrier mother. The carrier carries the recessive haemophilia gene but, since she also carries the normal gene, does not show any symptoms. There is a 50% chance one of the woman's children will inherit the recessive gene. If the child is a male, he will display haemophilia. If the child is a female, she will not display haemophilia but, as a carrier, could pass it down to her children. If the children inherit the normal X chromosome from their mother, they will be normal being neither carriers nor displaying the disease.

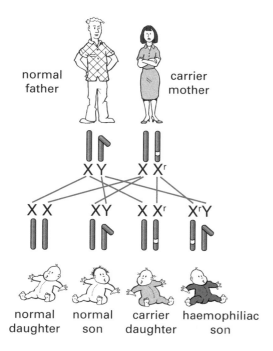

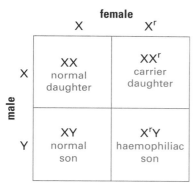

	female	
	X	X^r
X	XX normal daughter	XX^r carrier daughter
Y	XY normal son	X^{r}Y haemophiliac son

Figure 1.38 Normal father × carrier mother (X^r indicates X chromosome carries recessive haemophilia gene)

Diagrams such as these show probable scenarios, not definite outcomes. It may be, for example, that such parents have three children and all are normal (don't display the disease, nor are carriers).

1.11 Watson and Crick and the structure of DNA

In England in 1953, scientists James Watson and Francis Crick used X-ray data obtained by Rosalind Franklin to discover the structure of the molecule that encodes our genetic information. This is the DNA molecule. They won a Nobel Prize (1962) 'for their discoveries concerning the molecular structure of nucleic acids and its significance for information transfer in living material'.

DNA: structure and replication

DNA is an acronym for deoxyribose nucleic acid. The shape of the DNA molecule is a double helix.

Structure

The two strands of the double helix resemble a spiral staircase. The separate strands are composed of molecules called nucleotides. Nucleotides are composed of three parts:

- a phosphate group
- a deoxyribose sugar molecule
- a nucleobase, also called a nitrogen base.

The 'spiral steps' are composed of the nucleobases (nitrogen bases). The sides of the 'spiral staircase' are composed of the phosphate groups and deoxyribose sugar molecules. There are four types of nucleobases:

- cytosine (C)
- guanine (G)
- thymine (T)
- adenine (A).

Two nucleobases linked together construct the 'spiral steps'.

- Cytosine (C) always bonds with guanine (G).
- Thymine (T) always bonds with adenine (A).

Think of a lock-and-key arrangement; the shapes of their molecules are such that C links with G, T links with A.

A simplified model of a short section of the DNA structure is shown in Figure 1.39 (on the next page).

Replication

Prior to normal cell division, each DNA molecule must make a copy of itself. In this way each new cell will have an exact copy of each DNA molecule. This process is called replication.

The following are the steps in replication.

1. The nucleobases (nitrogen bases) that form the 'spiral steps' start to split apart at one end of the DNA ladder.
2. New nucleotides are transported into place and linked together to produce a complementary strand according to the rule for base pairing (i.e. C with G, T with A).
3. Two new double helices form when this process is completed.

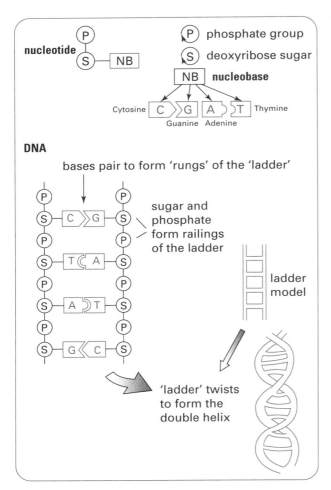

Figure 1.39 Structure of nucleotides and DNA

Figure 1.40 shows a simplified model of the first stage of this replication process.

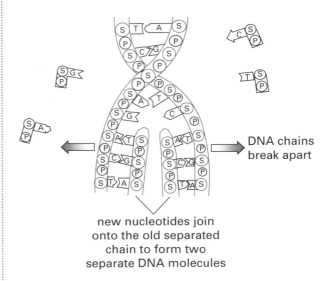

new nucleotides join onto the old separated chain to form two separate DNA molecules

Figure 1.40 DNA replication

1.12 DNA mutations

Genes contain information that is used by the cells to control growth, development and proper functioning. The information they carry is in the form of a chemical code. Sometimes that code may be faulty. We are all born with several faulty gene copies (estimate about half a dozen defective genes) and

 Case study 1: The fruit fly *Drosophila melanogaster*

The fruit fly, *Drosophila melanogaster*, is a small insect about 3 mm long often found around spoiled fruit. It is very popular with geneticists and is one of the most commonly used model organisms in biology because of the following reasons.

➤ It is small, and doesn't take up much room.

➤ It is easy to breed.

➤ It has a short breeding cycle (about 10 days at room temperature) so several generations can be studied within a few weeks.

➤ Females lay up to 100 eggs per day, and up to 2000 in a lifetime.

➤ Males and females are easily distinguished. Males have a distinct black patch on their abdomen.

➤ It is easy to study.

Drosophila has four pairs of chromosomes in each of its cells: the X/Y sex chromosomes and the autosomes (non-sex chromosomes) numbered 2, 3 and 4. (The fourth chromosome is very tiny.) Its genome contains around 14 000 genes.

Part A: Crossing normal-winged flies with vestigial-winged flies

Vestigial-winged flies cannot fly since they have a defect in their 'vestigial gene', located on the second chromosome. Flies with normal wings have them fully developed and are able to fly. Suppose a pure-breeding normal-winged female was crossed with a pure-breeding vestigial-winged male (see Figure 1.41).

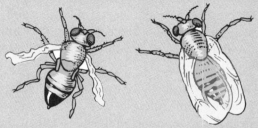

vestigial-winged male   normal-winged female

Figure 1.41 Normal-winged female × vestigial-winged male

Figure 1.42 shows a representative sample of the F_1 generation.

Figure 1.42 The F_1 generation

Let us consider the following questions and answers about Figure 1.42.

Q1: Which trait is dominant: normal wings or vestigial wings? How do you know?

A1: Since all flies have normal wings, then the normal-wing allele is dominant and the vestigial-wing is recessive.

Q2: Use a Punnet square to determine the genotype of the F_1 generation.

A2: Assume W represents the normal-wing allele and w represents the vestigial-wing allele. The normal-winged female can only produce W for her gametes, while the vestigial-winged male produces w for his gametes. Being pure-breeding, the flies are homozygous for their respective genes (see Figure 1.43 for the Punnett square).

All of the offspring in the F_1 generation are heterozygous, and have the genotype Ww. Two flies from the F_1 generation were used to produce the F_2 generation. Figure 1.44 shows a representative sample of the F_2 generation.

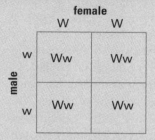

Figure 1.43 Punnett square, F_1 generation

Figure 1.44 The F_2 generation

Q3: What is the ratio of the wing types normal:vestigial?

A3: 6:2 = 3:1

Q4: Use a Punnet square to determine the genotypes and phenotypes of the F_2 generation.

A4: All flies from the F_1 generation have genotype Ww (see Figure 1.45).

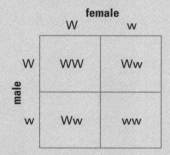

Figure 1.45 Punnett square, F_2 generation

In the second generation, the genotype ratio is WW:Ww:ww = 1:2:1, with phenotypes normal:vestigial wings = 3:1. Since W dominates w, the presence of just one W will produce flies with normal wings.

Q5: Suppose in the F_1 generation, consisting of 14 flies, the wing ratio for normal:vestigial was found to be 5:2, not 3:1. Account for the discrepancy.

(cont.)

A5: This is a small sample of 14 flies. Punnett squares are used as predictive tools and determining the likelihood of inheriting genes. Which of the two parental copies of a gene is inherited depends on which sex cell is inherited, and this is a matter of chance. The ratio 5:2 is close to 6:2 = 3:1. Using much larger samples, the ratio will more closely approximate the theoretical value.

Part B: Sex-linked characteristics

Wild-type fruit flies have brick red eyes and transverse black rings across their abdomen, and are yellow-brown in colour. This is their normal appearance in nature.

The example in Part A showed that inheritance patterns of genes on the autosomes produce male and female progeny in the same proportions of phenotypes. However, if the gene for a particular trait is located on a sex chromosome, then a pattern of inheritance related to sex will be shown. That is, crosses following the inheritance of genes on the sex chromosomes will often show male and female offspring with different ratios of phenotypes.

Suppose a white-eyed pure-breeding female fly was mated with a pure-breeding wild-type male fly (see Figure 1.46). It is known that the gene controlling eye colour resides on the X sex chromosome.

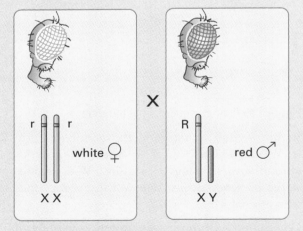

Figure 1.46 Sex-linkage in *Drosophila* eye colour (♀ = female; ♂ = male)

Let R represent the allele for red colouring and r represent the absence of red colouring (i.e. white eyes). A Punnet square for this cross could look like Figure 1.47.

Since in males the allele for eye colour resides on the X chromosome, then its gametes will either contain an X chromosome, with the R allele, or the Y chromosome, without the R allele (shown as o on the Punnett square). (You can also draw your Punnett square using $X^rX^r \times X^RY$, as was done similarly earlier with the haemophilia examples.)

female

	r	r
R	Rr red-eyed ♀	Rr red-eyed ♀
o	or white-eyed ♂	or white-eyed ♂

(male)

Figure 1.47 Punnett square, F_1 generation

Q6: What is the phenotype and genotype for the F_1 generation from this cross?

A6: All the female flies will have genotype Rr and have phenotype red eyes. All the male flies will carry just one allele of this gene, r, and exhibit white eyes.

Q7: While allele is dominant? Which is recessive?

A7: When white-eyed males are crossed with red-eyed females, all the F_1 progeny have red eyes if they contain the R allele, and white eyes if they don't. This shows that the allele for red (R) is dominant and the white (r) is recessive.

Q8: How is this different from the normal- and vestigial-wing cross experiment?

A8: All flies in the previous example had normal wings in the F_1 generation, regardless of gender. In this example, being a sex-linked trait, females exhibited one phenotype and males another.

Q9: What would a Punnett square cross for the F_2 generation be?

A9: The female flies can produce R or r in their gametes. The male flies can produce r in half of their gametes, with the other half having no allele (o) for eye colour.

Q10: Interpret the Punnett square shown in Figure 1.48.

A10: All the red-eyed females have genotype Rr (they are heterozygous), but the white-eyed females have genotype rr (they are homozygous). Of the males, about half are red-eyed with genotype Ro, while the other half are white-eyed with genotype or. There are four genotypes Rr, Rr, Ro and or in approximately equal numbers. Phenotypes are red:white = 1:1.

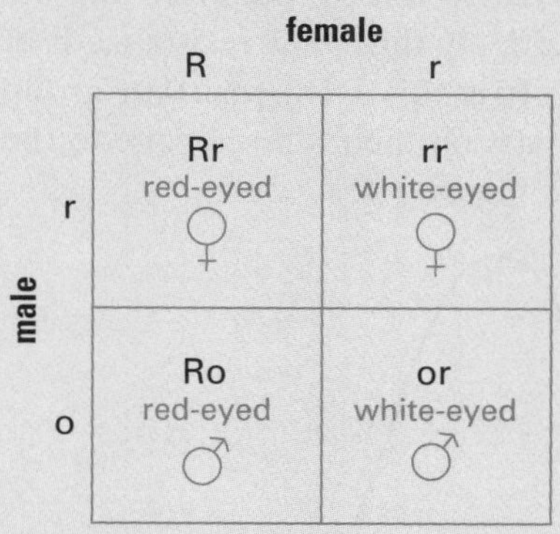

female

	R	r
r	Rr red-eyed ♀	rr white-eyed ♀
o	Ro red-eyed ♂	or white-eyed ♂

(male)

Figure 1.48 Punnett square, F_2 generation

In *Drosophila*, eye colour has nothing to do with sex determination. In other words, genes on the sex chromosomes are not necessarily related to sexual function. The same holds for humans, where there are many X-linked genes, of which few could be interpreted as being connected to some sexual function.

these usually cause no problem. Since the nucleus of each of our cells contains over 20 000 genes, the occasional 'spelling mistake' is bound to happen. Most of us do not suffer any harmful effects from our defective genes because we carry two copies of nearly all genes. If the potentially harmful gene is recessive, then its normal counterpart will carry out all the tasks assigned to both.

If these faulty genes are in the egg or sperm cells, they can be passed on to children (inherited). The faulty gene may be in these cells because:

- that person inherited it from one or both parents
- a mutation can sometimes occur in an egg or sperm cell.

If the second of these reasons occurs, the individual conceived from that egg or sperm cell will be the first in the family to have the condition. This gene may then be passed down to his or her children and on to future generations.

Such gene changes are not always harmful. They allow new versions of DNA combinations to occur, which can be harmful, benign or beneficial.

- Harmful changes are usually self-eliminating. In the wild, if that trait is somehow disadvantageous,

the animal is unlikely to survive to breeding age and so does not pass the gene on.

- Benign changes usually do not influence the species. They are neither good nor bad, but merely different (for instance, the wide variety of colours in randomly bred flower varieties). While they don't currently confer a survival advantage, they aren't disadvantageous. However, should the environment change, those genes might prove advantageous or disadvantageous.

- Beneficial changes can create improved varieties of the organisms, making it more successful in its environment and allowing it to leave more descendents. This results in greater diversity and therefore greater adaptability in the species. The prevalence of the gene will increase in the wild, and may even outnumber, or replace, the unaltered version.

Example: DDT resistance

Suppose in a population of flies or mosquitoes there is a random change to one of the genes controlling resistance to the synthetic insecticide DDT. This change may confer, say, greater DDT resistance. But if there is no DDT in the environment then the change is harmless, and the gene will be passed along to the next generation of flies or mosquitoes, just like its non-altered counterpart. Now if the insects' environment is sprayed with DDT those insects that have a low resistance will be killed, leaving the minority behind. Suddenly this DDT resistance is of advantage to them. It is this DDT-resistant group that will survive to pass on their altered gene to the next generation (see Figure 1.49).

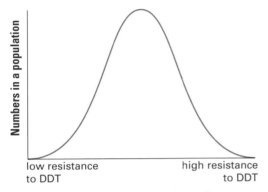

Before DDT is introduced to the environment

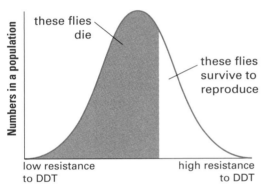

After DDT is introduced to the environment

Figure 1.49 Effects of DDT on a fly population

So with the next spraying, greater concentrations will need to be used for any significant effect. DDT-resistant mosquitoes were first detected in India in 1959, and they have increased so rapidly that when a local spraying program is initiated there is now very little effect.

The insecticidal properties of DDT were discovered in 1939, and it was used with great success in the second half of World War II to control malaria and typhus among civilians and troops. However, over the years resistance has greatly reduced DDT's effectiveness and today it is not often used.

DNA replication errors

The process of DNA replication may go wrong. This results in a change in the sequence of nucleobases (nitrogen bases) in the DNA molecule. This change in the code is called a DNA mutation.

There are a number of ways in which DNA mutations can occur, including the following.

> Deletion. If a nucleobase is omitted during replication, the nucleobase sequence changes.
Original sequence
= CCT GTC GGA GCA ACA …
C is omitted in GTC.
New sequence = CCT GTG AGC AAC A …

> Substitution. Sometimes a nucleobase is not copied properly and a different base is substituted.
Original sequence
= CAA CTA CCC ATA AAA …
G is substituted for the first C in CCC.
New sequence = CAA CTA GCC ATA AAA …

When the DNA code is changed in these ways, the information transmitted to the cell is also altered (see Figure 1.50).

Chromosomes and genes

The DNA molecule is one of a number of molecules located in the chromosomes of the nucleus. The sequence of nucleobases in the DNA is a code that the cell uses to construct protein molecules required for life functions. Protein molecules are very large molecules (polymers) that are constructed from smaller molecules called amino acids. The amino acids link together to form the long chains of the protein.

> Sets of three nucleobases form a triplet code.

> Each amino acid has a number of alternative triplet codes (e.g. CCC and CCT both code for the amino acid called glycine).

Example: Triplet codes

The sequence of triplet codes
                    CCC TTT AAA GAG
leads to the following sequence of linked amino acids in a protein chain:
    —glycine—lysine—phenylalanine—leucine—

Genes

Genes are codes that contain information about inheritance. Here are some key points about genes.

> Genes are segments of the DNA molecule containing many triplet codes.

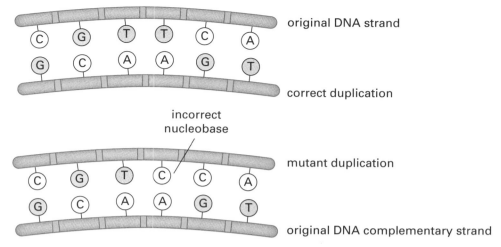

Figure 1.50 How a mutation can occur by nucleotide substitution

- Each gene is responsible for the production of a certain protein.
- Gene segments of the DNA strands are separated from one another by other non-coding segments.
- Genes do not function at all times. They can be turned 'on' or 'off'.
- Each gene may have two alternative forms called alleles.

Environmental effects

The inheritance of particular gene combinations can lead to features that are more suitable in certain environments. The following environmental factors influence the characteristics of a population.

- Availability of food and water. Poor diets and nutritional disease will affect the survival of weaker members of a population.
- Infectious disease. Individuals with high natural immunity have a greater chance of survival when infectious diseases appear.
- Latitude and sunlight. Individuals with darker skins can survive in equatorial latitudes where there is strong solar radiation.

Example 1: Light brown and dark-coloured moths

Light brown moths have a mottled body that helps to camouflage them in their natural woodland environment. Dark-coloured moths have a gene mutation that leads to dark-coloured bodies. They are easily seen by birds in the woodlands and are therefore more likely to be eaten. Consequently, a woodland population of moths usually has more mottled light brown moths than dark moths. The features of the population of moths have been affected by the environment. These two types of moth are shown in Figure 1.51.

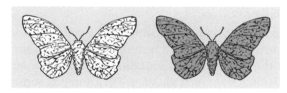

Figure 1.51 Light and dark forms of the peppered moth

Example 2: Salt-tolerant plants

Some plant species are able to colonise coastal dunes because they have inherited genes to deal with high-salinity environments. Seeds from non-salt-tolerant plants will quickly die after germination in such environments.

In some parts of Australia, increases in soil salinity (due to poor farming practices) have led to a change in the characteristics of native vegetation. The proportion of salt-tolerant plants increases at the expense of non-salt-tolerant plants.

Causes of mutations

Many mutations occur naturally, such as when DNA fails to copy accurately. Mutations can also be caused by external influences, such as exposure to specific chemicals or radiation, including ultraviolet light and nuclear radiation. These agents cause the DNA to break down. Sometimes the cell tries to repair the DNA, but might not do a perfect job of it. Hence, the cell ends up with DNA slightly different to the original DNA: a mutation.

Mutations and evolution

Evolution depends on mutations since this is the only way that new alleles are created. Genetic mutations that improve the survival and reproduction of the organism become more common in the population and remain in successive generations.

Mutations occur randomly. Whether a particular mutation happens or not, or when it happens, is not related to how useful that mutation might be. Since every cell of our bodies contains genes, there are many places where mutations can occur. But the ones that matter for evolution are those occurring in our reproductive cells (egg and sperm), which can be passed on to the next generation. The effects can vary.

> Some mutations don't have any noticeable effect on the phenotype of an organism; for example, where a mutation occurs in a stretch of DNA having no function.

> Small change occurs in phenotype; for example, curly ears in dogs or cats, changes in eye colour, or larger flowers.

> Big change occurs in phenotype. In extreme cases a harmful mutation can be lethal to the organism. On the other hand, a mutation can improve an individual's survival changes. For example, some people are resistant to HIV infection and AIDS as they possess a certain mutant allele.

1.13 Genetic testing and counselling

Much research has occurred over the last few decades (and is continuing to occur) into the structure and function of genes, which is increasing our understanding of their role in maintaining health and causing disease. This knowledge is creating ongoing opportunities and increased roles for genetic testing.

The purpose of genetic testing

Human genotypes are alike in many ways, but small differences make us unique beings in both appearance and genetic makeup and help to identify us as individuals. Sometimes minor differences in our genotype are related to disease or to the difficulty or inability to metabolise or to normally break down certain drugs. A genetic disorder is a condition caused by changed genetic material. An error in just one gene can be the cause of a serious medical condition or disability, such as those listed in Table 1.4. These kinds of genetic variations may be either inherited or occur spontaneously.

A genetic test is one that reveals this genetic information. Testing is done on DNA, RNA or protein (the 'gene product'), but may also involve measuring a chemical substance that indirectly indicates how a gene functions. For example, haemoglobin electrophoresis can diagnose carriers of thalassaemia. Measuring blood cholesterol levels in a child may assist in diagnosing a family history of high cholesterol levels.

Some individuals who are given a particular therapeutic drug to treat certain symptoms or to keep symptoms from occurring may have a severe over-reaction to the drug or, at the other extreme, experience very little effect. This may be related to the genetic makeup of the individual. Genetic testing can play a role in determining likely responses to a drug. By comparing the precise area on a specific chromosome to the 'normal' DNA, genetic variations can be found that may play a role in the over- or under-responsiveness to a particular drug. Such testing can determine an individual's resistance or sensitivity to the effectiveness of certain drugs used in viral therapy (e.g. drugs for HIV or hepatitis C).

Example: Thalassaemia—a genetically transmitted disease

Thalassaemia is an inherited blood disorder passed down through families where the body makes an abnormal form of haemoglobin, the protein in red blood cells that carries oxygen. This results in an increased destruction of red blood cells, leading to

Table 1.4 Some specific genetic diseases or disorders

Alzheimer's disease	breast cancer	colon cancer	colour blindness
cri du chat	cystic fibrosis	Down syndrome	Duchenne muscular dystrophy
haemochromatosis	haemophilia	leukaemia	lymphoma
neurofibromatosis	osteoarthritis	ovarian cancer	phenylketonuria
sickle-cell anaemia	Tay–Sachs disease	thalassaemia	Turner's syndrome

anaemia. Figure 1.52 shows how haemoglobin usually works.

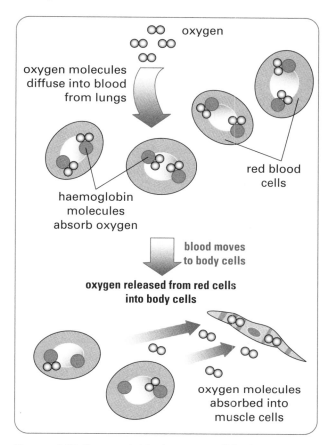

Figure 1.52 Haemoglobin is responsible for carrying oxygen through the body to all organ systems.

There are many forms of thalassaemia, including:

- thalassaemia major
- thalassaemia minor.

A defective (abnormal) gene inherited from both parents results in thalassaemia major. Thalassaemia minor occurs by inheriting the defective gene from only one parent. Persons with this form of the disorder are carriers of the disease and usually do not show any symptoms.

The most severe form of thalassaemia causes stillbirth (death of the unborn baby during birth or the late stages of pregnancy). Children born with thalassaemia major are normal at birth, but develop severe anaemia during the first year of life. Other symptoms include:

- bone deformities in the face
- fatigue
- growth failure

- shortness of breath
- yellow skin (jaundice).

Treatment for thalassaemia major often involves regular blood transfusions and iron chelation therapy. Even so, severe thalassaemia can cause early death due to heart failure, usually between the ages of 20 to 30.

Genetic counselling

If there's a chance that you or a family member has some genetic disorder, or are at risk of one, you may be referred for genetic testing. The testing can be done at any stage in life. This testing can determine the presence of genes for certain inherited disorders and to look for predispositions to disease or any gene abnormalities.

Genetic counselling is mainly about communicating, educating and supporting. During counselling the condition is explained, along with its possible consequences, the probability of developing or transmitting it and possible methods to prevent it. Issues discussed during counselling include:

- identifying family members at risk; alternatively, they may be reassured to find that they do not have, or are unlikely to develop, the particular condition
- estimating the risks that other family members, or future children, will be affected by the condition
- discussing the condition's impact and possible effects on the individual and their family, including management strategies and referral to appropriate community resources and support groups
- discussing appropriate prenatal testing and other reproductive options so that any decision is made on an informed basis (many genetic conditions can be diagnosed before birth)
- if a genetic condition is identified in a prenatal diagnosis; an informed decision can be made regarding the continuation of the pregnancy or termination.

Screening of newborn children for treatable diseases such as phenylketonuria or congenital hypothyroidism should certainly be done. People with a family history of a heritable disease should consider genetic testing as a precautionary measure. Early testing for such diseases allows for early treatment and can minimise many discomforts and uncertainties.

1.14 Genetic technologies and privacy

Gene technology is a relatively new study referring to a range of activities concerned with understanding the function and interaction of genes, taking advantage of natural genetic variation, altering genes and transferring them to new hosts. Through gene technologies, human and animal health can be improved and a safer and more sustainable food supply can be created. Genetic technologies have also been termed genetic engineering or genetic modification.

It is possible for a gene for a particular characteristic to be identified in one organism. Genes within a species can be modified, or genes can be moved from one species to another. This gene can be inserted into a chromosome of another organism, after some modification, causing the organism to adopt this new characteristic. The gene inserted into the DNA of the new organism becomes a permanent part of the organism's genetic makeup.

For example, it is possible to take the gene that produces vitamin A from a crop, such as corn, and introduce this into rice. This would result in rice seeds enhanced with vitamin A.

On the other hand, this technology can also be used to silence (turn off) certain genes. For example, silencing viral genes can prevent infections in animals and plants.

The following are some benefits of gene technology.

> More effective therapies can be developed for diseases like cancer, diabetes, hepatitis C and influenza; for example, microorganisms such as yeast and bacteria have been modified to produce vaccines for hepatitis B and insulin for diabetics.

> A malaria vaccine could be developed by genetically modifying the malaria parasite *Plasmodium falciparum*. (This vaccine is currently undergoing trials.)

> Scientists can locate and study genes causing genetic diseases, or which make some people prone to heart disease, Alzheimer's disease, motor neurone disease, some cancers, rheumatoid arthritis and lupus.

> Crops such as cotton, soybean, canola, corn, sugar beet and potato have been modified to be insect resistant, herbicide tolerant or both. This allows farmers to use less herbicide and pesticide on their farms, thereby reducing costs and causing less environmental pollution.

> Soybeans have been modified for increased oleic acid content, a healthy mono-unsaturated fat.

> Currently there are trials in Australia on pineapple, papaya, wheat, barley and sugarcane which have been genetically modified for insect resistance, herbicide tolerance, colour, sugar composition, oil production, flowering and fruit development.

Plantings of genetically modified (GM) crops are increasing around the world. Currently over 1 billion hectares has been planted with the largest area by far being in the United States.

Example: Genetically engineered insect-resistant corn

A century ago it was noticed that a commonly occurring soil bacterium *Bacillus thuringiensis* is lethal to certain insects. In the 1930s *B. thuringiensis* was grown in large quantities and sprayed onto corn crops to prevent damage. It has since been found that this is due to a protein (called Bt protein) produced by these bacteria.

The 'blueprint' for the Bt protein is encoded in a specific DNA sequence (gene). The Bt protein gene has been isolated from this bacterium and inserted into corns' genetic material, as shown in Figure 1.53. The corn now produces its own Bt protein. Chewing insects (such as the European corn borer or the Western corn rootworm) trying to eat the corn absorb the active toxic ingredient. While resistance may develop over time, for the moment insecticides will no longer be needed to control these pests.

Artificial selection of Bt strains has led to the successful targeting of many insect pests. Because no toxic effects of Bt on humans have been detected, it is now considered an acceptable pest control measure in growing food crops.

Privacy issues

While information about genetic modification or genetic engineering of plants or animals is reasonably well documented, gene technologies also provide a new opportunity for individuals to know more about the potential risk of disease for themselves and their families. Once informed about their genetic status, these individuals can take proactive steps to protect

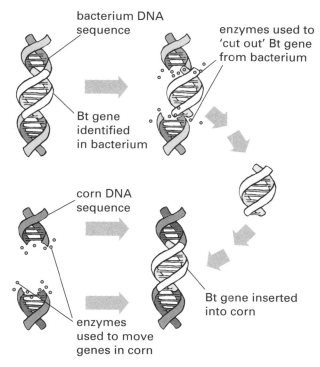

bacterium DNA sequence

enzymes used to 'cut out' Bt gene from bacterium

Bt gene identified in bacterium

corn DNA sequence

Bt gene inserted into corn

enzymes used to move genes in corn

Figure 1.53 Engineering insect-resistant corn

their health, enhance their wellbeing and lower health care costs for themselves and society as a whole.

But two emerging and closely-related issues have arisen:

- genetic privacy (the protection of individual genetic information)
- genetic discrimination (treating individuals differently on the basis of actual or presumed genetic differences).

There are concerns as to how this genetic information may be used by third parties, especially if it is prejudicial to a person's interests. Questions that need answering include the following.

- Who should have access to personal genetic information, and how will it be used?
- Who owns and controls genetic information?
- How does personal genetic information affect an individual and society's perceptions of that individual?

Governments will be required to enact legislation to deal with such cases. Anti-discrimination laws are needed to ensure, for example, that genetic information cannot be used by employers for hiring and firing purposes or by health insurers to decline coverage.

 ## Experiment 1

Investigating human traits

Aim

- To survey the class and close family members to determine the frequency of various traits

Method

Part A: Surveying the class

1. Use Table 1.5 to determine the proportion of the class possessing these dominant or recessive characteristics.

2. Count the number of students with the dominant characteristic and the number with the recessive characteristic for each trait (see also Figure 1.54 on the next page). Record your class results in a copy of the table.

Table 1.5 Proportion of dominant and recessive characteristics

Dominant trait	Number	Percentage	Recessive trait	Number	Percentage
brown eyes			blue eyes		
right-handed			left-handed		
able to bend thumb joint			cannot bend thumb joint		
free-hanging earlobe			attached earlobe		
able to roll tongue into U-shape			cannot roll tongue into U-shape		
second toe shorter than big toe			second toe longer than big toe		
round face			long face		
straight hairline			peaked hairline		

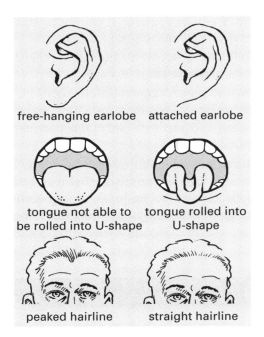

free-hanging earlobe   attached earlobe

tongue not able to   tongue rolled into
be rolled into U-shape   U-shape

peaked hairline   straight hairline

Figure 1.54 Some human genetic traits

3. Complete the table by working out the proportions as percentages (express your answers to the nearest whole numbers).

Part B: Surveying the family

1. If you have sufficient family members to survey, draw up a similar table and record your results. Collect information where possible from parents, brothers, sisters, aunts, uncles and cousins.

2. Compare your results with your class results.

Analysis

1. For the class results, which traits were the most frequent?

2. For which characteristics was the recessive trait the most frequent?

3. Using appropriate codes for dominant and recessive genes, write the possible genotypes for each trait. For example, FF or Ff could be the genotypes for free earlobes and ff would be the genotype for attached earlobes.

4. If you have been able to survey sufficient family members then perform steps 1 to 3 above to analyse the family results.

Go to p. 227 to check your answers.

Conclusion

Write a suitable conclusion.
Go to p. 227 to check your answer.

(Note: Some of the characteristics in this experiment are not controlled by a single gene. For example, left-handedness is less common than right-handedness, with various studies suggesting that 8 to 15% of the world's population is left-handed. However, handedness is not inherited from parents in a simple way. Even when both parents are left-handed, there is only about a ¼ chance of their children being left-handed. Genes aren't the whole story; you might then need some sort of environmental trigger for it to happen. And the situation is complicated further over the centuries by parental and societal pressures with many suffering unfair discrimination. Even in English, the word for the direction 'right' also means 'correct' or 'proper'. The Latin word *sinistra* means 'left' as well as 'unlucky' and this double meaning also survives in other European languages, and in the English word 'sinister'.)

 ## Experiment 2

Modelling genetic crosses

Aim

⊘ To investigate Mendel's laws of inheritance

Materials

⊘ Two sets of different-coloured plastic disks (e.g. 30 black and 30 white)

⊘ Two plastic containers (such as old margarine tubs)

Method

Part A: Crossing hybrid parents

1. Let the black disks represent guinea pigs with black coats and the white disks represent guinea pigs with white coats. Black (B) is dominant to white (b).

2. Place 15 black disks and 15 white disks in the first container. This is the female hybrid parent. The disks represent her ova (eggs).

3. Place 15 black disks and 15 white disks in the second container. These disks represent the sperm of the male hybrid parent.

4. Randomly select a pair of disks, one disk from each container. The pair represents the offspring after fertilisation. Record the colours you select. Determine the genotypes and phenotypes of the offspring.

5. Return the disks to the containers after each draw. Mix the disks.

6. Repeat for a total of 20 draws.

7. Copy and complete Table 1.6 for all 20 draws.

Table 1.6 Hybrid experiment results

Run	Colour of selected disk	Genotype of offspring	Phenotype of offspring
1			
2			
3			

Part B: Mixed crosses

1. Repeat Part A using parents with the following genotypes. In each case consider how many disks of each colour you will have in your two containers.

   a) Bb (male) × bb (female)

   b) Bb (male) × BB (female)

2. Tabulate your results.

Analysis

1. For each experiment, calculate the total number of black-coated and white-coated guinea pigs born.

2. Express your results as a simple ratio to the closest whole number (number of black:white).

3. Draw up a Punnett square for each cross shown in Figure 1.55 and predict the ratio of black to white that would be expected. Compare your experimental results with the predicted outcome. Explain any variations.

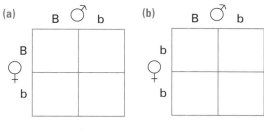

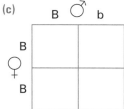

Figure 1.55 Using Punnett squares to predict black to white coat ratios

Go to **p. 227** to check your answers.

Conclusion

Write a suitable conclusion.

Go to **p. 227** to check your answer.

Experiment 3

Sex, genes and chromosomes

Aim

⊙ To investigate the inheritance of sex-linked genes

Materials

⊙ Three sets of different-coloured plastic disks (20 red, 10 green and 10 white)

⊙ Two plastic containers (such as old margarine tubs)

⊙ Non-permanent marker pen

Method

In this experiment, you will determine the chance of producing a male or female.

1. Label 20 red disks with the letter X using a marker pen. Place the 20 red disks in a plastic container labelled 'eggs'. These represent the egg cells that contain the X chromosome.

2. Label 10 green disks with an X and 10 white disks with a Y and place them in a second container labelled 'sperm'.

3. Draw a disk from each container and record the combination (XX or XY).

4. Replace the disks and repeat nine more times. Tally your results.

5. Combine the class results into a table. Calculate the proportion of XX and XY combinations as a percentage.

Analysis

1. Tabulate your results and the class results.

2. What percentage of females and males were produced in this simulation?

3. Why is it better to use the total class results rather than only your own group's results?

4. Do your results confirm that the world's population of males and females is close to 50:50?

Go to **p. 227** to check your answers.

Conclusion

 Write a suitable conclusion.

Go to p. 227 to check your answer.

(Note: Male to female ratios can vary quite significantly throughout the world. While men outnumber women, there are many countries, especially in Europe, where women outnumber men. Currently there are over 7 billion people on this planet. Estimates are that the current worldwide sex ratio at birth is 107 boys to 100 girls. Gender imbalances may arise due to various reasons ranging from natural factors and war casualties to intentional gender control and deliberate 'gendercide'. Consequently, the sex ratio tends to reduce as age increases, and among the elderly there is usually an excess of females.)

Test yourself 2

Part A: Knowledge

1. Gene technologies have produced insect-resistant cotton, reducing pesticide use by up to 80%. This in turn means *(1 mark)*

   A fewer chemicals in the environment.

   B less harm to friendly insects.

   C reduced farming production costs.

   D all of the above.

2. Figure 1.56 shows an example of a *(1 mark)*

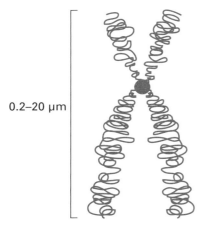

0.2–20 μm

Figure 1.56 Diagram to identify

   A chromosome.

   B chromatid.

   C DNA molecule.

   D gene.

3. The structure of DNA could be described as *(1 mark)*

   A a large polymer molecule.

   B a double helix.

   C a large protein molecule.

   D two of the above.

4. The process used to insert normal genes into human cells to correct disorders is known as *(1 mark)*

   A gene therapy.

   B sequencing genomes.

   C vaccination.

   D immunisation.

5. Genes are *(1 mark)*

   A the triplet code of nucleobases.

   B segments of the DNA molecule that code for a particular protein.

   C found attached to one of each pair of chromosomes.

   D composed of five consecutive triplet codes.

6. Complete the following restricted-response questions using the appropriate word. *(1 mark for each part)*

   a) .... chromosomes are pairs of chromosomes which are present in diploid cells and have the same appearance and function.

   b) The number, size and shape of all the chromosomes in a cell is called the .... and is characteristic for a species.

   c) The process of .... is involved in the production of gametes, which have a haploid number of chromosomes.

   d) The process of combining two gametes to produce a zygote is called ....

   e) James .... and Francis .... were the co-discoverers of the structure of DNA in 1953.

7. Use the code letters to match the terms or phrases in each column. *(1 mark for each part)*

Column 1		Column 2	
A	deoxyribonucleic acid	F	constriction point
B	pure breeding	G	sex cell
C	gamete	H	pea experiments
D	centromere	I	DNA
E	Gregor Mendel	J	homozygous

Part B: Skills

8. Pedigrees are sometimes called family trees. They can be used to show the relationship between individuals in an extended family and they can show genotypes or phenotypes, and the path along which some genes have been inherited. Figure 1.57 shows the pedigree of three generations of a particular family. The squares represent males and the circles represent females. The pedigree shows the inheritance of long and short eyelashes in this family.

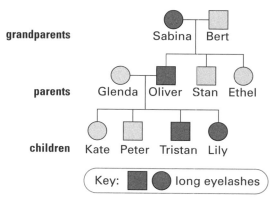

Figure 1.57 Pedigree for three generations of a family

a) Name Peter's grandmother. *(1 mark)*
b) Name Bert's daughter-in-law. *(1 mark)*
c) How many nieces does Ethel have? *(1 mark)*
d) Does Kate have long or short eyelashes? *(1 mark)*
e) If long eyelashes (E) is dominant to short eyelashes (e), determine the genotypes of
   i) Bert *(1 mark)*
   ii) Oliver *(1 mark)*
   iii) Lily *(1 mark)*

9. Figure 1.58 shows part of the family tree for Queen Victoria. Coloured-in squares indicate that the individual suffered from haemophilia.
   a) What indication is there that haemophilia is a sex-linked characteristic? *(1 mark)*
   b) Identify each of the following individuals by referring to either their number or name.
      i) One of Queen Victoria's sons, Leopold, was affected with haemophilia and died following a fall at the age of 31 years as a result of a cerebral haemorrhage. Who had he married? *(1 mark)*
      ii) Leopold, through his daughter, had an affected grandson, who died at age 20 years. What was his name? *(1 mark)*

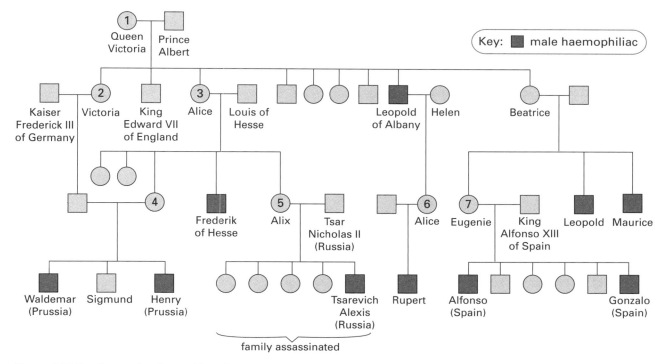

Figure 1.58 Family tree for Queen Victoria

iii) Alice married the Duke of Hesse (in Germany) and had one affected son, Frederick, and two carrier daughters, Irene and Alix. Who is Irene? *(1 mark)*

iv) Irene married into the Prussian royal family and had two affected sons. What were their names? *(2 marks)*

v) Beatrice married into the Spanish royal family. She had two affected sons. What were their names? *(2 marks)*

vi) Beatrice also had a daughter, Eugenie, who married King Alfonso of Spain and in turn had two affected sons, the older of whom was also called Alfonso. Who is the other son? *(1 mark)*

vii) Alix, a daughter of Alice, married the Russian Tsar, Nicholas II, with whom she had four daughters and a single son. What was the name of the son? *(1 mark)*

c) Two daughters of Queen Victoria, Alice and Beatrice, proved to be carriers of haemophilia. How do you know? *(1 mark)*

d) Queen Victoria was a carrier of the haemophilia gene. However, none of her ancestors is known to have been affected. Suggestion a possible way she could have become a carrier. *(1 mark)*

e) Queen Elizabeth II is the daughter of King George VI. George VI was the grandson of Edward VII (shown on the family tree). None of these men had haemophilia.

i) What is the relationship of Queen Elizabeth II and Queen Victoria? *(1 mark)*

ii) Is Queen Elizabeth II a carrier of the haemophilia gene? *(1 mark)*

10. A human female carrier who is heterozygous for the recessive, sex-linked trait causing red–green colour blindness marries a normal male. What proportion of their male progeny will have red–green colour blindness? *(2 marks)*

11. a) Where do each of the two copies of a gene in a diploid cell come from? *(2 marks)*

b) Why is the outcome of any breeding experiment that is not sex-linked the same regardless of which of the parents provides the eggs and which provides the sperm? *(1 mark)*

12. Figure 1.59 shows some pure-breeding experiments involving red- and white-coated Shorthorn cattle.

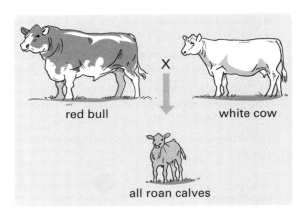

Figure 1.59 Crossing red-coated and white-coated Shorthorn cattle

All the F_1 generation are roan coloured. Their coats contain red hairs intermixed with white. Does this experiment indicate that either red or white coat is dominant? Explain. *(2 marks)*

13. Figure 1.60 shows three of the 23 pairs of chromosomes in a body cell of a human male. The locations of the three genes on these chromosomes are shown. These genes control nose shape, type of hair and earlobes.

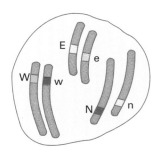

Key:
W = wavy hair
w = straight hair
E = unattached earlobes
e = attached earlobes
N = narrow nose
n = wide nose

Figure 1.60 Genes on chromosomes

a) Write the genotype for this individual for these three traits. *(2 marks)*

b) When sperm is produced, the number of chromosomes halves. Each sperm cell receives one of each chromosome pair. Write the genotypes of all the possible genotype combinations that this person will have in their sperm for these three traits. *(2 marks)*

c) A sperm cell has the genotype WEn. This sperm fertilises an egg with the genotype WeN. What will be the genotype and phenotype of the offspring? *(4 marks)*

14. In a pea-breeding experiment, both parent plants shown in Figure 1.61 are homozygous.

   a) Why would all of the F_1 generation plants have yellow pea seed phenotypes? *(1 mark)*

   b) What accounts for the green pea seed in the F_2 generation? *(1 mark)*

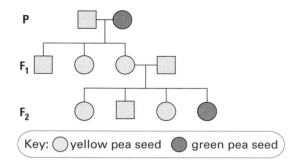

Key: ◯ yellow pea seed ● green pea seed

Figure 1.61 Results of pea-breeding experiment

Go to pp. 228–229 to check your answers.

Summary

1. Darwin studied variation among living things and fossilised remains of extinct organisms.

2. Darwin concluded that organisms had changed or evolved over the long periods of geological time.

3. Darwin developed the theory of natural selection to explain his observations.

4. Darwin proposed that favourable characteristics in a given environment make an organism reproductively fit.

5. There is considerable evidence that organisms have evolved over time.

6. Various factors in the environment may change and this may lead to new selection pressures.

7. Humans have used artificial selection in the domestication of animals and plants.

8. Antibiotic resistance in bacteria is an example of artificial selection.

9. Within the nuclei of cells are chromosomes, which carry the genes.

10. Each human cell contains 46 pairs of chromosomes.

11. Genes are the components on chromosomes that play an important role in determining physical and other traits about individuals.

12. Meiosis is a special type of cell division important for sexual reproduction; in animals, meiosis produces gametes.

13. Gregor Mendel built the founding principles of hereditary and genetics.

14. Genes exist in alternative forms, called alleles. They contain information that is used by the cells to control growth, development and proper functioning.

15. Genotype refers to the genetic composition of an individual. Phenotype refers to the characteristic shown by that individual.

16. Punnett squares are used by biologists to predict the probability of possible genotypes of offspring.

17. A pedigree can refer to the lineage or genealogical descent of people or of animals.

18. Sex-linkage associates a characteristic with gender, because the gene controlling the chromosome is located on a sex chromosome.

19. James Watson and Francis Crick discovered the structure of the DNA molecule that encodes our genetic information as a double helix.

20. A mutation occurs when a gene is damaged or changed in such a way as to alter the genetic message carried by that gene.

21. The purpose of genetic testing or screening is to confirm the diagnosis in patients with certain symptoms and to advise other family members of the diagnosed patient whether they also have the disease.

22. There are concerns about the possible use or misuse of genetic profiles, with calls for restricting the accessibility of this information and ensuring confidentiality.

Are you able to answer every syllabus question in this chapter? Tick each question as you go through the list if you are able to answer it. If you cannot answer it, turn to the appropriate page in the guide as is listed in the column to find the answer.

	For a complete understanding of this topic	Page no.	✓
1	Can I recall the observations made by Darwin that demonstrated natural variation?	3	
2	Can I explain why Darwin concluded that organisms had changed or evolved over the long periods of geological time?	3	
3	Can I recall the major points of Darwin's theory of natural selection?	3	
4	Can I recall the connection that Darwin placed on favourable characteristics and reproductive fitness?	3	
5	Can I list the considerable evidence that organisms have evolved over time?	4–8	
6	Can I explain how various factors in the environment may change and how this may lead to new selection pressures?	8–9	
7	Can I explain how humans have used artificial selection in the domestication of animals and plants?	9–10	
8	Can I explain how antibiotic resistance in bacteria is an example of artificial selection?	11–12	

	For a complete understanding of this topic	Page no.	✓
9	Can I explain the relationship between genes and chromosomes?	15–17	
10	Can I identify how many chromosomes a human has?	16	
11	Can I explain the connection between genes and individual physical traits?	17	
12	Can I describe the importance of meiosis?	18	
13	Can I explain the importance of Gregor Mendel's work?	19–21	
14	Can I explain what is meant by the term 'allele'?	21	
15	Can I explain the difference between genotype and phenotype?	21–22	
16	Can I explain how to use a Punnett square?	22	
17	Can I explain what a pedigree is?	23	
18	Can I explain the importance of Watson and Crick's work?	25–26	
19	Can I explain what a mutation is?	26–32	
20	Can I explain the purpose of genetic testing or screening?	32–33	
21	Can I list some concerns about the possible use or misuse of genetic profiles?	34–35	

Chapter test

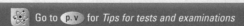 Go to **p. v** for *Tips for tests and examinations*   80 min

Part A: Multiple-choice questions

(1 mark for each)

1. Which of the following statements is part of the theory of natural selection as proposed by Charles Darwin?
   A Over time the characteristics of a population change as the favourable characteristics are preserved.
   B Humans have evolved from their ape-like ancestors.
   C Structural changes in an organism during its lifetime are preserved and are passed onto the next generation.
   D Mutations in the cellular DNA are inheritable and lead to evolution of species.

2. Which one of the following statements is correct?
   A By 500 million years ago, the great majority of the life forms of today existed.
   B Birds, mammals and flowering plants made their appearance in the fossil record in the Mesozoic Era.

C The first land organisms were amphibians that appeared in the Devonian period about 400 million years ago.

D By the middle Palaeozoic, the oceans swarmed with giant fish and aquatic mammals.

3. According to Darwin's tree of life, which of the following groups branched away from the main trunk at the earliest date in the evolution of life?

A mammals

B protista

C fungi

D green plants

4. The following statements concern the Australian bilby. Which of these statements would enable you to decide whether this bilby made a contribution to the evolution of its species?

A It was significantly larger than other members of its species.

B It ate considerable quantities of food.

C It lived for 4 years.

D During its lifetime it ran a lot and had muscular legs.

5. On his trip to the Galapagos Islands, Darwin observed populations of finches. He used these observations as evidence for evolution. The observation that provided this evidence was that

A the fossils discovered on the islands showed that the living finches were different.

B the older the island, the more the finches resembled the mainland finches.

C each island had different species of finches.

D DNA differences between each finch population.

6. If a known test animal is homozygous recessive for a trait (tt) and another test animal is homozygous dominant for a trait (TT), the percentage of the offspring that will be homozygous recessive is

A 0%.

B 25%.

C 50%.

D 100%.

7. The features of an organism

A are determined only by the genes they inherit.

B are determined only by the environment in which they live.

C that are acquired during their life can readily be inherited by their children.

D are determined both by its inherited genes and its interaction with the environment.

8. DNA fingerprint patterns for a disputed parental case are shown in Figure 1.62.

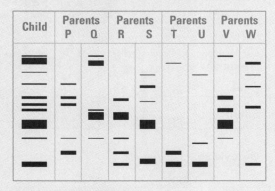

Figure 1.62 DNA patterns

Which pair of parents' DNA matches the child's DNA?

A P and Q

B R and S

C T and U

D V and W

9. Which of these is the first step in the process to producing a genetically modified organism?

A Attach the DNA fragment to a carrier.

B Clone double-stranded DNA fragments.

C Transfer the DNA fragment into the host organism.

D Isolate the foreign DNA fragment.

10. Hybrid plants are

A crosses between individuals of unknown genotype with individuals of known genotype.

B offspring that are homozygous.

C the offspring of parents that have different forms of a trait.

D the process of selecting the best characteristics of an organism.

Part B: Short-answer questions

11. Figure 1.63 shows the range of four invertebrates over an approximate 300-million-year time scale. The range represents the

total geological life span of a distinct group of organisms.

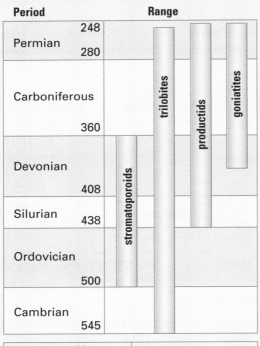

Figure 1.63 Geological life span of four organisms (times are measured in millions of years ago)

a) What geological era is represented by this diagram? *(1 mark)*

b) Which of the four organisms appeared first in the fossil record? *(1 mark)*

c) Which organisms became extinct in the Permian period? *(1 mark)*

d) Which organisms do not appear in the fossil record of the following periods?
   i) Silurian *(1 mark)*
   ii) Cambrian *(1 mark)*

e) How would a palaeontologist distinguish fossilised rock layers from the Carboniferous and the Cambrian? *(2 marks)*

12. Biogeography is the study of the distribution of organisms. Figure 1.64 shows the locations of continental masses that formed Gondwana at two different times in Earth's history.

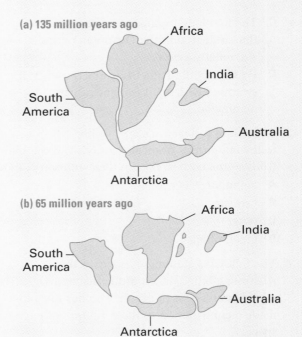

Figure 1.64 Gondwana break up

Use this information to explain the following.

a) Fossil marsupials have been found in Australia and South America but none have been found in Africa. *(1 mark)*

b) It is likely that fossil marsupials will eventually be found in Antarctica. *(1 mark)*

c) Most living marsupials are found in Australia, with only two species found in South America. *(1 mark)*

13. Domesticated cats have many different breeds, whereas there are few natural breeds of wild cats. Use Darwin's theory to explain this observation. *(2 marks)*

14. Figure 1.65 shows a proposed evolutionary tree for five living species of frogs (A, B, C, D and E). Use this diagram to explain how modern DNA analysis could be used to support the hypothesis that only C, D and E have the extinct species X as their common ancestor. *(2 marks)*

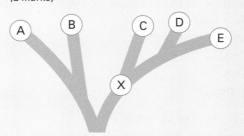

Figure 1.65 Evolutionary tree

15. Consider the following account of the formation of new species of frogs in Australia. Answer the questions that follow.

About 1 million years ago, glacial periods created cool, moist conditions across the whole of southern Australia. Wet areas linking the eastern and western coastlines of southern Australia allowed a continuous population of frogs to interbreed. When the glacial period ended, the climate became much drier and this led to the formation of the Nullarbor Plain in southern central Australia. This desert zone prevented frogs in the south-east from interbreeding with the south-western frogs. Today the two populations show distinct differences in their appearance and in their reproductive behaviour.

a) Explain how these environmental changes can lead to evolutionary change in the frogs. *(2 marks)*

b) Compare the original gene pools of the eastern and western frogs at the time when the Nullarbor Plain formed. *(1 mark)*

c) How will gene mutations in both populations ensure that the two groups become two new species? *(1 mark)*

d) The western zone is much drier than the eastern zone. How will these different environments select the favourable characteristics in each population? *(2 marks)*

16. Species are often divided into subspecies called 'races'. We are familiar with the different racial characteristics in humans. These different races can interbreed. Suggest a mechanism for the development of races in a human population. *(3 marks)*

17. *Escherichia coli* is a common bacterium. If a natural population is cultured in a laboratory in the presence of an antibiotic, we find that most but not all the bacteria are killed. The survivors are collected and cultured again in the presence of the antibiotic. This time most survive and few are killed.

a) What conclusion can one draw about the natural population of bacteria? *(1 mark)*

b) Explain why the antibiotic is a selecting agent. *(1 mark)*

18. Figure 1.66 shows the evolutionary tree for the land plants. Use this diagram to answer the following questions.

a) How long ago did ferns, tree ferns and horsetails share a common ancestor? *(1 mark)*

b) How long ago did ferns and conifers (pines) share a common ancestor? *(1 mark)*

c) Which modern group of land plants was the first to evolve? *(1 mark)*

d) How long ago did all land plants share a common ancestor with aquatic plants? *(1 mark)*

e) Which major plant group was the last to evolve? *(1 mark)*

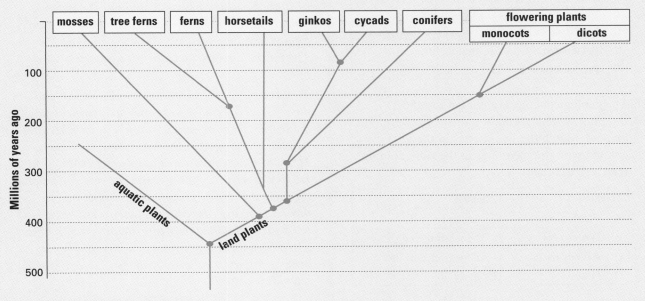

Figure 1.66 Evolutionary tree for plants

19. Are the following statements true or false?
    (1 mark for each part)
    a) In nature, only animals struggle for existence.
    b) In a species, all members of the population are identical.
    c) 'Survival of the fittest' refers to the ability of organisms with favourable characteristics to survive so they can reproduce.
    d) Over time, populations of organisms gradually become better adapted to their environment through the process of natural selection.
    e) Two populations of magpies that are prevented from breeding will soon develop into new species.
    f) According to Darwin, humans are descended from monkeys and apes.
    g) In the tree of life, the simplest organisms are near the base of the tree.
    h) The Precambrian rocks contain evidence of vertebrate life forms.
    i) There was a rapid explosion in life forms in the Cambrian period.
    j) The Mesozoic era was dominated by mammals.

20. The eras of Earth's history are given names to reflect events or sequences. Match the era in the left column with its meaning in the right column. *(1 mark for each part)*

Column 1		Column 2	
A	Cenozoic	E	ancient life
B	Mesozoic	F	before the Cambrian
C	Palaeozoic	G	middle life
D	Precambrian	H	recent life

21. The geological eons are named to reflect the time of their formation or the life forms present. Match the list of eons in the left column with the meanings in the right column. *(1 mark for each part)*

Column 1		Column 2	
A	Phanerozoic	E	ancient
B	Proterozoic	F	beneath the earth
C	Archaean	G	appearance of life
D	Hadean	H	early life

The following text is used to answer Questions 22 and 23.

Wilberforce and Darwin

Darwin's On the Origin of Species *was published on 24 November 1859. All 1250 first edition copies were sold out on the first day. A storm of protest immediately erupted. The* Quarterly Review *strongly criticised Darwin's theories as they were counter to the word of God as set out in the Bible. Although Darwin had not yet published his views on the origin of humans, he did add a concluding sentence at the end of his book: 'Much light will be thrown on the origin of man and his history'. This last sentence provoked the greatest furore. Some commentators vilified Darwin for believing that humans had descended from monkeys. Darwin was denounced for degrading men to the same level as the beasts of nature. By June 1860, the outrage from various sectors of society was growing. At the meeting of the British Association for the Advancement of Science, Bishop Samuel Wilberforce took the dais to denounce Darwin and his theories. Although Darwin was not present, Wilberforce attacked Thomas Huxley, who was one of Darwin's supporters. Wilberforce triumphantly asked of Huxley: 'Was it through his grandfather or his grandmother that Huxley claimed descent from an ape?' When it was Huxley's turn to speak, he defended Darwin at length and concluded by saying that he would never be ashamed to have an ape as an ancestor, but he would be ashamed of an eminent and famous man who tried to argue about an area of study on which he knew nothing. The meeting quickly developed into a slanging match. Women fainted and men on each side shouted at each other. The hatred directed at Darwin's supporters was bitter.*

To this day, people speak out about Darwin and his theory. You only have to search the internet using the words 'Darwin' and 'evolution' to quickly find that the tirade against Darwin's views continues. Many of these articles would be described by Huxley as writings of those who do not understand the meaning and implications of evolutionary theory. In many cases, the arguments are based on religious faith alone. Scientific theories cannot be tested by faith and personal belief. A theory can only be found to be false by the processes of the scientific method.

22. Thomas Huxley believed in Darwin's theory of natural selection. In his argument with Bishop Wilberforce, what point of view did he promote? *(1 mark)*

23. Why is the theory of natural selection a scientific theory and not one based on faith? *(1 mark)*

The following text is used to answer Questions 24 and 25.

Lamarckian evolution

About 40 years before the publication of Darwin's theory of evolution by natural selection, Jean Baptiste Lamarck (1744–1829) proposed a different theory of evolution.

> *Citizens, go from the simplest to the most complex and you will have the true thread that connects all the productions of nature; you will have an accurate idea of progression; you will be convinced that the simplest things have given rise to all others.*

Lamarck's theory of evolution was largely ignored or attacked during his lifetime. But Charles Darwin acknowledged Lamarck as a great biologist and as an early proponent of evolution. Like Darwin, Lamarck argued that the Earth was extremely old. Lamarck believed that the environment acted on all organisms and caused them to change their behaviour. He believed that changes in behaviour led to increasing or lesser use of certain body structures. The changes in these structures acquired during the lifetime of an organism could be inherited. Over many generations, the change would become permanent. Thus, a giraffe that continually stretched its neck to reach the higher leaves in a tree would pass this favourable characteristic onto the subsequent generations. Similarly, the ancestors of snakes gradually lost their legs as they adopted a habit of crawling on the ground. The lack of use of their legs led to their gradual disappearance. The needs of the animal in terms of the environment in which it lived dictated the direction in which evolution occurred. Lamarck's theory is called evolution by acquired characteristics. There is only very limited support for Lamarckian evolution today. It is hard to understand how characteristics acquired by parents could be passed onto their sex cells and then through to their offspring. Darwin's theory explains the increase in the size of the necks

of giraffes in terms of variation in the natural population, competition and natural selection.

24. Explain the phrase: 'evolution by acquired characteristics'. *(1 mark)*

25. How did Darwin explain the evolution of the neck of giraffes? *(1 mark)*

26. Explain why the fruit-fly *Drosophila melanogaster* is widely used by geneticists for breeding experiments in the laboratory. *(4 marks)*

27. Table 1.7 gives the ratios of purple to white grains for six corn cobs in the F_2 generation of a breeding experiment.

Table 1.7 Results of grain colour on corn cob experiments

Trial	Number of purple grains	Number of white grains	Total number of grains	Ratio purple : white
1	399	145	544	2.75 : 1
2	474	152	i)	3.12 : 1
3	387	ii)	508	3.20 : 1
4	iii)	144	569	2.95 : 1
5	390	136	526	iv)
6	411	130	541	v)

a) Complete the values shown by Roman numerals in the table. *(5 marks)*

b) Which colour grain is dominant: purple or white? *(1 mark)*

c) One of the most striking features of these biological results is their variability between cobs. Why isn't the ratio exactly 3 : 1, the theoretical value? *(1 mark)*

28. The sequence of nucleobases along one strand of a DNA molecule is: CCTGTGAGCAAC. Write the sequence of bases on the complementary DNA strand. *(2 marks)*

29. Name two ways in which the DNA code can be mutated. *(2 marks)*

30. A black-coated male guinea pig has two dominant genes (BB) inherited from its parents. This guinea pig mates with a white-coated female (bb).

a) If all the sperm produced by the male contains B genes, what gene do all the eggs from the female contain? *(1 mark)*

b) All the baby pigs in the litter contain the same gene pairs for coat colour. What is this gene pair? *(1 mark)*

31. Malaria can be prevented by killing local mosquito populations. Insecticides have been used for this purpose, such as DDT, which is a lethal nerve poison. In a field experiment, mosquito samples were regularly captured over a number of months and sprayed with a 4% solution of DDT. The results were observed over time (see Figure 1.67) to determine what percentages of mosquitoes were killed.

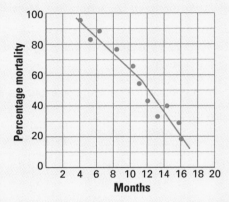

Figure 1.67 DDT effect on mosquitoes over time

a) Describe the shape of the graph. *(1 mark)*

b) Explain the results. *(2 marks)*

32. The triplet codes in the DNA molecule are each associated with a particular amino acid.

a) Use Table 1.8 to determine the amino acid sequence in a protein chain made by decoding the following set of triplet codes: TGA GAG CCC CTA AAA ACA. *(2 marks)*

Table 1.8 Amino acid codes

Triplet code	Amino acid	Triplet code	Amino acid
AAA	phenylalanine	GCT	arginine
AAT	leucine	TAA	isoleucine
AGA	serine	TGA	threonine
ACA	cysteine	CAA	valine
ACC	tryptophan	CGT	alanine
GAG	leucine	CTA	aspartic acid
GGA	proline	CTC	glutamic acid
GTA	histidine	CCC	glycine

b) A mutation in the DNA code occurs so that the previous sequence now becomes: TGA GAG CCC CAA AAA ACA

i) What type of mutation has occurred? *(1 mark)*

ii) What change in amino acids will occur in the protein chain? *(1 mark)*

33. Haemophilia in humans is due to an X-chromosome mutation.

a) Draw a Punnett square to show the results of mating between a normal (non-carrier) female and a haemophilic male. *(3 marks)*

b) Which of the following statements is true? *(1 mark)*

A. Half of daughters are normal and half of sons are haemophilic.

B. All sons are normal and all daughters are carriers.

C. Half of sons are normal and half are haemophilic; all daughters are carriers.

D. All daughters are normal and all sons are carriers.

E. Half of daughters are haemophilic and half of daughters are carriers; all sons are normal.

c) Would any of the children exhibit haemophilia? Explain. *(2 marks)*

34. Figure 1.68 shows two cell nuclei, each with three pairs of chromosomes. Other chromosomes are not shown. Some genes are shown on each chromosome.

a) Cell nucleus (1) has the following gene combination sequence (or genotype): BBRrss. Write the gene combination sequence for cell nucleus (2). *(1 mark)*

b) Use the following information about each gene to determine the appearance (phenotype) of people containing each type of cell. *(2 marks)*

B = brown eyes, b = blue eyes, R = round face, r = long face, S = straight hairline, s = peaked hairline

c) What will be the appearance (phenotype) of a person with the following gene combination in their cells: bbrrss? *(1 mark)*

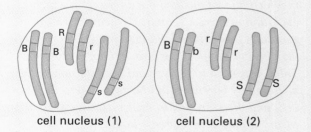

cell nucleus (1)   cell nucleus (2)

Figure 1.68 Two cell nuclei with three chromosomes

35. Chromosomes occur in pairs called homologous pairs. In humans there are 23 pairs. Figure 1.69 shows a pair of homologous chromosomes. Bands along each chromosome represent genes.

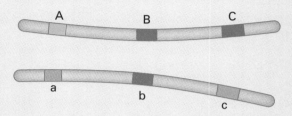

Figure 1.69 A homologous pair of chromosomes

a) Gene 'b' is found on one of the chromosomes.
   i) What allele is found on the other chromosome? *(1 mark)*
   ii) If gene 'B' represents brown eyes and 'b' represents blue eyes, what coloured eyes will this person have? *(1 mark)*
b) What generalisation can be made about the location of the gene pairs on the chromosome? *(1 mark)*

36. Cell division is an important process in all living things. Match the code letters in column 1 to the example provided in column 2. *(3 marks)*

Column 1	Column 2
A growth	P a cut on the skin gradually improves and eventually disappears; new red blood cells are generated in the bone marrow
B repair	Q can occur by mitosis or meiosis
C reproduction	R cells multiply in numbers and grow to their maximum size

37. In a natural woodland exists a population of mottled, light-brown moths and dark moths. The mottled, light-brown moths are 90% of the total population. Moths are part of the diet of the native bird population.

a) Why is the population of dark moths so low in this woodland? *(1 mark)*
b) A coal-burning power plant is established near the woodland. Over many years the black soot from the power plant is blown by the wind into the woodland and the tree trunks gradually become quite black. How will this change in the environment affect the moth population? *(2 marks)*

38. a) The potential benefits of gene technology are immense. List at least three. *(3 marks)*
   b) What are some criticisms of gene technology? *(2 marks)*

39. Figure 1.70 shows the components of a section of one strand of a DNA molecule. Z is a component known as a phosphate group.

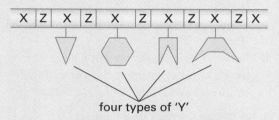

Figure 1.70 Section of a DNA molecule with coded sections X, Y and Z

a) Identify the parts labelled by the code letters (X and Y). *(2 marks)*
b) What general name is given to the structure comprising X, Y and Z? *(1 mark)*
c) Why is DNA described as a polymer? *(1 mark)*

40. Darier's disease is a rare genetic disorder that is indicated mainly by changes in the skin. It is characterised by dark crusty patches on the skin, sometimes containing pus. Onset usually occurs in adolescence and it is usually chronic. Darier's is inherited in an autosomal dominant pattern by a change (mutation) in the gene on chromosome number 12. Only one copy of the gene is sufficient to cause the disorder, when inherited from a parent who has the disorder.

Figure 1.71 shows the disease inherited in a certain family.

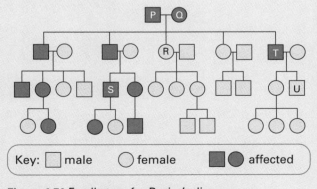

Key: ☐ male   ○ female   ■● affected

Figure 1.71 Family tree for Darier's disease

a) How do you know this is not a sex-linked disorder? *(1 mark)*

b) Persons marked P and Q are both heterozygous for the disease. How do you know? *(2 marks)*

c) Given D represents the Darier's disease allele and d represents the normal allele, what is the genotype for person marked R? *(1 mark)*

d) What is the genotype for person marked S? *(1 mark)*

e) What is the genotype for person marked T? *(1 mark)*

f) Person U marries a woman who does not have Darier's disease. Could any of their children have Darier's disease? *(3 marks)*

Go to pp. 229–232 to check your answers.

CHAPTER 2

Atomic structure and chemical reactions

Overview

In this chapter you will learn about:

- ☑ historical development of the periodic table
- ☑ classifying elements
- ☑ structure of the atom
- ☑ the modern periodic table
- ☑ trends in properties of the elements
- ☑ reactivity of metals
- ☑ chemical word equations and symbolic equations
- ☑ valency and chemical formulae
- ☑ ionic and covalent compounds
- ☑ balancing equations for simple chemical reactions
- ☑ decomposition and precipitation reactions
- ☑ rates of chemical change
- ☑ factors affecting the rate of corrosion and rusting
- ☑ useful substances.

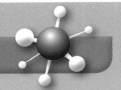

Glossary

Atom—the smallest unit of an element; composed of protons, neutrons and electrons

Atomic number (Z)—the number of protons in the nucleus of an atom

Biofuel—a type of renewable fuel whose energy is derived from biological carbon fixation

Biomass—any material which is recently derived from plant and animal material such as wood from forests, material left over from agricultural and forestry processes, and organic industrial, human and animal wastes

Catalyst—a substance that speeds up a reaction, but is chemically unchanged at the end of the reaction

Corrosion—a process in which a solid, such as a metal, is eaten away and changed by a chemical action

Covalent bond—a form of chemical bonding that is characterised by the sharing of pairs of electrons between atoms

Decomposition—the breakdown of a substance into simpler substances

Effervescence—gas bubbles in a liquid

Electron—a negatively charged subatomic particle located outside and moving around the nucleus

Electron configuration—the arrangement of electrons in their shells

Group—a column of the periodic table containing a family of related elements

Ionic bond—a type of chemical bond formed through an electrostatic attraction between two oppositely charged ions

Isotopes—atoms with the same atomic number but different mass numbers

Law of mass conservation—matter can neither be created nor destroyed, but can be changed in form

Mass number (A)—the number of protons plus neutrons in the nucleus of an atom

Neutron—a neutral subatomic particle found in the nucleus

Nucleus—the central positive core of an atom

Octet—a group of eight valence electrons surrounding an atom; all noble gases are stable, having an octet of valence electrons, except helium

Period—a row of elements of the periodic table

Periodic table—the arrangement of the elements according to increasing atomic number

Pharmacology—the science of drugs, including their composition, uses and effects

Polyatomic ion—a charged species (ion) made up of two or more atoms covalently bonded (also known as a molecular ion); for example, SO_4^{2-}, NH_4^+

Polymer—a large molecule (macromolecule) composed of repeating structural units, typically connected by covalent chemical bonds

Precipitation—the formation of an insoluble solid on mixing solutions of ionic compounds

Proton—a positively charged subatomic particle located in the nucleus

Rust—any of various powdery or scaly reddish-brown or reddish-yellow hydrated iron oxides and hydroxides formed on iron and iron-containing materials; in order to occur, rusting requires water and oxygen

Salt—ionic compounds that result from the neutralisation reaction of an acid and a base

Valence shell—the outermost shell of an atom consisting of the valence electrons

Valency—the combining power of an element in a compound

2.1 Historical development of the periodic table

In 1660, the English scientist Robert Boyle was the first person to distinguish between elements and compounds. By the late 18th century, chemists had identified numerous substances that they classified as elements. Boyle believed that an element was a chemical substance that could not be broken into simpler substances by any known chemical means. Thirty-three of these substances are still classified as elements today whereas others were in fact compounds that resisted all attempts by these early chemists to break them down. Water and salt are such examples.

Law of mass conservation

French chemist Antoine Lavoisier (1743–1794) is often called the father of modern chemistry. In 1789, he stated that elements were the building blocks of all other substances. Lavoisier believed in the importance of accurate measurements and his experiments supported the law of mass conservation.

Lavoisier performed the experiment shown in Figure 2.1. He placed some red mercury oxide in an evacuated glass vessel. The tap was closed and the vessel heated. The red substance broke down to form mercury and a colourless gas that Lavoisier named oxygen. He weighed the vessels before and after the reaction and found that there was no change in mass.

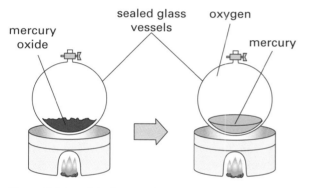

Figure 2.1 Lavoisier's experiment

The experiment showed there was no change in mass during the reaction. The vessel was sealed and so no products could escape from it. The reactant's mass was therefore the same as the mass of the products. This is an example of the law of mass conservation in a chemical reaction.

Using careful weighing procedures, Lavoisier found that 217 g of the red oxide of mercury produced 201 g of mercury (Hg). The difference in mass was 16 g. Lavoisier reasoned that this mass difference was due to the mass of oxygen produced.

The law of mass conservation states that in a chemical reaction, the total mass of the products equals the total mass of the reactants.

The atomic theory

In 1808, the English chemist John Dalton (1766–1844) proposed the atomic theory of matter. He based his theory on a proposal by the Greek philosopher Democritus (460–370 BC) that matter was made up of indivisible atoms. Some of the important ideas of Dalton's atomic theory are that:

> all matter is made of atoms

> atoms are indivisible, and they cannot be destroyed or created

> all atoms of the same element are exactly alike, but different from the atoms of all other elements.

Although many scientists of Dalton's time were not convinced by the idea of atoms, the increasing experimental evidence meant that within a few years the atomic theory became one of the foundation stones of modern chemistry. Today we believe that all the matter in nature is composed of elements and that each element is made up of its own kind of atoms which are different from the atoms of all other elements. Sometimes these elements exist in nature as separate substances and sometimes they are combined with other elements. The element sulfur, for example, differs from the element oxygen because its atoms are different; the weight of sulfur atoms is greater than the weight of oxygen atoms.

Atomic weight

Dalton investigated the relative weights of the atoms of different elements. Consider the following experiments similar to those that Dalton conducted to find the relative atomic weights of elements.

Experiment 1

Dalton found that carbon (C) would burn in variable amounts of oxygen (O) to form two different gaseous compounds. Twelve-gram samples of carbon were prepared and reacted with oxygen under these different conditions. The product gases in each reaction were then weighed.

> Reaction 1: 12 g of carbon → 28 g of gaseous compound (1)

> Reaction 2: 12 g of carbon → 44 g of gaseous compound (2)

Hypothesis

Atoms combine to form compounds in simple whole-number ratios. (In other words, one carbon atom, for instance, can only react with 1, 2, 3 and so on, atoms of oxygen. It can't, for example, react with 1½ oxygen atoms.) Therefore, the weight of a compound is the sum of the atomic weights of each component element.

Prediction

- Compound 1 is CO (i.e. one atom of C and one atom of O)
- Compound 2 is CO_2 (i.e. one atom of C and two atoms of O)

Figure 2.2 shows models of the two oxides of carbon.

compound 1 is called carbon monoxide

compound 2 is called carbon dioxide

Figure 2.2 Oxides of carbon

The only difference between the two compounds is an 'O' atom. The difference in reacting weights is 44 – 28 = 16 g. Therefore, if the relative atomic weight of carbon is 12 units then the relative atomic weight of oxygen is 16 units. The atomic weight units are given the symbol 'u'. Thus the atomic weight of oxygen is 16 u.

Experiment 2

Sulfur reacts with oxygen to form two different gaseous compounds.

- Reaction 1: 32 g of sulfur → 64 g of gaseous compound (A)
- Reaction 2: 32 g of sulfur → 80 g of gaseous compound (B)

The difference in weight between A and B is 16 g. This difference is most likely due to a difference of one oxygen atom in each molecule. This data is consistent with the following atom ratios:

- Compound A, S:O = 1:2
- Compound B, S:O = 1:3

If the atomic weight of oxygen is 16 u, then the atomic weight of sulfur is 32 u. The formula of compound A is SO_2 and the formula of compound B is SO_3.

Relative atomic weight

In this way, chemists gradually developed tables of the atomic weights of all known elements. They were hampered by a lack of accurate weighing devices. It was not until the 20th century that chemists could weigh individual atoms using a machine called a mass spectrometer. Individual atoms have very small masses. For example, the lightest atom, hydrogen, has a mass of 1.67×10^{-24} g. This information is used to define the atomic mass unit:

$$1\ u = 1.67 \times 10^{-24}\ g$$

These actual masses are so small that chemists prefer to use the relative weight scale. Therefore, the atomic weight of an element is a relative weight, not an absolute weight. An example of this is shown in Figure 2.3. Each hydrogen atom has a mass of 1 u and thus the carbon atom has a mass of 12 u.

carbon atoms are 12 times heavier than hydrogen atoms

Figure 2.3 Comparing the mass of carbon atoms to hydrogen atoms

Classifying elements

In the 1860s and 1870s, attempts were made to classify the known elements according to their atomic weights.

John Newlands

John Newlands (1837–1898) was an English chemist who investigated ways in which the known elements could be arranged in tabular format based on increasing atomic weight. In early versions of his table of elements he left spaces for undiscovered elements but in later versions he did not. His 1863 table (published in 1864/5) contained seven rows and eight columns. Related elements appear in the rows of Newlands' table. He proposed the law of octaves, which stated that every eighth element after a given one had similar chemical properties to the one selected. For example, Figure 2.4 shows a version of Newlands' table and if we select magnesium (Mg) as the first element and count to eight down the column and then down the next column, we reach calcium (Ca) which has similar physical and chemical properties to magnesium. Thus, Newlands became the first person to introduce the idea of periodicity or repeating properties of the elements. However, many scientists at the time were not impressed by this law of octaves and his achievement was not universally recognised. It was not until 1998 that he was recognised by the Royal Society of Chemistry as the originator of the concept of the periodic table.

beryllium (Be)

F (fluorine) not yet discovered

H		Cl	Co/Ni	Br	Pd	I	Pt/Ir
Li	Na	K	Cu	Rb	Ag	Cs	Tl
G	Mg	Ca	Zn	Sr	Cd	Ba/V	Pb
Bo	Al	Cr	Y	Ce/La	U	Ta	Th
C	Si	Ti	In	Zn	Sn	W	Hg
N	P	Mn	As	Di/Mo	Sb	Nb	Bi
O	S	Fe	Se	Ro/Ru	Te	Au	Os

boron (B)

Figure 2.4 Newlands' periodic table of 1863. Note the elements are arranged in vertical columns according to atomic weight. Some elements occupy the same cell. The atomic weights of some elements were inaccurate and so they are misplaced in the table. 'Di' stands for didymium which was believed to be an element but was found later to be a mixture of neodymium and praseodymium. 'Ro' stands for rhodium (Rh).

Dmitri Mendeleev

Four years after Newlands published his periodic table, Russian scientist Dmitri Mendeleev (1834–1907) produced his own version of the periodic table. He was unaware of the Newland's table. His table gained wide acceptance as he left spaces for elements yet to be discovered. Mendeleev's table was based on increasing atomic weight. If the atomic weight was not accurately known then the element was placed in a position consistent with its chemical properties. His revised 1871 table consisted of eight columns (called groups) and 12 rows (called series), as shown in Figure 2.5. The vertical groups contained elements with similar properties and therefore formed a chemical family.

The success of Mendeleev's periodic table was also due to its ability to predict the properties of undiscovered elements. Two of these elements were gallium (Ga) and germanium (Ge) which are in the same group as aluminium and silicon respectively. In 1871, these elements had not yet been discovered so Mendeleev left spaces for them (see Figure 2.6). He made some predictions about the expected properties of these elements using chemical and physical data of elements around them.

When gallium was discovered in 1875, its properties were very close to those predicted by Mendeleev. In 1887 the element germanium was discovered and its properties were also found to be similar to the predictions of Mendeleev. Eventually, Mendeleev had to expand his table to create a new group when the noble gases (helium, neon, argon and so on) were discovered at the end of the 19th century.

Series	Group							
	I	II	III	IV	V	VI	VII	VIII
1	H (1)							
2	Li (7)	Be (9)	B (11)	C (12)	N (14)	O (16)		
3	Na (23)	Mg (24)	Al (27)	Si (28)	P (31)	S (32)	Cl (35.5)	
4	K (39)	Ca (40)		Ti (48)	V (51)	Cr (52)	Mn (55)	Fe (56)
								Co (59)
								Ni (59)
								Cu (63)
5		Zn (65)			As (75)	Se (78)	Br (80)	

Figure 2.5 The first five rows of Mendeleev's 1871 table. Fe, Co, Ni and Cu have all been placed in Series 4, Group VIII.

Al	Si	P
?	?	As
In	Sn	Sb

Figure 2.6 Gallium and germanium had not been discovered in 1871.

2.2 Structure of the atom

The New Zealand scientist Ernest Rutherford (1871–1937) was an early pioneer in the use of radioactivity as a tool to investigate matter. His experiments with radioactivity led him to propose that most of the mass of an atom is located in a small central core of the atom called the nucleus. He proposed that positive protons were located in the nucleus together with neutral particles which became known as neutrons. The neutrons were eventually discovered in 1932. Rutherford imagined that the negative electrons orbited the nucleus like planets around the Sun. It soon became apparent that electrons could not remain stable in this way and so an alternative theory was required. In 1913, the Danish physicist Niels Bohr (1885–1962) proposed the shell model of the atom in which electrons occupied stable energy levels around the nucleus.

Figure 2.7 illustrates Bohr's shell model. In this model, electrons occupy specific shells or energy levels extending outwards from the nucleus. These shells are labelled K, L, M, N and O. There is a maximum electron population (MEP) in any shell and this is calculated using the following formula:

$$MEP = 2n^2$$

Thus, the K shell ($n = 1$) has a maximum of two electrons [$2(1)^2$]. The L shell ($n = 2$) has a maximum of eight electrons [$2(2)^2$]. The M shell ($n = 3$) has a maximum of 18 electrons [$2(3)^2$].

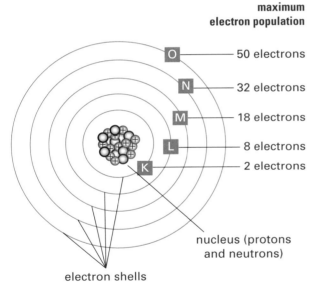

maximum electron population

O — 50 electrons
N — 32 electrons
M — 18 electrons
L — 8 electrons
K — 2 electrons

nucleus (protons and neutrons)

electron shells

Figure 2.7 Shell model of the atom

Figure 2.8 shows the nucleus and the two electron shells for an oxygen atom. In oxygen the eight electrons are arranged so that two electrons exist in the K shell and six electrons are present in the L shell.

The outermost shell of an atom that contains electrons is called the valence shell. The electrons in that shell are called valence electrons. The arrangement or pattern of electrons in the electron shells is called the electron configuration. The number of electrons is written in order starting with the K shell.

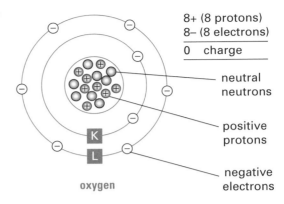

8+ (8 protons)
8– (8 electrons)
0   charge

neutral neutrons

positive protons

negative electrons

oxygen

Figure 2.8 Electrons shells and nucleus in a neutral oxygen atom (not to scale)

The following are some examples of elements and their electron configuration.

>> Fluorine is a gaseous element. It has nine protons in its nucleus and nine electrons in its electron shells. The first two electrons occupy the K shell which is now full. The remaining seven electrons are located in the L shell. These seven electrons are valence electrons. Fluorine's electron configuration is therefore 2, 7.

>> Sodium is a reactive metallic element. It has 11 protons in its nucleus and 11 electrons in its electron shells. The first two electrons occupy the K shell which is now full. The next eight electrons are located in the L shell, which is now full. The remaining electron is located in the M shell. This single electron is the valence electron. Sodium's electron configuration is therefore 2, 8, 1.

2.3 The modern periodic table

With the discovery of the subatomic particles of the atom in the late 19th and early 20th centuries, the method of arranging elements in the periodic table changed. A quantity called the atomic number (Z) was used to arrange the elements rather than the atomic weight. The term mass number (A) was then defined in terms of the total number of particles inside the nucleus.

>> Atomic number (Z) means the number of protons in the nucleus of an atom.

>> Mass number (A) means the number of protons plus neutrons in the nucleus of an atom.

The simplest atom is hydrogen, with one proton in its nucleus. So the atomic number of hydrogen is 1.

Uranium is a heavy element with 92 protons in its nucleus. Its atomic number is 92. An element can exist in a variety of forms called isotopes. This is due to differing numbers of neutrons. Isotopes have the same atomic number (Z) but different mass numbers (A). For example, hydrogen (Z = 1) has three isotopic forms with mass numbers 1, 2 and 3.

The outline map in Figure 2.9 shows the structure of the modern periodic table. The complete periodic table appears in the inside front cover of this book.

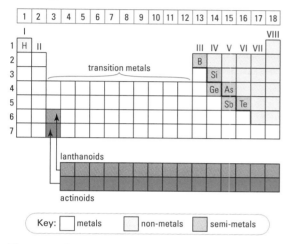

Figure 2.9 Outline map diagram of the periodic table. Note that the vertical groups can be numbered using Roman numerals (I to VIII) or numbers from 1 to 18. This last method is now the preferred method of group numbering.

Each family in the periodic table forms a vertical column or group. The family of alkali metals, which includes sodium and potassium, forms Group 1 (or I). Elements such as chlorine, bromine and iodine belong to Group 17 (or VII). The noble gases belong to Group 18 (or VIII).

Each horizontal row of the table is called a period. The first period contains only two elements, hydrogen and helium. Periods 2 and 3 each have eight elements. Periods 4 and 5 contain 18 elements. Period 6 has 32 elements including the lanthanoid series (Z = 57 to 71) of elements. Period 7 has 32 elements including the radioactive actinoid series (Z = 89 to 103) of elements.

The groups of the periodic table also indicate something about electron configuration. Elements of Group 1 (or I) have one valence electron. Elements of Group 13 (or III) have three valence electrons. All Group 15 (or V) elements have five valence electrons. For example, arsenic (Z = 33) is a member of Group 15 (or V) as its electronic configuration is: 2, 8, 18, 5.

Six elements (B, Si, Ge, As, Sb, Te) are classified as semi-metals. They separate the metallic elements from the non-metallic elements.

Eighteen elements are classified as non-metals. This includes hydrogen which is a gaseous element placed in Group 1 (I) as it has one valence electron. Some non-metals are gases (hydrogen, fluorine, chlorine and all the noble gases). Bromine is a fuming liquid and the rest of the non-metals are solids at room temperature.

Most of the elements of the periodic table are metals. One metal (mercury) is liquid at room temperature. The centre zone of the periodic table is called the transition metals. Included in the transition metals are the lanthanide and actinide series of metals. Elements from Z = 84 to Z = 92 are naturally radioactive. Metals after uranium (Z = 92) are radioactive and synthetic. As scientists continue their research, new synthetic elements will be created. These new elements will occupy Period 8.

Predicting trends in the properties of elements

The periodic table demonstrates various trends in properties down a group and across a period.

Metallic properties

The following trends are exhibited in the periodic table:

> metallic properties increase down a group
> metallic properties decrease across a period.

This trend is mainly exhibited in groups on the right of the periodic table. Consider Groups 15 (V) and 16 (VI). Down each of these groups, the elements change from non-metals to semi-metals to metals (see Table 2.1).

The trend in metallic properties across Periods 2 and 3 is shown in Table 2.2. The trend is from metals to semi-metals to non-metals.

Table 2.1 Metallic properties in Groups 15 (V) and 16 (VI)

Group 15 (V)	Classification	Group 16 (VI)	Classification
N	non-metal	O	non-metal
P	non-metal	S	non-metal
As	semi-metal	Se	non-metal
Sb	semi-metal	Te	semi-metal
Bi	metal	Po	metal

Table 2.2 Metallic properties across Periods 2 and 3

Li	Be	B	C	N	O	F	Ne
metal	metal	semi-metal	non-metal	non-metal	non-metal	non-metal	non-metal

Na	Mg	Al	Si	P	S	Cl	Ar
metal	metal	metal	semi-metal	non-metal	non-metal	non-metal	non-metal

Metal reactivity

Some metals are more reactive than others. Potassium is a very reactive metal whereas gold is quite unreactive.

The following trends are exhibited in the periodic table.

⊜ In Groups 1 (I) and 2 (II), reactivity increases down the group.

⊜ In the transition metals, reactivity tends to decrease down a group.

⊜ Across a period, metal reactivity tends to decrease.

These trends tell us that the most active metals are at the bottom left of the periodic table. Ignoring the radioactive metals in Period 7, the least-reactive transition metals are elements such as mercury, platinum and gold.

Non-metal reactivity

In Groups 14 (IV) to 17 (VII) the reactivity of the non-metal:

⊜ decreases down the group

⊜ increases across the period.

In Group 18 (VIII):

⊜ the noble gases are all quite unreactive although reactivity does increase slightly down the group.

These trends show that fluorine is the most reactive of the non-metals and helium is the least reactive.

Melting point

There are no simple trends with regard to the melting points of the elements. Figure 2.10 shows a bar graph of the melting points of the elements in Periods 1 to 4.

The melting points tend to rise along a period and then decrease. This correlates with the change from metals to semi-metals and then non-metals. Carbon, boron and silicon have very high melting points.

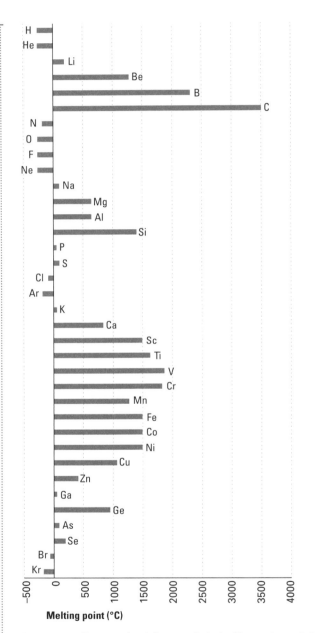

Figure 2.10 Bar graph of the trends in boiling points of the first 36 elements of the periodic table

2.4 Reactivity of metals

Metals vary in their reactivity. Various experimental tests can be done to rank the metals in a reactivity order. Metals are reacted with water, acids and oxygen and the rate of each reaction is compared. The results of these experiments allow the activity series of metals to be determined. Table 2.3 shows the activity series of some common metals. In this table, the activity decreases from left to right.

Reactive metals such as potassium, sodium and calcium will react with cold water, producing bubbles of hydrogen gas. This production of gas bubbles is known as effervescence. With magnesium, a few bubbles are observed if the water is hot. Iron can be made to react if heated in an atmosphere of steam. The word equation is given below. (For more information on word equations, see page 61.)

potassium + water → potassium hydroxide
+ hydrogen

Acids such as dilute sulfuric acid and hydrochloric acid increase the rate of reaction. The active metals react very rapidly, generating hydrogen gas. Zinc will react moderately fast with these acids but for lead the reaction is very slow. Copper, silver and gold do not react with dilute acids.

Word equation:

magnesium + hydrochloric acid
→ magnesium chloride + hydrogen

Experiment 1

Activity series of metals

Aim

To rank metals according to their reactivity with various reagents

Method

1. Set up five test tubes in a test-tube rack. Half-fill each tube with hot water from a hot water tap.

2. Place a small piece of one of the following metals in each tube: copper, magnesium, zinc, calcium, iron.

3. Compare the rate of gas evolution for each metal. Use a five-point rating scale. If there is no reaction, use a dash ('—').

4. Repeat steps 1 to 3 with dilute hydrochloric acid.

Results

The results of each experiment are shown in Table 2.4.

Table 2.4 Results of reactivity experiment

	Metal				
	copper	magnesium	zinc	calcium	iron
Reaction with hot water	—	xx	x	xxxxx	—
Reaction with dilute hydrochloric acid	—	xxx	xx	xxxxx	x

Go to p. 233 to check your answer.

Conclusion

Write a suitable conclusion.
Go to p. 233 to check your answer.

Test yourself 1

Part A: Knowledge

1. An element with the electronic configuration 2, 8, 5 *(1 mark)*
   A is a metal.
   B has an atomic number of 15.
   C has a mass number of 15.
   D is very unreactive.

2. Select the set of elements that are all metals. *(1 mark)*
   A calcium, aluminium, germanium
   B potassium, zinc, mercury
   C gold, silver, sulfur
   D hydrogen, phosphorus, bromine

3. The element that belongs to Period 4 and Group 16 (VI) of the periodic table is *(1 mark)*
   A Hf.
   B Se.

Table 2.3 Activity series of metals

K	Na	Ca	Mg	Al	Zn	Fe	Sn	Pb	Cu	Ag	Au

C Te.

D Po.

4. Select the set of elements that contains a metal and a semi-metal. *(1 mark)*

   A Mn, As

   B K, U

   C B, Xe

   D He, Si

5. Select the set of elements that contains a non-metal and a member of the lanthanoid series of elements. *(1 mark)*

   A Kr, Np

   B P, No

   C Br, Gd

   D W, Sm

6. Complete the following restricted-response questions using the appropriate word.
   (1 mark for each part)

   a) The first element of Group 17 (VII) in the periodic table is ....

   b) The majority of elements in the periodic table are good electrical conductors and are classified as ....

   c) The region of the periodic table between Group 2 (or II) and 3 (or III) is called the .... metals.

   d) Iron is a member of Period .... of the periodic table.

   e) In the activity series of metals, ... is more active than sodium.

7. Use the code letters to match the terms or phrases in each column. *(1 mark for each part)*

Column 1		Column 2	
A	Period 1	F	sodium
B	Group 1 (I)	G	helium
C	noble gas	H	Be
D	beryllium	I	radioactive elements
E	actinoids	J	two elements

Part B: Skills

8. Based on their position in the periodic table, classify the following elements as metals, non-metals or semi-metals.

   a) rhodium *(1 mark)*

   b) radon *(1 mark)*

   c) rubidium *(1 mark)*

   d) arsenic *(1 mark)*

   e) tantalum *(1 mark)*

9. Use the periodic table to identify the following unknown elements.

   a) six valence electrons; member of Period 5 *(1 mark)*

   b) member of Period 3; yellow-green gas; reactive *(1 mark)*

10. Three consecutive elements of Period 3 (X, Y and Z) have the properties shown in Table 2.5.

Table 2.5 Three consecutive elements of Period 3

	Element		
	X	Y	Z
melting point (°C)	44	113	−101
boiling point (°C)	280	445	−34
colour	white	yellow	yellow-green

   a) Determine the physical state of each element at 25 °C. *(3 marks)*

   b) By examining the pattern of solids, liquids and gases in the periodic table, identify X, Y and Z. *(3 marks)*

11. Figure 2.11 shows a blank map diagram of the periodic table.

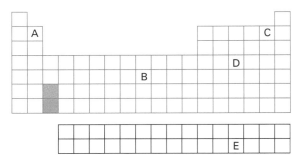

Figure 2.11 Periodic table map

Elements have been identified with code letters (A, B, C, D and E).

   a) Identify the period to which element A belongs. *(1 mark)*

   b) Classify element B as a metal, semi-metal or non-metal. *(1 mark)*

   c) Classify element C as a solid, liquid or gas at room temperature. *(1 mark)*

d) Name another element that is a member of the same family as element D and which has a greater atomic weight than D. *(1 mark)*

e) Is element E natural or synthetic? *(1 mark)*

12. Identify the following elements from their descriptions.

    a) a yellow-green gas that is used in solution to disinfect swimming pools *(1 mark)*

    b) a colourless gas which is abundant in the atmosphere; it rekindles a glowing splint of wood *(1 mark)*

    c) a colourless, very unreactive gas that is the third most abundant element in the atmosphere *(1 mark)*

    d) a Group 17 (VII) element that exists as a fuming red-brown liquid at room temperature and pressure *(1 mark)*

13. An isotope of element E has the following symbol: $^{40}_{18}E$.

    a) Use the periodic table to identify E. *(1 mark)*

    b) Calculate the number of neutrons in the nucleus of E. *(1 mark)*

    c) Write the electron configuration for E. *(1 mark)*

    d) How many electrons does E possess in its valence shell? *(1 mark)*

    e) Discuss the reactivity of E. *(1 mark)*

14. Identify which of the following statements are true and which are false.

    a) Sodium is a metal in Group 2 (II) of the periodic table. *(1 mark)*

    b) Mendeleev arranged the elements in the periodic table according to increasing atomic number. *(1 mark)*

    c) The elements of Group 17 (or VII) have seven valence shell electrons. *(1 mark)*

    d) Iron is a transition element. *(1 mark)*

    e) Newlands was the originator of the periodic table concept. *(1 mark)*

Go to pp. 233–234 to check your answers.

2.5 Word equations and symbolic equations

A new chemical substance is formed whenever a chemical change has occurred. In chemical reactions, atoms are neither created nor destroyed but are rearranged to form new substances. This is just stating the law of conservation of matter.

Word equations describe chemical reactions using words. They are written in the following manner:

reactant 1 + reactant 2 + ...
→ product 1 + product 2 + ...

The reactants are the substances that react together. The names of the reactants are listed before the arrow in a word equation. The products are the substances formed as a result of the reaction. The names of the products are listed after the arrow in a word equation. The arrow just means 'react together to form'. For example:

> Magnesium metal burns in oxygen gas with a bright white light, forming a white powder called magnesium oxide.

magnesium + oxygen → magnesium oxide

> Gaseous hydrogen and gaseous oxygen react together explosively, producing water vapour.

hydrogen + oxygen → water

Symbolic equations

When it comes to writing symbolic equations (chemical equations using chemical symbols), you need to know not only the chemical symbols but how each substance is composed. For example, oxygen gas and hydrogen gas are examples of diatomic molecules (molecules consisting of two atoms, such as H_2, N_2, O_2, F_2, Cl_2, Br_2 and I_2). The chemical formula for water is H_2O.

So for the reaction:

hydrogen + oxygen → water

the unbalanced chemical equation for this reaction is:

$$H_2 + O_2 \rightarrow H_2O$$

There are two hydrogen atoms on each side of this equation. Now count up the oxygen atoms on each side of the chemical equation. The left side of the equation has two oxygen atoms but the right side has only one.

This is obviously not equal, violating the law of conservation of matter. Now look at the balanced equation:

$$2H_2 + O_2 \rightarrow 2H_2O$$

Now the number of atoms on each side of the equation for each substance is equal. That is,

4 atoms H + 2 atoms O → 4 atoms H + 2 atoms O. The reaction can be shown diagrammatically as in Figure 2.12.

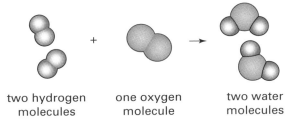

two hydrogen molecules   one oxygen molecule   two water molecules

Figure 2.12 Diagrammatic representation of the reaction $2H_2 + O_2 \rightarrow 2H_2O$

In words, two hydrogen molecules (each consisting of two hydrogen atoms) react with one oxygen molecule (consisting of two oxygen atoms) to form two water molecules (each consisting of two hydrogen atoms chemically linked to one oxygen atom). Chemists don't just work with single atoms or molecules, but with very large numbers of them. However, the ratios remain the same: every two hydrogen molecules react with one oxygen molecule, forming two water molecules (see Figure 2.13).

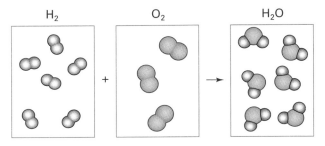

H_2 O_2 H_2O

Figure 2.13 The ratio $H_2:O_2:H_2O$ in the reaction forming water is always 2:1:2.

The following are examples of the steps used to produce a balanced chemical equation from a word equation.

⊙ Word equation:
  magnesium + oxygen → magnesium oxide
  Unbalanced chemical equation:
  $Mg + O_2 \rightarrow MgO$
  Balanced chemical equation:
  $2Mg + O_2 \rightarrow 2MgO$

⊙ Word equation:
  aluminium + oxygen → aluminium oxide
  Unbalanced chemical equation:
  $Al + O_2 \rightarrow Al_2O_3$
  Balanced chemical equation:
  $4Al + 3O_2 \rightarrow 2Al_2O_3$

⊙ Word equation:
  sodium carbonate + hydrochloric acid
    → sodium chloride + carbon dioxide + water
  Unbalanced chemical equation:
  $Na_2CO_3 + HCl \rightarrow NaCl + CO_2 + H_2O$
  Balanced chemical equation:
  $Na_2CO_3 + 2HCl \rightarrow 2NaCl + CO_2 + H_2O$

Look carefully at each of these examples and you will see that to balance the equations, the numbers of each type of atoms on each side are made the same.

Figure 2.14 is an example of the burning (combustion) of methane.

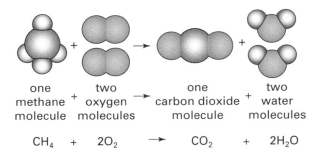

one methane molecule + two oxygen molecules → one carbon dioxide molecule + two water molecules

$CH_4 + 2O_2 \rightarrow CO_2 + 2H_2O$

Figure 2.14 Visualising the reaction between methane and oxygen

Once you have had some practice at balancing chemical equations, other questions in chemistry become easier to solve. Remember, in balancing equations you can only write numbers *before* the molecule. You can't change numbers inside the formula for a substance.

Questions

Before proceeding further, practise balancing these equations.

1. $Zn + HCl \rightarrow ZnCl_2 + H_2$
2. $S_8 + F_2 \rightarrow SF_6$
3. $C_2H_6 + O_2 \rightarrow CO_2 + H_2O$
4. $AgNO_3 + LiOH \rightarrow AgOH + LiNO_3$
5. $Mg + Mn_2O_3 \rightarrow MgO + Mn$
6. (harder) $NH_3 + O_2 \rightarrow NO + H_2O$

Answers

1. $Zn + 2HCl \rightarrow ZnCl_2 + H_2$
2. $S_8 + 24F_2 \rightarrow 8SF_6$
3. $2C_2H_6 + 7O_2 \rightarrow 4CO_2 + 6H_2O$
4. $AgNO_3 + LiOH \rightarrow AgOH + LiNO_3$ (this equation is balanced)
5. $3Mg + Mn_2O_3 \rightarrow 3MgO + 2Mn$
6. $4NH_3 + 5O_2 \rightarrow 4NO + 6H_2O$

Summary

1. Write a word equation.
2. Write an unbalanced symbolic equation, making sure to get the formula for each chemical correct.
3. Identify the different elements in the chemical equation.
4. Count the number of atoms of each element on both sides of the arrow.
5. Adjust the coefficients of the compounds that contain this element to balance the count on each side. (You can only write numbers in front of each formula. You can't change the formula of reactant or product molecules.)
6. Repeat the last two steps for each element identified.

This process is called 'balancing the equation'.

2.6 Valency and chemical formulae

Many inorganic compounds are composed of charged atoms.

⊘ Charged atoms are called ions.
⊘ Positive ions are called cations. They are formed when an atom of a metal loses one or more valence electrons.
⊘ Negative ions are called anions. They are formed when an atom of a non-metal gains one or more electrons into its valence shell.

Table 2.6 lists some of the common cations and anions and their periodic table group.

The table shows the following.
⊘ Metal ions have positive charges equal to their group number in the periodic table. This is also the number of electrons in their valence shell.
⊘ Non-metal ions have negative charges equal to their group number (in Roman numerals) minus eight (e.g. Group VI: charge = 6 − 8 = −2).
⊘ The name of the anion ends with the suffix 'ide'.

⊘ Ionic compounds are composed of cations and anions. The attraction between these oppositely charged ions is called an ionic bond.
⊘ Generally:

metal + non-metal → ionic compound

Example 1: Reaction of sodium with chlorine

A sodium atom (Na) readily forms a sodium ion (Na^+) by the loss of the single electron in its valence shell. This can be represented by a simple equation:

$$Na \rightarrow Na^+ + e^-$$

A chlorine atom (Cl) readily forms a chloride ion (Cl^-) by gaining one electron to make a stable octet in its valence shell. This can be represented by a simple equation:

$$Cl + e^- \rightarrow Cl^-$$

The sodium ion and chloride ion attract one another and form an ionic compound called sodium chloride (Na^+Cl^- or simply NaCl).

Figure 2.15 shows a model of this process.

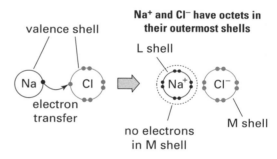

Figure 2.15 Formation of the ionic compound NaCl

The following points are important for a full understanding of electron configuration and bonding.

⊘ The outermost occupied shell of an atom is called the valence shell. The electrons that are found in this shell are called valence electrons. Each element is said to have a valency or combining

Table 2.6 Some of the common cations and anions in the periodic table

Group 1 (I)	Group 2 (II)	Group 3 (III)	Group 15 (IV)	Group 16 (VI)	Group 17 (VII)
sodium ion Na^+	magnesium ion Mg^{2+}	aluminium ion Al^{3+}	nitride ion N^{3-}	oxide ion O^{2-}	fluoride ion F^-
potassium ion K^+	calcium ion Ca^{2+}		phosphide ion P^{3-}	sulfide ion S^{2-}	chloride ion Cl^-

power. This refers to its ability to react with other elements to form compounds.

> The octet rule states that atoms lose, gain or share electrons in order to attain a stable valence shell of eight electrons. (Hydrogen is an exception because it can hold a maximum of only two electrons in its valence shell.) This gives them the same electronic configuration as most noble gases. This eight-electron configuration is especially stable.

Example 2: Reaction of magnesium with chlorine

Magnesium has two electrons in its outermost (valence) shell. Chlorine has seven electrons in its outermost shell. Magnesium can give up two electrons:

$$Mg \rightarrow Mg^{2+} + 2e^-$$

But each chlorine atom can only accept one electron to complete its octet. So two chlorine atoms are needed:

$$2Cl + 2e^- \rightarrow 2Cl^-$$

The attraction between the three ions keeps them together as magnesium chloride, $MgCl_2$. This is shown diagrammatically in Figure 2.16.

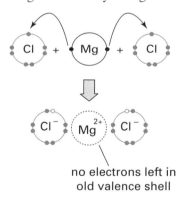

no electrons left in old valence shell

Figure 2.16 Magnesium is able to donate two electrons, one to each chlorine atom.

Valency table

Table 2.7 is a list of common charges and valencies of various ions. The table divides ions into groups with the following charges and valencies: +1, +2, +3, −1, −2 and −3.

For example, the valency of magnesium is +2, and its ion is written as Mg^{2+}. Some atoms form common groups and behave as if they were the one element; for example, the ammonium (NH_4^+) and sulfate (SO_4^{2-}) ions. These ions are called polyatomic ions.

Table 2.7 Some common valencies of ions

Name of ion	Symbol	Name of ion	Symbol
lithium	Li^+	hydride	H^-
sodium	Na^+	fluoride	F^-
potassium	K^+	chloride	Cl^-
silver	Ag^+	bromide	Br^-
ammonium	NH_4^+	iodide	I^-
hydrogen	H^+	nitrate	NO_3^-
		hydroxide	OH^-
magnesium	Mg^{2+}	oxide	O^{2-}
calcium	Ca^{2+}	sulfide	S^{2-}
iron(II)	Fe^{2+}	sulfate	SO_4^{2-}
barium	Ba^{2+}	carbonate	CO_3^{2-}
zinc	Zn^{2+}		
mercury	Hg^{2+}		
tin(II)	Sn^{2+}		
lead(II)	Pb^{2+}		
copper(II)	Cu^{2+}		
aluminium	Al^{3+}	nitride	N^{3-}
		phosphate	PO_4^{3-}

Chemical formulae

The valencies of metals and non-metals can be used to predict the chemical formulae of ionic compounds formed between these elements. There is just one rule: for an ionic compound, the sum of the valencies of component elements is zero.

Examples

1. Potassium bromide
   * Valency of K is +1.
   * Valency of Br is −1.
   * Sum of valencies is (+1) + (−1) = 0.

   As the valencies add to zero, potassium bromide is composed of one K and one Cl. So the formula is KBr.

2. Aluminium sulfide
   * Valency of Al is +3.
   * Valency of S is −2.
   * Two ions of aluminium are needed to react with three sulfur ions for the valencies to add to zero.
   * Sum of valencies is (+3) + (+3) + (−2) + (−2) + (−2) = 0.

   The formula for aluminium sulfide is Al_2S_3.

3. Calcium hydroxide
   * Valency of Ca is +2.

- Valency of OH is –1.
- So two hydroxide ions react with each calcium ion.
- Sum of valencies is $(+2) + (-1) + (-1) = 0$.

The formula for calcium hydroxide is $Ca(OH)_2$.

(Notice how the hydroxide ion, behaving as one group, is written in parentheses.)

In naming ionic compounds, the metal (or positive ion) is named first followed by the non-metal (or negative ion) with the appropriate suffix.

Questions

Before proceeding further, practise writing formulae for the following compounds.

1. silver chloride
2. zinc iodide
3. copper(II) sulfate
4. aluminium oxide
5. lithium carbonate
6. ammonium sulfate

Answers

1. $AgCl$
2. ZnI_2
3. $CuSO_4$
4. Al_2O_3
5. Li_2CO_3
6. $(NH_4)_2SO_4$

Table 2.8 lists some ionic compounds.

Table 2.8 Ionic compounds

Ionic compound	Chemical formula	Cation present	Anion present
zinc oxide	ZnO	Zn^{2+}	O^{2-}
magnesium chloride	$MgCl_2$	Mg^{2+}	Cl^-
copper sulfide	CuS	Cu^{2+}	S^{2-}
potassium bromide	KBr	K^+	Br^-
calcium iodide	CaI_2	Ca^{2+}	I^-
aluminium oxide	Al_2O_3	Al^{3+}	O^{2-}

2.7 Covalent compounds

When non-metals react with other non-metals to form a compound, there is no gain or loss of electrons. Instead, electron pairs are shared between atoms.

- This sharing of electron pairs is called a covalent bond.
- The atoms in a covalent compound are linked by covalent bonds.

Generally:

non-metal + non-metal → covalent compound

For example, hydrogen atoms have one valence electron and chlorine atoms have seven valence electrons. When hydrogen atoms bond with chlorine atoms they share an electron pair to form the covalent bond. Figure 2.17 shows a model of the formation of the covalent bond in hydrogen chloride (HCl).

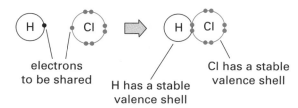

electrons to be shared

H has a stable valence shell

Cl has a stable valence shell

Figure 2.17 Covalent bonding in hydrogen chloride

Table 2.9 lists some common covalent compounds.

Table 2.9 Covalent compounds

Covalent compound	Chemical formula
water	H_2O
ammonia	NH_3
ethylene	C_2H_4
nitrogen dioxide	NO_2
carbon monoxide	CO

Follow these rules to name covalent compounds.

- Name the non-metal with the lower periodic group number first.
- Name the non-metal with the higher periodic group number second.
- Use Greek prefixes to indicate the number of each type of atom (mono = 1; di = 2; tri = 3; tetra = 4; penta = 5).
- Delete the last few letters of the second non-metal's name and substitute '-ide'.

Examples

1. CO = carbon monoxide
2. NO_2 = nitrogen dioxide
3. PCl_3 = phosphorus trichloride
4. CF_4 = carbon tetrafluoride
5. N_2O_4 = dinitrogen tetroxide

2.8 Balancing equations for simple chemical reactions

Before attempting to write formula equations for reactions, you need to know what kind of reaction occurs in any particular situation. A chemical equation shows not only what the reactants and products are, but also how much of each reactant combines to form how much of each product.

Here are some common reaction types.

> metal + acid → salt + hydrogen
>
> e.g. magnesium + hydrochloric acid
> → magnesium chloride + hydrogen
> $$Mg + 2HCl \rightarrow MgCl_2 + H_2$$
>
> e.g. zinc + sulfuric acid → zinc sulfate + hydrogen
> $$Zn + H_2SO_4 \rightarrow ZnSO_4 + H_2$$

> acid + base → salt + water
>
> (This reaction is often called neutralisation.)
>
> e.g. phosphoric acid + sodium hydroxide
> → sodium phosphate + water
> $$H_3PO_4 + 3NaOH \rightarrow Na_3PO_4 + 3H_2O$$
>
> e.g. hydrochloric acid + ammonium hydroxide
> → ammonium chloride + water
> $$HCl + NH_4OH \rightarrow NH_4Cl + H_2O$$

> acid + carbonate → salt + water + carbon dioxide
>
> e.g. nitric acid + calcium carbonate
> → calcium nitrate + water + carbon dioxide
> $$2HNO_3 + CaCO_3 \rightarrow Ca(NO_3)_2 + H_2O + CO_2$$
>
> e.g. hydrochloric acid + iron(II) carbonate
> → iron(II) chloride + water + carbon dioxide
> $$2HCl + FeCO_3 \rightarrow FeCl_2 + H_2O + CO_2$$

> Some salts are insoluble in water. So if solutions of two soluble salts are mixed, the ions may simply rearrange to form a precipitate of an insoluble salt.
>
> e.g. silver nitrate + calcium chloride
> → silver chloride + calcium nitrate
> $$2AgNO_3 + CaCl_2 \rightarrow 2AgCl + Ca(NO_3)_2$$
>
> Silver nitrate, calcium chloride and calcium nitrate all dissolve easily in water. But silver chloride is insoluble in water and so will precipitate out.

> Combustion is the burning of a substance so that its elements combine with oxygen.
>
> e.g. magnesium + oxygen → magnesium oxide
> $$2Mg + O_2 \rightarrow 2MgO$$

e.g. iron + oxygen → iron(III) oxide
$$4Fe + 3O_2 \rightarrow 2Fe_2O_3$$

> Fuels containing carbon and hydrogen burn in oxygen to produce carbon dioxide and water.
>
> e.g. methane + oxygen → carbon dioxide + water
> $$CH_4 + 2O_2 \rightarrow CO_2 + 2H_2O$$
>
> e.g. propane + oxygen → carbon dioxide + water
> $$C_3H_8 + 5O_2 \rightarrow 3CO_2 + 4H_2O$$

> Sometimes two or more simple compounds combine to produce a more complex one. This is often called a synthesis reaction.
>
> e.g. iron + sulfur → iron sulfide
> $$Fe + S \rightarrow FeS$$
>
> e.g. potassium + chlorine gas → potassium chloride
> $$2K + Cl_2 \rightarrow 2KCl$$

> Sometimes a complex molecule breaks down, forming simpler ones. These decomposition reactions are the opposite of synthesis reactions.
>
> e.g. water → hydrogen + oxygen
> $$2H_2O \rightarrow 2H_2 + O_2$$
>
> e.g. potassium chlorate → potassium chloride + oxygen
> $$2KClO_3 \rightarrow 2KCl + 3O_2$$

For most people, salt simply refers to table salt (sodium chloride), the stuff you sprinkle over fish and chips. However, to a chemist a salt refers to an ionic compound produced by reacting an acid with a base. Hydrochloric acid (HCl) produces chlorides, sulfuric acid (H_2SO_4) produces sulfates, and nitric acid (HNO_3) forms nitrates.

Table 2.10 lists some common bases and their chemical formulae.

Table 2.10 Some common bases

Base	Formula
sodium hydroxide	NaOH
ammonium hydroxide	NH_4OH
calcium oxide	CaO
potassium hydroxide	KOH
magnesium hydroxide	$Mg(OH)_2$

Neutralisation reactions (the reaction between an acid and base) can be used to relieve indigestion. In antacid tablets, weak bases such as sodium hydrogen carbonate, $NaHCO_3$ or magnesium hydroxide, $Mg(OH)_2$ neutralise excess stomach acids.

Decomposition

Decomposition reactions require energy in the form of heat, light or electricity to break down the reactants. A reason many medicines have an expiration date stamped on the packet or bottle is that they start to decompose. For example, aspirin decomposes especially in high humidity. Decomposing aspirin has the smell of vinegar. This decomposition is shown in Figure 2.18.

In chemistry, decomposition can be represented by:

$$AB \rightarrow A + B$$

Metal carbonates such as copper carbonate break down when heated strongly. This is called thermal decomposition, as heat is used to initiate the reaction. That a reaction occurs is obvious as copper carbonate is green and becomes copper oxide which is black:

$$\text{copper carbonate} \xrightarrow{\text{heat}} \text{copper oxide} + \text{carbon dioxide}$$

$$CuCO_3 \rightarrow CuO + CO_2$$

This reaction is illustrated in Figure 2.19.

Another example is the decomposition of silver chloride. There is enough energy in sunlight to pry the particles apart. White silver chloride turns grey (fine particles of silver) in sunlight (see Figure 2.20):

$$\text{silver chloride} \rightarrow \text{silver} + \text{chlorine gas}$$

$$2AgCl \rightarrow 2Ag + Cl_2$$

Silver bromide reacts the same way:

$$2AgBr \rightarrow 2Ag + Br_2$$

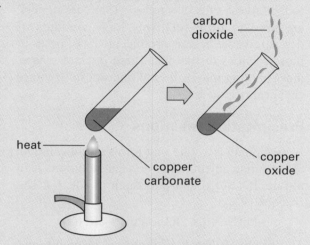

Figure 2.19 Decomposition of copper carbonate

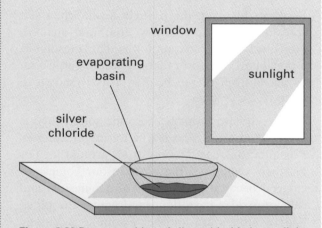

Figure 2.20 Decomposition of silver chloride by sunlight

A typical black-and-white photographic film contains tiny crystals of very slightly soluble silver chloride or silver bromide. Grains of these salts are suspended in a gelatine matrix. When exposed

Figure 2.18 The chemical decomposition (or hydrolysis) of aspirin in water

(cont.)

to light, these salts decompose. Then 'developers' are used to form relatively large amounts of deposited free silver producing dark areas in those sections of the film. These days, of course, most photography is digital and doesn't require chemical reactions.

Precipitation reactions

A precipitate is a solid that forms out of solution; for example, mixing the two clear solutions lead nitrate, $Pb(NO_3)_2$ and potassium iodide, KI. The reaction is:

$$Pb(NO_3)_2 + 2KI \rightarrow PbI_2 + 2KNO_3$$

The bright yellow lead iodide is insoluble and settles out at the bottom (see Figure 2.21).

Look at this from the particle level. When salt solutions are mixed, new combinations are possible. If a combination forms that is insoluble, a precipitate will form that eventually settles out at the bottom of the beaker. This is shown in Figure 2.22.

The precipitate forms because the solid (PbI_2) is insoluble in water. This is true for all precipitates. Precipitation reactions occur all around us. For instance, sometimes the pipes in our homes get clogged because precipitates of magnesium and calcium oxides have deposited within the pipes. Kidney stones are another example. A kidney

stone is just a precipitate, often of calcium ions and oxalates. It is often recommended that a good way to avoid kidney stones is to drink plenty of water to dilute these salts, and so prevent any potential deposits.

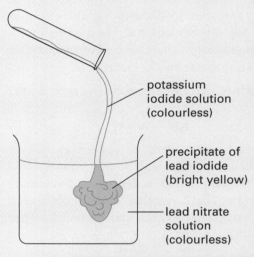

Figure 2.21 Lead nitrate reacting with potassium iodide

Cholesterol is only slightly soluble in water, so it can dissolve and travel in the aqueous bloodstream at very small concentrations. Over time, and with increased cholesterol levels, plaques may develop as shown in Figure 2.23. Plaques in blood vessels are a complex of cholesterol, various cells and other chemicals that precipitate from the

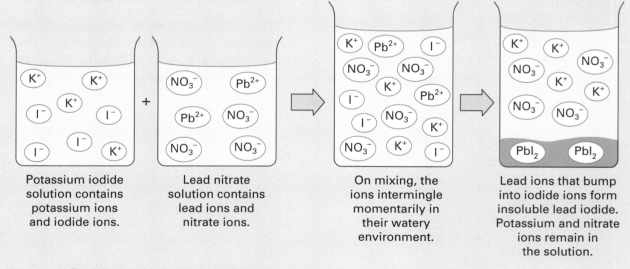

Potassium iodide solution contains potassium ions and iodide ions.

Lead nitrate solution contains lead ions and nitrate ions.

On mixing, the ions intermingle momentarily in their watery environment.

Lead ions that bump into iodide ions form insoluble lead iodide. Potassium and nitrate ions remain in the solution.

Figure 2.22 Particle reaction between lead nitrate and potassium iodide

bloodstream and build up in the walls of blood vessels. This is similar to salts precipitating out and clogging water pipes. These can lead to heart attacks.

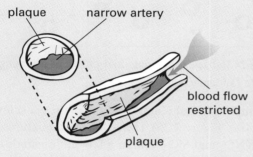

Figure 2.23 Narrowing of artery

Precipitation reactions are also useful. They can be used for making pigments, removing salts from water in water treatment, and for isolating various chemicals from a solution. Many precipitates can be made to form pure crystals.

When you add ammonium sulfate to a protein solution, the ammonium sulfate competes with the protein to bind with water. This can dehydrate the proteins and precipitate them from solution. Precipitation can also be achieved by adding an organic solvent or by changing the pH to alter the nature of the solution. Precipitation is widely used to separate and recover organic molecules, especially proteins.

 Experiment 2

Precipitation reactions

Aim

▷ To determine whether changing the concentration of potassium iodide changes the mass of lead iodide formed between the reaction of lead nitrate and potassium iodide

Solutions required

▷ A 150-mL $Pb(NO_3)_2$ solution made up to a concentration of 300 g $Pb(NO_3)_2$ per litre of solution. (This is more than enough lead nitrate for all the following potassium iodide solutions to completely react.)

▷ Solution A: 50 mL distilled water. This represents a concentration of 0 g KI per litre of solution.

▷ Solution B: 50 mL solution of KI made up to a concentration of 50 g KI per litre of solution.

▷ Solution C: 50 mL solution of KI made up to a concentration of 100 g KI per litre of solution.

▷ Solution D: 50 mL solution of KI made up to a concentration of 150 g KI per litre of solution.

▷ Solution E: 50 mL solution of KI made up to a concentration of 200 g KI per litre of solution.

▷ Solution F: 50 mL solution of KI made up to a concentration of 250 g KI per litre of solution.

▷ Solution G: 50 mL solution of KI made up to a concentration of 300 g KI per litre of solution.

Method

1. Label appropriate beakers with the letter of the solution it contains.

2. Measure 10 mL of the $Pb(NO_3)_2$ solution using a measuring cylinder and pour this amount into each of seven labelled beakers A-1, B-1 and so on to G-1. (This indicates the solutions that will be used in trial number 1.)

3. Measure 10 mL of the KI solution A using a measuring cylinder and pour this amount into beaker A-1.

4. Repeat this with solution B, pouring it into beaker B-1 and so on.

5. You should now have six beakers showing a yellow precipitate and one remaining clear.

6. Take seven filter papers and, along one edge, write A-1, B-1, …, G-1 to distinguish them.

7. Pour the products of each reaction through the respectively labelled filter papers to filter out the solid lead iodide.

8. Repeat steps 2 to 7 for trial 2. This time your beakers and filter papers will be labelled A-2, B-2, C-2, …, G-2.

9. Leave these 2 × 7 amounts of lead iodide to dry overnight so that there is the least amount of water present as possible.

10. Weigh a piece of clean filter paper to determine its mass. (You can assume this is the mass of each of the filter papers in your experiment.)

11. Record the mass of the lead iodide minus the mass of filter paper in the table below.

Analysis

1. Complete Table 2.11. Calculate the average mass of PbI$_2$: ½(mass from trial 1 + mass from trial 2).

Table 2.11 Results of precipitation reaction experiment

KI concentration, g/L	Mass of lead iodide, Trial 1, g	Mass of lead iodide, Trial 2, g	Average mass of lead iodide, g
0 (A)	0	0	0
50 (B)			
100 (C)			
150 (D)			
200 (E)			
250 (F)			
300 (G)			

2. Plot a graph of the (average) mass of lead iodide formed versus the concentration of potassium iodide.

Go to p. 233 to check your answers.

Conclusion

 Write a suitable conclusion.

Go to p. 233 to check your answer.

2.9 Rate of chemical change

Particles are constantly moving: vibrating, rotating or moving around (especially in liquids and gases, as shown in Figure 2.24). Some move faster, some move slower, and the motion will vary as particles bump into each other and into the walls of any container they are in.

The rate of a chemical reaction is how fast it happens. If a reaction has a low rate, the molecules combine at a slower speed than for a reaction with a higher rate. How quickly reactions occur depends on the type of molecules that are combining. Some reactions take hundreds, maybe even thousands, of years while other can occur almost instantaneously.

An example of a slow reaction is the tarnishing of silver. Sulfur-containing materials generally cause silver to form a dull, grey or black film or coating (patina) over the metal.

$$2Ag + H_2S \rightarrow Ag_2S + H_2$$

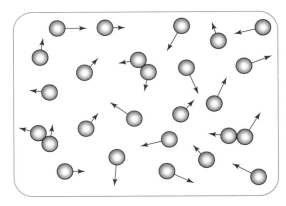

Figure 2.24 Particles in liquids and gases have enough energy to randomly move around.

An example of a fast reaction occurs in the car safety air bag (see Figure 2.25). Here there is a mixture of NaN$_3$, KNO$_3$ and SiO$_2$. Within a few milliseconds of impact, an electric impulse triggers the first reaction:

$$2NaN_3 \rightarrow 2Na + 3N_2(g)$$

The sodium azide decomposes to sodium and nitrogen gas. The gas issues at a speed of around 320 km/h (90 m/s) to fill a nylon or polyamide bag.

Sodium metal is very reactive, so potassium nitrate then reacts to remove it. This reaction produces more N$_2$ gas:

$$10Na + 2KNO_3 \rightarrow K_2O + 5Na_2O + N_2(g)$$

Both potassium oxide and sodium oxide are highly reactive, so a final reaction is used to eliminate these chemicals. They react with silicon dioxide to produce a harmless and stable silicate glass:

$$K_2O + Na_2O + 2SiO_2 \rightarrow K_2SiO_3 + Na_2SiO_3$$

The whole process, from the impact of the crash to full inflation of the air bags, takes only about 40 milliseconds.

Figure 2.25 Ideally, the driver's body should not hit the air bag while it is still inflating.

A number of factors affect the overall speed of a reaction.

Temperature

As the temperature of a system increases, the molecules bounce around faster since they have more energy. Therefore, they are more likely to collide and combine. As the temperature drops, the molecules slow down and collide less. That temperature drop lowers the rate of the reaction. This is shown in Figure 2.26.

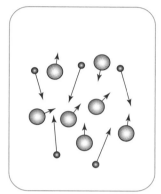

At low temperatures gas particles move at slower average speeds. Heavier particles move slower than lighter particles.

At high temperatures gas particles move at greater average speeds. Heavier particles move slower than lighter particles.

Figure 2.26 The speed of gas molecules depends on their temperature.

Also, at any particular temperature, only a portion of the reacting molecules have the minimum energy for reaction to take place. Therefore, when the temperature is increased, more molecules are able to move faster. This means more of them will have the minimum energy needed so when they slam into each other they react, rather than just bouncing off each other.

Concentration

If there are more of the reacting substances in a system, there is a greater chance that molecules will collide and speed up the rate of the reaction. If there is less of the substance, there will be fewer collisions and the reaction will probably occur at a slower speed. This is illustrated in Figure 2.27.

Pressure

Pressure affects the rate of reaction, especially with gases (see Figure 2.28). With greater pressure,

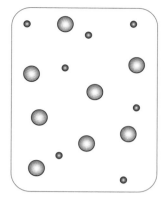
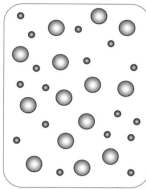

Figure 2.27 When particles are crammed in together (greater number of particles per unit volume) they have more chance of bumping into each other.

molecules have less space in which to move. Molecules crammed in together are more likely to collide. As the pressure decreases, the molecules are further apart and don't hit each other as often. The lower pressure decreases the rate of reaction.

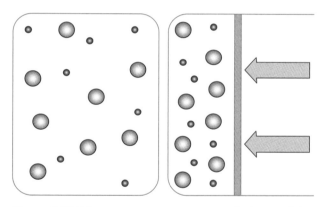

Figure 2.28 When gases are compressed, the particles are closer together and the chance of an effective collision is greater.

Catalysts

A catalyst is a substance, usually used in small amounts, that modifies and increases the rate of a reaction without being consumed in the process. When the reaction has finished, there is exactly the same mass of catalyst as at the beginning.

For example, hydrogen peroxide (H_2O_2) is a clear liquid. As it is an oxidising agent, it is often used for bleaching or for cleaning. Hydrogen peroxide spontaneously decomposes slowly into water and oxygen gas:

$$2H_2O_2 \rightarrow 2H_2O + O_2$$

The reaction can be further slowed at lower temperatures. This is why hydrogen peroxide is often stored in a refrigerator. But adding a small quantity of manganese dioxide (MnO_2, also called manganese(IV) oxide) makes the reaction bubble vigorously as O_2 is formed.

So, why does this happen? Chemical reactions involve breaking and/or forming chemical bonds. Successful collisions causing reactions only occur if the particles collide with a certain minimum energy. Most particles don't have enough energy, and will simply bounce apart. Increasing the rate of a reaction means increasing the number of these successful collisions. One possible method of doing this is to provide another way for the reaction to occur. Adding a catalyst affects this pathway (see Figure 2.29). It provides an alternative route for the reaction so more particles can react.

 Experiment 3

Investigating rusting of steel wool

Aim

> To investigate some factors that affect the rusting of steel wool

Preamble

Rusting is a very common chemical reaction which happens to iron and metals containing iron. Corrosion of iron (rusting) is a major problem, as it destroys the structural integrity of the metal, and replacing rusted iron objects can be a major expense. Rust is a series of red oxides that form from the reaction of iron. Steel wool is mainly iron and will need to be cleaned with detergent to remove oil and prevent rusting, and then dried thoroughly before use in this experiment.

Method

1. Take some new (or freshly cleaned) steel wool and cut it into equal-sized small pieces.
2. Label six flasks as follows, and place the required contents in each.
   Flask 1: Leave empty and dry.
   Flask 2: Half-fill with tap water.
   Flask 3: Half-fill with boiling water, then allow to cool. (Boiling water drives most of the dissolved oxygen out.) Before leaving the flask overnight, place a layer of oil on top to prevent air re-entering the water.
   Flask 4: Half-fill with tap water that has a teaspoon of salt dissolved.
   Flask 5: Half-fill with tap water that has a teaspoon of bicarbonate of soda dissolved.
   Flask 6: Half-fill with tap water that has a teaspoon of vinegar dissolved.
3. Place a piece of the steel wool in each of the jars, making sure all the steel wool is in the liquid.
4. Place corks or rubber bungs on the jars and leave overnight.
5. Check the jars the following day and write down your observations.

Analysis

1. Which flasks show the most rusting?
2. Which flasks show the least rusting?
3. Which flask acts as the control?
4. In another experiment, both vinegar and bleach are added to the water. It is observed that the steel wool rusts at a rapid pace. Explain.

Go to **p. 233** to check your answers.

Conclusion

Write a suitable conclusion.
Go to **p. 233** to check your answer.

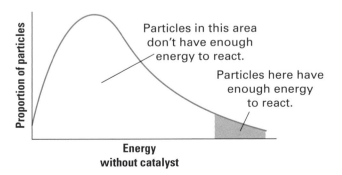
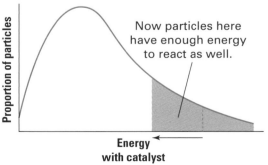

Figure 2.29 The effect of a catalyst on the number of reacting particles

2.10 Useful substances

Early in history, and even up to recent times, humans only had natural materials available to them. But technology has moved on and so, especially over the last century, many materials have been developed with useful properties. This section will look at some of these developments.

Metals

The least reactive metals were the easiest to isolate and were the first to be widely used by humans. For example, copper was among the first metals mined and crafted by humans. It was available in large quantities and was initially extractable almost at the surface of the Earth. As well, it was suitable to use for weapons, tools, art objects and ornaments. Later it was found that by mixing it with other metals (alloying), different properties could be obtained. For instance, bronze = copper + tin; brass = copper + zinc. Our 'gold' and 'silver' coins are mostly copper.

Aluminium

Aluminium is so widely used in today's modern world that it is almost impossible to imagine it not being around. Its unique qualities give it a huge array of possible applications from transport, packaging, electrical applications and medicine through to construction of homes and furniture. Around the home we know it as soft drink cans, alfoil, cooking utensils and window frames.

Aluminium is extraordinarily strong, malleable and ductile. It is easily machined and cast, lightweight and doesn't corrode. This is because once it is exposed to air its surface quickly develops a thin, microscopic

Case study 2: Factors that affect the rate of corrosion and rusting

Corrosion is the breakdown of some manufactured material by chemically reacting with its surroundings. This produces a deterioration of the material and its properties. Often corrosion refers to metals reacting with oxygen. Rusting iron and steel forming iron oxides is a common example. This type of damage typically produces oxide(s) and/or salt(s) of the original metal. Corrosion can also occur in materials other than metals.

Only a few metals occur naturally as elements, such as gold, platinum and silver. This is because they are not very reactive. Many metals and alloys corrode simply by being exposed to moisture in the air, but the process can be strongly affected by exposure to other liquids and gases and even by bacteria.

Rusting is the corrosion of iron (or steel, an alloy of iron) to form hydrated iron(III) oxide; that is $Fe_2O_3 \times xH_2O$. (Note: x is typically 1 or 2.) This flaky substance is commonly known as rust:

$$\text{iron} + \text{oxygen} + \text{water} \rightarrow \text{rust}$$

Both oxygen and water are necessary in this process. When iron rusts it flakes off, exposing fresh metal underneath. Rust takes up a greater volume than metallic iron and consequently splits and cracks. It is also porous to water and oxygen, so these substances can reach the underlying metal and allow more rust to be formed.

The rate of rusting of iron is accelerated when:

- it is in or near seawater
- the water, or moisture, it is in contact with is acidic
- it is in contact with a less active metal such as copper or tin
- the iron contains impurities
- it is under mechanical stress
- the temperature increases.

Iron and steel objects such as cars are painted and undercoated mainly to prevent and/or delay these corrosive reactions. This puts a barrier between the steel and moisture and oxygen. However, as these paints and coatings break down or are damaged, bare steel can be exposed. This makes the metal immediately vulnerable to corrosion. Coating the exposed metal with oil or grease significantly reduces the chances of developing rust in iron. This is because grease or oil forms a protective layer, just like paint does, preventing rust formation.

(cont.)

The Sydney Harbour Bridge contains 52 800 t of steelwork (see Figure 2.30). Constant painting and other maintenance is required. Each coat on the bridge requires around 30 000 L of paint.

Figure 2.30 The Sydney Harbour Bridge requires constant painting and other maintenance to prevent corrosion.

Sometimes, factories will soak the body of a car or boat in chemicals to create layers of rust protection. Also, galvanising (adding a coating of zinc) to car bodies before the primer coat of paint is added forms an extra layer of protection.

Another way to prevent steel from rusting is to use sacrificial anodes (see Figure 2.31). These more reactive metals corrode first, thus protecting the more useful metal.

There are many products on the market that work against rust forming. A simple homemade recipe is to dip the metal into one part anhydrous lanolin with five parts paint thinner.

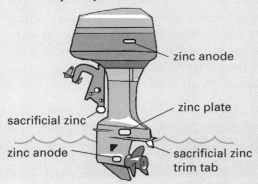

Figure 2.31 Zinc is more reactive than steel. Outboard motors can be protected from rusting by attaching zinc strips which corrode first; these can be replaced regularly, saving on costly motor repairs.

layer of oxide over its top, which renders the metal almost completely resistant to corrosion. Because of these properties, aluminium comprises about 80% of an aircraft's unloaded weight. NASA space shuttles are made from 90% aluminium. It is also used to make cars, trucks and trains.

In the mid-1800s, French Emperor Napoleon III spent enormous amounts of money to develop pure aluminium. He could see the potential in lightweight armour for his troops. But after 2 years of effort he had only a little more than 2 kg of metal. It was so rare and expensive (more expensive than gold or silver) that he used it to make the first set of aluminium cutlery used by visiting monarchs.

It was not until 1886 that it was discovered how to obtain aluminium metal from the electrolysis of aluminium ore. However, it is only in recent times that industry has become sufficiently skilled at isolating and refining aluminium at a reasonable cost for everyday use.

Titanium

Titanium is a silvery chemical element with a low density, and is strong, lustrous and corrosion resistant. It can be combined with a number of metals to produce strong, lightweight alloys for aerospace, military, industrial process, automotive, medical prostheses and implants, mobile phones and other applications.

Because it is difficult and expensive to refine, pure metallic titanium was not prepared until 1910, and it was not used outside the laboratory until 1932. As it is non-toxic and is not rejected by the body, titanium is used in a variety of medical applications including surgical implements and implants (such as joint replacement for hip balls and sockets and for knee replacement as shown in Figure 2.32) that can remain in place for several decades.

Fuels

Burning plant materials such as wood, peat moss, charcoal, bagasse (sugar cane waste) and animal and

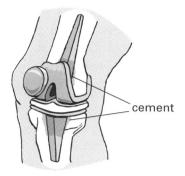

Figure 2.32 In a total knee replacement, metal implants are cemented into place at the tibia and femur.

vegetable wastes have long been used. Even in this century, some 40% of the world's population still relies on this traditional use of biomass for cooking.

The main purpose of fuel is to use the tremendous amount of stored energy to generate heat or perform mechanical work, such as powering an engine. Fuels may also be used to generate electricity, which can then be used for heating, lighting or other purposes.

Petroleum is a widespread modern fuel allowing travel both locally and across the world in a way not previously possible. It brings the world's produce to our doorstep, can warm us in winter and is the raw material for many plastics, medicines, pesticides, paints and clothing. However, there is only a finite amount of petroleum in the ground (it is a non-renewable resource) and, at the rate we are pumping it out and using it, it will only last for a short period longer. Therefore, alternative fuels will need to be found.

One of these is biofuels. This is produced from renewable resources, especially plant biomass, vegetable oils, and treated municipal and industrial wastes. The most obvious of these are bioethanol and biodiesel as they are convenient fuels for storing and transporting energy. An Australian company is showing promise in this area by being able to convert discarded biomass, such as agricultural wastes, sawdust and pond weed, into oil in less than half an hour using a process called catalytic hydrothermal reaction. Advantages include solving a waste disposal problem, and not competing with land or agricultural crops for feedstock.

Ethanol can be produced from both biomass and most commonly through fermenting sugars. Enzymes can be used instead of fermentation. Ethanol is already being used extensively as a fuel additive and the use of ethanol fuel alone, or as part of a mix with petrol, is increasing around the world. In Australia ethanol is used as a fuel additive and E10 is petrol containing 10% ethanol. Some countries can use upwards of 85% ethanol in their fuels. Biodiesel is currently being used in some bus fleets around Australia.

Algae-based biofuels is another area of research aiming to solve transportation problems. Algae has the potential to yield more than 20 000 L/ha per year of fuel, and it is currently being trialled in the United States. Also, algae-based plastics can reduce waste and the cost is expected to be cheaper than traditional plastic prices.

Research is continuing. Studies show that jojoba oil (from the shrub *Simmondsia chinensis*) makes up about 50% of the weight of the jojoba seed. It may prove to be a viable substitute to fossil fuel and can even power-up large vehicles like buses and trains. Cultivating jojoba oil in large quantities would require huge funding as well as large areas set aside for the plant. Another promising plant is *Jatropha curcas*, an ugly and fast-growing poisonous weed, which can grow in marginal lands. Crushed jatropha seeds produce oil that can be processed to a high-quality biodiesel fuel for standard diesel vehicles, while the residue (press cake) can be turned into a biomass feedstock to power electricity plants or used as a fertiliser. It is claimed the plant may yield more than four times as much fuel per hectare as soybean, and more than 10 times that of corn; around 2000 L/ha of fuel!

Over the next few decades, vehicles using biofuels or hybrid cars using hydrogen fuel cells or electricity will become much more common. Figure 2.33 shows a hydrogen/oxygen fuel cell.

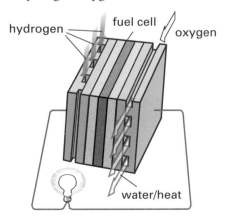

Figure 2.33 A typical fuel cell uses hydrogen and oxygen to produce electricity.

Pharmaceuticals

Aboriginal peoples sometimes had need of bush medicines. Many of these remedies used the chemical or physical action to heal. Aromatic herbs, tannin-rich inner barks and kino gum have variously effective healing properties. They didn't know why it worked; it just did! Other plants undoubtedly harboured alkaloids or other compounds with these therapies. But there were also many ineffective cures steeped in mysticism and tradition.

Aspirin

The ancient Greek physician, Hippocrates (5th century BC), wrote about a bitter powder extracted from willow bark (a plant of the genus *Salix*), that could reduce fevers and ease aches and pains. Ancient texts from Assyria, Sumer and Egypt record the leaves and bark of the willow tree as a remedy for aches and fever. Even Native Americans relied on it as a basis for their medical treatments.

A couple of centuries ago, scientists figured out that the active part of willow bark is a chemical known as salicin. It is converted by the body into salicylic acid. This chemical was isolated and manufactured in the laboratory and is now sold as aspirin (which is actually acetylsalicylic acid). Today, aspirin is one of the most widely used medicines in the world, with over 40 000 t being produced each year.

Artemisinin

Artemisia annua has been used by Chinese herbalists for over 2000 years to treat many illnesses, including malaria. The active ingredient, artemisinin, and its derivatives are a group of drugs that possess the most rapid action of all current drugs against malaria. But its discovery in the Western world was not made until just a few decades ago. Treatments containing this drug are now standard worldwide for the disease.

The plant and animal world is still a rich source of chemicals yet to be discovered and their properties established. This is an important reason for preserving the biodiversity of our forests and animal life.

Modern pharmacology

Pharmacology, which is the science of drugs and their composition, uses and effects, has become increasingly sophisticated. Biotechnology now allows the development of drugs targeted towards specific physiological processes. These can also be designed to be compatible with the patient and so reduce side-effects. The study of human genetics is now having an increased influence on medicine. As the genes controlling many genetic disorders are identified, and as techniques in molecular biology and genetics are developed, a new generation of drugs is emerging.

Producing insulin

One of the earliest uses of biotechnology was in 1978 using recombinant DNA technology to modify *Escherichia coli* bacteria to produce human insulin. Before the development of this technique, insulin was extracted from the pancreas glands of cattle, pigs and other farm animals. While generally effective in treating diabetes, animal-derived insulin is not identical to human insulin, and so may produce allergic reactions in some people. By inserting the human genes that produce insulin into bacteria, scientists are able to manufacture insulin that is compatible with humans.

Figure 2.34 shows how this is done. A plasmid is a small, circular piece of DNA found in bacterial cells. Once inside a bacterium, it can multiply making several dozen copies (including the inserted insulin-producing gene sequence) of itself. Bacteria multiply on average every 20 minutes, so it won't be too long before there are many millions of bacteria to harvest for insulin.

Vaccine for cancer?

Cancer is a scourge that affects peoples of all ages and from all walks of life. Cancer is not just one disease, but more than 100 different types which can affect every organ of the body. Generally, it is an abnormal growth of cells that tend to multiply in an uncontrolled way and, in some cases, to spread (see Figure 2.35). Each type of cancer is unique with its own causes, symptoms and methods of treatment. So it is no wonder researchers around the world are tackling it on many fronts.

As more is learned about how the body works, especially at the molecular level, more can be done to fight diseases and other conditions. For instance, the human papillomavirus (HPV) can sometimes lead to cervical cancer in young women. This link was made by the German researcher Harald zur Hausen in 1983 (he won the Nobel Prize in 2008). Many researchers around the world collaborated to further this work. Eventually a cancer-preventing vaccine was found. The Australian Professor Ian Frazer is credited as a creator of the HPV vaccine against cervical cancer. Gardasil is designed to prevent HPV infections by

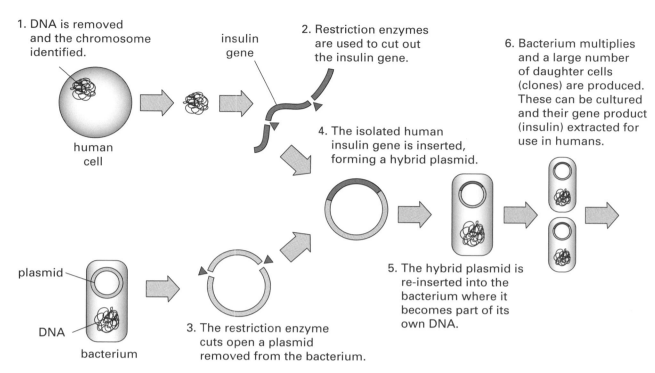

1. DNA is removed and the chromosome identified.

insulin gene

2. Restriction enzymes are used to cut out the insulin gene.

6. Bacterium multiplies and a large number of daughter cells (clones) are produced. These can be cultured and their gene product (insulin) extracted for use in humans.

human cell

4. The isolated human insulin gene is inserted, forming a hybrid plasmid.

plasmid

DNA

bacterium

3. The restriction enzyme cuts open a plasmid removed from the bacterium.

5. The hybrid plasmid is re-inserted into the bacterium where it becomes part of its own DNA.

Figure 2.34 Cloning the insulin gene

preventing the transmission of four strains of HPV. This vaccine was licensed in Australia in 2007.

In another study in the United States, researchers focused on a particular protein that is made in larger quantities in cancerous cells than in healthy ones. On this protein is a sugar with a distinctive shape. A vaccine is being developed to trigger the immune system to recognise this rogue sugar and attack the cancer. Early tests showed it shrunk breast tumours by 80%, and researchers believe it could also tackle prostate, pancreatic, bowel and ovarian cancers. Promising results on mice with breast tumours allow the researchers to now try the drug on human cancer cells in a dish. Years of large-scale human trials would need to follow before the drug was judged safe and

effective for widespread use in hospitals. If all goes well, the vaccine could be on the market by 2020.

These examples show that much modern scientific research is a collaborative effort by scientists around the world, with results often taking many years.

Polymers and new materials

Plastics such as polyethylene and polyvinyl chloride are products of the petrochemical industry. They consist of long-chain molecules that are composed of repeating subunits called monomers. When hundreds or thousands of these monomers are linked in straight, branching or linked chains then a polymer is formed. Figure 2.36 shows a section of a polyvinyl chloride (PVC) polymer. Its monomer is CH_2CHCl.

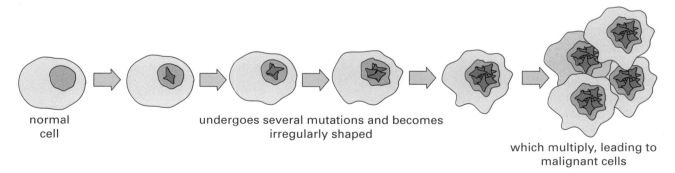

normal cell

undergoes several mutations and becomes irregularly shaped

which multiply, leading to malignant cells

Figure 2.35 How a normal cell can mutate to become cancerous

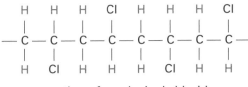

section of a polyvinyl chloride
(PVC) polymer chain

Figure 2.36 Section of a polyvinyl chloride (PVC) polymer chain

Scientists are continually striving to develop new materials that will do the job better or faster or cheaper. Sometimes an accidental development is made with a use being found afterwards. New materials are often at the centre of new designs. Giant strides in design fields are often linked with the innovation of a material that changes not only the possible solutions but the very nature of design problems. Here are some of those stories.

Post-it notes

Sticky notes, or Post-it notes, are partially adhesive, detachable note papers that seem to be everywhere in the office and home. These memo notes or place markers are stuck on desks, computers, books, files, folders, refrigerators and telephones. They have been around since the 1980s but their development started about 20 years earlier. A chemist who had became interested in a new family of polymers mixed an unusually large quantity of the monomer with the reaction mixture seemingly at random. He had discovered a totally unique phenomenon; a new polymer that was only partly sticky. This polymer would stick the note paper to other surfaces thus holding them together, but permitting easy separation without damaging either surface or leaving any marks or residue.

But this was not the end of the story. A use had to be found for poorly sticking polymer glue and machinery needed to be created to apply the substrate and glue to the paper. However, within 4 years of production Post-it notes became the 3M Company's most successful new product. Now sticky note pads are not just available in their initial yellow colour but also come in a variety of colours, sizes and styles, including pre-printed notes. In 2003, the company introduced a stronger glue that adheres better to vertical and non-smooth surfaces. Figure 2.37 is an example of how Post-it notes are now an accepted part of our culture.

Figure 2.37 When the founder of Apple computers, Steve Jobs, died in 2011 sticky notes with condolence messages were placed on many Apple stores worldwide.

NovoSorb polymer glue sticks bone

Hip and knee joint replacement requires using metallic pins and screws. This can be painful during recovery, and with follow-up surgery to remove these metallic objects. An Australian discovery, a polymer called NovoSorb, has been found to be more efficient and less painful. This polymer can be designed as a gel, liquid, rubbery substance or as hard as bone. It can also be made porous and injected with cells and drugs to assist repair and healing.

Introduced to a fracture, the polymer gel cures and glues the fractured bone together and mechanically supports it while the chemicals in it foster the healing process. The polymer is designed to naturally break down at the same rate as healing. In a diseased joint, the gel can be cured into a rubber-like substance able to bear the load without pain while cells carried in the polymer repair the injury.

This substance is still in the trial stages, with further applications being investigated. If all goes well the polymer should be available in a few years.

New building materials

Not all new innovations require inventing new chemicals. New combinations of existing materials can provide the desired outcomes.

A new process for making strong, but very light, concrete wall panels is being developed in Melbourne. These cellular aerated panels are as strong as standard concrete but much lighter, more durable, have a higher thermal insulation (about five times greater) and can reduce costs. They are suitable for both load-bearing and non-load-bearing walls. They are also fire-resistant and non-porous with a smooth, weather-resistant surface that can be used as a natural external finish, painted or rendered. The lower weight of these panels leads to other savings, such as reduced building foundation, structure and transport costs.

In Sydney, fly ash waste (fine particulate pollution generated in coal furnaces from coal-fired power stations) is being converted into a new range of high-strength, lightweight building materials. This drastically reduces the quantity of cement needed to achieve high-strength concrete structures. In addition, it takes pressure off disposing of this waste product since it is now being recycled. The fly ash bricks and pavers are about 20% lighter and stronger than their clay counterparts. This translates into further emissions savings because less steel and shallower concrete foundations are required for the same-sized structures. The bricks, pavers and aggregates are being produced in China.

 ## Test yourself 2

Part A: Knowledge

1. Select the response that correctly names a compound and its chemical formula. *(1 mark)*
   A sodium chloride, $NaCl_2$
   B calcium chloride, $CaCl_2$
   C nitrogen trioxide, N_2O_3
   D sulfuric acid, HNO_3

2. Consider the following word equation.
   sulfur + oxygen → sulfur dioxide
   This reaction could be classified as a *(1 mark)*
   A precipitation reaction.
   B neutralisation reaction.
   C decomposition reaction.
   D combustion reaction.

3. Consider the following word equation.
   magnesium oxide + sulfuric acid → magnesium sulfate + water
   This reaction is classified as a *(1 mark)*
   A neutralisation reaction.
   B precipitation reaction.
   C decomposition reaction.
   D combustion reaction.

4. Sodium carbonate and nitric acid are allowed to react. What is the name of the gas that evolves from this reaction? *(1 mark)*
   A water
   B carbon dioxide
   C nitrogen dioxide
   D hydrogen

5. Figure 2.38 shows a particle model of a chemical reaction.

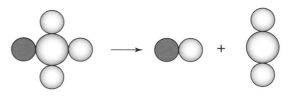

Figure 2.38 Particle model of a chemical reaction

The type of chemical reaction shown in this particle model is *(1 mark)*
   A a decomposition reaction.
   B an acid on a metal.
   C an acid on a carbonate.
   D a precipitation reaction.

6. Complete the following restricted-response questions using the appropriate word.
   (1 mark for each part)
   a) Calcium bromide is an example of an .... compound.
   b) The atoms in ammonia molecules are joined by .... bonds.
   c) The correct name for N_2O_5 is dinitrogen ....
   d) An .... is observed when magnesium is added to sulfuric acid.
   e) When magnesium burns in oxygen, the product is called magnesium ....

7. Use the code letters to match the terms or phrases in each column. *(1 mark for each part)*

Column 1		Column 2	
A	covalent bond	F	explosive combustion
B	hydrogen burns in air	G	shared electron pair
C	rusting	H	reactive metal
D	magnesium	I	strong base
E	sodium hydroxide	J	corrosion

Part B: Skills

8. Figure 2.39 shows an atomic model for a number of compounds. Use the key provided to answer the following.
   a) Name the compounds. *(3 marks)*
   b) Write their chemical formulae. *(3 marks)*
   c) Classify the compounds as ionic compounds or covalent compounds. *(3 marks)*

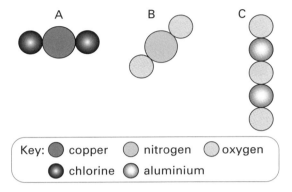

Figure 2.39 Atomic models of different compounds

9. The list below shows some common observations made during chemical reactions.
   A. A substance dissolves.
   B. Effervescence occurs.
   C. The reaction mixture changes colour.
   D. The reaction mixture gets hot or cold.
   E. A precipitate forms when solutions are mixed.
   F. Flames are produced or an explosion occurs.

   Consider the reactions that occur when the following substances are combined. From the list above, choose the observations that would be made in each case. Use the code letters.
   a) A piece of magnesium ribbon is placed in a beaker of dilute sulfuric acid. *(1 mark)*
   b) Ethanol is burnt using a spirit burner. *(1 mark)*
   c) Copper carbonate is heated strongly over a Bunsen burner flame. *(1 mark)*

10. The following information was collected concerning compounds of silver and sodium.
    - *Silver chloride is an insoluble ionic compound whereas silver nitrate is soluble. Both sodium chloride and sodium nitrate are soluble in water.*
    - *All substances in the solid state are white.*
    - *All their solutions are colourless.*

A solution of sodium chloride and a solution of silver nitrate are mixed together in a beaker.
   a) Describe what a student would observe on mixing these solutions. *(1 mark)*
   b) Classify the type of reaction occurring. *(1 mark)*
   c) Write a word equation for the reaction. *(2 marks)*
   d) Convert the word equation into a balanced symbolic equation. *(2 marks)*

11. Figure 2.40 shows the results of an experiment in which different iron nails are subjected to a range of environmental conditions.

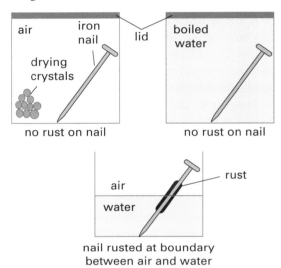

Figure 2.40 Iron nail experiment

   a) What type of chemical change is the student investigating? *(1 mark)*
   b) What conclusions can be drawn from these experiments? *(2 marks)*

12. Figure 2.41 shows a ball-and-stick model of a chemical reaction involving molecules.

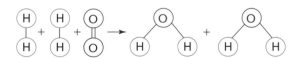

Figure 2.41 Ball-and-stick model of a chemical reaction

   a) What major scientific idea is illustrated by this equation? *(1 mark)*
   b) Classify the types of molecules according to the number of atoms per molecule. *(2 marks)*

c) What type of reaction does this model represent? *(1 mark)*

13. Two test tubes containing dilute hydrochloric acid and drops of universal indicator were set up in a test-tube rack. Each tube also contained a thermometer. Two white powdered solids (X and Y) were slowly added separately to each tube until no further changes were observed. The results of the experiment are summarised in Table 2.12.

Table 2.12 Results of experiment

Powder	Observations
X	• The white solid dissolves and the solution turns from red to green and then blue-violet. • The temperature of the mixture increases.
Y	• The white solid dissolves and the solution turns from red to green and then green-blue. • Effervescence occurs. • The temperature of the mixture increases.

a) Classify the type of reaction occurring when X and Y combine with the hydrochloric acid. *(1 mark)*

b) What is the purpose of the universal indicator? *(1 mark)*

c) Why does the temperature rise in each case? *(1 mark)*

d) One substance is magnesium oxide and one is magnesium carbonate. Use the results to determine which substance is magnesium carbonate. Justify your answer. *(2 marks)*

e) What can one conclude about the pH of the final mixture in each tube? *(2 marks)*

14. Read the following description of substance Q.
  • *Q is a colourless liquid.*
  • *Q reacts with calcium metal with the release of a colourless gas that explodes in the presence of a flame.*
  • *Q reacts with iron carbonate to produce a yellow solution and a colourless gas. The colourless gas turns limewater white.*
  • *Q conducts an electrical current.*

a) Suggest two chemical substances that could produce the reactions described. *(2 marks)*

b) Write the chemical formulae for the substances named in a). *(2 marks)*

c) Name the gas that explodes in the presence of a flame. *(1 mark)*

d) Name the gas that turned the limewater white. *(1 mark)*

Go to p. 234 to check your answers.

Summary

1. Mass is conserved in all chemical reactions.
2. John Dalton proposed the modern atomic theory.
3. John Newlands and Dmitri Mendeleev arranged elements into a periodic table using their atomic weights.
4. In the modern periodic table, the elements are arranged according to their atomic numbers.
5. Different elements have different atomic weights and the relative weights of different atoms can be compared.
6. Atoms combine to form compounds in simple whole number ratios.
7. A simple structure of the atom can be envisaged as a small, very dense nucleus containing protons and neutrons, with electrons orbiting in electron shells around this nucleus.
8. The physical and chemical properties of elements show trends down a group and across a period.
9. Metals can be arranged in an activity series based on their rates of reaction with other substances.
10. Word equations and equations written in chemical symbols describe the reactants and products of a chemical reaction.

11. In chemical reactions, atoms are neither created nor destroyed but are rearranged to form new substances.

12. Valency allows you to work out the chemical formula for a substance, and is a measure of how many electrons an atom can either accept or give up.

13. Covalent compounds share electron pairs.

14. In order to write formula equations for reactions, you need to know what kind of reaction occurs in any particular situation.

15. Chemical equations can be written in words (word equation) or using chemical symbols (symbolic equations).

16. Decomposition reactions occur when complex molecules break down, forming simpler ones.

17. A precipitation reaction occurs where soluble ions in separate solutions are mixed together to form an insoluble compound that settles out of solution.

18. There are a number of factors that determine the rate (how fast) a chemical reaction occurs. These include temperature, concentration, pressure and whether or not a catalyst is present.

19. Rusting is a chemical process that takes place in metals exposed to the atmosphere. Certain conditions in the air around a metal have to be present for iron to rust, and this can be prevented.

20. Technological advances have enabled humans to develop new and useful materials.

Syllabus checklist

Are you able to answer every syllabus question in this chapter? Tick each question as you go through the list if you are able to answer it. If you cannot answer it, turn to the appropriate page in the guide as is listed in the column to find the answer.

	For a complete understanding of this topic	Page no.	✓
1	Can I explain why mass is conserved in a chemical reaction?	53	
2	Can I recall the proposals in John Dalton's atomic theory?	53	
3	Can I explain the differences between the periodic tables constructed by John Newlands and Dmitri Mendeleev?	54–55	
4	Can I recall how the elements of the modern periodic table are arranged?	56–58	
5	Can I explain the trends in various properties of the elements across a period and down a group?	57–58	
6	Can I list common metals in an activity series from most active to least active?	58	
7	Can I write word equations and simple chemical symbolic equations?	61–63	
8	Do I understand the law of conservation of matter?	61	

	For a complete understanding of this topic	Page no.	✓
9	Do I understand valency and how it can be used to write the chemical formula for a substance?	63–65	
10	Do I understand what a covalent bond is?	65	
11	Do I understand some simple reaction types and can I write equations for the common reaction types?	66	
12	Do I understand what decomposition reactions are?	67–68	
13	Do I understand what precipitation reactions are?	68–69	
14	Can I list the factors that determine the rate of a reaction?	71–72	
15	Do I understand what conditions promote rusting, and how it may be prevented?	73–74	
16	Can I appreciate the technological advances that are occurring to develop new and useful materials?	77–79	

Part A: Multiple-choice questions

(1 mark for each)

1. Which of the metals listed below is the most active?
   A zinc
   B lead
   C copper
   D sodium

2. Which of the non-metals listed below is the most reactive?
   A fluorine
   B neon
   C sulfur
   D nitrogen

3. Identify the semi-metal in the following list.
   A selenium
   B krypton
   C boron
   D nitrogen

4. Select the set that contains a reactive metal and an unreactive non-metal.
   A potassium; xenon
   B lead; fluorine
   C silver; oxygen
   D sodium; sulfur

5. The scientist who developed the atomic theory in the 18th century is:
   A Dmitri Mendeleev.
   B John Dalton.
   C John Newlands.
   D Antoine Lavoisier.

6. What number should be written in front of the oxygen in the following equation to make it a balanced equation?
   $$C_2H_5OH + O_2 \rightarrow CO_2 + H_2O$$
   A 1
   B 2
   C 3
   D 4

7. When an acid is neutralised by a base, the new substance formed is
   A hydrogen gas and a salt.
   B a salt and water.
   C sodium chloride.
   D carbon dioxide.

8. The gas which is released when magnesium reacts with hydrochloric acid is
   A carbon dioxide.
   B oxygen.
   C chlorine.
   D hydrogen.

9. A covalent bond is formed when atoms
   A gain or lose electrons.
   B gain or lose protons.
   C share electrons.
   D fuse together.

10. The chemical formula for pentane is C_5H_{12}. Which statement is correct?
    A One molecule contains 17 atoms.
    B There are 17 atoms of hydrogen in this molecule.
    C There are more carbon atoms than hydrogen atoms.
    D This is a penta-atomic molecule.

Part B: Short-answer questions

11. Figure 2.42 shows an outline of the periodic table.

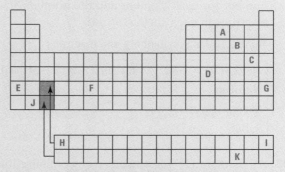

Figure 2.42 Outline diagram of the periodic table

a) To which group does element A belong? *(1 mark)*

b) Is element B a metal, semi-metal or a non-metal? *(1 mark)*

c) Is element C a gas, liquid or solid at room temperature? *(1 mark)*

d) Is element D a metal, a non-metal or a transition metal? *(1 mark)*

e) What is the melting point trend for elements E, F and G? *(1 mark)*

f) Which element is naturally radioactive? *(1 mark)*

g) Which element is synthetic? *(1 mark)*

h) Which element is the heaviest member of the lanthanoid series? *(1 mark)*

12. a) Why did Dmitri Mendeleev create a table of elements that contained gaps? *(1 mark)*

b) In what way does the modern periodic table differ from Mendeleev's table? *(1 mark)*

13. Use the periodic table to answer the following questions.

a) In which group of the table do the following elements belong?
   i) magnesium *(1 mark)*
   ii) aluminium *(1 mark)*
   iii) oxygen *(1 mark)*
   iv) carbon *(1 mark)*
   v) argon *(1 mark)*

b) In which period of the table are the following elements found?
   i) potassium *(1 mark)*
   ii) sulfur *(1 mark)*
   iii) helium *(1 mark)*
   iv) lead *(1 mark)*
   v) silver *(1 mark)*

14. Complete Table 2.13 by writing the atomic number for each element and the number of electrons in each shell. *(3 marks)*

Table 2.13 Atomic numbers and electrons

Element	Z	K shell	L shell	M shell
Nitrogen				
Magnesium				
Sulfur				

15. An element (X) has the electron configuration 2, 8, 6.

a) To which group in the periodic table does this element belong? *(1 mark)*

b) Is this element a metal, semi-metal or non-metal? *(1 mark)*

c) What is the normal valency of this element? *(1 mark)*

d) X reacts with sodium. Will the compound be ionic or covalently bonded? *(1 mark)*

16. A 40.08-g mass of calcium metal completely reacts with 16.00 g of oxygen. Calculate the mass of the calcium oxide that forms. *(1 mark)*

17. An element has the electron configuration: 2, 8, 18, 8, 1.

a) What is the atomic number of this element? *(1 mark)*

b) Name this element and write its chemical symbol. *(2 marks)*

c) Classify this element as a metal, semi-metal or non-metal. *(1 mark)*

18. For each of the following sets of elements, identify a common feature they all possess.

a) Am, Cf, No *(1 mark)*

b) Xe, Kr, Rn *(1 mark)*

c) Si, Ge, Sb *(1 mark)*

d) Ir, Nb, Mn *(1 mark)*

19. A positive ion is commonly formed when a metal loses one or more electrons. For each of the following ions, determine the number of protons, neutrons and electrons.

a) $_{20}^{40}\text{Ca}^{2+}$ *(3 marks)*

b) $_{13}^{27}\text{Al}^{3+}$ *(3 marks)*

20. A negative ion is commonly formed when a non-metal gains one or more electrons. For each of the following ions, determine the number of protons, neutrons and electrons and identify which element of the periodic table each one is.

a) $_{16}^{32}\text{X}^{2-}$ *(4 marks)*

b) $_{9}^{19}\text{Q}^{-}$ *(4 marks)*

21. Arrange the following metals in the correct order of the activity series from most active to least active: zinc; lead; aluminium; copper; gold; magnesium; potassium; iron. *(1 mark)*

22. a) For which of the following reactions does:
   i) effervescence occur? *(1 mark)*
   ii) a precipitate form? *(1 mark)*
   If no reaction occurs, write 'no reaction'.
   Reaction 1: lead nitrate solution is mixed with sodium sulfate solution.
   Reaction 2: lead metal is added to dilute hydrochloric acid.
   Reaction 3: calcium carbonate (marble chips) is added to dilute nitric acid.

b) Write word equations for the reactions in a). *(2 marks)*

23. Between 1807 and 1817 three elements of the periodic table (sodium, potassium and lithium) were discovered. Table 2.14 provides information about these three elements.
   a) To what group of the periodic table do these elements belong? *(1 mark)*
   b) How do these elements demonstrate the trends in properties that Newlands and Mendeleev observed in the 19th century? *(3 marks)*

Table 2.14 Properties of lithium, sodium and potassium

Property	Lithium	Sodium	Potassium
appearance	soft, silvery, lustrous	soft, silvery, lustrous	soft, silvery, lustrous
atomic weight (u)	6.94	22.99	39.10
density (g/cm³)	0.53	0.97	0.86
melting point (°C)	180	98	63
boiling point (°C)	1342	883	760
reaction with water	rapid bubbling; hydrogen released	very rapid bubbling, hydrogen released explosively	violent bubbling reaction, hydrogen explodes
chemical formula of chloride compound	LiCl	NaCl	KCl

24. Complete Table 2.15. *(11 marks)*

25. Table 2.16 shows the boiling points and atomic radii of elements of Period 2.

Table 2.16 Boiling points and atomic radii of Period 2 elements

Element	Z	Boiling point (°C)	Atomic radius (pm)
Li	3	1330	152
Be	4	2477	112
B	5	3930	88
C	6	4630	71
N	7	−196	73
O	8	−183	74
F	9	−188	71
Ne	10	−246	69

   a) State the trend in boiling point across this period. *(1 mark)*
   b) State the trend in atomic radius across this period. *(1 mark)*
   c) Classify these elements as metals, semi-metals and non-metals. *(1 mark)*

26. Name the following compounds and classify them as ionic or covalent:
   a) CaI_2 *(1 mark)*
   b) SCl_2 *(1 mark)*
   c) HI *(1 mark)*
   d) HgO *(1 mark)*

27. The nine cards in Figure 2.43 (on the next page) represent a 3 × 3 block of elements in the periodic table. The cards are randomly placed. Your job is to change their positions so they form the correct pattern for the periodic table. *(9 marks)*

Table 2.15 Properties of some elements

Element	Z	K shell	L shell	M shell	N shell	O shell	Valency
Co	27	2	8	15	2		+2
K					1		
O							
Ca				8			
N							
F							
		2	8	18	7		
		2	8	18	2		
		2	8	18	18	7	
Ag					18	1	
	26						+2

Colourless unreactive gas	Yellow-green gas	Grey solid or red solid
MP = –249 °C BP = –246 °C • used in coloured lights • no compounds exist	MP = –101 °C BP = –34 °C • used as a bleach and disinfectant • its anion is abundant in sea water	MP = 217 °C (grey) 170 °C (red) decomposes BP = 685 °C (grey) • conductivity of grey form increases on exposure to light • used in ruby glass
1	**2**	**3**

Colourless gas	Yellow solid	Colourless unreactive gas
MP = –219 °C BP = –183 °C • rekindles a glowing splint • most abundant element in Earth's crust	MP = 113 °C BP = 445 °C • found near volcanic vents • burns with a violet flame to produce an acidic oxide	MP = –157 °C BP = –152 °C • a difluoride and tetrafluoride have been prepared • six stable isotopes
4	**5**	**6**

Yellow gas	Colourless unreactive gas	Red-brown fuming liquid
MP = –220 °C BP = –188 °C • very strong oxidising agent • its soluble alkali salts used in water supplies	MP = –189 °C BP = –186 °C • used as a non-corrosive atmosphere in incandescent lights • third most abundant gas in air	MP = –7 °C BP = 59 °C • its silver salt is used in photography • present in halons (ozone-destroying chemicals)
7	**8**	**9**

Figure 2.43 A 3 × 3 block of elements of the periodic table; the cards are arranged randomly.

28. Write the symbols for the ions in the following ionic compounds and name each compound (refer to the periodic table).
    a) $BaCl_2$ *(1 mark)*
    b) $Ga(NO_3)_3$ *(1 mark)*
    c) RbF *(1 mark)*

29. Determine the valency of the indicated elements in each of the following covalent compounds.
    a) X in X_2O_3 *(1 mark)*
    b) Y in YCl_5 *(1 mark)*
    c) Z in H_2Z *(1 mark)*

30. Yellow sulfur burns in a gas jar of pure oxygen with a pale mauve flame. A colourless gas is formed. The gas dissolves in water and the solution formed turns blue litmus red.
    a) What are the indicators of a chemical change in the combustion process? *(2 marks)*
    b) Name the gas formed in the combustion reaction. *(1 mark)*
    c) Write a word equation for the combustion reaction. *(2 marks)*
    d) Write a balanced symbolic equation for the combustion reaction. *(2 marks)*
    e) What can one conclude about the acid–base properties of the colourless gas? *(1 mark)*

31. Ethane (C_2H_6) burns in oxygen to form carbon dioxide and water.
    a) How many atoms are present in one molecule of ethane? *(1 mark)*
    b) Write a word equation for the combustion reaction. *(2 marks)*
    c) Write a balanced symbolic equation for the combustion reaction. *(2 marks)*
    d) How could a student prove that carbon dioxide is released in the combustion process? *(2 marks)*
    e) Why is an ignition (or heat) source not required after the combustion reaction has begun? *(1 mark)*

32. Name the salts produced in each of the following reactions with acids.
    a) Zinc dissolves in sulfuric acid. *(1 mark)*
    b) Calcium oxide dissolves in nitric acid. *(1 mark)*

c) Sodium carbonate dissolves in hydrochloric acid. *(1 mark)*

33. Magnesium carbonate is converted into magnesium oxide when the white solid is heated over a Bunsen flame.
    a) What type of chemical reaction is described above? *(1 mark)*
    b) What other product will form in this reaction? *(1 mark)*
    c) Write a word equation and a balanced symbolic equation for this reaction. *(2 marks)*

34. When nitric acid is added to sodium sulfide (Na_2S), a foul-smelling gas called hydrogen sulfide is released. The sodium sulfide dissolves to form a colourless solution of sodium nitrate. The experiment was conducted with two equal mass samples (X and Y) of sodium sulfide. The volume and temperature of the acid were the same in each experiment. The volume of gas released was measured each minute and recorded, and the data was plotted as a line graph. Figure 2.44 shows the results of these experiments.

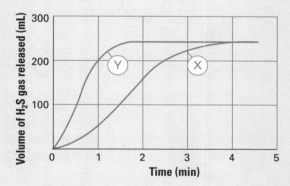

Figure 2.44 Volume of hydrogen sulfide gas released as a function of time

    a) Which reaction has the greater initial rate? *(1 mark)*
    b) Explain why the rates of the reaction were different in each container. *(1 mark)*
    c) Write a word equation for the reaction. *(1 mark)*
    d) Write a balanced symbolic equation for the reaction. *(1 mark)*
    e) Figure 2.45 shows four possible structures for the foul-smelling gas released in the reaction. Which model is consistent with the experimental information and the symbolic equation? *(1 mark)*

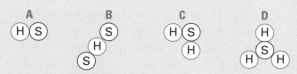

Figure 2.45 Possible models for the foul-smelling gas

35. Table 2.17 lists some solubility rules for ionic compounds.

Table 2.17 Solubility rules for some ionic salts

Type of salt	General solubility rule	Exceptions to the rule
Group 1(I) salts	soluble	–
nitrate salts	soluble	–
chloride salts	soluble	silver chloride, AgCl
		lead chloride, $PbCl_2$
sulfate salts	soluble	barium sulfate, $BaSO_4$
		lead sulfate, $PbSO_4$
		calcium sulfate, $CaSO_4$
carbonate salts	insoluble	Group 1 (I) carbonates
		ammonium carbonate, $(NH_4)_2CO_3$

Use the table to answer the following questions.
    a) Determine whether the following compounds are soluble or insoluble in water.
       i) calcium chloride *(1 mark)*
       ii) iron carbonate *(1 mark)*
       iii) barium nitrate *(1 mark)*
       iv) sodium sulfate *(1 mark)*
    b) Solutions of the following ionic compounds are mixed together. Predict whether a precipitate will form.
       i) silver nitrate and potassium chloride *(1 mark)*
       ii) ammonium sulfate and barium chloride *(1 mark)*
       iii) sodium nitrate and copper sulfate *(1 mark)*

36. Figure 2.46 shows an experiment in which a student passes an electric current (via platinum electrodes) into water containing a small amount of sodium sulfate. The sodium sulfate

is added to make the water conductive but it does not alter the reaction. (Sulfuric acid is also suitable for this purpose.) Gases collect in inverted test tubes (initially filled with water).

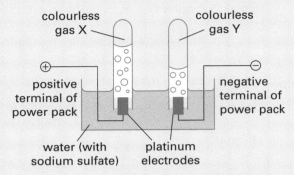

Figure 2.46 Passing an electric current through water

a) Compare the volume of the gas released from the negative electrode Y to the volume of gas from the positive electrode X. *(1 mark)*

b) The gas Y from the negative electrode is tested and found to explode in the presence of air and a flame. What is this gas? *(1 mark)*

c) The gas X from the positive electrode is tested and found to relight a glowing wooden splint. What gas is this? *(1 mark)*

d) Explain, with the aid of a word equation, the type of reaction that is occurring. *(2 marks)*

e) Write a balanced symbolic equation for this reaction. *(1 mark)*

f) How do the different gas volumes (see Figure 2.46) support the balanced equation? *(1 mark)*

37. Nicholas is performing an experiment heating some solid lead nitrate (see Figure 2.47).

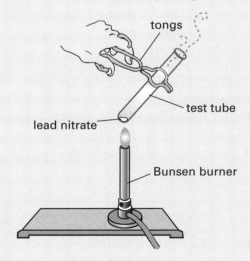

Figure 2.47 Heating lead nitrate

a) Explain three of the things the student is doing correctly in Figure 2.47. *(3 marks)*

b) After a little while the student observes brown fumes of nitrogen dioxide. What kind of reaction is this? *(1 mark)*

c) Another gas, odourless and colourless, is also released. What might this gas be? *(1 mark)*

d) At the end of the experiment the student is left with a mass of lead oxide in the test tube. Write a balanced equation for the reaction. *(1 mark)*

38. The experiment shown in Figure 2.48 is performed to determine whether two soluble antacid tablets will dissolve at the same rate if one is crushed. A solid antacid tablet is dropped into a beaker of water at the same time as a crushed tablet is dropped into another beaker of water. The time for each to completely dissolve is recorded.

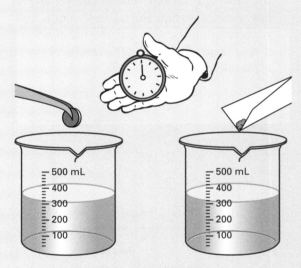

Figure 2.48 Dissolving antacid tablets

a) Explain why it is important for the following to remain the same:
   i) volume of water in each beaker *(1 mark)*
   ii) temperature of the water *(1 mark)*
   iii) mass of antacid table used. *(1 mark)*

b) Does it matter if one is stirred and the other is not? Explain. *(1 mark)*

c) It was found that the crushed tablet dissolved faster than the uncrushed tablet. Explain. *(2 marks)*

d) Which should dissolve faster in hot tea: a sugar cube, plain sugar or icing sugar (very finely powdered sugar)? *(1 mark)*

39. Corrugated galvanised iron is a common roofing material in Australia. The sheeting is covered with a protective zinc coating to prevent the mild steel from rusting.

a) Which of the following statements describes a way of giving added protection to the iron? Explain your decision, and explain why the other alternatives are poor choices. *(3 marks)*
  - being used on roofs near the seaside
  - being used in city locations where rainfall is sometimes acidic
  - painting the roof
  - punching copper nails through the sheeting to secure it

b) Consider the following information.

The zinc coating on galvanised iron prevents the protected metal from corrosion by forming a physical barrier, and by acting as a sacrificial electrode if this barrier is damaged. In the atmosphere, zinc reacts with oxygen forming zinc oxide. This oxide further reacts with water or moisture, forming zinc hydroxide. Finally, zinc hydroxide reacts with moist carbon dioxide (which forms weak carbonic acid, H_2CO_3) in the atmosphere producing a thin, impermeable, tenacious and quite insoluble dull grey layer of zinc carbonate. This adheres extremely well to the underlying zinc, so protecting it from further corrosion.

Write three balanced equations for the reactions described in this passage. *(3 marks)*

40. Hydrogen peroxide decomposes very slowly at room temperature. The presence of a catalyst may cause it to decompose quickly.

a) Write a balanced equation for the decomposition of hydrogen peroxide (H_2O_2). *(1 mark)*

b) From Graph A in Figure 2.49, how do you know that hydrogen peroxide ordinarily decomposes very slowly? *(1 mark)*

c) How can you determine how much oxygen is produced in an experiment? Draw a diagram to show how you can measure the volume of this gas. *(3 marks)*

d) On Graph A, both P and Q represent the same catalyst. One is present in greater quantity that the other. Which letter shows the greater quantity? *(1 mark)*

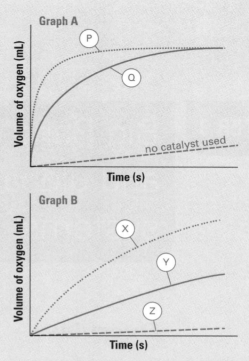

Figure 2.49 The decomposition of hydrogen peroxide

e) Is it true that the more catalyst there is, the more oxygen gas you'll get? Explain. *(2 marks)*

f) Describe the shape of the curves P and Q, and what it means, in Graph A. *(2 marks)*

g) Graph B in Figure 2.49 shows three different catalysts that can be used in this reaction: manganese dioxide, MnO_2; zinc oxide, ZnO; and copper(II) oxide, CuO. CuO is better than ZnO, but not as good as MnO_2. Identify each of these catalysts in Graph B. *(3 marks)*

h) The rate of reaction can also be determined using the apparatus shown in Figure 2.50. Explain how this can be done. *(2 marks)*

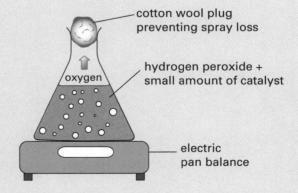

Figure 2.50 Alternative apparatus for experiment

Go to pp. 234–238 to check your answers.

CHAPTER 3

Big Bang theory and global systems

Overview

In this chapter you will learn about:

- the Big Bang theory
- evidence for the Big Bang theory
- evolution of the universe
- the life of stars
- the fate of the universe
- astronomy
- natural cycles in the biosphere
- the greenhouse effect and climate change
- atmospheric pollution
- CFCs and the ozone layer.

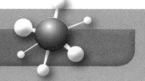

Glossary

Astronomical unit—the average distance between Earth and the Sun (1 AU = 150 million km)

Azimuth—the angular position of an object in the sky measured from north in a clockwise direction

Big Bang theory—a theory of the origin of the universe; states that the universe came into existence about 13.7 billion years ago due to the creation of space-time and the partial conversion of energy into matter

Biodiversity—the variety of life in the world or in a particular habitat or ecosystem

Biosphere—the part of the Earth's crust, waters and atmosphere that supports life

Carbon sequestration—the process of removing carbon from the atmosphere and depositing it in a reservoir, for long-term storage of CO_2

Cosmic background radiation—the electromagnetic radiation in space that remains following the Big Bang; this radiation cooled as the universe expanded and is now at an average temperature of 3 degrees above absolute zero (i.e. −270 °C)

Elevation—angular position of an object above the Earth's plane

Eutrophication—the process by which a body of water becomes enriched in dissolved nutrients (such as nitrates or phosphates), which stimulate the growth of aquatic plant life and thereby usually result in the depletion of dissolved oxygen

Exoplanet—a planet outside our solar system that orbits a star other than Earth's Sun

Galaxy—vast collections of stars that are held together by gravitational forces

Interstellar—between the stars

Light-year (ly)—the distance light travels in one Earth year

Nuclear fusion—the process in which nuclei of light elements join together, with the release of large amounts of energy

Phytoplankton—minute, free-floating aquatic plants

Plankton—a variety of small or microscopic organisms, including algae and protozoa, that float or drift in great numbers in fresh or salt water, especially at or near the surface, and serve as food for fish and other larger organisms

Red shift—the shift in frequencies of visible spectral lines towards the red end (low frequency) of the electromagnetic spectrum; used as evidence of an expanding universe

Spectrum—the range of visible and non-visible light

Stratosphere—a layer in the atmosphere situated between about 15 km and 50 km altitude above the Earth's surface

Thermohaline circulation—the large-scale ocean circulation driven by global density gradients created by surface heat and freshwater variations

Transpiration—the process by which water that is absorbed by plants is evaporated into the atmosphere from the plant's surface, such as through leaf pores

Troposphere—the lowest layer of Earth's atmosphere, beginning at Earth's surface and up to a height of 15 km above sea level; most of the mass of the atmosphere is in the troposphere, and almost all weather occurs here

Zenith—the highest point in the heavens (directly above you)

3.1 The Big Bang theory

The Big Bang theory is currently the most favoured theory about the beginning and subsequent evolution of the universe. This theory was proposed in 1948 by George Gamow, and states that about 13.7 billion years ago space and time came into existence as a 'singularity'. The exact nature of this singularity is not fully understood but one can imagine it as a superdense point from which time and space emerge. One cannot talk of what was before the Big Bang as time and space did not exist. From this singularity, the universe formed and then inflated and expanded. There was no actual explosion. In terms of Einstein's equation ($E = mc^2$), the energy that came into existence was partly converted to matter and antimatter over a short period of time. Antimatter is composed of particles that destroy matter particles when they collide. Following a period of such collisions, all the antimatter was destroyed and an excess of matter was left. Space became filled with hot matter that inflated and expanded rapidly and cooled as it expanded. The sequence of events that followed the formation of the universe can be summarised in Table 3.1.

Figure 3.1 summarises the key events following the Big Bang and the expansion of the universe.

Table 3.1 Events since the Big Bang

Time after the Big Bang	Event
0	The Big Bang occurs: space and time form.
10^{-12} to 10^{-6} seconds	Space inflates and becomes filled with radiation. Temperature = 100 billion °C. Subatomic particles (e.g. quarks and electrons) and antimatter particles have formed.
10^{-6} to 1 seconds	The universe cools as it expands. Protons and neutrons form as well as their antimatter forms. The temperature is now 10 billion °C.
1 to 10 seconds	Most of the matter and antimatter particles annihilate each other, leaving an excess of protons, neutrons and electrons.
3 to 10 minutes	Universe continues to cool and atomic nuclei form from protons and neutrons. The temperature is now 1 billion °C.
377 000 years	Atoms (mainly hydrogen and helium) have formed as nuclei combine with electrons. Light waves have escaped to fill the expanding universe. The temperature of the universe has dropped to 3000 °C.
377 000 years to 13.7 billion years	Gravitational forces lead to the formation of stars, galaxies and planets. The first stars probably formed about 100 to 200 million years after the Big Bang. A nebula began to form about 9 billion years after the Big Bang. From this nebula, our Sun and solar system began to form. The universe continues to expand and cool.
13.7 billion years	Today ($\sim 10^{10}$ years after the Big Bang) the intergalactic temperature is only 3 degrees above absolute zero (i.e. –270 °C; absolute zero is –273 °C).

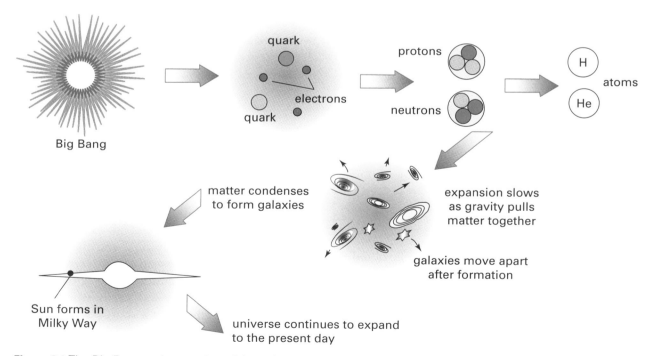

Figure 3.1 The Big Bang and expansion of the universe

3.2 Evidence for the Big Bang theory

In the first 30 years of the 20th century, various scientists (including Einstein, Lemaître and Friedmann) developed theories that suggested that the universe was expanding. No experimental evidence had been collected at the time to show this expansion. The concept of an expanding universe implied that the universe must have been originally much smaller than its current size. From this idea and Einstein's theory concerning the equivalence of mass and energy, the Big Bang theory developed.

Here is some of the evidence gathered which supports the theory of an expanding universe.

- Red shift of stars and galaxies. Astronomers analysed the light from distant stars and galaxies with a spectroscope. A spectroscope is an instrument that detects different wavelengths or frequencies of light and displays them on a screen as a series of coloured lines rather like a barcode. Each element in a star produces its own characteristic pattern or spectrum of coloured lines. When astronomers looked at various elements in these sources, they found the characteristic frequencies of key lines of the spectrum were shifted towards the red end (low-energy end) of the visible spectrum. This observation was made by Edwin Hubble in the late 1920s and indicated that these stars and galaxies were moving away from us (and from each other). They are moving away because space itself is expanding. Figure 3.2 shows a model to demonstrate the expanding universe. Imagine that the dots are galaxies. As the shape enlarges (expanding universe) all dots within the shape are moving away from the central dot. But, at the same time, they are also moving away from each other. Figure 3.3 shows an example of the red shift of hydrogen spectral lines from a source in a distant galaxy compared to a hydrogen source in a laboratory on Earth.

- Cosmic background radiation. In 1965 two astronomers (Penzis and Wilson) detected uniform microwave radiation emanating from intergalactic space. This radiation was equivalent to a background temperature of −270 °C (or 3 degrees above absolute zero). In 1989 the Cosmic Background Explorer satellite (COBE) studied this background radiation and found

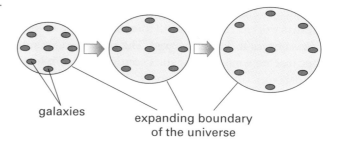

galaxies expanding boundary of the universe

Figure 3.2 Demonstrating the expanding universe

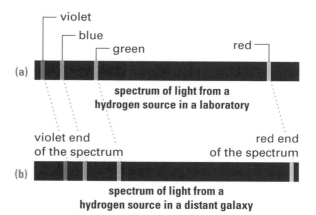

violet
blue
green
red

(a)

spectrum of light from a hydrogen source in a laboratory

violet end of the spectrum
red end of the spectrum

(b)

spectrum of light from a hydrogen source in a distant galaxy

Figure 3.3 Hydrogen spectral lines measured from a source on Earth (a) and a source in a distant galaxy (b).

small amounts of matter irregularly scattered in the intergalactic spaces (see Figure 3.4). These observations were consistent with the expansion and cooling of space following the formation of space and time billions of years ago.

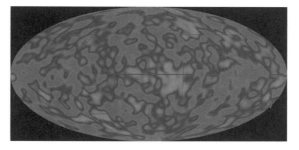

Figure 3.4 COBE map of the universe showing zones of different temperatures caused by the formation of stars and galaxies about 1 million years after the Big Bang

- Calculations of the relative proportions of hydrogen and helium in the universe based on the Big Bang theory have been confirmed by astronomical measurements. This is further evidence for the Big Bang theory.

Before the development of the Big Bang theory, another theory called the steady state theory (Gold,

Hoyle, Bondi, 1948) proposed that the universe always existed and that it will forever continue to look the same as it did in the past. The universe expands because new matter and stars continue to form from a reservoir of energy. There is therefore a balance between expansion and star/galaxy formation.

Opponents of the steady state theory have made the following criticisms.

- The discovery of the variable distribution of galactic radio sources and very distant and very bright quasars implies that the early universe looked different to the current universe. This is inconsistent with the steady state theory.
- The discovery of cosmic background radiation cannot be explained by the steady state theory.

However, since 1996 the Hubble Space telescope has taken photographs of the most distant regions of space, showing mature galaxies similar to our local ones. This is consistent with the steady state theory.

Problems with the steady state theory began to surface in the late 1960s, when observations showed that the universe was in fact changing. So the steady state model is now largely discredited.

3.3 Evolution of the universe

Following the Big Bang, the matter that formed spread out as space expanded. This matter was not uniformly spread but irregularly scattered. By 1 billion years after the Big Bang, gravity began to pull matter together to form various astronomical structures. Gaseous clouds of hydrogen and dust collapsed under gravity to form galaxies. Inside these galaxies, stars began to form and illuminate space with their light. The Sun and the solar system began to form from a planetary nebula about 4.6 billion years ago. The nuclear fusion reactions in its core were initiated when the gravitational heating reached 10 million degrees. Nuclear fusion is a process in which the nuclei of light atoms (such as hydrogen) are converted into heavier nuclei (like helium) with the release of vast amounts of energy. Circling this young star were protoplanets which formed from the spinning disk of condensed matter. These protoplanets became the planets of our solar system. Star formation continues today in distant parts of the universe.

Stars, galaxies and deep space objects

Stars

Astronomers think stars are born in groups or clusters which are made from large quantities of interstellar (between the stars) hydrogen gas and sooty dust left from dying stars. Slowly, over many billions of years, this matter is pulled together by gravity to form a protostar which begins to glow a dull red as its temperature increases. Spinning flattens the protostar into a disc. At this stage, planets may form from the rings in the disk. If the temperature in the central core increases to 10 million °C, nuclear reactions fuse hydrogen into helium and the star is formed. Stars like our own Sun then shine for about 10 billion years.

Our Sun contains 98% of all the mass of the solar system. It is largely composed of hydrogen and a smaller amount of helium. It has a diameter of 1 390 000 km, which is about a hundred times greater than Earth's, and a mass about 300 000 times greater. Yet it is smaller than the average star. Inside the Sun, hundreds of huge nuclear explosions occur each second. But because of the huge gravitational forces, the Sun does not blow itself apart. The energy from the nuclear reactions occurs deep inside the core of the Sun. Here the temperature is at least 14 million °C. The energy produced in the core moves outwards through the radiation zone over a period of about a million years to the convection zone, where the energy is transferred to the surface. The outer surface is a cool 5600 °C and is known as the photosphere. Visible light is emitted from the surface, as well as other forms of radiation such as infra-red, ultraviolet and gamma rays.

The universe is composed of many stars. Our star, the Sun, is one of 100 billion stars in our galaxy, the Milky Way. And, in turn, our galaxy is just one of the billions of galaxies in the universe.

Galaxies

A galaxy is a vast collection of stars, gas and stellar dust (see Figure 3.5). Some galaxies are elliptical and some have irregular shapes. Galaxies are organised into local clusters and superclusters that are hundreds of millions of light-years across. Our solar system is located in the end of one of the arms of a spiral galaxy called the Milky Way. The Milky Way has a diameter of about 100 000 light-years (ly) and our solar system is about 32 000 ly from the galactic centre. Some galaxies, such as our Milky Way galaxy, have black holes at their centres.

1 light-year (ly) = the distance light travels in a year
= 9 500 000 000 000 km

Our galaxy is part of the local group, which includes the Large Magellanic Cloud, Small Magellanic Cloud and the Andromeda galaxy, and a few dozen other galaxies. The local group is part of the Virgo supercluster, a huge system of galaxies 100 million ly across.

Figure 3.5 Galaxies of stars

Deep space objects

Beyond the galaxies and superclusters are deep space objects. The following are some common objects found in deep space.

> Nebulae. These are clouds of gas and stellar dust. Some glow brightly and others are dark. The southern sky contains the Coalsack Nebula near the Southern Cross (Crux) constellation of stars (see Figure 3.6). This nebula is dark.

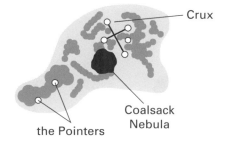

Figure 3.6 The Coalsack Nebula

> Novae and supernovae. Novae are formed by explosions that shear off the outer layers of stars. This causes the star to shine more brightly than normal. In supernovae, the explosions tear the whole star apart and there is a short period where the exploding star shines billions of times more brightly. Eventually a nebula is left behind with a rapidly spinning pulsar or neutron star at its centre.

The most famous supernova occurred in AD 1054; it produced the Crab Nebula. The Crab Nebula is made up of a rapidly spinning (30 times each second) pulsating neutron star, called a pulsar, in the centre, and glowing ejections of gases flying outward in an irregular fashion. In the years since, these gases have spread out at least 10 ly across. The supernova was seen in one of the horns of the constellation Taurus. The explosion was recorded by the Chinese and Koreans. Rock paintings discovered in Arizona and New Mexico suggest it may also have been seen by south-western Native Americans. It was bright enough to be seen during the day, and its great brilliance lasted for weeks.

> Pulsars are very small (~20 km) and very dense objects that are about as heavy as the Sun. They emit pulses of radio waves as well as short bursts of X-rays and gamma rays along the direction of their magnetic axes (see Figure 3.7) . We detect the pulsar if its pulses are directed towards us.

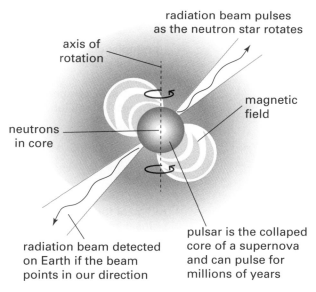

Figure 3.7 Model of a pulsar

> Quasars and black holes. Quasars are at vast distances in deep space. They are the centres

of violent galaxies. They emit huge amounts of energy in jet streams at right angles to a spinning hydrogen gas disc as shown in Figure 3.8. It is these bright jet streams of radio waves that we detect if they point in our direction. The spiralling gas is subjected to the intense gravity of a black hole at the centre. Black holes are extremely massive objects equivalent to billions of suns. They are so massive that nothing, not even light, can escape.

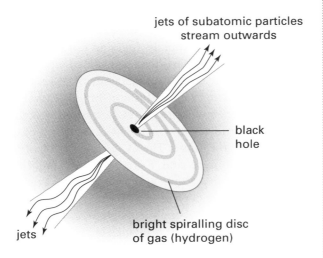

Figure 3.8 Artist's impression of a quasar and black hole

The life of stars

Eventually, a star like our Sun will start running out of hydrogen in its core and begin to shrink. This process causes it to become even hotter. Now a new series of nuclear reactions will occur, producing a helium shell around the core. While the core is contracting and heating, the shell will expand and cool down. It might get as much as 100 times bigger than what it was before. It will then be a red giant. Aldebaran is a red giant in the Taurus constellation. The core, however, will continue contracting and may reach a temperature well over 100 million °C. The red giant will rapidly use up its remaining fuel and eject its outer layers to form a planetary nebula. The nebula will drift off and the exposed core will then be a white dwarf. Its size will be no larger than the Earth and its temperature only about 100 000 °C, but it will be a very heavy star. In fact, it will be millions of times heavier than Earth. Its life is effectively over, and for the next billion years or so it will slowly cool down until a cold black dwarf is formed. The process of evolution of a star like our Sun is shown in Figure 3.9.

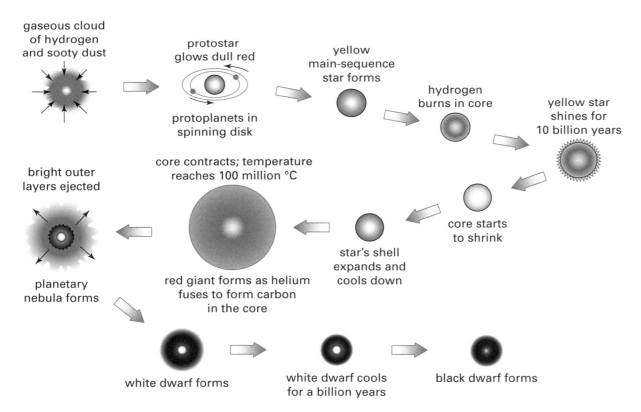

Figure 3.9 Evolution of stars like our Sun

Very heavy stars (two to six times as massive as the Sun) burn their fuel for about 1 million years. Their cores are so hot that they glow a bright blue. Eventually, these massive stars run out of fuel and swell to form red supergiants. Betelgeuse is a red supergiant in the Orion constellation. The core of these huge stars will have turned to iron, the end as far as nuclear reactions are concerned. Though several billion degrees Celsius, this star gets much hotter as it collapses in on itself in a supernova. The huge gravitational attraction causes it to collapse at about 50 000 km per second. In one second more energy is thrown out than the Sun can produce in its whole lifetime. Its mass is squeezed into a space of about 20 km in diameter. A very bright object appears in the night sky for a few days and then fades. Afterwards, the only sign such a star existed is the pulsar (or neutron star) it leaves behind. Very massive stars eventually swell to form very large red supergiants before they explode to create a supernova. The core that is left collapses in on itself to produce a dense, dark star called a black hole. The gravitational attraction of black holes is so large not even light can escape.

Stars that are less than half the size of the Sun are called red dwarfs. They have very long lives, and never evolve into red giants. Many of these common stars are almost as old as the universe. They fuse hydrogen into helium, but their small size prevents any further nuclear events. After they have exhausted their hydrogen, they cool and darken to form black dwarfs. Their lifetimes are estimated to be 100 billion years. Proxima Centauri (the closest star to the solar system) is a very small star with a mass about 15% of the Sun's mass.

Figure 3.10 shows the evolutionary path of different types of stars.

Formation of the solar system

About 9 billion years ago, in an outer part of the Milky Way galaxy, gas and dust particles began to collapse and spin. A massive nebula was forming. As its internal temperature increased, a point was reached where thermonuclear reactions began and a dull red protosun was formed. Over time, this protosun attracted more dust from space, which began to form planets, asteroids and comets. As hydrogen atoms fused together in the thermonuclear reactions, the Sun grew brighter and a yellow star was formed. Our Sun and its family of planets, the Solar

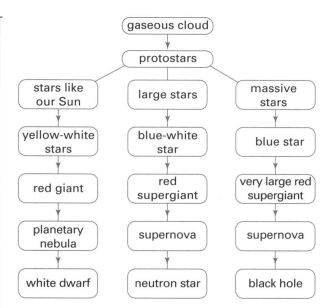

Figure 3.10 Star evolution

System, was created about 4.6 billion years ago. This process is shown in Figure 3.11.

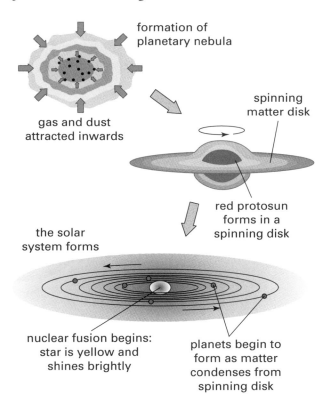

Figure 3.11 The formation of the Sun and solar system

Formation of the Earth

The primitive Earth formed about 4.6 billion years ago. Initially, it was cold compared to its current internal heat. As gravity compressed the matter of the primitive planet, the compression led to a gradual rise in temperature. Radioactive elements such as uranium also released energy as they decayed and so the internal temperature of the Earth rose further. New compounds began to form as the temperature increased. Eventually, parts of the Earth's interior began to melt. Convection currents carried lighter materials towards the surface of the Earth where they cooled to form a solid crust.

The heavier minerals such as iron and nickel remained at the Earth's core in both solid and liquid forms. An atmosphere was formed as gaseous elements and compounds were explosively released through the solidifying crust (see Figure 3.12). Scientists believe this atmosphere consisted of nitrogen, carbon dioxide, water vapour, ammonia and methane. Over the next few billion years, the interaction between ultraviolet rays from the Sun and the Earth's atmosphere led to chemical reactions in the atmosphere. Ammonia decomposed into nitrogen and hydrogen and water vapour decomposed into oxygen and hydrogen. The hydrogen gas was so light that it escaped gradually into space. Most of the oxygen in the atmosphere, however, did not arise until living things such as photosynthetic protists and plants evolved billions of years after the Earth was formed. Continued cooling of the Earth's surface led to the condensation of water vapour into liquid water, which covered much of the Earth's surface. Carbon dioxide dissolved in the liquid water and eventually precipitated in the form of insoluble carbonates such as limestone rocks. Much of the carbon dioxide of this early atmosphere is now locked up in carbonaceous rocks.

The fate of the universe

Various theories have been proposed concerning the fate of the universe, including the following.

> The open universe theory. This suggests that the universe will continue to expand and cool forever. (There is evidence that the distant regions of the universe are expanding at an ever-increasing rate.) Ultimately, the stars will redden and die (~100 trillion years) as they exhaust their nuclear fuel and the universe will become very dark and very cold.

> The closed (pulsating) universe theory. The universe will expand for a time but will eventually stop expanding and contract as gravity draws

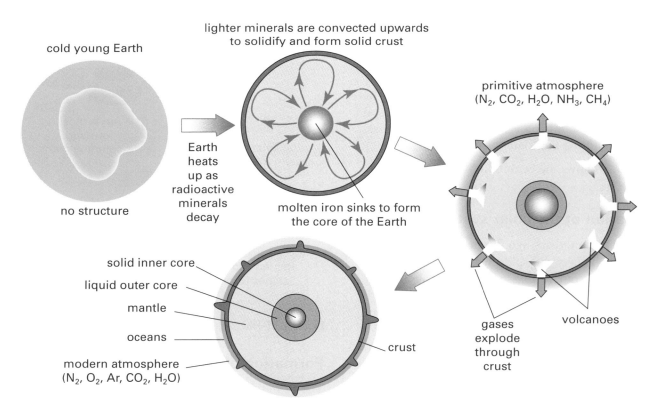

Figure 3.12 The formation of the Earth

matter back together. This scenario ends in a big 'crunch' followed by a new Big Bang. This process repeats itself forever.

3.4 Exploration and study of the universe

Electromagnetic spectrum and astronomy

Astronomers use various bands of the electromagnetic spectrum to investigate the universe. Table 3.2 shows some of the applications.

Table 3.2 Electromagnetic waves used to study the universe

Electromagnetic band	Uses in astronomy
radio	Radio telescopes are large dishes (e.g. Parkes in NSW) that collect radio waves from space. The weak radio signals are amplified and analysed. Radio astronomy is used to: • observe objects that emit mainly radio waves rather than visible light (e.g. dark nebulae, quasars, pulsars) • observe clouds of hydrogen in deep space.
infrared	Infrared telescopes and their spectrometers are used to: • detect objects that are too cool to emit visible light • measure the temperature of the atmosphere of solar system planets • determine the temperature of the background radiation in deep space.
visible	Ground-based optical telescopes and spectrometers as well as space telescopes such as the Hubble are used to: • observe and measure various optical sources such as planets, comets, stars and galaxies • measure the red shift of space objects such as galaxies to determine the extent of expansion of the universe • measure the colour and temperature of stars.

Since 1945, many Australian universities and CSIRO have made huge strides in radio astronomy to the point that we are now recognised as one of the world leaders. Radio waves coming from space are very weak and large instruments with very sensitive detectors are needed to collect them. Radio waves are collected by a large curved dish that reflects the signals onto a detector suspended above the centre of the dish. The weak signals are changed into electrical pulses and amplified. They can then be stored by computer for later study. Unlike light telescopes, which can only examine the heavens at night, radio telescopes can pick up signals at any time of day or night.

There are three main reasons for using radio telescopes.

- They can show where clouds of cool hydrogen are located between stars. These clouds are where new stars are born and produce no light of their own.
- Radio signals can pass through matter that stops light. They can come to us from far across the galaxy unhindered and give us information which would otherwise be hidden from view.
- Some objects in the universe don't give out much light but are very rich in radio waves. Some of the furthest objects in the universe can only be detected by the radio waves they emit.

Problems in obtaining information in astronomy

Ground-based telescopes

Ground-based astronomy is faced with many difficulties, including the following.

- Earth's atmosphere. The atmosphere absorbs various components of the electromagnetic spectrum to different extents. Infrared, ultraviolet and X-rays are significantly absorbed by the atmosphere. Visible light is scattered and refracted by the atmosphere and clear images are hard to obtain. Locating telescopes on high mountains and using modern adaptive optics improves the quality of the signals detected. The Keck telescopes (in a dormant volcano in Hawaii) have the largest computer-controlled mirrors in the world. At this site the air is very still. The Keck telescopes can see fainter sources than the Hubble space telescope.

- Light pollution. Cities emit so much visible light at night that telescopes have to be built (where possible) in sparsely populated areas where there is little visible light pollution.
- Radio wave pollution. Mobile phones, microwave sources and pay-TV transmissions make it more difficult for radio astronomers to detect weak radio signals from space.
- Solar storms. Solar flares release bursts of electromagnetic radiation that interfere with other electromagnetic sources from space.
- Optical systems in telescopes. Lenses and mirrors in telescopes produce some degree of distortion of images. Telescopes are limited by their resolution. Resolution is the ability of an optical system to distinguish between two close objects. Space satellites and space probes have been launched to overcome these problems. They are not subject to the problems of Earth's atmosphere and pollution from various ground-based electromagnetic sources.

Space telescopes

Because space telescopes are located above Earth's atmosphere, they do not suffer the atmospheric problems of ground-based telescopes. They can also use other bands of the electromagnetic spectrum that cannot be used on the ground. Some of these new-generation telescopes include the following.

- The Hubble space telescope. This telescope was launched in 1990 and can detect fine detail of visible and ultraviolet sources in nearby stars and distant galaxies.
- The Chandra X-ray observatory. This facility was placed in orbit in 1999 and can examine X-ray sources, such as black holes, in deep space.
- The RadioAstron space telescope. This Russian radio telescope was launched in July 2011. It will search for supermassive black holes, dark matter and dark energy.
- The James Webb space telescope. Due to be launched in 2018, the James Webb telescope will search for the earliest galaxies that formed after the Big Bang and the stars that are starting to form planetary systems. The space telescope will be located in an orbit 1.5 million km from Earth when operational.

The construction of these telescopes is a team effort using the expertise of astronomers, physicists and engineers.

The International Space Station

The International Space Station (ISS) shown in Figure 3.13 is maintained in an orbit around the Earth at an altitude of between 278 and 460 km. The first components of the ISS were launched into orbit in 1998 and since then it has undergone continued construction to include a total of 15 pressurised modules. All this work has been the combined effort of many people from different scientific and engineering backgrounds. The ISS is a research laboratory which operates in a microgravity environment.

Areas of research on the ISS include:

- monitoring the long-term effects of microgravity and radiation on the human body
- monitoring bone loss and muscle atrophy over the long term
- space medicine including remotely guided ultrasound scanning
- maintenance and repair of space craft during extended journeys and future missions to Mars
- cell and tissue growth in microgravity.

Figure 3.13 International Space Station

Australian astronomy

Australian Square Kilometre Array Pathfinder (ASKAP)

CSIRO is building the next generation of radio telescopes. It will ultimately consist of 36 radio antennas (each 12 m in diameter) linked together so they function as one telescope. This will enable the radio telescope array to detect hundreds of times more galaxies than current technology allows. The radio antennas are being built in a remote location near Murchison in Western Australia (see Figure 3.14). This region has a low population and does not suffer significant radio noise from communication systems. The construction period is 2010 to 2013.

Figure 3.14 CSIRO's ASKAP radio antennas at Murchison in Western Australia

Eventually ASKAP will become part of a world project called the Square Kilometre Array (SKA) which is due to be completed by 2024. Twenty countries will be involved and thousands of receptors will be built across a radius of 3000-km radius from a central core region to be sited in New Zealand, Australia and South Africa. The SKA will then become the world's most sensitive telescope and it will allow astronomers to investigate the first stars and galaxies that formed after the Big Bang.

Australian astronomers: Brian Schmidt and Penny Sackett

Penny Sackett is an astronomer whose major interest is the use of gravitational microlensing in the search for planets outside our own solar system. Gravitational microlensing involves the bending of light waves from a distant star when a planet passes between the star and the Earth, as seen in Figure 3.15. Periodic changes in the brightness of the star are observed. Professor Sackett became Australia's Chief Scientist but she resigned this position in 2011.

Exoplanets are planets outside our solar system that orbit a star other than the Earth's Sun. Several hundred of these exoplanets have now been discovered since the first one was detected back in the 1990s. Some astronomers are searching for planets orbiting distant stars at the right distance to support surface water and life. These 'goldilocks' planets need to have a suitable mass and atmosphere.

Brian Schmidt is an astronomer who works at the Australian National University's Mount Stromlo Observatory in Canberra. His work has involved the study of Type IA supernovae. These supernovae all have the same absolute brightness but their apparent brightness decreases with distance. Their distance in space can be calculated by investigating their brightness. The greater their distances, the further

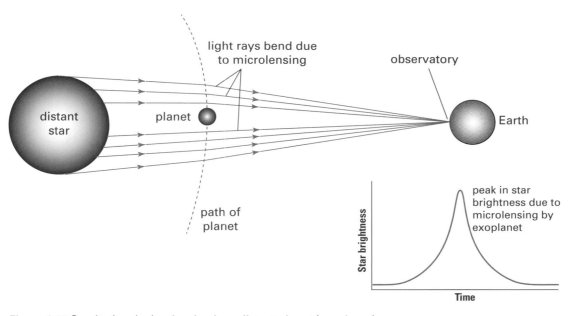

Figure 3.15 Gravitational microlensing by a distant planet (exoplanet)

back in time that these stars formed. In 1998 the team found that the further away these stars were, the greater the speed they were travelling. This meant that the expansion of the universe is accelerating and not slowing down. In 2011, Brian Schmidt shared the Nobel Prize for Physics for this discovery.

Currently Brian Schmidt is working on the SkyMapper project using a wide-angle telescope at Siding Springs. Its aim is to survey and digitally map the southern sky using a precision 1.35-m Cassegrain optics and a $2.5 million camera which can capture 268 million pixels per minute in a region of the sky 29 times the size of the Moon. It is hoped that these maps will identify the mysterious dark matter of the universe.

 ## Experiment 1

Plotting star positions on star charts

Aim

⊃ To plot the azimuth and elevation of stars on a two-dimensional star chart

Background

⊃ The azimuth of an object in the sky is the angular direction of an object compared to north. The elevation of an object in the sky is the angle of the object above the horizontal direction. This is shown in Figure 3.16.

Method

A star chart is a flat (two-dimensional) representation of half the celestial dome. The perimeter of the dome represents the horizon. Look at the star chart in Figure 3.17 and note the important features.

⊃ The azimuth is plotted across the bottom of the star chart.

⊃ The elevation is plotted along the curved sides of the star chart.

⊃ Z is the zenith (i.e. directly overhead of the observer, O).

⊃ Star A has an azimuth of 30° (i.e. east of north) and an elevation of 60°.

⊃ Star B has an azimuth of 300° (i.e. west of north) and an elevation of 30°.

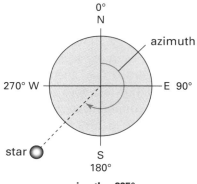

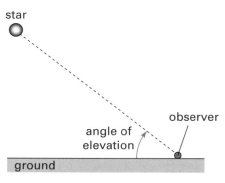

Figure 3.16 Azimuth and elevation

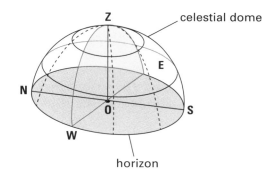

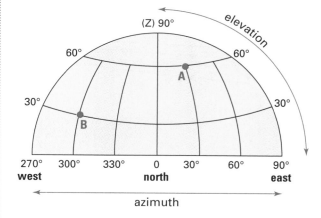

Figure 3.17 Celestial dome and star chart

Analysis

1. Use the star chart in Figure 3.18 to plot the positions of the nominated stars. The observer is looking south.

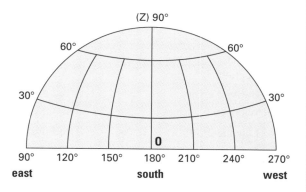

Observer: Canberra (10 pm) 35°S (mid-July)
Star X: azimuth (120°) elevation (45°)
Star Y: azimuth (225°) elevation (15°)

Figure 3.18 Star chart

2. Use the information in the star chart in Figure 3.19 to determine the azimuth and elevation of the three stars and the Southern Cross constellation. The observer is looking south.

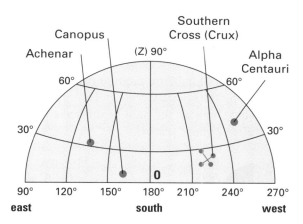

Observer: Canberra (9 pm)
35°S (mid-September)

Figure 3.19 Azimuth and elevation of stars and Crux

Go to p. 238 to check your answers.

Conclusion

Write a suitable conclusion.

Go to p. 238 to check your answer.

 Test yourself 1

Part A: Knowledge

1. Which of the following is the most abundant element in the universe? *(1 mark)*
   A hydrogen
   B helium
   C carbon
   D water

2. Astronomers have inferred our universe is *(1 mark)*
   A expanding.
   B contracting.
   C static.
   D expanding but will ultimately contract.

3. Black holes are ultimately formed when *(1 mark)*
   A a planetary nebula forms.
   B a white dwarf explodes.
   C a yellow star expands.
   D massive red supergiants explode.

4. The observed red shift of stars and galaxies is evidence for *(1 mark)*
   A cosmic background radiation.
   B an expanding universe.
   C star evolution.
   D red giant stars about to become supernovae.

5. Ground-based astronomy is faced with many difficulties. Select the statement that correctly identifies a problem and its cause. *(1 mark)*
   A Earth's atmosphere strongly absorbs infrared and ultraviolet light and consequently these emissions from space are difficult to study.
   B Cities emit too much light but astronomers must operate from cities where computing systems are available to analyse results.
   C Mobile phones emit so much infrared radiation that astronomers are experiencing interference with the infrared signals from space.
   D Clear images can only be obtained if the telescopes are mounted on very high mountains where the air is very still for most of the year.

6. Complete the following restricted-response questions using the appropriate word.
   (1 mark for each part)
   a) Pulsars emit regular pulses of .... waves.
   b) The Sun was formed from vast clouds of .... gas and interstellar dust.
   c) When red supergiant stars use up their fuel, they collapse and explode, producing a bright ....
   d) A light-year is the .... light travels in one Earth year.
   e) The open universe theory predicts that the universe will continue to .... and cool forever.

7. Use the code letters to match the terms or phrases in each column. *(1 mark for each part)*

Column 1		Column 2	
A	Big Bang theory	F	X-ray sources
B	Edwin Hubble	G	ground-based observatory
C	light pollution	H	red dwarf star
D	Chandra observatory	I	red shift of stars/galaxies
E	Proxima Centauri	J	expanding universe

Part B: Skills

8. Examine Tables 3.3 and 3.4 which show data for the seven closest stars to our Sun.
   a) Copy and complete the plot of star distances in Figure 3.20 using the tabulated data. *(6 marks)*
   b) Use the tabulated data about the surface temperature of stars and their colours to determine which are the hottest and coolest stars closest to the Earth. *(2 marks)*
   c) The star Rigel is a whitish-blue supergiant star. It is about 800 million ly from our Sun. Estimate the possible range of surface temperatures of this star. *(1 mark)*

Table 3.3 Distances and colours of closest stars

Star	Distance from the Sun (ly)	Star colour
Proxima Centauri	4.24	red dwarf
Alpha Centauri A	4.35	yellow-white
Alpha Centauri B	4.35	yellow-orange
Barnard's Star	5.98	red dwarf
Wolf 359	7.78	red dwarf
Lalande 21185	8.26	red dwarf
Sirius A	8.55	white

Table 3.4 Colours of stars and their surface temperatures

Surface temperature (°C)	Colour
< 3 500	red
3 500–4 800	orange
4 800–6 000	yellow
6 000–8 000	yellow-white
8 000–11 000	white
11 000–30 000	white to whitish-blue
> 30 000	blue

9. a) What is meant by the term 'light-year'? *(1 mark)*
   b) Beams of light are emitted from the Sun. Copy the scale diagram in Figure 3.21 to show how far the light beams have travelled after 2 years. *(1 mark)*

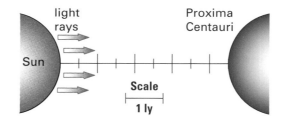

Figure 3.21 Light rays from the Sun

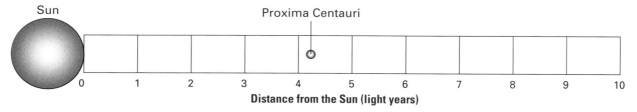

Figure 3.20 Distances from the Sun

c) How long will the beams of light take to reach Proxima Centauri? *(1 mark)*

10. Examine the diagram of the night sky in Figure 3.22.

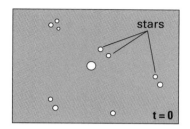

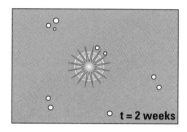

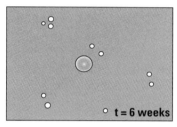

Figure 3.22 What caused this event?

What could account for the changes in these stars? *(1 mark)*

11. Sirius is the brightest star in the night sky. It is 26 times brighter than the Sun. It is found in the constellation Canis Major. Sirius is 83 300 000 000 000 km from Earth.
   a) Light rays travel at 300 000 km/s. Calculate the time for light rays from Sirius to reach Earth. Express your answer in:
      i) seconds *(1 mark)*
      ii) years (assume 1 year = 365.25 days). *(1 mark)*
   b) What is the distance from Sirius to Earth in light-years? *(1 mark)*
   c) Radio signals travel at the speed of light. If a radio signal was sent to Sirius and then relayed back to Earth, how long would the round trip take? *(1 mark)*

12. Figure 3.23 shows a jumbled sequence of events in the evolution of a star like our own Sun. Place these images in the correct sequence. *(1 mark)*

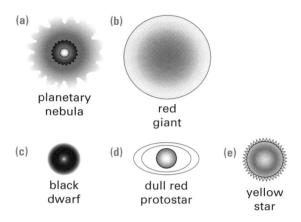

Figure 3.23 Jumbled sequence

13. Figure 3.24 shows a simplified diagram of the rotation of the Milky Way galaxy at two time intervals. The position of the Sun is marked. Use this information to calculate the time for one complete revolution of the galaxy. *(2 marks)*

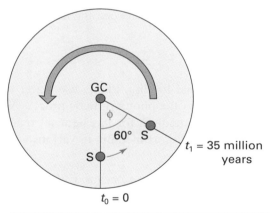

Key: GC = galactic core (Milky Way)
S = Sun
φ = angular rotation in 35 million years

Figure 3.24 Rotation of the Milky Way

14. Use the code letters to place the following jumbled statements in the correct sequence. *(2 marks)*

The Big Bang
A. Gravitational forces cause matter to condense to form stars and galaxies.

B. Some energy is converted to subatomic matter.

C. The very hot primitive universe cools as it expands.

D. Atomic nuclei start to form.

E. The expansion and cooling of the universe continues to the present day.

F. Space and time come into existence.

G. Atoms of hydrogen and helium form as nuclei and electrons combine.

H. Space inflates and expands.

Go to pp. 238–239 to check your answers.

3.5 Natural cycles in the biosphere

Apart from food and energy, other materials such as water, carbon, oxygen and nitrogen need to be transferred around an ecosystem. There has not been any change in the chemical make-up of the biosphere for millions of years. The biosphere is the part of the Earth's crust, waters and atmosphere that supports life. As the biosphere does not run short of raw materials, elements and other chemicals must be continually recycled between the living and non-living world.

Water cycle

Water is essential for life. Plants use water as an important part of the photosynthetic process. Water also provides a medium for biochemical reactions in cells and a transport medium in various vascular systems.

Liquid water is present in oceans, rivers and lakes. Water absorbs solar energy and evaporates into the atmosphere to form invisible water vapour. As the water vapour cools, clouds containing tiny water droplets form. Eventually, the water is returned to Earth as rain, snow or ice. Some water soaks into the ground and supports life in the soil; other water collects in oceans, rivers and lakes. Figure 3.25 shows the water cycle; any pollutants in the air will dissolve in the precipitation and be washed into the oceans or lakes.

Living things take in more water than they actually use. Plants, for instance, use only a small fraction of the water absorbed through their roots. A large portion transpires through their leaves. It is not

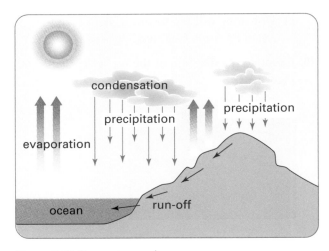

Figure 3.25 The water cycle

uncommon for crops to transpire the equivalent of many tens of centimetres of rainfall each growing season.

Transpiration is the process by which water vapour and oxygen exit through stomata (singular: stoma) on the underside of plant leaves, while carbon dioxide enters through these small openings. As shown in Figure 3.26, guard cells on either side of each stoma control their size. The source of the energy for the water cycle comes directly from our Sun.

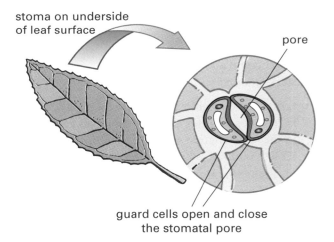

Figure 3.26 Transpiration in plant leaves

Carbon–oxygen cycle

Carbon and oxygen are important elements in ecosystems. The bodies of living things are composed of compounds of carbon, hydrogen, oxygen and nitrogen. Oxygen is used by animals and plants for cellular respiration. Plants use carbon dioxide and water, in the process of photosynthesis, to make energy-rich nutrients (e.g. glucose). Oxygen is released into the atmosphere in this process. The carbon and oxygen atoms in the glucose are then converted to thousands of other chemical compounds in cellular reactions in plants and animals. On their death these carbon–oxygen compounds are recycled by decomposers back into the environment. Combustion of fossil fuels by humans also returns carbon (in the form of carbon dioxide and carbon monoxide) to the atmosphere. Figure 3.27 shows the carbon–oxygen cycle.

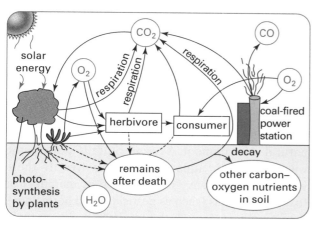

Figure 3.27 The carbon–oxygen cycle

Small amounts of carbon dioxide also enter the atmosphere from other sources:

> volcanoes
> weathering of some rocks, such as limestone
> burning of fossil fuels
> loss from the sea.

Nitrogen cycle

Nitrogen is also an important element in nature. Nitrogen is an essential element in proteins that form cell membranes. It is also a vital component of DNA in the nucleus of each cell. Figure 3.28 shows the nitrogen cycle. Nitrogen is present in the soil in various compounds including nitrate and ammonium salts. These are absorbed by plants through their roots. Nitrogen is incorporated into many nitrogen compounds in plants. Nitrogen compounds make their way through food chains via the various feeding relationships in ecosystems.

After the organism's death, decomposers return nitrogen compounds to the soil. Nitrogen can be returned to the air by denitrifying bacteria in the

soil. Nitrogen can also be converted to nitrogen compounds by nitrifying bacteria in the soil and in specialised root nodules in some plants such as legumes. Lightning can also cause nitrogen fixation in the atmosphere. The high energy of the lightning bolt leads to the formation of nitrogen compounds.

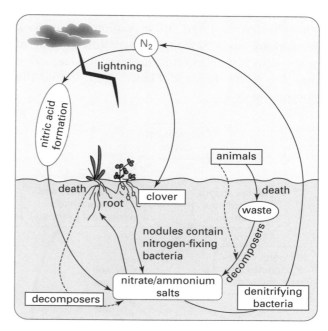

Figure 3.28 The nitrogen cycle

Approximately 78% of the air we breathe in consists of nitrogen. However, this nitrogen has no effect on the workings of our body and so it is just exhaled.

Phosphorus cycle

Phosphorus is an essential nutrient for living things in the form of ions. It is a part of DNA molecules and molecules that store energy, and is found in the fats of cell membranes. Phosphorus is also found in other parts of our bodies, such as bones and teeth.

Phosphorus is located in water, soil and many types of sediment, but is not found in the air (except in very small dust particles). Phosphorus cycles from the non-living to the living world and back again very slowly; it is the slowest one of the matter cycles described here.

Phosphorus is found in rock formations and ocean sediments as phosphate salts. These salts are released from rocks through the action of weathering. They usually dissolve in soil water and are absorbed by plants. Since there are only very small amounts of phosphorus in the soil, it is often a limiting factor in plant growth. Hence, farmers and gardeners often apply phosphate fertilisers on their lands. Animals absorb phosphates by eating plants or plant-eating animals.

Eventually, when animals and plants die, phosphates are returned to the soils or oceans during decay. Phosphorus may end up in sediments or rock formations again, remaining there for millions of years, until it is released again through weathering and the cycle repeats. Figure 3.29 shows the phosphorus cycle.

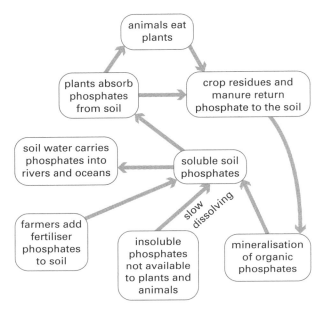

Figure 3.29 The phosphorus cycle

Humans influence the phosphate cycle through the use of commercial synthetic fertilisers. Around half of all crops worldwide use commercial fertilisers, which are essential for high-yield harvests. The phosphate is obtained through mining certain deposits of calcium phosphate called apatite, and by using commercial products such as super phosphate.

Applying excessive amounts of fertiliser has negative environmental effects, wastes the growers' time and money, and throws other soil nutrients out of balance. If plants are not able to utilise all of the phosphate fertiliser applied, much of it may be lost from the land through water run-off, resulting in problems in streams and rivers. For example, phosphorus in surface waters can lead to eutrophication. Eutrophication is the process whereby water is enriched in dissolved nutrients, stimulating aquatic plant overgrowth that depletes dissolved oxygen. Phosphate levels greater than 1.0 mg/L may interfere with coagulation in drinking water treatment plants.

3.6 Impact of human activities in ecosystems

Humans often upset the balance of nature. As human populations grow, they require space for their houses and so natural ecosystems are disturbed or destroyed as new homes are built. Farms and mines also contribute to the destruction of the environment. We will now look at some examples of the impact of humans on ecosystems.

Waste

The wastes that humans generate can pollute the natural environment. Sewage outfalls pollute the water in which aquatic organisms live. If these wastes contain heavy metals (such as mercury) or toxic compounds (such as pesticides and herbicides), then organisms low on the food chain absorb these pollutants and pass them on to organisms higher up the food chain. In so doing, their concentration becomes magnified. Many large fish species have been shown to contain toxic levels of heavy metals.

Acid rain

Acidic gases (such as sulfur dioxide) from factories and metal smelters cause damage to ecosystems by the formation of acid rain. When acidic gases dissolve in raindrops, acid rain is formed. Acid rain can leach valuable minerals from soils and so plants will not grow. Acid rain damages tree leaves so that they cannot photosynthesise. Lakes and rivers can become so acidified that fish eggs will not hatch.

Algal blooms

The use of fertilisers in farming can be detrimental to the surrounding environment. Rain can wash fertiliser into rivers and creeks. These nutrients cause algae to grow excessively, leading to an algal bloom. The algal blooms upset the normal balance in this ecosystem. When these algae die, the decomposition of their bodies uses up the dissolved oxygen in the water and this leads to the death of other aquatic organisms. This process is shown in Figure 3.30.

(a) run-off

run-off, fertilisers and sewage

balanced ecosystem has an increase in nutrients from run-off

(b)

run-off continues

plants, algae, animals increase in numbers; more O_2 in water; aerobic bacteria break down dead plants and animals and add more nutrients to water

(c)

at critical level all oxygen is removed from water by plants, algae, bacteria and animals

(d)

phew!

anaerobic bacteria move into the river to break up dead organisms

Figure 3.30 Algae bloom in a river

Introduced animals and plants

The introduction of non-native plants and animals can have a devastating impact on local ecosystems. The introduction of rabbits to Australia in the early 1800s led to widespread problems. Rabbits reproduced so quickly that their large numbers stripped the land bare of grass and so deprived sheep and native animals of food. The introduction of special viruses into wild rabbit populations has been the only way to control them.

The introduction of the prickly pear cactus as a fodder plant also caused a similar problem. As the prickly pear had no natural predators, it quickly proliferated and took over valuable land, making it unsuitable for farming. The plant was eventually controlled by the release of a moth that laid its eggs on the cactus. The caterpillars that hatched from the eggs ate its flesh and so controlled the numbers of cacti.

Loss of habitat

The removal of trees by farmers has led to a loss of habitat for many communities. Some living things have become endangered or extinct because of these human activities.

Salinity

In many parts of rural Australia, mineral salts are rising to the surface as trees are removed by farmers. The salts rise with the rising water table. Salt kills plants and so renders the land useless for farming.

Farming and urban development

Land has to be cleared so that farms and towns can exist. Many forests have been lost due to urbanisation.

3.7 The greenhouse effect and climate change

Gases such as carbon dioxide (CO_2), methane (CH_4), nitrous oxide (N_2O) and water vapour (H_2O) are very important in our atmosphere. They are responsible for trapping solar radiation and warming our atmosphere. Without these gases, Earth would be very cold like the planet Mars. This is called the greenhouse effect because the atmosphere is trapping heat just like the glass of a gardener's greenhouse traps heat to keep plants alive in cold climates, or a car parked outside is hot when you enter it (see Figure 3.31).

2. Solar radiation hits the fabric/upholstery inside and is changed to longer wavelength heat waves.

3. Heat waves unable to pass out through the glass are trapped inside the car.

1. Short wavelength solar radiation passes through the car window.

Figure 3.31 Greenhouse effect inside a car

Light from the Sun strikes the surface of the Earth. Different molecules within the atmosphere vibrate in response to the various frequencies of the light. Carbon dioxide and other greenhouse gases strongly absorb the infra-red component of sunlight, their molecules vibrate and the heat energy produced is mostly reflected back into space. The small amount not reflected is retained in the atmosphere. As the amount of carbon dioxide increases, more heat is retained and the global temperature rises. Each year 20 billion t of carbon dioxide enters the atmosphere. Not all of this carbon dioxide can be absorbed by plants or the hydrosphere and so it accumulates in the atmosphere. As Figure 3.32 shows, the greenhouse effect keeps the Earth's climate warm and habitable.

As long as the amount of greenhouse gases in the atmosphere remains the same, and as long as the amount of heat arriving from the Sun is constant, equilibrium is established. That is, as much energy is lost into space as is gained from the Sun. In this equilibrium, the natural greenhouse effect maintains the Earth's average temperature at around 14 °C.

Enhanced greenhouse effect

Since the industrial revolution, the amount of carbon dioxide and methane has been increasing. Today there is 25% more carbon dioxide in the atmosphere than 200 years ago (see Figure 3.33). In this same time the amount of methane in the atmosphere has doubled. Nitrous oxide has increased because of the large increase in the use of fertilisers and the burning of organic matter. This has led to a slight rise in global warming.

Strengthening of the greenhouse effect through human activities is known as the enhanced (or anthropogenic) greenhouse effect. This increase is mainly due to increased atmospheric carbon dioxide levels. Current projections suggest that atmospheric carbon dioxide levels could reach 450 parts per million (ppm) by 2050 unless action is taken to reduce emissions. The overload of greenhouse gases is believed by most scientists to be a cause of climate change.

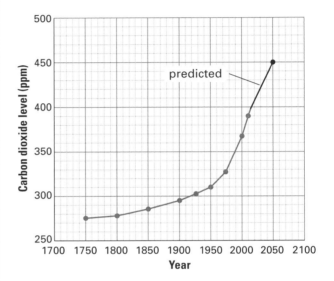

Figure 3.33 Atmospheric carbon dioxide levels since the industrial revolution

Changes to permafrost, sea-levels, sea ice and biodiversity

Increased levels of carbon dioxide come from a major human source: burning fossil fuels. Another

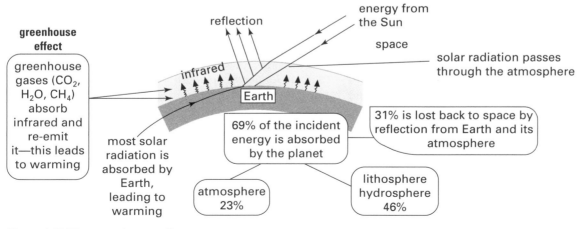

Figure 3.32 The greenhouse effect

Case study 1: Palaeocene–Eocene Thermal Maximum

Atmospheric carbon dioxide levels have varied over the many millions of years of Earth's history. Some argue that what we are witnessing is a natural phenomenon; others argue that human contributions are exacerbating whatever natural events there might be.

During the Palaeocene (a geologic epoch that lasted from about 65.5 to 56 million years ago) the Earth was already warmer. Around 56 million years ago (at the beginning of the Eocene epoch) there was a geologically sudden massive injection of carbon dioxide into the atmosphere. How much and where it originated is still being researched, but it is estimated to being the equivalent of burning off all our remaining fossil fuels. Global temperatures rose by about 6 °C over a period of 20000 years. Sea levels rose by some 20 m, while some of the deepest points of the ocean became oxygen starved and acidified. All this forced plants and animals to migrate, adapt or die.

This lasted for around 150000 years until the excess carbon dioxide was reabsorbed by the forests, oceans and sediments. In the meantime it created droughts, floods and insect plagues. Many sea creatures and land mammals became extinct, but numerous other modern mammalian orders emerged. Almost half of the ocean's foraminifera (a type of plankton species found especially in deeper waters) became extinct over a period of around 1000 years. Foraminifera is a species of plankton, which are a variety of small or microscopic organisms found in fresh or salt water and are food for fish and other large organisms.

While life survived, it was drastically altered. As well, large-scale changes in the climate system occurred; such as in the patterns of atmospheric circulation, vapour transport and rainfall, and disruption to deep-ocean circulation.

Figure 3.34 compares temperature rise from the enhanced greenhouse effect with the Palaeocene–Eocene Thermal Maximum.

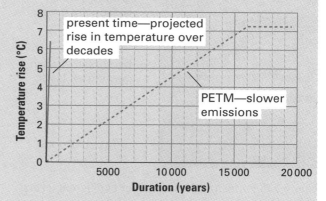

Figure 3.34 Temperature rise from the enhanced greenhouse effect versus the Palaeocene–Eocene thermal maximum (PETM)

This case study helps illustrate how global warming due to greenhouse gases can quickly lead to drastic disruptions to climate, and to biological and other important changes around the world. Although these events unfolded millions of years ago and spanned thousands of years, the findings provide clues to help better understand the long-term impacts of today's human-influenced climate change.

greenhouse gas is methane. While this is naturally present in the Earth and through microbial decay of organic matter, human sources produce greater amounts of this gas. Examples include coal mining and landfills, but the prime worldwide source is animal agriculture, producing more than 100 million t of methane each year.

Methane is a more powerful greenhouse gas than carbon dioxide, but as there is over 200 times more carbon dioxide in the atmosphere, the amount of

warming methane contributes is only a quarter of that which carbon dioxide contributes.

As temperatures rise, other factors come into play. These include changes to permafrost, sea level, sea ice, ocean acidification and biodiversity.

Changes to permafrost

Permafrost is soil at or below the freezing point of water for two or more years. Ice is not necessary, but it frequently occurs. Most permafrost is found in high latitudes (i.e. land near the North and South Poles), but alpine permafrost can exist at high altitudes in much lower latitudes. It accounts for about a quarter of the exposed land in the northern hemisphere. Most of the world's permafrost has been frozen for millennia and can be up to several thousand metres thick. As Figure 3.35 shows, permafrost has a number of different layers.

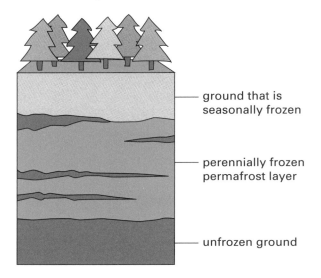

ground that is seasonally frozen

perennially frozen permafrost layer

unfrozen ground

Figure 3.35 Permafrost has a number of different layers

It is estimated that much of Earth's permafrost will likely disappear by 2200 due to warming temperatures, unleashing vast quantities of carbon (CO_2 and CH_4) into the atmosphere. When permafrost formed, plant material, mainly roots, were trapped and frozen in soil. These have not had the opportunity to rot, but this will occur as they thaw out. Predictions for carbon release between now and 2200 are about one-fifth of the total amount of carbon in the atmosphere today.

Peat bogs cover almost a quarter of the Earth's land surface to a depth of 25 m. As they thaw due to rising temperatures, they have the potential to release billions of tonnes of methane trapped by ice below the surface. Worldwide, peat bogs contain at least 2 trillion t of CH_4.

So global warming increases the vulnerability of these soils. For example, heat generated from increased microbial activity could lead to sustained and long-term chronic emissions of carbon dioxide and methane. These, in turn, will feed into more global warming, amplifying the problem.

Changes to sea level

Since the mid-19th century, the sea level has been rising, most likely through human-induced climate change. Global average sea levels rose at a rate of around 1.7 mm per year over in the last 50 years, with the average rise being double that during the last decade. While this doesn't sound like much, it is expected to continue for centuries. Projected sea level rises of between 18 and 59 cm are expected for this century. As sea levels rise, many cities along the coasts will be threatened. Millions of people will be displaced and many low-lying islands could disappear altogether. Currently there are over 600 million people who live in coastal areas which are less than 10 m above sea level.

The problem is not only confined to humans. Effects will include coastal erosion, wetland and coastal plain flooding, salinity of aquifers and soils, and a loss of habitats for plants, fish, birds and other wildlife. It is estimated that up to a third of the current coastal land and wetland habitats are likely to be lost in the next century if ocean levels continue to rise at the present rate.

So, what is the cause? Glaciers and ice sheets cover about 10% of the world's land area and exist on every continent except Australia. Over the past century, most of the world's mountain glaciers and the ice sheets in both Greenland and Antarctica have lost mass. The melting of glaciers and ice sheets adds water to the oceans, contributing to sea levels rising. During the second half of the 20th century, a 2 to 5 cm rise in sea level can be attributed to mountain glaciers and ice caps melting. Loss of ice from the Greenland and Antarctic ice sheets added around 1 cm to the sea level. If all the ice on Greenland were to melt, requiring hundreds if not thousands of years, the sea level would rise by roughly 7 m!

Another contributor is the expansion of liquids with heat. As climate change increases ocean temperatures, first at the surface and over centuries at much greater depths, the water expands. So thermal expansion contributes to sea level rise; around 2.5 cm during the second half of the 20th century (see Figure 3.36).

Changes to sea ice

The Arctic sea ice covers an area of some 14 million km^2. The surface of the ice reflects solar energy away from the Earth, acting as the planet's natural refrigerator. Around 80% of the sunlight is reflected. Ice and melt water from the Arctic Ocean have important effects on ocean circulation patterns and from there to oceans and other climate systems elsewhere.

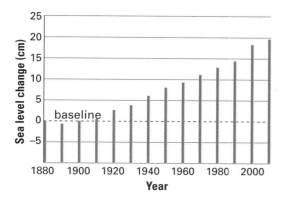

Figure 3.36 Recent changes to sea levels (the year 1900 is taken as a base line)

The Arctic's sea ice is home to a wide variety of wildlife, including polar bears, arctic foxes, seals, walruses and whales, fish species and sea birds. It is also an important transportation route by caribou and musk ox, as well as a traditional hunting ground for the Inuit.

However, the melting back of sea ice and floating ice shelves don't directly contribute to sea level rise since this ice is already floating on the ocean. (It is already displacing its mass of water.) Nevertheless, this melting can lead to a reduction in the surface reflectivity allowing for greater absorption of solar radiation. This accelerates warming, and so increases the melting back of snow and ice on land. In addition, as the floating ice shelves break up there is a faster flow of ice on land into the oceans, thereby adding to sea level rise.

The ice that forms over the Arctic sea is shrinking so rapidly that it could vanish altogether in several years' time during summer. Although it would reappear again in winter, its absence during the peak of summer would rob polar bears of their summer hunting ground and threaten them with extinction. The loss of sea ice in the Arctic is unprecedented in its duration and magnitude, indicating human-influenced climate change.

Ocean acidification

Carbon dioxide is slightly soluble, forming carbonic acid: $CO_2 + H_2O \rightarrow H_2CO_3$. Atmospheric carbon dioxide dissolves in the ocean, being transferred deep below as shown in Figure 3.37. Increased carbon dioxide emissions over the last two centuries have led to an increase in the amount of carbon dioxide being dissolved in the ocean. This makes the ocean more acidic. Over the last few hundred million years, the ocean's pH has remained fairly constant at 8.17 ± 0.6 (slightly alkaline). Marine organisms have evolved in this fairly stable environment.

So as the ocean waters become more acidic, it puts stress on marine life and their survival. The most obvious impact is to reduce the amount of calcium carbonate ($CaCO_3$) available. Calcium carbonate is the substance used by many marine organisms (such

atmospheric CO_2 dissolves in ocean

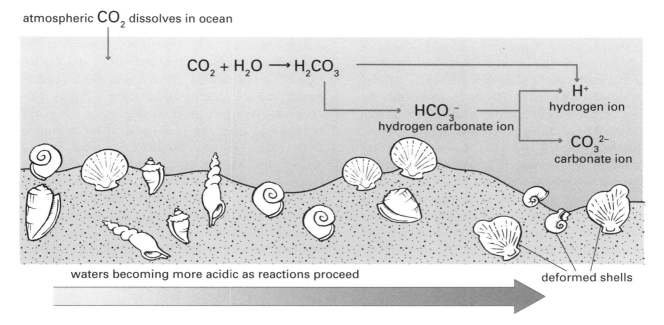

Figure 3.37 Up to half of the CO_2 released by burning fossil fuels over the past 200 years has been absorbed by the world's oceans.

as coral, shellfish, crustaceans and molluscs) to build their shells. If the expected pH drop of 0.5 occurs during this century, it is estimated there would be 60% less calcium carbonate available as the calcium carbonate would dissolve to produce soluble calcium hydrogen carbonate. Figure 3.38 summarises this process.

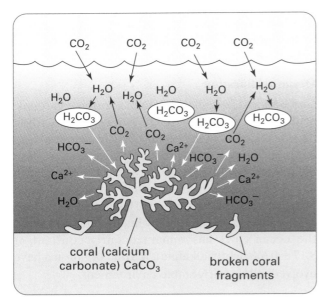

Figure 3.38 Calcium carbonate in coral reacts with carbonic acid forming soluble calcium hydrogen carbonate.

Changes to biodiversity

Climate change impacts on biodiversity, which is the variety of life in a particular habitat or ecosystem. For example, there is the series of large tracts of bleached coral on the Great Barrier Reef resulting from unusually warm summers. Bleaching affects coral growth and makes it more vulnerable to disease, causing a significant die-off in some locations. Queensland's green ringtail possum lives in tropical rainforests. It cannot control its body temperature when the air temperature rises above 30 °C. Hence, an extended heatwave could kill off a large part of its population. Another threat to its population is the distribution of these rainforests, which is already severely limited by rainfall and temperature. Small changes could be catastrophic.

Many of our natural systems are already under severe stress due to humans modifying the landscape and reducing habitats. Add into the mix introduced species and diseases that threaten many species in these restricted and modified habitats, and this will lead to more damage to native biodiversity under the influence of changing climates.

With warmer climates, some species will be forced to migrate as they can no longer survive in their current locations. But such migration might not always be possible because of unsuitable soils, natural and human barriers, or severe competition from organisms already there.

With climate change will come changes in the intensity, frequency and extent of disturbances such as fire, cyclone, drought and flood. This will place existing vegetation under stress, force animals to migrate or die out, and favour species able to rapidly colonise denuded areas. This will most likely mean major changes in the distribution and abundance of many indigenous species, and the spread of weeds that are more tolerant of these changes. As temperatures increase, insects carrying tropical diseases will move further south (or northwards in the northern hemisphere), and into higher altitudes in mountainous regions, thereby spreading diseases over a larger area.

Climate change could have dramatic effects on a wide range of plants and animals in Australia and worldwide, especially for some particularly vulnerable species.

Effects of deep ocean currents on climate and marine life

The density of sea water depends on temperature and salinity, and it can vary across the globe. These differences arise from heating and cooling at the sea surface and from the evaporation and sea ice formation (enhancing salinity) and from rainfall, runoff and ice melting (decreasing salinity). This drives a conveyor belt of moving water across the oceans, and from top to bottom. It takes around 1600 years to go once around the system. In cold regions the highest surface water densities are reached, resulting in convective mixing and sinking of deep water. On their journey, the water masses transport both energy (as heat) and matter (solids, dissolved substances and gases) around the Earth. For example, upwelling from the ocean's bottom brings up nutrient-rich colder waters that promote a flourishing marine life.

The circulation is key to providing nutrients to marine life on the ocean surface. For example, phytoplankton (minute, free-floating aquatic plants)

Case study 2: The mountain pygmy possum (*Burramys parvus*)

The mountain pygmy possum is the world's only hibernating marsupial (see Figure 3.39). Its distribution is limited to alpine and subalpine regions, in New South Wales' Kosciusko National Park and in Victoria's Alpine National Park, where there is a continuous period of snow cover for up to 6 months. Its total habitat covers less than 10 km², with only 3000 remaining adults.

This possum needs a snow depth over winter of at least 1 m to provide enough insulation to keep it warm during hibernation. However, with global warming, snow cover in Australia's mountain areas is predicted to decline dramatically. An average temperature rise of only 3 °C could entirely eliminate all snow. Add to this pressure from skiers in the ski fields, and a declining bogong moth population (the possum's food source and also a casualty of global warming), and the possum could well be threatened with extinction.

Figure 3.39 The mountain pygmy possum, weighing in at 45 g

are found on the surface of the ocean living largely off the energy from natural sunlight. When they die they slowly sink to the ocean floor, decomposing and carrying nutrients that make it back up to the surface on this conveyor belt. Without enough nutrients, phytoplankton growth could be limited, cutting off the bottom of the food chain for marine ecosystems.

This circulation is called the thermohaline circulation and is shown in Figure 3.40. It has a large impact on

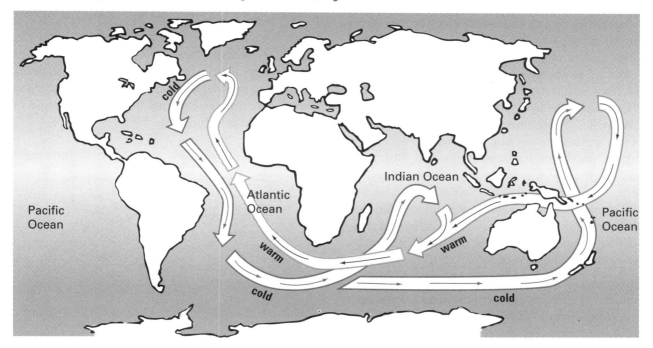

Figure 3.40 Thermohaline circulation around the globe

the climate of the Earth and plays an important role in supplying heat to polar regions, thereby regulating the amount of sea ice in these regions. But as glaciers melt and release fresh water (such as in the north Atlantic Ocean), the saltier waters are diluted. This will likely slow, or even stop (low probability and the worst-case scenario) the conveyor belt since fresh water will not be able to sink, thus affecting deep ocean currents. The melting of the Greenland ice sheet is suspected to cause a major disruption in the deep water formation and variation in the North Atlantic. Climatologists estimate the global conveyor belt will slow by 10 to 50% within the next 100 years. This will impact on marine life as there will now be less nutrient-rich material for them to feast on.

Without the current thermohaline circulation, one of the biggest impacts would be on the temperature over the North Atlantic and Europe. These northerly regions have annual temperatures that are about 9 °C above the average for their latitude. While all of this is not due to the thermohaline circulation, certainly northern Europe would significantly cool if the circulation were to collapse.

Use of computer modelling to investigate climate change

How do we know what the enhanced greenhouse effect or global warming will do to this planet? Part of the answer lies in observing the subtle changes now occurring, or the large-scale changes that have occurred in the past (such as the Palaeocene–Eocene Thermal Maximum). Another is by predicting the amount of warming using computer modelling. Modelling is a way of simplifying the real world, allowing problems to be solved and finding answers to 'What if ...?' scenarios. It takes very powerful supercomputers to carry out the many and necessary complex mathematical computations. But this modelling is only as good as the information gone into its programming. If an assumption is false, or if an estimate is incorrect, the results could be slightly or wildly out. And then there is the fact that modelling predicts what *might* occur, given certain conditions, not what *will* occur.

Computer models, for instance, suggest that a doubling of the concentration of the main greenhouse gas, carbon dioxide, may raise the average global temperature between 1 and 3 °C. But increasing temperature will increase evaporation and cloud cover. These extra clouds would then reflect a greater proportion of the Sun's energy back to space. Hence, less would reach the Earth's surface. This could then counteract the greenhouse effect. How much, if any, will this affect the temperature? It is not just the amount of cloud that is important, but also the detailed properties of the cloud.

Climate models attempt to copy the way in which the Earth's climate actually behaves. There are many factors to consider:

- daily variations
- seasonal variations
- atmospheric circulations and temperatures
- variations on the land in coastal, alpine or desert regions as well as from the tropics to polar regions
- ocean depths, salinity, temperature and circulation.

All of these components interact with each other in complicated ways, some having greater effects than others. So you can see there are many variables and processes to be considered.

Over long periods of observations, scientists know how the major air and sea currents move, how heat moves into and out of the atmosphere, how often evaporation and precipitation of water occurs, chemical reactions in the atmosphere, volcanic effects, and when and where cyclones are likely to occur. Complex mathematical equations are built for each of these based on well-established physical laws that define the behaviour of the weather and climate.

Then a three-dimensional grid is placed over the Earth or, as with the CSIRO model, a grid over Australia, and measurements are made at each point. Points may be, say, 500 km from each other and many thousands of measurements taken. An example of this is shown in Figure 3.41.

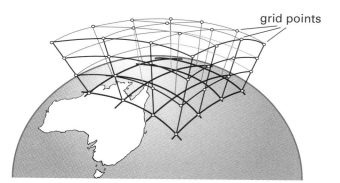

Figure 3.41 Grid points are made on the land, the atmosphere and the ocean.

This is fed into a supercomputer capable of performing more than 500 million calculations each second! The model calculates how the conditions would change at each point, and then runs the calculations again for the next period in time. It might take several hours of computer time to run a scenario spanning a whole year. How well this model predicts is determined by comparing the results with the actual events as they unfold for that year.

Modelling can be used:

> to reproduce the climate of the recent past, both in terms of the average and variations in space and time

> to reproduce what we know about ancient climates (which are more limited)

> to predict what the climate might be like at some future time period

> with more regional detail to produce the weather forecasts for each day.

As computers become faster, and equations become more detailed, grid points can be spaced closer together. Then the results can more closely mimic reality, and more detail about regional changes in climate obtained. So far the best models have performed well but, of course, they are not complete.

3.8 Atmospheric pollution

The atmosphere is the most sensitive of the spheres to pollution. Any pollutants are quickly spread by winds and eventually end up in the water or on the land as a result of the water cycle. The Earth can handle a small amount of naturally occurring pollutants, as the atmospheric winds and ocean currents eventually spread it over a larger area. While some pollutants are from natural causes such as dust and windblown soil or the results from volcanic activity, pollution is often understood to be the results of human activity. Humans constantly create pollution events on a grand scale in terms of both the amount of pollution and the time over which it is produced (see Figure 3.42).

Causes of atmospheric pollution

Incomplete combustion

When hydrocarbon fuels are burnt in a restricted air (or oxygen) supply, a mixture of products including carbon monoxide, carbon dioxide, carbon (soot) and water are formed:

hydrocarbon + air → carbon monoxide
+ carbon dioxide + carbon + water

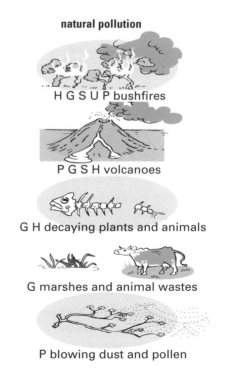

manufactured pollution

vehicles P G N H S U

factories P G N H S U

fires P G H S U

aeroplanes P G N H S U

atmosphere

Key:
P particles
G gases
N noise
H heat
S smoke
U unburned fuels

natural pollution

H G S U P bushfires

P G S H volcanoes

G H decaying plants and animals

G marshes and animal wastes

P blowing dust and pollen

Figure 3.42 The ways pollutants gets into the atmosphere

Carbon dioxide production will accelerate global warming. Carbon monoxide is a dangerous pollutant because it can lead to suffocation and death. Carbon monoxide is absorbed by red blood cells in preference to oxygen. Soot particles may be deposited in the environment, leading to the blackening of buildings and trees. Soot particles may also contain dangerous cancer-causing agents (carcinogens).

Release of acidic oxides

Fossil fuels often contain sulfur impurities. When these fuels are burnt, the sulfur is also burnt to form sulfur dioxide gas. In the atmosphere, the sulfur dioxide can also be oxidised to sulfur trioxide. These oxides of sulfur are acidic oxides. They combine with moisture in the air to form droplets of acid rain.

sulfur + oxygen → sulfur dioxide (SO_2)

sulfur dioxide + oxygen → sulfur trioxide (SO_3)

sulfur dioxide + water → sulfurous acid (H_2SO_3)

sulfur trioxide + water → sulfuric acid (H_2SO_4)

Acidic oxides of nitrogen can also be formed in the engines of cars and trucks. These oxides are emitted in the exhaust and contaminate the environment. They also contribute to acid rain.

nitrogen + oxygen → nitrogen monoxide (NO)

nitrogen monoxide + oxygen → nitrogen dioxide (NO_2)

nitrogen dioxide + water → nitrous acid + nitric acid (HNO_2, HNO_3)

Particulate matter

Particulates are tiny particles of solid or liquid suspended in a gas. They can occur naturally (volcanoes, dust storms, forest and grassland fires, sea spray and living vegetation) or from human activities (burning of fossil fuels in vehicles, power plants and various industrial processes). Smog (smoke + fog) results from a mixture of smoke and sulfur dioxide. Modern smog often comes from vehicular and industrial emissions that are acted on in the atmosphere by ultraviolet light forming secondary pollutants.

Volatile organic compounds

Volatile organic compounds (VOCs) are an important outdoor air pollutant. One of these is methane, an extremely efficient greenhouse gas contributing to enhanced global warming. Other hydrocarbons can promote greenhouse gases in their role of creating

ozone and in prolonging the life of methane in the atmosphere. These include compounds such as benzene, toluene and xylene which are suspected carcinogens and may lead to leukaemia through prolonged exposure. Another dangerous compound often associated with industrial uses is 1,3-butadiene. The chemical diagrams for some VOCs are shown in Figure 3.43.

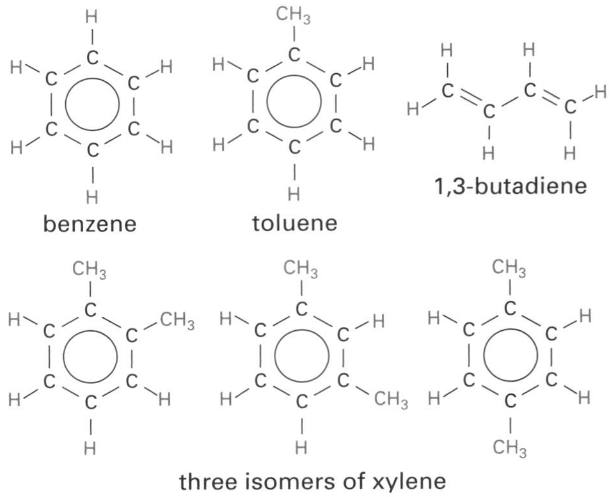

Figure 3.43 Some volatile organic compounds

In the atmosphere, light reacts with these volatile organic compounds forming two important by-products in the lower atmosphere: ozone and organic aerosol. These have important consequences for air quality and climate. Both these chemicals are harmful to our respiratory system. Ozone is an important gas in the stratosphere, but is harmful to humans and animals when produced close to the ground.

While human-produced VOCs can be harmful, the majority are produced naturally. These are not considered pollutants. Most of these are made by plants, the main compound being isoprene, $CH_2=C(CH_3)CH=CH_2$. Others are produced by animals, microbes and fungi (including moulds). The strong odour emitted by many plants consists of VOCs. Emissions are affected by a variety of factors, such as temperature and sunlight, and occur almost exclusively from the leaves, in particular the stomata.

Methods of reducing carbon dioxide pollution

Some people argue that carbon dioxide is not a pollutant as it is a natural component of the atmosphere and needed by plants in order to carry out photosynthesis. Others argue that carbon dioxide in excess threatens the wellbeing of an ecosystem, so it should be considered to be a pollutant.

Up until recently, the amount of carbon dioxide taken out of the atmosphere every year by plants was almost perfectly balanced by the amount of carbon dioxide put back into the atmosphere through respiration and decay. This is part of the carbon cycle. But over the last couple of centuries the atmospheric carbon dioxide has been increasing. There are several reasons for this.

> Deforestation. Tropical forests are being cut down, and with a reduction in vegetation, there is a reduction in photosynthesis. So less carbon dioxide is removed from the atmosphere.

> Burning fossil fuels. The carbon in fossil fuels was laid down over millions of years and taken out of circulation. Since the organisms did not decay completely, the carbon was never released into the atmosphere as carbon dioxide. Now humans are burning fossil fuels at an increasing rate. This is the largest source of carbon dioxide emissions globally.

> Ocean warming. The solubility of gases decreases as temperature rises. The huge amounts of carbon dioxide trapped in the oceans are steadily released as sea temperatures rise.

Several methods are being tested and evaluated in an attempt to trap and remove carbon dioxide from the atmosphere.

> Carbon sequestration. This is a process by which growing trees and plants absorb or remove carbon dioxide from the atmosphere and turn it into biomass. There are financial incentives in Australia for companies which unavoidably release carbon dioxide into the atmosphere to buy carbon credits where trees are planted to counteract the pollution produced.

> Geologic sequestration. This involves collecting and transporting concentrated carbon dioxide gas from large emission sources, such as power plants, and injecting it into deep underground reservoirs, such as depleted oil or gas reservoirs. Storage in a variety of other reservoirs may increase as technologies continue to develop. In 2008 a demonstration plant near Nirranda, south-western Victoria, has stored over 65 000 t of carbon dioxide-rich gas injected into a depleted natural gas reservoir approximately 2 km below the surface.

> Ocean sequestration. It may be possible to store some excess carbon dioxide in oceans or in ocean sediments (see Figure 3.44). But this has yet to be implemented. Questions to be answered include: how much can the ocean hold; how will pH be affected; how well can oceans store this carbon dioxide?

Various governments are taking measures to limit emissions of carbon dioxide and other greenhouse

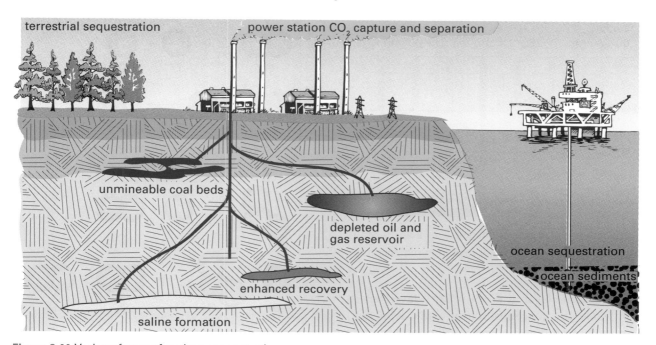

Figure 3.44 Various forms of carbon sequestration

gases. One method is to put taxes on carbon emissions (carbon tax) or increase taxes on petrol and diesel, so that people and companies will have greater incentives to conserve energy and pollute less. It will also give incentives to develop alternative, non-polluting fuels and spur the development of more-efficient and less-polluting methods of production.

3.9 CFCs and the ozone layer

The atmosphere can be divided into a number of layers. The lowest layer is the troposphere which extends from the surface to an altitude of 15 km. Above this is the stratosphere which extends to an altitude of 50 km. The ozone layer is located in Earth's stratosphere approximately 20 to 30 km above Earth (see Figure 3.45). The layer consists of relatively high concentrations of ozone (O_3). Unlike oxygen gas (O_2), ozone is poisonous. Ozone absorbs some 97 to 99% of the Sun's high-frequency ultraviolet light. If this energetic radiation were to reach the surface, it could be potentially damaging to life forms on Earth. Ultraviolet damages DNA, thereby causing skin cancer and eye damage in humans and some other animals, as well as being harmful to crops and plankton. The ozone layer varies seasonally and geographically in thickness.

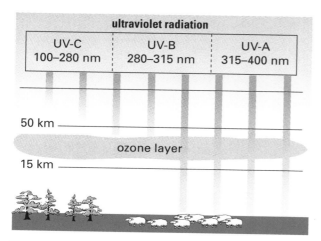

Figure 3.45 Ozone in the atmosphere is able to stop various frequencies of ultraviolet rays from reaching the ground.

Called the ozone layer, it is not really a layer but a region where the concentration of ozone is higher than normal. And that is a very small concentration since only around 10 molecules out of each million

in the air are ozone. Ozone in the atmosphere is mainly concentrated in the lower stratosphere (see Figure 3.46).

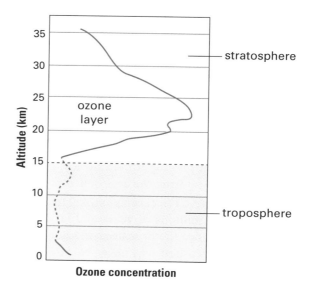

Figure 3.46 Concentration of ozone in the atmosphere

In the stratosphere, small amounts of ozone are constantly being made by the action of sunlight on oxygen. The total amount of ozone usually stays relatively constant from year to year because it is being broken down by natural processes at about the same rate. Figure 3.47 illustrates the formation and destruction of ozone.

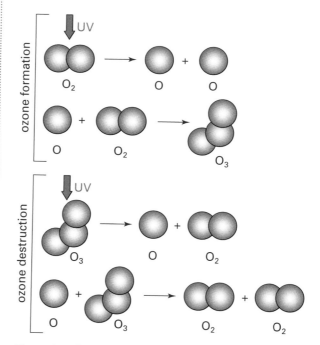

Figure 3.47 Formation and destruction of ozone

Human activity has recently changed that natural balance of ozone formation and depletion. Certain chemicals (such as chlorofluorocarbons and hydro chlorofluorocarbons) can destroy stratospheric ozone faster than it can be formed.

Structure of chlorofluorocarbons

Chlorofluorocarbons (CFCs) are carbon compounds that contain only chlorine and fluorine (no hydrogen). Some examples of CFC molecules are shown in Figure 3.48. A common subclass is the hydrochlorofluorocarbon (HCFC), which contains hydrogen as well. Another group, halons, are also carbon compounds containing only bromine and other halogens (no hydrogen). CFCs were popular for a variety of uses.

- As they are gases at room temperature, they can be easily liquefied. And because they are stable and non-toxic, they are used as fluids in refrigerators and air conditioners.
- They are used as insulation and packing materials.
- They are used as foaming agents to make polystyrene and polyurethane foam plastics.
- As they are fairly unreactive and non-flammable, they are used as propellants in spray cans.
- As they are dense, non-flammable liquids, halons are often used in fire extinguishers.

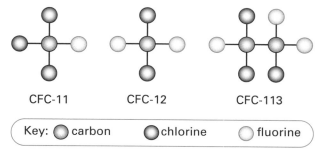

CFC-11   CFC-12   CFC-113

Key: ● carbon   ● chlorine   ○ fluorine

Figure 3.48 Some examples of CFC molecules

CFCs were developed in the 1930s as safe, non-toxic, non-flammable alternatives to other dangerous substances like ammonia and sulfur dioxide for use in refrigeration and spray can propellants. As they became inexpensive to manufacture, and had the right properties, their usage grew enormously over the years.

By the late 1960s they were standard in many applications. However, concern was beginning to be expressed about the impact of these chemicals on the ozone layer. As a result of a dramatic seasonal depletion of the ozone layer over Antarctica, the Montreal Protocol was begun in 1987. This was an international treaty designed to protect the ozone layer by phasing out the production of ozone-depleting chemicals. A complete elimination of all CFCs by the year 2000 was later voted on, and by 2010 most CFCs have been eliminated from developing countries as well. Australia has met or exceeded all of its phase-out obligations under the Montreal Protocol.

Destruction of the ozone layer by CFCs

The most important CFCs are CFC-11 and CFC-12, compounds which are not very chemically reactive and which can therefore remain in the stratosphere and cause harm to the ozone layer for decades. Ozone loss is greatest over Antarctica, and this depletion is commonly referred to as the ozone hole.

Two chemists, Mario Molina and Sherwood Rowland, were awarded the 1995 Nobel Prize for their work about how CFCs attack the ozone layer. The first CFC reaction in the stratosphere is the photo-induced breaking of a C–Cl bond:

$$CCl_3F \rightarrow CCl_2F\bullet + Cl\bullet$$

The chlorine atom (radical), written as Cl•, behaves very differently from the chlorine molecule (Cl_2). The Cl• radical is long-lived in the upper atmosphere, where it catalyses the conversion of ozone into O_2 (see Figure 3.49). Researchers calculate that each chlorine atom can destroy many thousands of ozone molecules. With less ozone, there is less protection from ultraviolet radiation, so more ultraviolet light reaches the Earth's surface.

Measuring ozone

If ozone is an almost colourless gas many kilometres above us, and in very low concentration, how do we know if there is more or less of it? Scientists can measure the amount of ozone in a given vertical column of atmosphere by using various instruments.

- A balloon carries an ozonesonde instrument more than 30 km high to the stratosphere. Here it sucks in a sample of air and tests the amount of ozone gas using an electrochemical concentration cell.
- Some aircraft can reach the lower stratosphere to measure the ozone in the air.
- A Total Ozone Mapping Spectrometer (TOMS) on a satellite determines the amount of ozone present

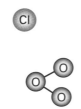

1. In the upper atmosphere, UV radiation rips off a chlorine radical from a CFC molecule.

2. The chlorine radical is free to wander, eventually coming into contact with an ozone molecule.

3. The chlorine radical destroys ozone by breaking one of its bonds.

7. The free chlorine radical is now available to attack another ozone molecule, repeating steps 3 onwards. This cycle can occur many thousands of times.

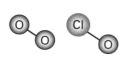

4. This forms an oxygen molecule and a chlorine monoxide (ClO) radical.

5. An oxygen atom in the atmosphere breaks the ClO bond.

6. The free oxygen radical joins with oxygen atom from ClO producing oxygen gas. The chlorine radical is released again.

Figure 3.49 How a chlorine radical from a CFC can destroy many thousands of ozone molecules

in the ozone layer by measuring backscattered ultraviolet light. The TOMS program closed in 2007 after the instruments failed, but it gave valuable information for 30 years.

> There are instruments on other satellites, such as the Ozone Monitoring Instrument (OMI) on the Aura satellite; this also measures backscattered ultraviolet light.

> The Michelson Interferometer for Passive Atmospheric Sounding operates in the near to mid-infra-red where many of the atmospheric trace gases playing a major role in atmospheric chemistry have important emission features.

Solving the problem of CFCs

After the first warnings of damage to stratospheric ozone were announced, scientists went to work on developing safer alternatives to chlorofluorocarbons. As a stop-gap measure, until more permanent solutions could be found, HCFCs were (and still are) used. These compounds contain carbon, hydrogen, chlorine and fluorine. As HCFCs have shorter atmospheric lifetimes than CFCs, they deliver less reactive chlorine to destroy ozone. They are expected to be phased out by the 2020s.

Hydrofluorocarbons (HFCs) are compounds containing carbon, hydrogen and fluorine. Some of these chemicals are acceptable alternatives to CFCs and HCFCs on a longer-term basis. Since the HFCs contain no chlorine. they do not directly affect stratospheric ozone. Atmospheric lifetimes of the most commonly used HFCs are less than 12 years, but they have other adverse environmental effects.

Although there are currently many substitutes for CFCs, scientists continue to research new chemicals, which are less expensive, less destructive to the ozone layer and more practical for industry.

Because of the phase-out, CFCs are no longer accumulating in the atmosphere at an accelerating rate. There are some early signs of stratospheric ozone recovery, but the damage will take many decades to repair. If international agreements are adhered to, some estimate that the ozone layer is expected to recover around 2050.

 Experiment 2

The greenhouse effect

Aim

> To observe the temperature change in a model greenhouse

Equipment

> two small containers, identical in size (such as juice boxes)

- two spirit thermometers
- cotton wool (if using plastic drink bottles)
- sticky tape
- clear plastic
- sharp scissors

Method

1. Cut out one window in each of the two containers, as shown in Figure 3.50.

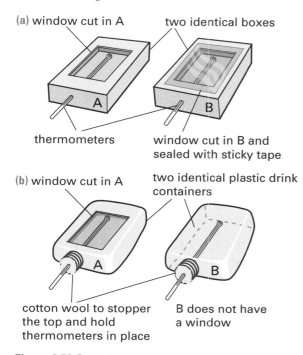

(a) window cut in A   two identical boxes

thermometers   window cut in B and sealed with sticky tape

(b) window cut in A   two identical plastic drink containers

cotton wool to stopper the top and hold thermometers in place   B does not have a window

Figure 3.50 Greenhouse set up

2. Cover one window with clear plastic. This represents the greenhouse. Leave the other window uncovered.
3. Place the thermometers in the two greenhouses so that the bulb of the thermometer is visible in the window.
4. If using a drink bottle, carefully stopper the mouth with cotton wool to prevent the thermometer from rolling around and air from entering the bottle at this point.
5. Take the initial temperature in the two containers.
6. Place them together in a sunny place and record the temperature in the containers every 2 minutes for at least 30 minutes (longer if possible).
7. Record the results in a table.

Analysis

1. Plot a line graph of your results. Plot both graphs on the same grid using different-coloured lines.

2. Explain these results.
3. Would you expect the same results if you had used glass instead of plastic?
4. What are the advantages to farmers of using plastic in their greenhouses instead of traditional glass?

Go to p. 238 to check your answers.

Conclusion

Write a suitable conclusion.

Go to p. 238 to check your answer.

Experiment 3

Acid rain on marble

Aim

- To observe the effect of acid rain on marble, a common component of buildings and statuary

Method

1. Place 50 mL of dilute hydrochloric acid (1 mol/L) in a beaker and label it A. This acid has a concentration of 1 unit.
2. Place 5 mL of hydrochloric acid in the 100 mL cylinder.
3. Pour 45 mL of distilled water in the cylinder so that the total volume is 50 mL. Mix.
4. Pour this diluted solution into a beaker and label it B (concentration 0.1 units).
5. Wash out your cylinders. Place 5 mL of the solution from beaker B into the measuring cylinder and add exactly 45 mL of distilled water. Stir thoroughly. Place in a beaker and label it C (concentration 0.01 units).
6. Continue in this way until you have six labelled beakers containing acid strengths 1.0, 0.1, 0.01, 0.001, 0.0001 and 0.00001 units.
7. Test samples of each solution with universal pH paper or universal indicator solution and record the colours. Relate these colours to pH using an indicator colour card.
8. Weigh out six pieces of marble chip nearly equal in size. Record the mass of each chip.
9. Place one chip of marble in each of the six beakers (see Figure 3.51). Record which chip has been added to which beaker.

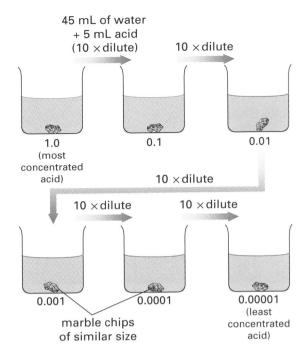

45 mL of water
+ 5 mL acid
(10 ×dilute)

10 ×dilute

1.0
(most
concentrated
acid)

0.1

0.01

10 ×dilute

10 ×dilute

10 ×dilute

0.001

0.0001

marble chips
of similar size

0.00001
(least
concentrated
acid)

Figure 3.51 Experimenting with marble chips and acids

10. Record any observations.

11. Let the beakers stand for several days, recording any observations you make each lesson.

12. Carefully decant the acids from each beaker in turn. Using tongs, wash any remaining marble with water. Dry thoroughly with paper towel or in a drying oven. Reweigh each piece.

13. Calculate the loss of mass for each chip in each beaker. Tabulate your results.

14. Plot your results on a column graph of mass lost versus acid strength.

Analysis

1. Describe your observations as the acid attacked the marble.

2. Describe the trend you see in your graph.

3. Relate the loss in mass to the pH of the acid solution.

4. Why is it important to minimise the formation of acid rain?

Go to p. 238 to check your answers.

Conclusion

Write a suitable conclusion.

Go to p. 238 to check your answer.

 Test yourself 2

Part A: Knowledge

1. Moisture falling to the ground from clouds is known as *(1 mark)*
   A condensation.
   B precipitation.
   C evaporation.
   D sublimation.

2. Which of these is *not* a greenhouse gas? *(1 mark)*
   A oxygen
   B methane
   C carbon dioxide
   D water vapour

3. Converting nitrogen gas to nitrates by bacteria is called *(1 mark)*
   A denitrification.
   B excretion.
   C nitrogen fixation.
   D mutualism.

4. The majority of the pollution in the oceans comes from *(1 mark)*
   A the ocean itself.
   B undersea volcanoes and earth movements.
   C the atmosphere.
   D the land.

5. Which statement is best supported by the carbon–oxygen cycle shown in Figure 3.52? *(1 mark)*

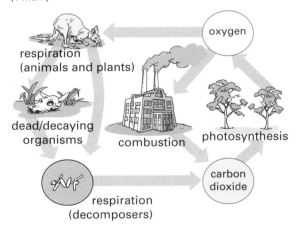

Figure 3.52 The carbon–oxygen cycle

A Consumers use CO_2 and generate O_2.
B Producers use CO_2 and generate O_2.

C In the combustion process, CO_2 is converted into O_2.

D Decomposers remove CO_2 from the atmosphere, replacing it with O_2.

6. Complete the following restricted-response questions using the appropriate word.
(1 mark for each part)

   a) In the greenhouse effect, shorter wavelengths are changed into longer wavelength .... waves.

   b) CFCs stands for .... fluorocarbons.

   c) A scientist who showed how CFCs attack the ozone layer is ....

   d) .... is the process where nitrogen and phosphorus enter ecosystems by fertilising water bodies, often leading to changes in animal and plant populations and degrading water and habitat quality.

   e) Gases enter and leave the leaves of plants through small openings called ....

7. Use the code letters to match the terms or phrases in each column. *(1 mark for each part)*

Column 1		Column 2	
A	halon	F	bleaching
B	ozone layer	G	fire extinguishers
C	acid rain	H	greenhouse gas
D	coral	I	sulfur dioxide
E	nitrous oxide	J	stratosphere

Part B: Skills

8. Consider Figure 3.53, which shows part of the nitrogen cycle.

   a) Use the figure to identify the letter where each of the following occur:

      i) nitrogen-fixing bacteria *(1 mark)*

      ii) bacteria which decompose wastes and dead organisms. *(1 mark)*

   b) 'The main purpose of denitrifying bacteria is to metabolise nitrogenous compounds, with the assistance of enzymes, turning them back into nitrogen gas.' Which letter describes where this occurs? *(1 mark)*

   c) Where did the cow get its nitrogen for this to appear in its wastes? *(1 mark)*

9. Figure 3.54 (on the next page) shows the concentration of carbon dioxide in the atmosphere over time.

   a) Describe the trend in this graph. *(1 mark)*

   b) What is the percentage increase in carbon dioxide in the atmosphere over the hundred years of the 20th century? *(2 marks)*

10. Transportation is responsible for significant carbon dioxide emissions in Australia. Table 3.5 (on the next page) shows the percentage contribution of various transport sectors to these carbon dioxide emissions.

   a) The data in this table has been tabulated poorly. Redraw the table so that the data is provided in descending order. *(2 marks)*

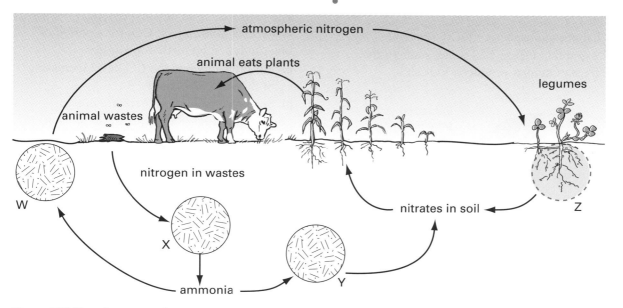

Figure 3.53 The nitrogen cycle

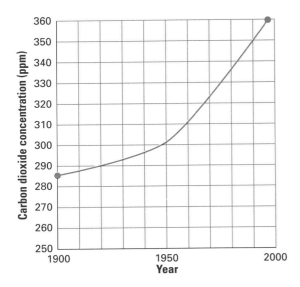

Figure 3.54 Carbon dioxide concentration in the atmosphere over time

b) Use your table to plot a divided bar graph of contributions of each sector to the carbon dioxide emissions. *(3 marks)*

Table 3.5 Percentage of CO_2 emissions per type of transportation

Transportation sector	Percentage of CO_2 emissions
aeroplanes	12
rail transport	5
cars	58
buses and trucks	19
shipping	6

11. a) What are atmospheric VOCs? *(2 marks)*
    b) The graph in Figure 3.55 shows some of the sources of human-produced VOCs.

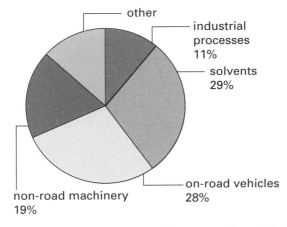

Figure 3.55 Some sources of human-produced VOCs

i) What is the percentage for 'other' uses? *(1 mark)*

ii) Where does about one-fifth of human-produced VOCs originate? *(1 mark)*

iii) In drawing this sector graph, what is the central angle for on-road vehicles? *(1 mark)*

c) Human VOC sources produce around 142 million t of carbon annually, while biological sources emit an estimated 1150 million t of carbon per year. What percentage of the total comes from human sources? *(2 marks)*

12. Figure 3.56 shows a modelling of sea level increases over several centuries.

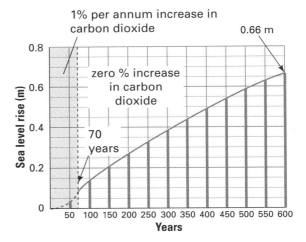

Figure 3.56 Modelling sea level changes

The model is based on a hypothetical 1% p.a. increase in atmospheric CO_2 for a period of time, and then no further increase.

a) For how long was the CO_2 level increasing in this model? *(1 mark)*

b) Sea level rises shown here are due to thermal expansion. Explain what this means. *(2 marks)*

c) Is it true that after CO_2 levels stop increasing, there is no further increase in sea level? Suggest possible reasons. *(2 marks)*

d) Calculate the average sea level change per year over these six centuries. *(2 marks)*

13. Permafrost is permanently frozen ground that occurs and persists where the mean temperature above ground is 0 °C or less. Figure 3.57 shows the modelled and projected loss of permafrost.

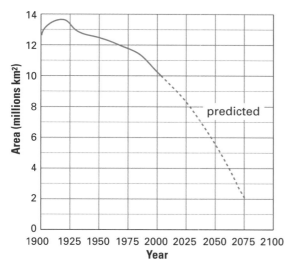

Figure 3.57 Area with permafrost (north of 45°N)

a) Describe the trend shown in the graph. *(2 marks)*

b) Suggest two reasons for this trend. *(2 marks)*

c) Part of this graph has been extrapolated.
  i) Explain extrapolation, and what it means in this context. *(2 marks)*
  ii) From when was the graph extrapolated? *(1 mark)*

d) The arctic tundra contains an estimated 1.5 trillion t of methane, stored far beneath the surface. How, if any, could this affect the area covered with permafrost? *(2 marks)*

14. Figure 3.58 shows the effects of atmospheric pollution. Write appropriate captions to replace the letters P, Q, R and S. *(4 marks)*

Go to pp. 239–241 to check your answers.

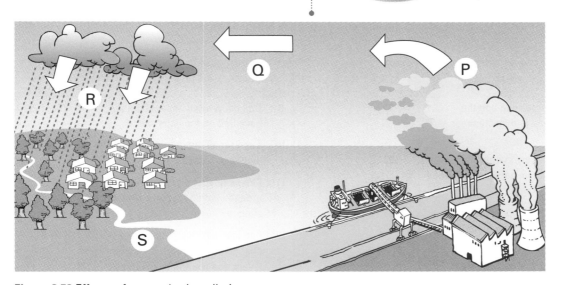

Figure 3.58 Effects of atmospheric pollution

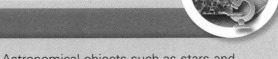

Summary

1. The Big Bang theory proposes that the universe came into existence 13.7 billion years ago.

2. Since the Big Bang, some energy was converted to matter and the universe has evolved and various astronomical objects were formed.

3. Evidence has been collected that supports the theory of the Big Bang.

4. Astronomical objects such as stars and galaxies have formed and continue to evolve.

5. There are theories about the fate of the universe.

6. Bands of the electromagnetic spectrum can be used to investigate the universe.

7. There are various problems associated with ground-based astronomy.

Summary cont.

8. There are natural cycles in the biosphere, such as the water cycle, carbon–oxygen cycle, nitrogen cycle and phosphorus cycle.

9. Humans have an impact on the ecosystem.

10. The greenhouse effect keeps our planet habitable.

11. Climate change is occurring, and this may be affected by the enhanced greenhouse effect.

12. Climate change has an effect on permafrost, sea levels, sea ice and biodiversity.

13. Deep ocean currents have an effect on climate and affect marine life.

14. Meteorologists use computer modelling to investigate climate change.

15. The atmosphere is the most sensitive of the spheres to pollution.

16. CFCs have a profound effect on the ozone layer.

Syllabus checklist

Are you able to answer every syllabus question in this chapter? Tick each question as you go through the list if you are able to answer it. If you cannot answer it, turn to the appropriate page in the guide as is listed in the column to find the answer.

For a complete understanding of this topic		Page no.	✓
1	Can I recall how long ago the universe came into existence in the Big Bang?	91	
2	Can I explain how matter and various astronomical objects formed after the Big Bang?	92	
3	Can I recall the evidence that supports the Big Bang theory?	93	
4	Can I recall the stages in the evolution of stars and galaxies?	94–95	
5	Can I recall the various theories about the possible fate of the universe?	98–99	
6	Can I describe how astronomers investigate the universe using the properties of electromagnetic radiation?	99	
7	Can I recall the problems in investigating space using ground-based astronomy?	99–100	
8	Can I recall the importance of the natural cycles in the biosphere, such as the water cycle, carbon-oxygen cycle, nitrogen cycle and phosphorus cycle?	106–108	

For a complete understanding of this topic		Page no.	✓
9	Do I know what impact humans have had on the ecosystem?	108–109	
10	Can I recall the greenhouse effect and what it does?	109–110	
11	Can I explain how the enhanced greenhouse effect can be related to climate change?	110	
12	Can I recall the effect climate change has on permafrost, sea levels, sea ice and biodiversity?	110–114	
13	Can I recall the effect deep ocean currents have on climate and marine life?	114–116	
14	Do I understand why meteorologists use computer modelling to investigate climate change?	116–117	
15	Can I state which sphere of the Earth is the most sensitive to pollution?	117	
16	Do I understand the need for and importance of world leaders and industries to remove CFCs from the environment?	119–120	
17	Do I understand the effect CFCs have on the ozone layer?	120–122	

Go to p.v for *Tips for tests and examinations*   80 min

Part A: Multiple-choice questions

(1 mark for each)

1. This object is the hot, compact and incredibly dense cinder which remains when an ordinary star several times heavier than the Sun explodes in a supernova. Which of the following could this object be?

   A dwarf star

   B pulsar

   C nebula

   D protostar

2. What is the colour of the hottest stars?

   A white

   B blue

   C yellow

   D red

3. Select the statement that is true of the Milky Way.

   A The Milky Way is an elliptical galaxy with the Sun close to its centre.

   B The Milky Way is a supernova that exploded about 12 billion years ago.

   C The Milky Way galaxy has a diameter of about 100 000 ly.

   D Pulsars and black holes are common in the Milky Way galaxy.

4. As the Sun ages, it will evolve into a giant star. What colour is that giant star?

   A yellow

   B white

   C blue

   D red

5. Identify the scientist(s) who discovered cosmic background radiation.

   A Hubble

   B Penzis and Wilson

   C Gold, Hoyle and Bondi

   D Sackett

6. The energy that powers the water cycle comes from

   A animals.

   B plants.

   C the ground.

   D the Sun.

7. Which of these does *not* aid the greenhouse effect?

   A deforestation

   B evaporation

   C increasing the number of cows

   D none of the above

8. If the Earth did not have the greenhouse effect, the average Earth temperature would be

   A below 0 °C.

   B 0 °C.

   C above 0 °C.

   D impossible to determine.

9. Which of the following cycles does *not* have a gaseous component?

   A carbon

   B nitrogen

   C phosphorus

   D water

10. Animals get their organic nitrogen compounds by

    A nitrogen fixation.

    B absorption.

    C breathing.

    D feeding.

Part B: Short-answer questions

11. a) Use the star chart in Figure 3.59 to determine the azimuth and elevation of the labelled stars (A, B and C). *(3 marks)*

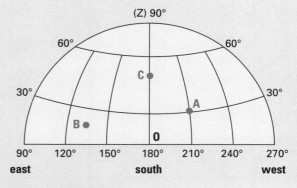

Figure 3.59 Star chart

b) Which direction is the observer facing in this star chart? *(1 mark)*

c) What does the symbol Z mean in this chart? *(1 mark)*

12. Match *some* of the following words with the list of definitions: Andromeda; binary star; black hole; galaxy; gamma rays; infra-red; Milky Way; nebula; nova; quasar; red giant star.

a) the name of our own galaxy *(1 mark)*

b) a collection of many stars, dust and gas held together by the force of their mutual gravity *(1 mark)*

c) an object that shines because of the release of energy in its core by nuclear fusion *(1 mark)*

d) the nearest spiral galaxy to the Milky Way and the most distant object visible to the naked eye *(1 mark)*

e) a cloud of dust and gas in space which is visible to observers on Earth because it emits, reflects or absorbs starlight *(1 mark)*

f) a star observed to brighten suddenly and then gradually decline back to its original brightness over a period of months *(1 mark)*

g) the highest energy form of electromagnetic radiation *(1 mark)*

13. Figure 3.60 shows the absolute brightness (or absolute magnitude) of some stars in relation to their surface temperatures. The more negative the absolute magnitude, the brighter the star. The curved lines are called the main sequence and represent the position of stars in which they spend the greater part of their evolution.

a) Work out the approximate surface temperature and absolute magnitude (brightness) of Proxima Centauri. *(2 marks)*

b) What type of object is Proxima Centauri? *(1 mark)*

c) White dwarfs are stars that are very hot but have a very low brightness. In which region (A, B, C or D) of the graph would you expect the white dwarfs to be plotted? *(1 mark)*

d) Three stars (X, Y and Z) are shown in the main sequence. Arrange these stars in order of age from youngest to oldest. (Hint: large, hot stars have short lives.) *(1 mark)*

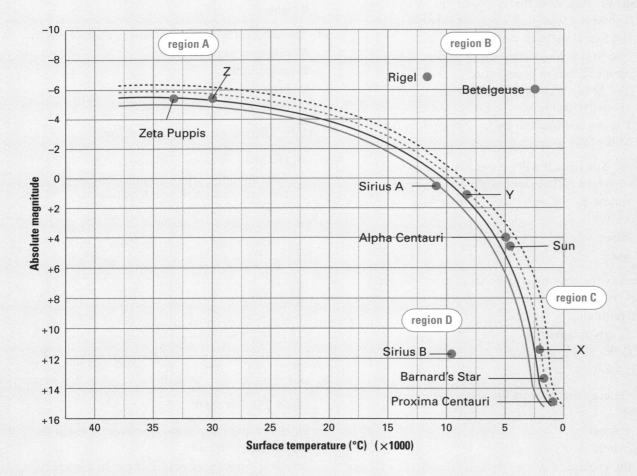

Figure 3.60 Brightness versus surface temperature

e) The Sun has a surface temperature of about 5600 °C. Estimate its approximate absolute magnitude. *(1 mark)*

f) State whether each of the following statements is true or false.
   i) Betelgeuse is a hotter, brighter star than Sirius B. *(1 mark)*
   ii) Alpha Centauri is not as bright as Zeta Puppis. *(1 mark)*
   iii) Rigel is brighter than the Sun when measured on an absolute magnitude scale. *(1 mark)*

14. One light-year is equal to 9461 billion km. Calculate the distance of the following stars from the Sun. *(2 marks)*
   a) Wolf-359 ($d = 7.7$ ly)
   b) Beta Crucis ($d = 353$ ly)

15. The stars of the Southern Cross form a constellation. In the sky, they appear to be close together. Their recently measured distances from the Sun are listed in Table 3.6.

Table 3.6 The distance from the Sun of stars in the Southern Cross

Star	Distance (ly)
Alpha Crucis	321
Beta Crucis	353
Gamma Crucis	88
Delta Crusis	364
Epsilon Crucis	228

a) Do these stars form a cluster in space? Explain. *(2 marks)*
b) The stars are listed in order of decreasing brightness as seen from Earth.
   i) Which star is the brightest as seen from Earth? *(1 mark)*
   ii) Beta Crucis has a higher surface temperature than Alpha Crucis. Why does it appear less bright than Alpha Crucis? *(1 mark)*

16. The surface temperature (T) of a star can be estimated from the wavelength (λ) using the following mathematical formula:
$$T \times \lambda = 3\,000\,000$$
Temperature is measured in absolute units (kelvin, K) and wavelength is measured in nanometres (nm).

a) Light from the Sun has a wavelength of 510 nm. Calculate the surface temperature of the Sun in absolute units. *(1 mark)*
b) Given that 0 °C = 273 K and 100 °C = 373 K, determine the temperature of the surface of the Sun in degrees Celsius. *(1 mark)*
c) Betelgeuse is a red supergiant star. Its surface temperature is about 4300 K. Calculate the wavelength of the light emitted from its surface. *(1 mark)*

17. Figure 3.61 is a graph of the penetration of various electromagnetic waves through the atmosphere.

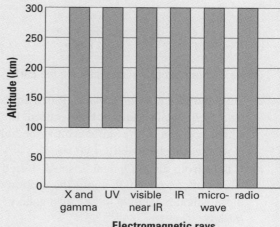

Figure 3.61 Penetration of electromagnetic rays through the atmosphere

a) Which rays are quickly filtered out by the upper atmosphere? *(1 mark)*
b) Which rays are able to penetrate below 20 km altitude? *(1 mark)*
c) Use the graph to name the two common types of ground-based astronomy. *(2 marks)*

18. Part (a) of Figure 3.62 shows three lines in the visible spectrum produced by light emitted from a star that is rotating around another star. These three lines (X, Y and Z) correspond to different directions of motion of the star relative to an observer on Earth. Part (b) of the figure shows the direction of motion of the star relative to Earth at different times in its cycle.
a) In which position in the star's orbit is the light from the star red-shifted? *(1 mark)*
b) Match the three spectral lines to the rotational direction of the star in part (b) of the diagram. *(3 marks)*

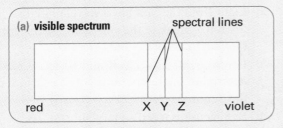

(a) **visible spectrum** — spectral lines

red   X Y Z   violet

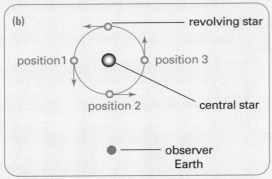

(b) revolving star — position1 — position 3 — central star — position 2 — observer Earth

Figure 3.62 Motion of a star relative to the Earth

c) Stars that are moving towards Earth emit light frequencies that are blue-shifted. In which position of the star's orbit is the light from this star blue-shifted? *(1 mark)*

d) If light from distant galaxies is red-shifted, what can one conclude about the motion of these galaxies relative to our own galaxy? *(1 mark)*

19. The normal units of distance measurement on Earth are replaced by larger units when describing distances in space outside our solar system. The astronomical unit (AU) is defined as the distance between the Sun and Earth. One astronomical unit = 150 million km. This unit is useful for measuring distances in the solar system.

Calculate the distance of the following planets from the Sun in kilometres.

a) Venus (*d* = 0.7 AU) *(1 mark)*

b) Saturn (*d* = 9.5 AU) *(1 mark)*

20. Figure 3.63 is a set of jumbled diagrams that show the evolution of a star such as the Sun. Use the code letters to place these diagrams in their correct sequence. *(2 marks)*

21. A student constructed the astronomical model shown in Figure 3.64 as part of an astronomy project. What name is given by astronomers to this structure? *(1 mark)*

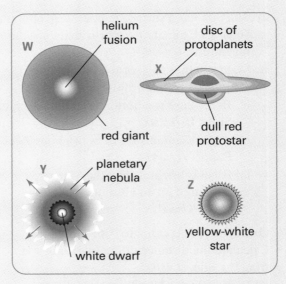

Figure 3.63 Jumbled diagrams of star evolution

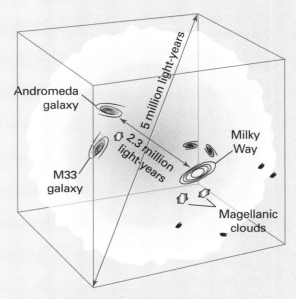

Figure 3.64 Astronomical model

22. The radius of the Earth is 6384 km. The Hubble space telescope orbits 650 km above the Earth's surface.

a) What is the radius of the orbit of the telescope? *(1 mark)*

b) What distance does it cover in travelling once around the Earth? (Remember, $C = 2\pi r$.) *(1 mark)*

c) If it circles once every 90 minutes, calculate its speed in km/h. *(1 mark)*

d) There are 8766 hours in a year. How many kilometres did the telescope travel in its first 10 years of operation? *(1 mark)*

23. Binaries or binary stars are often detected because the brightness of the system changes as one star eclipses the other. This is easiest to see when you look at their orbits edge-on. Look at Figure 3.65. One star is large and dim and the other is small and bright.

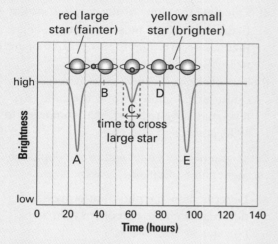

Figure 3.65 Binary stars

a) When is the binary system brightest? When is it faintest? (Choose between positions marked A, B, C, D and E.) *(1 mark)*

b) How long does it take the small star to cross the face of the large star? *(1 mark)*

c) How long does it take the small star to make one complete orbit? *(1 mark)*

24. a) The Big Bang theory is based on evidence collected by astronomers. Identify two pieces of evidence for this theory. *(2 marks)*

b) According to the Big Bang theory, what happened in the 10 minutes of the formation of the universe? *(2 marks)*

c) How old is the universe believed to be? *(1 mark)*

25. Match *some* of the following words with the list of definitions: asteroid; Big Bang; black hole; dark matter; infra-red; Milky Way; nebula; neutron star; nova; parallax; pulsar; quasar; red giant star.

a) a very compact object, far away and very bright, thought to be active galactic nuclei *(1 mark)*

b) a very large, bright and cool star having a diameter up to 100 times the Sun which, having exhausted all its useable hydrogen to form helium, is in the later part of its life *(1 mark)*

c) matter that is difficult to detect because of its very low brightness or lack of brightness, but vast quantities of it are thought to exist in the universe *(1 mark)*

d) the central remains of a star which has undergone a supernova explosion and is very dense *(1 mark)*

e) the theory that proposes the universe came into being in an instantaneous event about 13.7 billion years ago *(1 mark)*

f) any of the many rocky objects, most of which orbit the Sun between Mars and Jupiter *(1 mark)*

g) electromagnetic radiation with wavelengths longer than visible light *(1 mark)*

h) a spinning neutron star *(1 mark)*

i) the remains of a star so dense that not even light can escape from it *(1 mark)*

26. Figure 3.66 shows the yearly emissions of carbon dioxide into the atmosphere (units are arbitrary).

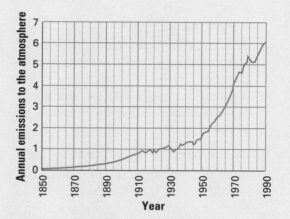

Figure 3.66 Yearly emissions of CO_2

a) Describe the trend shown in the graph. *(1 mark)*

b) List some of the places this CO_2 is coming from. *(7 marks)*

c) Do you expect this trend to continue? Explain. *(1 mark)*

d) What might be the number of units of CO_2 emitted into the atmosphere this year? *(1 mark)*

27. Figure 3.67 shows the concentration of carbon dioxide in the atmosphere using the very small unit parts per million (ppm).

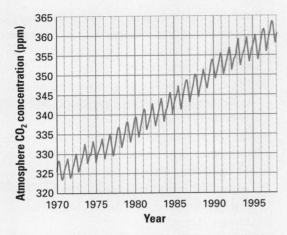

Figure 3.67 Atmospheric concentration of CO_2

a) How does this graph differ in what it shows from Figure 3.66 in the previous question? *(5 marks)*

b) What does the 'saw-tooth' pattern in the graph show? *(2 marks)*

c) What was the average CO_2 concentration in the following years?
   i) 1975 *(1 mark)*
   ii) 1995 *(1 mark)*

d) By what percentage amount has the CO_2 concentration increased in these 20 years? *(2 marks)*

e) What major effect would this increase in CO_2 concentration in the atmosphere have on this planet? *(1 mark)*

28. Figure 3.68 shows the mean sea level change over a number of years.

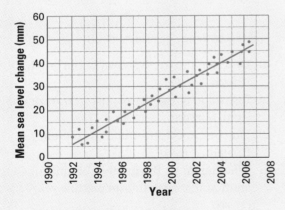

Figure 3.68 Mean sea level change

a) The line shown is the line of best fit. What is meant by this? *(2 marks)*

b) What year was taken as a point from which to measure sea level change? *(1 mark)*

c) If the line is extended further backwards before 1990, the sea level change would be negative. Does this mean that the sea level fell rather than increased? Explain. *(2 marks)*

d) Calculate the slope of the graph. *(2 marks)*

e) Estimate the total mean sea level change that has occurred up to this year, compared to 1990. *(2 marks)*

f) Sea level rise is expected to increase for centuries. Estimate by how much the sea level may have risen by 2090, compared to 1990. *(2 marks)*

29. Is the greenhouse effect and ozone depletion the same thing? Explain. *(3 marks)*

30. a) Describe how the phosphorus cycle is different from the carbon, oxygen and nitrogen cycles. *(2 marks)*

b) Phosphorus is found chiefly in sedimentary rocks. How is it released to take part in the cycle? What happens to it then? *(2 marks)*

31. On which organisms does ocean acidification put most stress? *(2 marks)*

32. Figure 3.69 shows how ozone is destroyed by CFCs in the stratosphere.

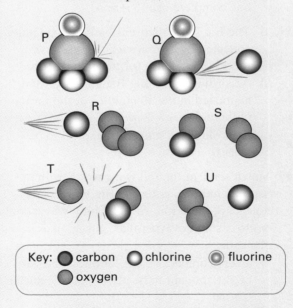

Figure 3.69 Ozone destruction in the stratosphere

Write a caption to go with each diagram. *(6 marks)*

33. a) What are CFCs? What do they contain? Why were they produced? *(3 marks)*

b) A free oxygen atom is involved in the reactions between ozone and CFCs. Where does this atom come from? Use a diagram, if necessary, in your answer. *(2 marks)*

34. a) Permafrost contains large quantities of stored methane. How did this methane originate? *(2 marks)*

b) What effect will this methane have as permafrost thaws? *(3 marks)*

c) What will be the effects on plant and animal life where the permafrost is now found? *(2 marks)*

d) What will be the effects on the landforms and human structures where the permafrost is now found? *(3 marks)*

e) Can this damage be prevented? Explain. *(2 marks)*

35. Figure 3.70 shows part of the water cycle. Replace the letters with the following words: condensation, groundwater, percolation, surface runoff, precipitation, transpiration, evaporation. *(7 marks)*

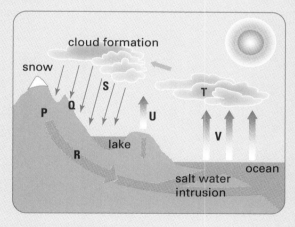

Figure 3.70 The water cycle

36. Sea level change can be difficult to measure. Sea levels are not constant as is, say, water in a bathtub.

a) List four things that can change the water level at any point in time. *(4 marks)*

b) What are some of the issues involved and how are some of the problems addressed? *(3 marks)*

37. Table 3.7 shows the sea level rises over a decade period, and the contribution each makes.

Table 3.7 Average sea level rise over a decade, by source

Source	Average sea level rise (mm per decade)
thermal expansion of ocean	16
melting glaciers and ice caps	8
melting Antarctic ice sheet	2
melting Greenland ice sheet	2
total increase	

a) Calculate the total increase. *(1 mark)*

b) What percentage of this increase is due to thermal expansion? *(2 marks)*

c) In the previous decade the sea level rose 11 mm in 10 years. Of that 38% was due to thermal expansion. How many millimetres did the ocean rise due to thermal expansion? *(2 marks)*

38. Ozone has been described as bad for our health and a saviour in the atmosphere. Comment on this apparent anomaly. *(2 marks)*

39. Table 3.8 shows the main sources of atmospheric carbon dioxide from fossil fuel combustion.

Table 3.8 Main fossil fuel combustion sources of atmospheric CO_2

Source	Contribution (%)
liquid fuels	36
solid fuels	35
gaseous fuels	20
cement production	3
other sources	

a) Complete the table for 'other sources'. *(1 mark)*

b) Draw a sector graph (pie diagram) showing this information. *(3 marks)*

40. Figure 3.71 shows a cross-section of the thermohaline 'conveyor belt' in the ocean.

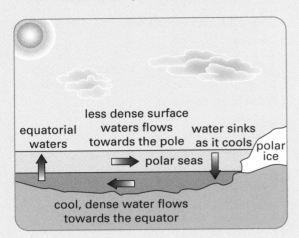

Figure 3.71 Thermohaline circulation

a) What is the thermohaline circulation? *(2 marks)*

b) Describe why water sinks at the poles. *(2 marks)*

c) What happens to the water near the equator? *(2 marks)*

d) What might interrupt this conveyor belt? *(2 marks)*

e) Are any chemicals carried by this circulation? Explain. *(2 marks)*

Go to pp. 241–245 to check your answers.

CHAPTER 4

Motion, force and energy

Overview

In this chapter you will learn about:

- ☑ motion and its measurement
- ☑ distance and displacement
- ☑ speed and velocity
- ☑ forces and acceleration
- ☑ gravitational acceleration
- ☑ Newton's laws of motion
- ☑ law of energy conservation
- ☑ kinetic and potential energy
- ☑ energy transfers and transformations
- ☑ energy changes in car crashes
- ☑ energy-efficient buildings
- ☑ innovative energy transfer devices in transport and communication.

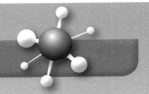

Glossary

Acceleration—a type of motion in which the speed continues to increase (unit = m/s^2, sometimes also written as ms^{-2})

Deceleration—a type of motion in which the speed continues to decrease (unit = m/s^2, sometimes also written as ms^{-2})

Energy efficiency—the percentage of total energy input to a machine or equipment that is consumed in useful work and not wasted as heat or other undesired energy form

Force—a push, pull or twist that changes the motion or shape of an object on which it acts (unit = newton, N)

Frangible—an object of low mass, designed to break, distort or yield on impact, so as to present a minimal hazard

Friction—a force that opposes motion when surfaces move over each other

Inertia—the tendency of all matter to resist any change to its motion

Mass—the amount of matter in a body (unit = kg, g)

Velocity—a measure of speed in a fixed direction (unit = m/s, sometimes also written as ms^{-1})

Weight—a force acting on a body due to gravity (unit = newton, N)

4.1 Measuring motion

In about 330 BC, the Greek philosopher Aristotle claimed that the four 'elements' of earth, water, air and fire had their natural places towards which they tend to travel. He argued that objects containing greater amounts of earth than others would fall towards the Earth faster and that their speed would increase as they neared their natural place. He also thought that each heavenly body followed a particular natural motion, unaffected by external causes or agents. These ideas and two other Aristotelian viewpoints were accepted for centuries: that a body moving at constant speed requires continuous force acting on it; and that force must be applied by contact rather than interaction at a distance. These views meant that the principles of motion were not properly understood.

Distance and speed

A large grassy field has been marked out by painted lines as shown in Figure 4.1. A student is jogging at a brisk, steady pace from point A to point C. She jogs along a straight path to B and turns right and jogs in a straight line towards C. The distance from A to B is 120 m and the distance from B to C is 160 m. Her jogging from A to B takes her 30 seconds and from B to C she takes 40 seconds. The total distance that the student jogs is 280 m and the total time she took is 70 seconds.

The student starts again and this time she ignores the painted lines and jogs directly in a straight line across the field from A to C. This distance is 200 m. This time it only takes her 50 seconds.

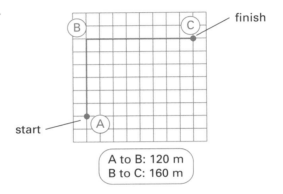

A to B: 120 m
B to C: 160 m

Figure 4.1 Student jogs along two paths at right angles

In each case she starts at A and ends at C, but the time taken to jog from A to B to C is longer than jogging directly in a straight line from A to C.

The speed at which she jogged can be calculated using the formula:

$$\text{speed} = \frac{\text{distance}}{\text{time}}$$

from A to B: speed $= \dfrac{120}{30} = 4$ m/s

from B to C: speed $= \dfrac{160}{40} = 4$ m/s

from A to C (directly): speed $= \dfrac{200}{50} = 4$ m/s

It is quite difficult to maintain a constant speed. In a car trip, the car has to stop for traffic lights and at other times the road is hilly and so travel times vary. For a car trip, one usually calculates an average speed rather than an absolute or instantaneous speed. The car's speedometer can tell you the instantaneous speed of the car at any moment but it cannot tell you the average speed for a journey. In order to calculate the average speed, you need to know the total distance travelled and the total time taken.

$$\text{average speed} = \frac{\text{total distance covered}}{\text{total time taken}}$$

Consider the car journey shown in the scale diagram in Figure 4.2. The time for the journey was 2.20 minutes (2 minutes 12 seconds).

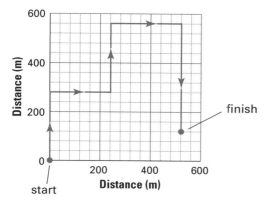

Figure 4.2 Car journey

Using the scale on the grid, the total distance travelled was 280 + 240 + 280 + 280 + 440 = 1520 m. The time for the journey was 2.20 minutes = 132 s.

$$\text{average speed} = \frac{1520}{132} = 11.5 \text{ m/s}$$

This average speed can be converted to the units of kilometres per hour:

$$11.5 \text{ m/s} = 11.5 \times \frac{3600}{1000} = 41.4 \text{ km/h}$$

In order to change from m/s to km/h, multiply by 3.6; to change from km/h to m/s, divide by 3.6.

Table 4.1 compares typical speeds for humans, animals and transport vehicles.

Table 4.1 Typical average speeds

Object	Typical average speed (m/s)
human walking	1
human running	7
athlete sprinting 100 m	10
car on an open highway	28
cheetah running	35
aeroplane	200

Displacement and velocity

Most people take speed and velocity to mean the same thing, but this is not so in science. It is useful to distinguish between the terms speed and velocity. Velocity is a term used by physicists to measure the change in motion of an object along a straight line in a particular direction. The speed of a body is independent of direction.

Example 1: Distance

Consider a straight road running east–west. A car travels along the road at a constant speed of 40 km/h. When it is travelling east, its velocity is said to be 40 km/h east. When it is travelling at the same speed west, its velocity is said to be 40 km/h west. While the speed is the same (40 km/h) the direction is different, and so the car will end up at a different place.

It is also important to distinguish between distance and displacement. Displacement is a term which refers to the straight line distance from the start to the end of the movement. In Figure 4.3, a student walks north from A to B and then turns east and walks from B to C. The distance he has walked is the sum of the distances AB and BC. The displacement of the student, however, is the straight line distance from A to C. The direction of this displacement from the start must also be stated.

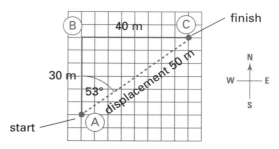

Figure 4.3 Distance and displacement

Answer:

distance travelled = 30 + 40 = 70 m
displacement = 50 m at 53° east of north

If we assume it took the student 40 seconds to walk from A to B to C, then we can work out his average speed and average velocity:

$$\text{average speed} = \frac{\text{distance}}{\text{time}} = \frac{70}{40} = 1.75 \text{ m/s}$$

$$\text{average velocity} = \frac{\text{displacement}}{\text{time}} = \frac{50}{40}$$
$$= 1.25 \text{ m/s at } 53° \text{ east of north}$$

It is interesting to note that if you walk to your friend's place, say 2 km, and then back again (another 2 km), the total distance you walked is 2 + 2 = 4 km. But your total displacement = 0 km, since your start and finish points are the same.

Example 2: Velocity

The journey from A to J shown in Figure 4.4 took 20 minutes ($^1/_3$ hour). Determine the displacement and the average velocity for the journey.

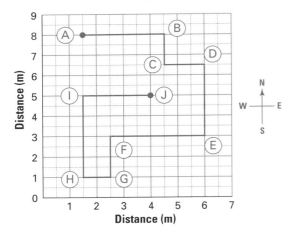

Figure 4.4 Car journey

Answer: The displacement of the car and the angle (θ) from south is shown in Figure 4.5.

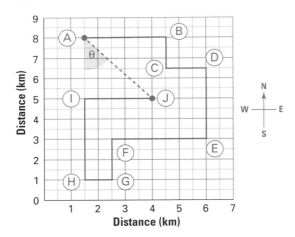

Figure 4.5 Determining displacement

The length of the displacement line can be found using Pythagoras' theorem or trigonometry.

displacement and angle:

$$AJ^2 = AI^2 + IJ^2 = 3^2 + 2.5^2 = 15.25$$
$$AJ = 3.91 \text{ km}$$

$$\tan \theta = \frac{2.5}{3} = 0.833$$
$$\theta = 39.8°$$

Therefore, the displacement of the car was 3.91 km at 39.8° east of south or 3.91 km S39.8°E.

$$\text{average velocity} = \frac{\text{displacement}}{\text{time}}$$
$$= \frac{3.91}{^1/_3}$$
$$= 11.7 \text{ km/h, S39.8°E}$$

Displacement–time graphs are useful in examining motion. Imagine a farm vehicle is travelling north along a straight dirt road on a grazing property for 30 seconds at a constant speed. The vehicle then stops and reverses backwards along the same road for 10 seconds and then stops for 10 seconds. The displacement–time graph in Figure 4.6 shows this motion. The graph shows that for the first 30 seconds (AB) the change in displacement with time is increasing at a constant rate. The line is straight with a constant slope. This means the vehicle is travelling with constant velocity. From B to C the vehicle has reversed direction and is travelling at a constant but lower velocity. Between C and D the vehicle is stopped as the displacement does not change with time.

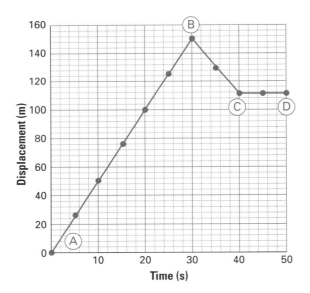

Figure 4.6 Displacement–time graph

Acceleration

When an object speeds up or slows down, it accelerates. Sometimes slowing down is called deceleration, but it can also be seen as negative acceleration. Positive acceleration occurs when the speed increases; negative acceleration occurs when the speed decreases.

Suppose a car increases its velocity from 8 m/s to 28 m/s in a northerly direction in 5 seconds. This is shown in Table 4.2.

Table 4.2 Velocity versus time

Time (s)	0	1	2	3	4	5
Velocity (m/s)	8	12	16	20	24	28

The velocity has changed by 20 m/s in 5 seconds; in other words, by $\frac{20}{5} = 4$ m/s every second. Its acceleration is therefore 4 m/s/s. It is more common to write this as 4 m/s^2.

Average acceleration can be calculated using the following formula:

$$\text{average acceleration} = \frac{\text{change in velocity}}{\text{change in time}}$$

This car's speed or velocity changes regularly, as it is accelerating at 4 m/s^2 (see Figure 4.7). If the acceleration ceases (i.e. acceleration now equals zero) after the 5 seconds, the car's velocity will remain at 28 m/s.

Like velocity and displacement, the acceleration of an object is directional. The direction of the acceleration must be stated. Acceleration is one measure of performance used by car manufacturers. They often give figures, called standing starts, that indicate how long it takes a car to reach a certain speed from a stationary position.

Example 1: Acceleration

A car starts from rest and reaches a velocity of 15 m/s in 5 seconds. Calculate its average acceleration.

Answer:
initial velocity = 0 m/s (i.e. at rest, stationary)
final velocity = 15 m/s
change in velocity = final velocity – initial velocity
$= 15 - 0 = 15$ m/s

time taken = 5 s
average acceleration $= \frac{15}{5} = 3$ m/s^2

Example 2: Deceleration

A car is travelling at 18 m/s, the brakes are applied and it comes to a stop in 4 seconds. Calculate its average deceleration.

Answer:
initial velocity = 18 m/s
final velocity = 0 m/s (i.e. at rest)
change in velocity = final velocity – initial velocity
$= 0 - 18 = -18$ m/s
time taken = 4 s
average acceleration $= -\frac{18}{4} = -4.5$ m/s^2

The negative sign indicates that the acceleration is negative. That is, the car is decelerating with an average deceleration of 4.5 m/s^2.

4.2 Force and acceleration

Forces cause all movements. Forces are pulls, pushes or twists that are applied to objects, and can cause a:

- change in speed; for example, pushing down on the accelerator pedal in a car will make the car move faster along a flat road
- change in direction; for example, twisting or turning the handlebars of a bicycle allows the bicycle to change direction
- change in shape; for example, squeezing a tennis ball will deform it and change its shape until you let go and it returns to its old shape.

Balanced forces

When an object is at rest, the forces acting on it are balanced and there is no net force. Consider the forces acting on a box resting on a wooden plank

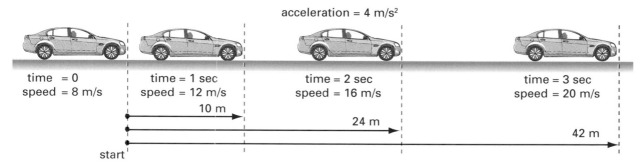

Figure 4.7 Car undergoing a constant acceleration in a northerly direction

on the floor, as shown in Figure 4.8. In this example, there are two balanced forces. One force is the weight (*W*) of the box pushing down on the plank. The plank pushes back on the box with a force equal to the weight force. This upwards force is called the reaction force (*R*). These two forces balance each other out and there is no motion of the box.

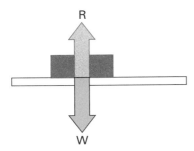

Figure 4.8 Balanced forces

When a body is travelling at constant velocity, there is no net force acting on it. For example, in order to travel at constant speed a bicycle rider must continue to pedal at a rate so that the applied force just balances all the frictional forces, which include road friction and air friction (see Figure 4.9). Friction is a force that causes objects to resist being moved across one another. If one object is pushed or pulled across another object, it experiences resistance caused by friction. Friction is often something that must be overcome, such as a squeaky door that needs oiling. But it has many important uses. You could not walk without friction. If you have ever walked with new leather-soled shoes across a slippery surface, you would appreciate this. The wheels of trains grip the rails of tracks by friction. Tyres on cars must, by law, have a certain amount of tread on them so that the amount of frictional force on the road is not reduced, causing the car to slide.

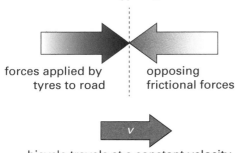

bicycle travels at a constant velocity
as the forces balance

Figure 4.9 A bicycle moving with constant speed has no net forces acting on it.

Unbalanced forces and acceleration

Speeding up or slowing down requires a net force to act. This net force is due to unbalanced forces acting on a body.

Figure 4.10 shows opposing forces acting on a body. Force F_1 is greater than force F_2 and so the net force is acting to the right. The length of the force arrow is a measure of the size of each force. If the net force is to the right then the body will accelerate to the right.

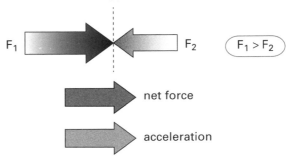

Figure 4.10 Unbalanced forces

When throwing a ball, you know you can make it go faster by throwing it harder. This just means you are applying a larger force to it. This larger force causes the ball to accelerate more, thereby achieving a greater speed as it leaves your hand.

An object will undergo uniform acceleration if a constant net force acts on it. The size of this uniform acceleration can be calculated from a knowledge of the initial and final velocities and the time it takes to change the velocity. If the object is accelerating in a south direction then the net force causing the acceleration must also be acting in the south direction.

Example: Uniform acceleration

A 10-kg mass initially moving along a flat surface at 10 m/s is uniformly accelerated for 3 seconds until its velocity is 16 m/s. Calculate its uniform acceleration. Answer:

initial velocity = 10 m/s

final velocity = 16 m/s

change in velocity = final velocity – initial velocity

$$= 16 - 10$$
$$= 6 \text{ m/s}$$

time taken = 3 s

uniform acceleration $= \dfrac{6}{3}$

$$= 2 \text{ m/s}^2$$

Accelerating by changing direction

Acceleration can also be due to changes in direction rather than changes in speed. A car that is travelling at a constant velocity of 10 m/s north turns a corner and continues on the new road to travel at a constant velocity of 10 m/s towards the west. At all times its speed has stayed constant at 10 m/s but due to its change in direction the car must have experienced a net force. Consequently, it must have accelerated to turn the corner.

Weight and gravitational acceleration

Weight and mass are another two words often assumed to mean the same thing, but scientists distinguish between the two. Weight is the force with which the Earth, or other object, attracts a mass (the amount of matter in a body, measured in units such as kg or g). Here is the equation linking the two:

weight = mass × acceleration due to gravity

or

$$W = m \times g$$

where W = the weight force (N)
m = mass (kg)
g = acceleration due to gravity (m/s^2)

On Earth, acceleration due to gravity is 9.8 m/s^2.

Weight is the name given to the force when the acceleration is that due to gravity. The force of gravity is classified as a field force. The field is a gravitational field and any mass in a gravitational field will experience a force. Other examples of fields include magnetic fields and electrostatic fields. Iron bodies experience a magnetic force in a magnetic field and charged bodies experience a force in an electrostatic field.

Consider a 60-kg girl, for example. Her mass is 60 kg. Her weight can be calculated as follows:

$$W = mg$$
$$= 60 \times 9.8$$
$$= 588 \text{ N}$$

The Earth is pulling her downwards with a force of 588 N. If she were to go to the Moon, where the acceleration due to gravity is only 1.6 m/s^2, her mass would still be 60 kg but her weight would now be less than 588 N:

$$W = mg$$
$$= 60 \times 1.6$$
$$= 96 \text{ N}$$

 ## Experiment 1

Speed and acceleration

Aim

> To investigate examples of motion involving constant speed and acceleration

Method

Walking at constant speed

This experiment uses an instrument called a ticker tape timer (see Figure 4.11). The vibrating arm on the ticker timer vibrates at 50 times a second. This pushes a raised dot on the underside of the arm against a carbon disk and leaves a small mark on the paper tape. As the tape moves, a series of dots is recorded on the paper tape. Analysis of these dots can reveal the motion of the body to which the tape is attached.

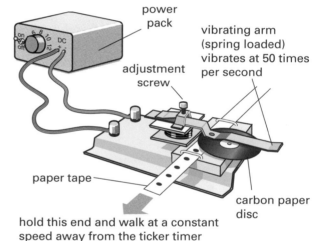

Figure 4.11 A ticker tape timer used to record motion

1. Set up the ticker timer. Adjust the tension of the screw to produce clear dots on the paper tape.

2. Hold one end of the paper tape and walk away very slowly at a constant speed so that the paper tape is pulled through the apparatus. Stop when you have got about 0.5 to 1 m of tape.

Falling weight

1. Clamp the ticker timer on a stand so the tape will pass through it in a downwards direction (see Figure 4.12).

2. Attach a mass to the end of the tape and let the weighted paper tape fall freely through the apparatus. Collect the pattern of dots.

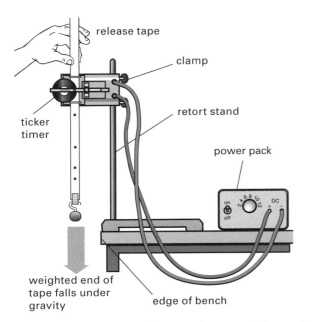

Figure 4.12 A ticker tape timer used to record the motion of a falling mass

Results and analysis

Sections of the ticker tapes collected in Experiments A and B are shown in Figure 4.13. Analyse these tape sections and explain what the dot pattern reveals about each type of motion.

(a) Student walking

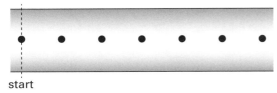

start

(b) Falling mass

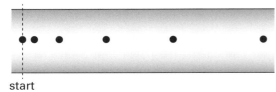

start

Figure 4.13 Results of Experiment 1

Go to p. 245 to check your answers.

Conclusion

Write a suitable conclusion.

Go to p. 245 to check your answer.

4.3 Newton's Laws

Isaac Newton (1642–1727) has been described as one of the greatest mathematicians and scientists of all time. He invented a new branch of mathematics, called calculus; showed that white light is made up of a rainbow of colours; invented the reflecting telescope; and showed, through his theory of gravitation, how the universe is held together.

He was born in England in the year Galileo died. Only 30 years after Galileo was censured for suggesting that the Earth revolved around the Sun, Newton had worked out the mathematics of how planets move. Up until Newton's time, people were consulting the writings of ancient philosophers to describe things around them. A quiet revolution then took place, with scientists starting to appeal to experiment and logic to find out about nature. As a child, Newton did not stand out. He was more interested in making mechanical devices than in studying, and was even considered a poor student. His mother was widowed before Newton was born, and he was raised by his grandmother when his mother re-married 2 years later. He attended Cambridge University, paid for by his uncle, and graduated with no particular distinction.

Newton's schooling was interrupted by the great plague in 1665, and he was later to say he did his best work in the 2 years following. One day, while drinking tea in his garden, he is said to have seen an apple fall from a tree. He immediately realised the same force was pulling on the apple as keeps the Moon in its orbit. He was able to calculate that the Moon's 'fall' towards Earth is what keeps it in its orbit. It was not until some 20 years later that Edmund Halley (after whom Halley's comet was named) convinced Newton to publish his discoveries. So, in 1687, Newton's discoveries on the laws of motion, mechanics and theories of gravitation were published in his book *Philosophiae naturalis principia mathematica* (Mathematical principles of natural philosophy). Scientists (or natural philosophers as they were known at the time) wrote all their major works in Latin, as this was a common language scientists in different countries could understand. This book represents one of the foundations of modern science and made Newton internationally famous. In 1704, he published another book, *Opticks*, dealing with light and lenses.

Newton's first law

Have you ever stood in a bus when it suddenly came to a stop? What happened? Did you feel yourself suddenly thrown forwards? Or what about when a car you are travelling in suddenly accelerates? Do you feel yourself being pushed more into your seat? This all has to do with inertia. Inertia is the tendency of all matter to resist any change to its motion.

A stationary object tends to remain stationary; a moving object tends to keep moving at the same speed and in the same direction. When a bus is travelling at constant speed you, and every other passenger in it, are carried along at the same speed. When the brakes are applied, the bus immediately slows down but your body keeps travelling at the original speed of the bus, so you are thrown forwards. Similarly, if you are stationary and the vehicle suddenly accelerates, you are thrown backwards as your body tries to maintain its initial position. The same is true when the vehicle suddenly turns a corner; you are thrown to one side because your body is still trying to go straight ahead.

The inertia of an object depends on its mass. The greater the mass, the greater is its inertia, or the greater is its resistance to a change in its motion. Because of inertia, an outside force must always be supplied to cause motion or slow it down. And, of course, the heavier the body, the greater must be the force. Supertankers on the ocean take over 10 km to stop when moving at normal speeds. If you are stopped at the traffic lights next to a large truck, you can accelerate much more quickly than the truck. As your car is much lighter, it requires less force to speed it up.

Figure 4.14 demonstrates the principle of inertia. If the paper is pulled out rapidly, the mass hardly moves due to its inertia.

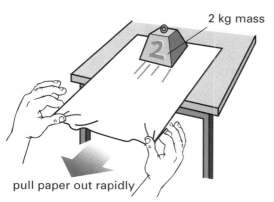

Figure 4.14 Demonstrating inertia

Newton was one of the first scientists to recognise inertia. His first law of motion is often called the law of inertia.

A body will stay at rest, or continue moving at a constant velocity in a straight line, unless an external force acts on the body.

Newton's second law

Experiments had shown that the more massive an object, the greater the force required to accelerate it. An object with twice the mass required twice the force to accelerate it to a certain velocity. So there are two factors that affect the acceleration of an object: the net force and the mass (see Figure 4.15).

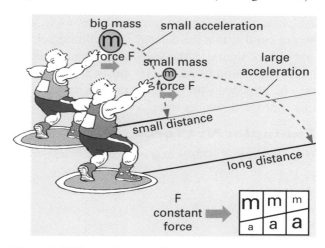

Figure 4.15 Newton's second law

Newton was the first person to work out a mathematical relationship between the force and the acceleration it produces on a body. The formula linking them is:

$$F = ma$$

where F = force, measured in newtons (N)

m = mass, measured in kilograms (kg)

a = acceleration, measured in metres/second^2 (m/s^2)

This equation is the mathematical expression of Newton's second law of motion.

The acceleration of a body depends directly on the size of the net force and inversely on the mass of the body.

Road designers and car manufacturers know how important forces are to saving lives. If a car travelling at speed hits a hard object (such as a wall, tree or other car), large forces are involved in bringing the car to a halt. The large change in speed in such a short time requires a large force. These forces cause extreme damage to the car and may kill its occupants. By building vehicles with crumple zones (which can absorb some of the impact), the time it takes to bring the car to a stop is increased. This lessens the forces produced and, hopefully, saves a few lives. Seatbelts are also important. These secure the occupants so as to reduce impact injuries that are caused by inertial motion. A sudden stop can lead to unrestrained occupants continuing to move forwards and crashing into the fixed parts of the car such as the dashboard or windscreen.

Poles and road signs are often located so that vehicles are unlikely to hit them. Many sign posts are frangible. That is, in the event of a vehicle collision the posts are designed to fracture, break away, give way or bend so that the damage to a colliding vehicle and risk of injury to the vehicle's occupants, upon impact, are minimised. Larger posts and supports may be provided with mechanisms designed to yield in a controlled manner upon collision.

Example: Net force

If a net force of 1000 N acts on a 200-kg body, what is its acceleration?

Answer:

$F = 1000$ N

$m = 200$ kg

$F = ma$

$1000 = 200a$

$a = 5$ m/s^2

 Experiment 2

Friction and acceleration

Aim

> To investigate the motion of an object sliding down smooth and rough inclined planes

Method

1. Assemble the apparatus as shown in Figure 4.16, using the smooth ramp first.

2. Before collecting any measurements, work out an appropriate angle (e.g. ~20°) at which to clamp each ramp so that the object slides smoothly down. Use this same angle for both experiments.

3. Start with the smooth ramp. Mark intervals of 10 cm along the ramp starting at the top.

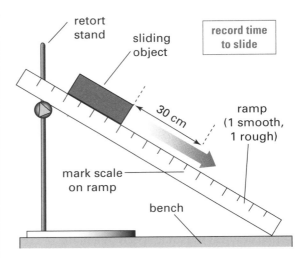

Figure 4.16 Testing for friction

4. Place the object at the top of the slope and release it. Use a suitable method to time how long it takes for the object to slide 30 cm, 60 cm, 90 cm and so on. Record the distance travelled and the time taken for each run.

5. Repeat this experiment using the ramp with the rough surface.

Results

Possible results are shown below:

> distance travelled (cm)

| 30 | 60 | 90 | 120 |

> time on smooth slope (s)

| 3.16 | 4.47 | 5.48 | 6.32 |

> time on rough slope (s)

| 3.87 | 5.48 | 6.71 | 7.75. |

Analysis

1. Use the collected data to copy and complete Table 4.3. Some data has been calculated for you.

Table 4.3 Friction and acceleration experiment

	Smooth surface	Rough surface
time to travel the first 30 cm (s)	3.16	
time to travel the second 30 cm (s)	4.47 − 3.16 = 1.31	
time to travel the third 30 cm (s)		
time to travel the last 30 cm (s)		

2. Determine the type of motion for each surface.

Go to pp. 245–246 to check your answers.

Conclusion

 Write a suitable conclusion.

Go to p. 246 to check your answer.

Newton's third law

Newton discovered that forces always occur in pairs. They are called action–reaction pairs. This idea is expressed in Newton's third law.

To every action there is an equal and opposite reaction.

Example 1: Ball fired from a cannon

A ball can be projected from a cannon by igniting gunpowder to produce an explosive force. This explosive force is the action force which acts on the ball as shown in Figure 4.17. At the same time, the ball exerts an equal and opposite reaction force on the cannon. Because a net force acts on the ball, it accelerates forwards out of the cannon. Because of the reaction force acting backwards on the cannon, the cannon recoils. In some modern weapons, including cannons, recoil dampening mechanisms inside the gun absorb some of this recoil force.

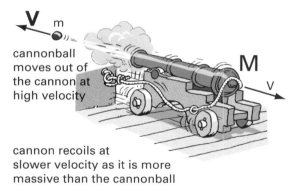

cannonball moves out of the cannon at high velocity

cannon recoils at slower velocity as it is more massive than the cannonball

Figure 4.17 A recoiling cannon. On wooden naval war ships, cannons were tied to the side of the ship with breech ropes to control the recoil.

Example 2: Sprinting from rest in a 100-m race

The muscles in the runner's legs and feet exert an action force (backwards) on the track. At the same time, the track exerts an equal and opposite reaction force on the runner. Because a net force acts on the runner, he will accelerate out of the blocks and along the track. The same thing happens at each contact with the ground. Note that the action force applied to the track is actually applied to the whole Earth, which is so massive that its acceleration is essentially unobservable.

Newton's third law of motion is used in propelling rockets. Rockets move forwards by expelling gases produced in a combustion chamber. The combustible propellant contains both fuel and an oxidiser. An oxidiser is a chemical that allows the fuel to burn without oxygen. A rocket engine, therefore, is self-contained and is the only type of device suitable for flight propulsion in outer space. The thrust is the force that pushes on the rocket to cause it to move. The amount of thrust developed by the rocket motor depends mainly on two factors:

- the speed the gases leave the combustion chamber
- the mass of the burning gases.

The biggest challenge is getting the rocket to escape the gravitational pull of the Earth. For this, powerful motors are needed as well as plenty of fuel. Rockets destined for space have two, three or four solid-fuel boosters side-by-side with the main engine. When the boosters have used up all their fuel, they are designed to fall away. The fuel in the main engine is also used up, about 10 minutes after lift-off. This first stage falls off and engines in the second stage take over. This way, the mass of the rocket can be minimised with the remaining fuel taking the rocket further afield once it has escaped Earth's gravity. Rockets that have parts designed to fall off are called multistage rockets. Figure 4.18 shows the action and reaction forces involved in the motion of a rocket.

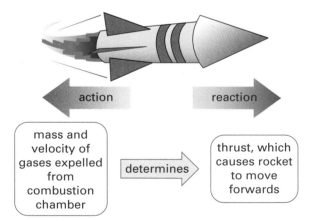

action   reaction

mass and velocity of gases expelled from combustion chamber → determines → thrust, which causes rocket to move forwards

Figure 4.18 Action and reaction forces act on different bodies.

Part A: Knowledge

1. The four-wheeled carriage shown below in Figure 4.19 was proposed as a practical illustration of Newton's third law of motion. It was powered by a jet of steam from a backward-pointing nozzle connected to a round boiler. Which of the following adjustments would have the *least* effect in making the carriage move faster? *(1 mark)*

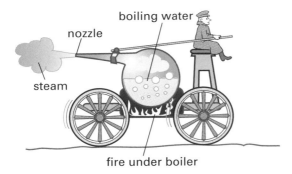

Figure 4.19 Steam-powered vehicle

A increasing the amount of water in the boiler
B increasing the heat under the boiler
C reducing the friction by having wheels with ball bearings
D making the nozzle narrower

2. Figure 4.20 shows the velocity of a cyclist over the first 25 seconds of a race. Which of the following statements is true? *(1 mark)*

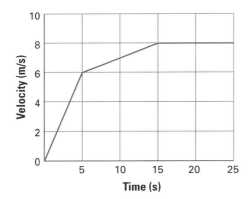

Figure 4.20 Velocity versus time for a cyclist

A The cyclist stopped accelerating after 15 seconds.
B The cyclist was travelling faster at first, but slowed down in stages.

C The distance covered in the first 5 seconds is greater than the distance between 20 to 25 seconds.
D The cyclist stopped cycling after 25 seconds.

3. A bicycle and its rider are moving along a smooth, straight road at a constant speed of 8 m/s. Which statement is true about the bicycle? *(1 mark)*
A The motion of the bicycle illustrates Newton's first law.
B The bicycle is subject to an unbalanced force.
C The force of friction on the road is greater than the force being applied to the wheels.
D The force of gravity acting on the bicycle is balanced by the force applied to the pedals.

4. A man applies a 50-N force to the side of a heavy crate which rests on the road. The crate does not move, even though the force is acting. Select the correct statement about the crate. *(1 mark)*
A There is a net force acting on the crate.
B The crate pushes back on the man with a force of 50 N.
C The force of gravity acting on the crate is 50 N.
D The frictional force between the floor and crate is much less than 50 N.

5. A heavy rock (weight = 800 N) is placed on a table and the tabletop sags under the weight of the rock. Eventually the tabletop stops sagging. Which statement is true? *(1 mark)*
A The weight of the rock is greater than the force applied by the table on the rock.
B There is an unbalanced force on the tabletop even when the sagging stops.
C Once the sagging stops, the force acting on the table is less than 800 N.
D After sagging stops, the force of the tabletop on the rock equals the force of the rock on the tabletop.

6. Complete the following restricted-response questions using the appropriate word.
(1 mark for each part)
a) A person could not walk along the ground without the assistance of .... forces.
b) The force acting on an iron bar in a magnetic field is an example of a .... force rather than a contact force.

c) The average speed of a moving vehicle is equal to the .... travelled divided by the time taken.

d) The statement 'For every action there is an equal and opposite reaction' is known as Newton's .... law.

e) A car is .... if its speed changes from 20 m/s to 15 m/s in 3 seconds.

7. Use the code letters to match the terms or phrases in each column. *(1 mark for each part)*

Column 1		Column 2	
A	acceleration	F	field force
B	gravity	G	balanced force
C	newton	H	reaction force
D	stationary object	I	change in velocity
E	cannon recoil	J	unit of force

Part B: Skills

8. The graph in Figure 4.21 shows the speed at which different objects fall through air, comparing it to freefall in a vacuum. If gravity acts equally for all objects, why are the graphs different for different things? *(2 marks)*

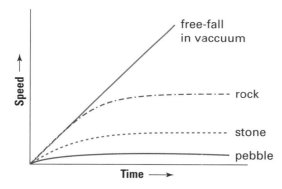

Figure 4.21 Speeds of falling objects

9. Rhiannon and Erin both leave home at 9 am. By 11 am, Rhiannon has covered twice the distance that Erin has. What can you say about the average speed of both girls? *(1 mark)*

10. A student set up the equipment shown in Figure 4.22.

a) Suggest an aim for this experiment. *(1 mark)*

b) List the steps of the method the student should have written in her notebook. *(2 marks)*

c) Draw the pattern of dots you would expect to see on the ticker tape. *(1 mark)*

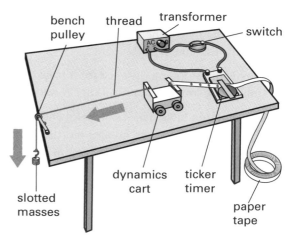

Figure 4.22 Motion experiment

11. A truck is dripping oil onto the road at a regular rate. Figure 4.23 shows the drips of oil at different times into the truck's journey.

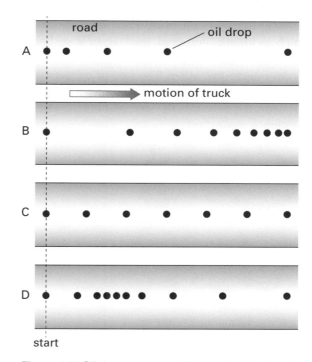

Figure 4.23 Oil drops on a road from a leaking truck

a) Which diagram shows the truck travelling at a constant speed? *(1 mark)*

b) Which diagram shows the truck getting faster? *(1 mark)*

c) Which diagram shows the truck decelerating? *(1 mark)*

d) Describe the truck's motion for the remaining diagram. *(1 mark)*

12. A fisherman trying to land a heavy fish often breaks the nylon line if he tries to bring it in too quickly. Explain. *(1 mark)*

13. Why is the stopping distance for a truck or a train much longer than for a car? *(1 mark)*

14. Two children have masses of 30 kg and 50 kg.
    a) Which child has the greater inertia? *(1 mark)*
    b) The two children are travelling in a car which suddenly brakes. Which child will show the greatest tendency to be thrown forwards? *(1 mark)*
    c) Suggest how inertia is related to whiplash injuries of the neck in car accidents. *(1 mark)*

Go to pp. 246–247 to check your answers.

4.4 Law of energy conservation

Energy in a system may take on various forms such as kinetic, potential, nuclear, heat or light (see Figure 4.24). These different forms can be changed from one to the other. The law of conservation of energy states that energy may neither be created nor destroyed. Therefore, the sum of all the energies in a system is a constant.

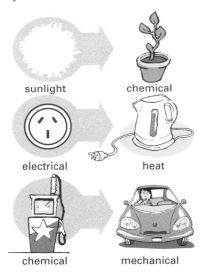

Figure 4.24 Examples of energy transformations

Calculating kinetic energy

The kinetic energy of an object is the energy which it possesses due to its motion. It is the work needed to accelerate a body of a certain mass from rest to a given velocity. It relies on two factors: its mass and how fast it is travelling.

The kinetic energy (KE) of a body of mass and speed of velocity is given by the formula:

$$KE = \tfrac{1}{2}mv^2$$

where m = mass, measured in kilograms (kg)
       v = velocity, measured in metres per second (m/s)

Kinetic energy is measured in joules (J).

Example 1: Kinetic energy

Calculate the kinetic energy of a body of mass 10 kg that is moving with a velocity of 6 m/s.

Answer:

$m = 10$ kg, $v = 6$ m/s

$$\begin{aligned} KE &= \tfrac{1}{2}mv^2 \\ &= \tfrac{1}{2} \times 10 \times 6^2 \\ &= 180 \text{ J} \end{aligned}$$

Example 2: Mass

Ball P of mass 4 kg is moving at 8 m/s. Ball R has the same kinetic energy as ball P but is moving at 4 m/s. What is the mass of ball R?

Answer:

Kinetic energy of ball P is

$$\begin{aligned} KE(P) &= \tfrac{1}{2}mv^2 \\ &= \tfrac{1}{2} \times 4 \times 8^2 \\ &= 128 \text{ J} \end{aligned}$$

Therefore, kinetic energy of ball R is KE(R) = 128 J

Now, $128 = \tfrac{1}{2} \times m \times 4^2$

Solve for m: $m = 2 \times \dfrac{128}{16}$

$= 16$ kg

The mass of ball R is 16 kg.

Example 3: Energy

A 1200-kg car is travelling at 65 km/h. Calculate its kinetic energy. How much energy is required to bring the car to rest?

Answer: In order to use the formula $KE = \tfrac{1}{2}mv^2$, mass needs to be in kg, and velocity in m/s. So change 65 km/h to m/s first.

$$\dfrac{65 \text{ km}}{h} = \dfrac{65 \text{ km}}{h} \times \dfrac{1000 \text{ m}}{1 \text{ km}} \times \dfrac{1 \text{ h}}{60 \text{ min}} \times \dfrac{1 \text{ min}}{60 \text{ s}}$$

$= 18$ m/s

And so $$\begin{aligned} KE &= \tfrac{1}{2} \times 1200 \times 18^2 \\ &= 194\,400 \text{ J (or 194.4 kJ)} \end{aligned}$$

This is the energy required to accelerate the car from rest to a speed of 65 km/h. And this amount of energy is required to return the car to the stationary position.

Calculating gravitational potential energy

The energy that is stored by an object in the gravitational field is called gravitational potential energy (GPE), or potential energy due to gravity. This is the energy an object has because of its position. The GPE of a body of mass held at a height above the ground on Earth where the acceleration due to gravity is $9.8 \, \text{m/s}^2$, is given by the formula:

$$\text{GPE} = mgh$$

where m = mass, measured in kilograms (kg)

h = height, measured in metres (m)

g = acceleration due to gravity, measured in metres/second^2 (m/s^2)

The value of g varies from one planet to another. It is much lower on the Moon compared with the Earth. On Earth the value of g also varies slightly from one place to another.

Example: GPE

Calculate the GPE of a 5-kg mass held at a position 100 m above the Earth's surface.

Answer:

m = 5 kg

g = 9.8 m/s^2

h = 100 m

GPE = mgh = 5 × 9.8 × 100 = 4900 J = 4.9 kJ

In this example, the GPE was compared to a point on the Earth's surface, which is arbitrarily taken to have a GPE of zero. In this case, the 5-kg mass has a GPE that is 4.9 kJ *more* than if it was placed at ground level. In some books the formula for GPE is given with h shown as Δh. The Greek letter delta, Δ, stands for 'change in'. So by moving the 5-kg mass from ground level to a height of 100 m ($\Delta h = 100$), it has acquired 4.9 kJ more energy. This is equal to the work done against gravity to bring a mass to a given point above ground level.

Comparing kinetic and gravitational potential energy

Part of the fun of a roller-coaster is its changing speed. The roller-coaster and its passengers are hauled to the top of the first and highest point on the ride. At this highest point the roller-coaster is initially stationary, so its kinetic energy is zero. But being at its highest point, its potential energy is at its maximum. Once it starts moving down the slope, some of this potential energy is converted into kinetic energy. So as the potential energy decreases, its kinetic energy, and hence the roller-coaster's speed, increases. At the bottom of the ride, the roller-coaster has attained its maximum kinetic energy. As the roller-coaster climbs, some of this kinetic energy is converted back to potential energy. This is illustrated in Figure 4.25.

But always: GPE + KE = constant. (In order to keep it simple, we assume all the energy transforms from GPE to KE and vice versa. Of course, in any real situation, there will be energy losses such as those due to friction, heat and sound.)

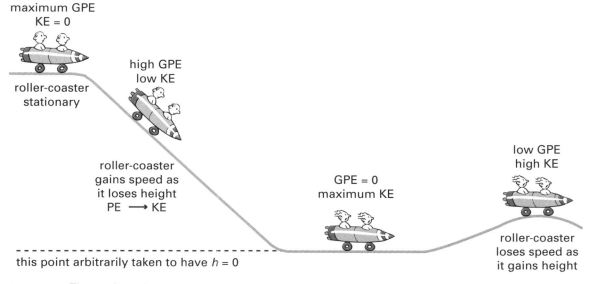

maximum GPE
KE = 0

roller-coaster
stationary

high GPE
low KE

roller-coaster
gains speed as
it loses height
PE ⟶ KE

GPE = 0
maximum KE

low GPE
high KE

roller-coaster
loses speed as
it gains height

this point arbitrarily taken to have h = 0

Figure 4.25 The total gravitational potential energy and kinetic energy remain constant.

Example: GPE and KE

A 10-kg object is dropped from a height of 100 m, as shown in Figure 4.26.

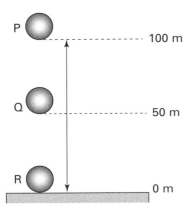

Figure 4.26 A 10-kg object dropped from 100 m

1. Calculate the gravitational potential energy of the object at positions P, Q and R.
2. Calculate the kinetic energy of the object at position Q. What assumption are you making?
3. Calculate the speed of the object at position Q.
4. What happens to the kinetic energy of the object once it hits the ground at R?

Answer:

1. At P, GPE $= mgh$
   $= 10 \times 9.8 \times 100$
   $= 9800$ J
   (Remember, on Earth $g = 9.8$ m/s^2).
   At Q, GPE $= mgh$
   $= 10 \times 9.8 \times 50$
   $= 4900$ J
   At R, GPE $= mgh$
   $= 10 \times 9.8 \times 0$
   $= 0$ J

2. It is assumed that the change in potential energy in dropping from P to Q is completely converted into kinetic energy. So:
   KE $= \frac{1}{2}mv^2$
   $= 9800 - 4900$
   $= 4900$ J

3. Since $\frac{1}{2}mv^2 = 4900$ J, then
   $\frac{1}{2} \times 10 \times v^2 = 4900$
   and so, $v^2 = \dfrac{4900}{5} = 980$
   $\therefore v = \sqrt{980} = 31.3$ m/s

4. As the object comes to a complete stop, the kinetic energy is transformed into sound and heat, deforming the ground and/or the ball.

4.5 Energy transfers and transformations

When energy is transformed from one form to another, some of the energy is always changed into some other form of energy that is not useful. For example, petrol contains stored chemical energy (chemical potential energy). Inside the car's engine, the chemical bonds containing this energy are broken and the energy released. Only about 15 to 25% of the energy from the fuel you put in your tank gets used to move your car down the road. The remaining energy is lost to engine and other inefficiencies, overcoming friction and resistance, heat and idling. The potential is there for car manufacturers to improve fuel efficiency with advanced technologies.

The same is true in generating and using electricity. This is why the Australian government has moved to replace incandescent light globes with compact fluorescent globes, where the overall efficiency increases significantly. Inefficient incandescent light bulbs were phased out by 2010. Only about 7% of the energy entering the power plant eventually lights this compact fluorescent bulb. The remaining 93% is lost along the way, mostly as heat (see Figure 4.27).

At every transformation, there will be energy losses. Improving the energy efficiency of appliances and products in all sectors (residential, commercial and industrial) has significant economic and environmental benefits.

Efficiency of machines

Energy conversion processes are never completely efficient. Considerable energy is usually wasted, often in the form of heat. The energy efficiency of a machine can be determined by comparing the useful output of energy to the input of energy. This efficiency is usually expressed as a percentage. If a machine is 80% efficient then 20% of the input energy is wasted, often in the form of heat.

Machines allow you to use your energy more conveniently, but they never save energy. A simple machine spreads the same amount of energy over a longer period of time, ultimately making the task easier. No matter how efficient the machine, the amount of energy put into the system is less than the amount of energy recovered. Energy is always wasted to overcome the friction in the system. No machine is 100% efficient.

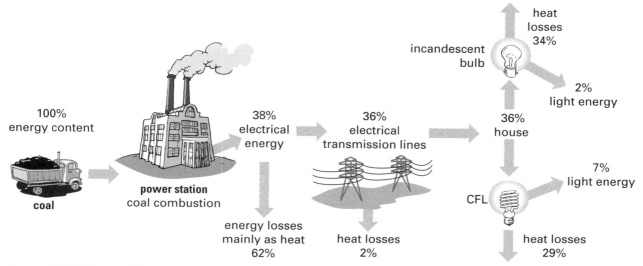

Figure 4.27 Efficiency of light bulbs.

How well a machine uses energy can be described in terms of its efficiency:

$$\text{efficiency} = \frac{\text{energy output}}{\text{energy input}} \times \frac{100}{1}$$

Here are some examples of energy efficiency.

Compact fluorescent lights

When a given quantity of electrical energy is supplied to a compact fluorescent light (CFL) bulb such as that shown in Figure 4.28, it is transformed into light energy and heat energy. For a CFL bulb, about 15 to 20% of the electrical energy is converted into useful light energy. Older-style incandescent lamps that produce light by heating a tungsten wire are about four times less efficient than CFL bulbs in converting electrical energy into light energy.

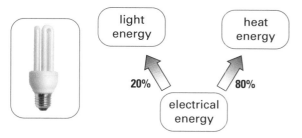

Figure 4.28 CFL bulbs waste less energy than incandescent lamps.

Car petrol engine

When a car engine burns petrol, only about 25% of the chemical potential energy of the fuel is transformed into useful kinetic energy in moving engine parts and rotating wheels. The remaining energy is not lost. It is converted into other energy forms such as heat energy and sound energy.

Dry cell battery

A torch dry cell battery is about 85% efficient in transforming chemical potential energy into useful electrical energy. The remaining 15% of the original energy is transformed into heat energy.

Power stations

There are various fuels that are used to generate electricity in power stations. Coal-fired power stations achieve efficiencies of 30 to 49% depending on the grade of coal. Natural gas-fired power stations achieve about 50% efficiency. Considerable amounts of heat energy are lost to the atmosphere.

Example 1: Energy input

A simple machine has an energy output of 200 kJ with 75% efficiency. Calculate the energy input to this machine.

Answer:

$$\text{efficiency} = \frac{\text{energy output}}{\text{energy input}} \times \frac{100}{1}$$

$$75 = \frac{200}{\text{energy input}} \times \frac{100}{1}$$

Therefore, energy input $= 200 \times \dfrac{100}{75} = 267$ kJ.

In the real world, the efficiency of a machine is never 100%. That is, a machine will never do work for you. The best you can hope for is that you do not have to put much more work into a machine than you get out. You can calculate efficiency by comparing work out to work in.

Example 2: Efficiency

A ramp is a simple kind of machine.

Use the following equation with the information supplied in Figure 4.29 to calculate the efficiency of using a ramp:

$$\text{efficiency} = \frac{\text{energy output}}{\text{energy input}} \times \frac{100}{1}$$

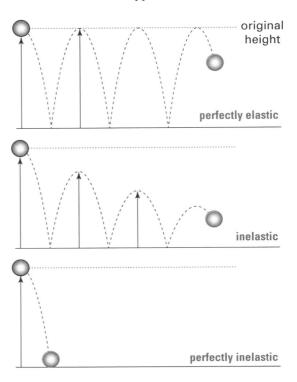

energy required = 10 J

energy required = 12 J

Figure 4.29 Energy required to lift a box with and without a ramp

Answer: In order to push the box up the ramp, you must do 12 J of work but really only get out the equivalent of 10 J.

$$\text{efficiency} = \frac{10}{12} \times 100$$
$$= 83.3\%$$

Even though ramps are not 100% efficient, they allow you to use less force while pushing the box through a greater distance.

An Australian government program, the Energy Rating Label, is an initiative to reduce greenhouse gas emissions, and for consumers to save on energy costs. This mandatory labelling covers major electrical appliances and requires that they display an energy star rating label (1 to 6 stars) as shown in Figure 4.30.

Figure 4.30 Energy labelling for major appliances in Australia was introduced in 1986 and modified in 2010 so that an appliance that was rated as 2.5 stars is now labelled as 1 star.

Energy changes in car crashes and pendulums

There are various types of collisions. An elastic collision is an encounter between two objects in which the total kinetic energy of the two bodies after the encounter is equal to their total kinetic energy before the encounter. Atoms bounce off each other in elastic collisions. But dropping a ball from a height is not perfectly elastic as the height reached after each bounce decreases. Energy is being lost to the system at each bounce and along the way. Dropping a lump of plasticine as shown in Figure 4.31 illustrates these three collision types.

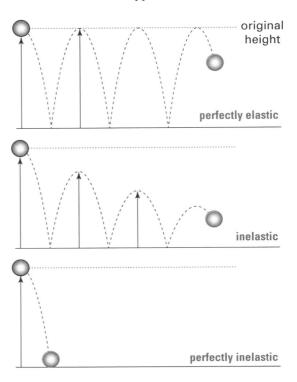

Figure 4.31 What can happen during a collision

Scientists study these types of collision and the energy transformations in them.

Car crashes

A typical car crash such as that shown in Figure 4.32 is an example of an inelastic collision. The car does not bounce off the tree, or another car, then goes on its merry way.

Consider a 1-t (= 1000 kg) car that is travelling at 90 km/h (= 25 m/s) when it hits a tree. The tree, being a large solid, does not give way and the front of the car crumples 1.5 m while the car is coming to rest.

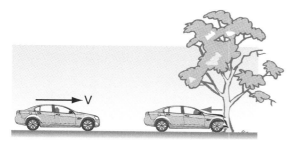

Figure 4.32 A car crashing into a tree

Before the collision, the kinetic energy of this car is:

$$KE = \frac{1}{2}mv^2$$
$$= \frac{1}{2} \times 1000 \times 25^2$$
$$= 312\,500 \text{ J}$$

After the collision, its kinetic energy is 0 J. This energy was transformed in the collision by damaging the tree, crumpling the car and making a lot of noise.

Crumple zones are a structural feature in modern vehicles. They are designed to absorb the energy from an impact by controlled deformation, and work by managing the energy in a crash, absorbing it within the outer parts of the vehicle. In this way it is not directly transmitted to the occupants, while also preventing intrusion into or deformation of the passenger cabin. Crumple zones are usually located in the front part of the vehicle, absorbing the impact of a head-on collision, though they may be found elsewhere.

As the car decelerates over a very short distance (and time), passengers and objects within the car will continue moving forwards at that direction and speed (Newton's first law of motion). Even small, unrestrained contents will continue forwards due to inertia. They may impact the interior of the vehicle, or passengers, with a force many times their normal weight. These missiles may become lethal.

Consider the car in the previous example. The car travelling at 25 m/s takes 1.5 m to come to rest. The deceleration required is 208 m/s² and the force applied to the 60-kg person is 60 × 208 = 12 480 N. This is over 20 times their weight force.

Another safety device is the seatbelt. Seatbelts restrain the occupants so they don't fly through the windshield (see Figure 4.33). They also absorb the passenger's inertial energy as they stretch during an impact. A person whose body is decelerated more slowly due to the crumple zone (and a stretching seatbelt) over a longer time period more often survives than a passenger whose body impacts a hard,

metal car body or dashboard that has come to a halt nearly instantaneously. A longer stopping distance decreases the impact force.

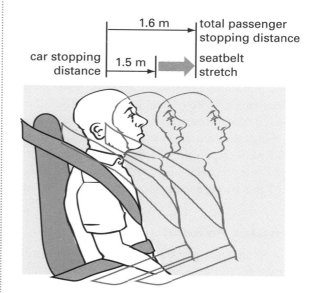

Figure 4.33 Seatbelt restraints

Suppose the seatbelt stretches 0.1 m during the crash. The passenger will stop in 1.5 + 0.1 = 1.6 m and the deceleration of the passenger is 195 m/s². The force on the person is F = 60 × 195 = 11 700 N. This improves the person's survival chances, while restraining the person in their seat.

A third safety feature is also incorporated. All new cars sold are required to have airbags on both driver and passenger sides. Tests show that airbags reduce the risk of dying in a direct frontal crash by over 30%. Now some cars have six or even eight airbags, to protect from crashes occurring from any number of directions. Airbags are designed to deploy as shown in Figure 4.34 so the driver or passenger has a soft cushion to strike, rather than a hard surface.

Figure 4.34 Airbags cushion a person's moving body, preventing sudden impact.

For over 30 years now, using technology developed for the aerospace and nuclear industries, car makers have used complex computer crash simulation studies to simulate the crash behaviour of individual car body components, and the car as a whole. This has led to improved and safer car designs.

A swinging pendulum

A simple pendulum consists of a weight suspended on a rod, string or wire of negligible mass. The other end is fixed. When the weight or bob is moved and let go, the pendulum will swing back and forth in a regular periodic motion. How fast the pendulum oscillates (moves back and forth) depends on the length of the string and on the acceleration due to gravity.

Example: Pendulum

Figure 4.35 shows a pendulum swinging backwards and forwards. The bob is released at A and swings down to B and then C. The bob then returns back to A. Identify the locations of maximum gravitational potential energy and kinetic energy and explain how this process illustrates the law of energy conservation.

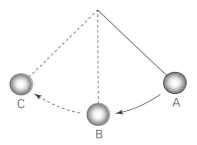

Figure 4.35 A swinging pendulum

Answer: A pendulum swinging back and forth changes gravitational potential energy into kinetic energy and back again. As Figure 4.36 shows, at A and C the gravitational potential energy is at a maximum and the kinetic energy of the bob is zero. At B the gravitational potential energy is zero and the kinetic energy of the bob is at a maximum as it is moving with its greatest speed at that point.

As time goes on, after each swing it doesn't return to the same height as before because friction and the resistance of the air use up some of the energy. These are damping forces. But this energy is not lost. It is merely changed in form. Energy is always conserved.

A swinging pendulum can be considered an isolated system. This is where there is no exchange of matter or energy between the system and its environment.

The fact that the pendulum ultimately loses energy to its surroundings indicates it is not completely isolated.

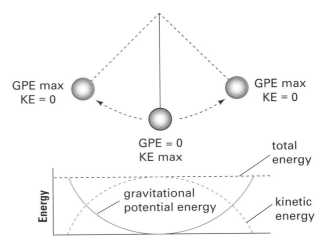

Figure 4.36 In a simple pendulum, energy oscillates between gravitational potential energy and kinetic energy; the total energy (ignoring minor losses) remains the same.

Energy-efficient buildings

Energy-efficient buildings (including houses) can make cost savings all around. Even if the costs of adopting energy-saving techniques are higher than conventional methods, they can be offset against the energy savings made over time. These buildings generally require less energy to construct, maintain, heat, cool, light and ventilate. Currently the energy used by Australian buildings accounts for around 20% of the country's greenhouse gas emissions, with half of that coming from homes.

Here are some factors to consider.

> A north-facing building (in the southern hemisphere, give or take up to 30° either side) allows maximum sunlight to enter through windows in the northerly wall in winter. It is also the easiest to prevent summer sunlight from entering. But most owners don't have control over the building's orientation.

> Insulation can be placed in the roof cavity as well as in hollow walls. Double-glazed windows can control temperature as do ceiling fans. Curtains and blinds are also useful in controlling the amount of heat. Figure 4.37 shows heat losses through a typical house.

> Draughts can allow heat to enter in summer and exit in winter. Use airtight construction detailing,

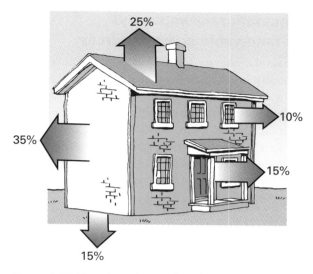

Figure 4.37 Most heat losses in a house occur through the ceiling and walls.

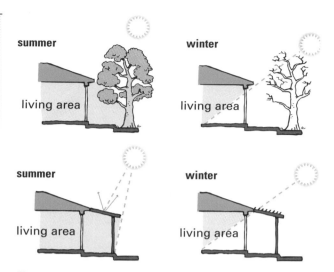

Figure 4.38 How plants and the Sun's angle determine the amount of heat entering a house

particularly at wall–ceiling and wall–floor junctions.

- For best performance during the colder winter in temperate climate zones, high thermal mass materials such as concrete, tiles and masonry walls can be used during building. These store heat energy during the day and release it back into the building at night.
- Building eaves, or some other shading, can be designed so that sunlight enters the building through the north-facing windows at the beginning of winter, but is prevented from entering during summer.
- Permitting winter sunlight entry into the building allows for a longer daily natural light, thereby cutting down on artificial lighting.
- Appropriate use of vegetation can shade building areas and/or naturally funnel cooling breezes to the building. Deciduous trees can provide much shade during summer while allowing light through in winter and provide passive heat (see Figure 4.38).
- A number of changes could be made to external lighting. It could be powered by solar energy. Energy-consuming halogen lights and older-style fluorescent tubes and incandescent lights could be replaced by LED lights. Little-used common areas could use motion sensors to trigger lights. Car parks could be more efficiently lit.
- Flow-controlled shower heads and tap fittings can be installed.

- Solar water heaters save energy by heating and storing water during daylight hours. Water heating is a major cost of any household. During low solar activity, the water temperature in the tank can be boosted with the aid of an electric element or gas booster, often operating during the less expensive off-peak periods.
- Black pipe pool heaters can heat the water in a swimming pool to around 40 °C. Black objects absorb more heat than light-coloured objects. A series of black pipes containing water are mounted on a roof and the Sun's energy heats the pipes and water. The warm water is then pumped between a storage tank and the pool.
- Solar space air heating systems allow heated air to circulate around cold rooms in winter. There are schemes where heated air can be stored during the day to be released at night.
- Photovoltaic (PV) power systems allow banks of solar cells to capture sunlight by striking a sandwich of semiconductor materials, thus generating electricity. This is of particular advantage for buildings in remote areas (see Figure 4.39).
- When buildings reach the end of their useful life, rather than demolishing and consigning to landfills, a method of deconstruction harvests what would be considered 'waste' and recycles it into useful building materials.

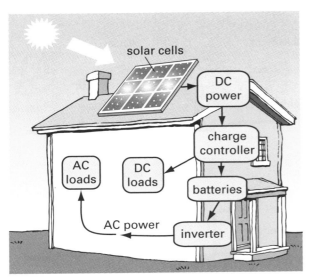

Figure 4.39 Making use of the free energy from the Sun

Comparing renewable and non-renewable energy sources

Renewable energy is self-sustaining energy and essentially inexhaustible. These sources include the Sun, water, wind and geothermal. Non-renewable energy sources are only available once and can't be replaced. The main sources include fossil fuels such as oil, coal and natural gas. As these fossil fuels are efficient energy sources, they are widely used. Table 4.4 outlines the features of some renewable and non-renewable energy sources.

However, in spite of their popularity, ease of use and relative low cost, non-renewable sources are polluting and contribute to excessive amounts of carbon in the atmosphere. On the other hand, renewable energy sources are cleaner, but can be difficult and often expensive to harness and currently are not as efficient.

Table 4.4 Some renewable and non-renewable resources

Non-renewable energy sources	Some features
oil	This is a fossil fuel formed more than 300 million years ago by decaying diatoms. These sea creatures, the size of a pin head, can convert sunlight directly into stored energy.
coal	Coal is abundant in Australia and considerably less costly than other energy sources. Black coal reserves are mostly in Queensland and New South Wales; brown coal is mostly in Victoria.
natural gas	This is made up mostly of methane, and is highly flammable. Usually found near petroleum underground, it often has no odour and is colourless.
nuclear	Mostly this form of energy comes from nuclear fission, when heavy radioactive nuclei break apart when struck by neutrons. It produces around 11% of the world's energy needs.
hydrogen	Modern rockets and space shuttles are powered by hydrogen. Its usefulness lies in its ability to store energy at high densities and to release it on demand.
coal seam gas	Australia has rich deposits of coal seam gas, currently providing 90% of Queensland's gas supplies. It consists of mainly methane with trace quantities of other gases. Gas is removed from underground coal seams by hydraulic fracturing.

Renewable energy sources	Some features
solar	Earth receives 5.6×10^{18} MJ (megajoules) of solar radiation each year. Some of this can be used to heat water or changed directly to an electric current by photovoltaic cells.
wind	The uneven heating of the Earth by the Sun causes air to move. The energy of this can be harnessed. Some areas are better placed for wind farms.
geothermal	Geothermal heat is stored in rock, especially in regions close to the boundaries of tectonic plates such as Japan and New Zealand. Australia's hot dry rock resources are in granite rock layers several kilometres underground.
tidal	The tide moves a huge amount of water twice each day, and harnessing it could provide a great deal of energy. While this supply is reliable and plentiful, converting it into useful electrical power poses challenges.
biomass	Living material (plants, animals, fungi, bacteria) represents an enormous store of energy. The original source of this energy is the Sun.
hydroelectric	Hydroelectricity is generated by using the gravitational force of falling or flowing water. It is the most widely used form of renewable energy, accounting for almost a quarter of all renewable sources.

It is for these reasons that the world has been slow to change. Non-renewable sources are polluting and contribute to excessive amounts of carbon in the atmosphere. Tables 4.5 and 4.6 list some of the pros and cons of each of these energy sources.

Nevertheless, people are experimenting with and using alternative energies. Governments and organisations, mindful of these depleting resources and of environmental damage to non-renewable energy sources, are funding research into alternative energy sources to fuel power stations and generate electricity. They are also funding the development of vehicles that utilise these fuels. Over half of the world's electricity is currently made by burning fossil fuels, a situation that is likely to change.

Bio-derived and synthetic fuels are being considered in the aircraft industry for their potential to replace or supplement conventional jet fuels, especially as current fuels are becoming more expensive. Biofuels show significant promise which could be easily integrated into present and future aircraft with little or no modification to current designs. While progress on alternative jet fuels is advanced, commercialisation is now the major challenge.

As non-renewable energy sources become scarcer and more expensive, and as research into alternative renewable energy sources makes them more efficient and cheaper, a point will come where environmentally friendly energy becomes the preferred option. The time to act is now; not when we have almost depleted our supply of fossil fuels. Alternative energy supply mechanisms need to be in place and functioning well before existing fuel supplies run out.

Table 4.5 Pros and cons of non-renewable energy sources

Advantages	Disadvantages
• They are cheap and easy to use. • Currently, these energy sources have little or no competition at all. They are widely available and relatively inexpensive. • It is fairly cheap to convert from one type of energy to another (e.g. burning coal to produce electricity). • Small amounts of nuclear fuel produce large amounts of power.	• Energy sources will be depleted at some time in the near future. • The rate at which such resources are being used can have serious environmental consequences. • These sources release toxic gases into the atmosphere when burnt and are the major cause for global warming. • Countries without an adequate supply are reliant on others for their energy sources. • Prices of these sources are increasing as they become scarcer.

Table 4.6 Pros and cons of renewable energy sources

Advantages	Disadvantages
• Energy sources are abundantly available and free to use. • The sources of energy are not limited and won't be depleted. • They have low carbon emissions and are therefore environment friendly. • They help to stimulate the economy and create job opportunities. • Australia isn't reliant on another country for the supply of energy sources. • In some instances, renewable sources can cost less than using energy derived from non-renewable sources. • Over time, with improvements in technology, renewable energy start-up costs will make them competitive with other energy forms. • Governments provide tax incentives and credit deductions for adopting renewable energy forms.	• Initial start-up costs can be quite steep • Some energy forms are not universal. For instance, wind farms can only be built where there is plentiful wind and no complaints from neighbours; tidal power is only practical along some coasts; hydroelectric power needs significant water and vertical drops. • Solar energy can be used during the daytime and not during night or rainy seasons. Storage batteries are required. • Geothermal energy can bring toxic chemicals beneath the Earth's surface to the top and can create environmental changes. • Building dams across rivers for hydroelectric power is very expensive and can affect natural water flow and wildlife. • Wind farms can affect bird populations as they are quite high.

4.6 Innovative energy transfer devices

For generations, household and industrial wastes were consigned to landfills. The biodegradable components of a landfill, such as paper and food wastes, decompose and emit methane, a greenhouse gas over 20 times more potent than carbon dioxide.

Now transfer stations offer an intermediate step to remove and sell recyclables (such as metals and plastics) with the remaining waste being shredded to make a 'fluff', which can be processed into alternative energy products (see Figure 4.40). Electricity is produced when the solid fluff is reacted with air under selected conditions, producing a clean fuel gas (syngas) in a process called gasification. Syngas contains CO, H_2, CO_2, H_2O and N_2. This fuel is then used in a gas engine, a gas turbine or in a steam boiler to produce electricity and/or steam.

Transport

Some 95% of all vehicle fuel in Australia is petrol and diesel. Liquefied petroleum gas (LPG), ethanol blends and biodiesel blends account for the remainder.

Alternative transport fuels provide benefits such as:

- potentially reducing vehicle emissions
- improving air quality
- providing alternative sources of supply thus supplementing mainstream fuels
- reducing our reliance on imported fuels.

LPG is a mixture of light hydrocarbon gases, mainly propane (C_3H_8) and butane (C_4H_{10}). It is a naturally occurring gas produced either directly through the processing of crude oil and natural gas or as a by-product of the petroleum refining process. It is significantly cheaper than petrol, and is supported by the federal government. Many commercial vehicles run on LPG.

Ethanol is typically used as a fuel extender and to increase octane levels in petrol. It is most commonly sold as E10 in Australia (10% ethanol, 90% petrol). There are currently three ethanol production plants in Australia: one in New South Wales and two in Queensland.

Biodiesel can be used in diesel engines, and is made from vegetable oils, animal fats and used cooking oil. It can also be produced from various non-food crops such as *Jatropha* and algae. It can be blended with conventional diesel fuel or used on its own.

Compressed natural gas (CNG) and liquefied natural gas (LNG) consist mainly of natural gas or methane (CH_4). It is produced either from gas wells or in conjunction with crude oil production. CNG and LNG are currently limited to use in heavy vehicles, such as metropolitan bus fleets, garbage trucks and line haulage.

Electric vehicles are becoming more popular. However, they currently only have a limited range before recharging. Given most daily trips are no more than 100 km, it is practical to plug the car in to a power outlet in the evening to recharge. It is feasible to use a system of battery replacements, when these are set up at petrol stations, rather

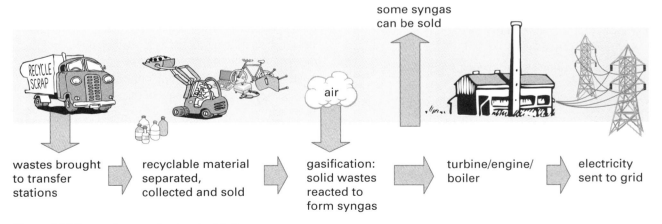

Figure 4.40 Converting wastes to electricity

some syngas can be sold

air

wastes brought to transfer stations → recyclable material separated, collected and sold → gasification: solid wastes reacted to form syngas → turbine/engine/boiler → electricity sent to grid

than battery recharging for longer journeys. One way around the problem is with hybrid vehicles (electric plus petrol). These are already successfully competing with conventional internal combustion powered cars. They have the ability to regenerate electricity when running downhill or when braking (regenerative braking). This energy is returned to the vehicle's battery.

In the mid-2000s a renewed interest in electric cars occurred mainly through concerns about rapidly rising oil prices and the need to limit greenhouse gas emissions. Vehicles powered by fuel cells are also currently getting a lot of attention.

Communication

Electricity is a convenient and versatile energy source. It was not until the advent of batteries that devices could become mobile and not fixed to where there was a power outlet. However, early batteries were large, heavy and did not deliver as much power. Especially in the last couple of decades, battery technology has improved making many devices, such as laptop computers, cameras, iPods and mobile phones smaller and easily portable. And these batteries are re-chargeable, whereas earlier batteries were not.

Mobile phones

The word 'phone' in mobile (or cell) phone is somewhat of a misnomer since these devices now are not just telephones, but game consoles, computers, cameras, app software devices and so on. But one thing is common; they all need power to work.

Nickel-cadmium batteries were very popular in the 1980s and 1990s, but they are much heavier than modern phone batteries. Some of the earlier mobile phones were attaché case size. Others were installed in vehicles due to the large battery requirements. Over the years, more energy-efficient electronics and the development of more advanced, smaller and lightweight batteries have made mobile phones hugely popular.

Additionally, due to increasing usage, the higher density of mobile phone cell sites meant that the average distance from phone to the base station became shorter. This led to increased battery life (you didn't need much transmission power) while on the move.

Current phones use many different types of batteries, the most common one being the lithium ion battery shown in Figure 4.41. These rechargeable batteries are also popular in consumer electronics. The batteries are small, light and are not affected by charging memory. That is, they can be charged without having to be fully discharged first. (Memory effect is especially observed in nickel-cadmium rechargeable batteries and causes them to hold less charge; these batteries gradually lose their maximum energy capacity if they are repeatedly recharged after being only partially discharged.) They also have one of the best energy densities, and a slow loss of charge when not in use. Table 4.7 (see the next page) lists some advantages and disadvantages of these types of batteries.

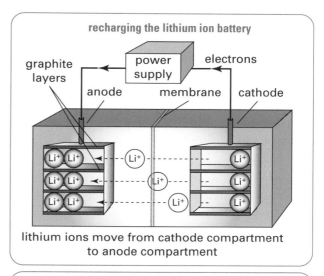

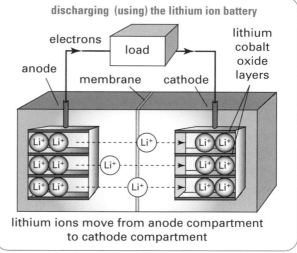

Figure 4.41 Charging and discharging a lithium ion battery

Table 4.7 Pros and cons of the lithium ion battery

Advantages	Disadvantages
• available in a wide variety of shapes and sizes • no memory effect • much lighter than other similar energy-equivalent batteries • self-discharge rate only around 5 to 10% per month • increased amount of power delivered with a low current	• limited life; capacity diminishes over time • internal resistance increases with each recharging and age • heat can increase capacity loss

Communications satellites

While mobile phones come with a charger so they can be plugged into a power outlet, communications satellites orbiting the Earth are too far away for that consideration. Communications satellites play a major role in expanding both international and domestic long-distance telephone calling, as well as television transmission, including direct broadcasts to home satellite dishes with digital television.

Satellites are powered by solar cells that have storage batteries to maintain that power when the Earth is between the satellite and the Sun (see Figure 4.42). The first spacecraft to use solar panels was launched by the United States in 1958, and the first communications satellite powered by solar cells to recharge storage batteries went into service in 1960.

Photovoltaic solar arrays are the main means of converting solar energy to electrical energy for satellites. This power is for two main purposes:

> run the sensors and other devices allowing the satellite to communicate with the Earth base
> power the propulsion system, thus keeping the satellite in its proper location.

The solar panels are closely packed with solar cells covering almost the total exposed surface. The panels themselves need a large surface area to optimise electricity generation. These panels can be pivoted as the satellite moves, thus ensuring they stay in the direct path of light rays. This can be done using a tracking mechanism. As satellite power requirements increase, efficiencies will need to be found to generate more electricity.

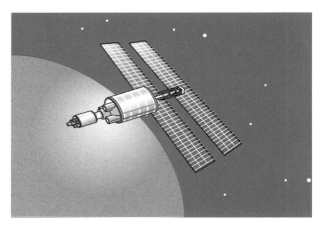

Figure 4.42 The most obvious feature of a communications satellite is its solar cell arrays to produce power.

 Experiment 3

Pendulum

Aim

> To observe energy transformations and calculate the period of oscillation of a pendulum

Method

1. Set up a simple pendulum as shown in Figure 4.43. Use a small, but heavy weight (bob) suspended using a very fine fishing line or cotton thread. Pass the line through a split cork which is clamped to the stand.

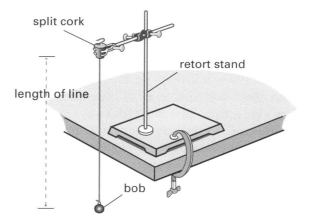

Figure 4.43 Setting up the simple pendulum

2. Look for the energy transfers as the pendulum bob swings from side to side. It goes from a gravitational store of energy at the top of its swing to kinetic energy which is greatest at the bottom of its swing. It then goes back to increasing

gravitational energy as it rises to the top of its swing on the other side.

3. Start with a length of 10 cm of line and, keeping the line taut, move the bob an angle of about 10° to one side and release. After one full swing, start the stopwatch and time 10 full swings back and forth.

4. Divide your time by 10 to calculate the time for one complete swing.

5. Adjust the lengths and repeat.

Analysis

1. What do you observe with the changing speed of the bob during its swing?

2. Complete Table 4.8 for the time of oscillation of your pendulum.

Table 4.8 Pendulum oscillation times

Line length (cm)	Time for one oscillation (s)	
10		
15		
20		
25		
30		
35		
40		
45		
50		
55		

3. Why were 10 oscillations timed, and not just one?

4. Plot your results on a grid.

5. What do you notice about the length of line and the time of each oscillation?

Go to p. 246 to check your answers.

Conclusion

Write a suitable conclusion.
Go to p. 246 to check your answer.

 Test yourself 2

Part A: Knowledge

1. Which of the following is a renewable fuel? *(1 mark)*

   A wood

   B coal

   C oil

   D uranium

2. Batteries store *(1 mark)*

   A electrical energy.

   B nuclear energy.

   C chemical energy.

   D gravitational potential energy.

3. In a hydroelectric power station, the sequence of energy transformations is *(1 mark)*

   A heat energy → electrical energy.

   B gravitational potential energy → kinetic energy → electrical energy.

   C gravitational potential energy → kinetic energy → heat energy → electrical energy.

   D solar energy → kinetic energy → electrical energy.

4. The fossil fuel that is the major source of energy for the production of electricity in Australia is *(1 mark)*

   A oil.

   B gas.

   C uranium.

   D coal.

5. The most versatile energy resource is *(1 mark)*

   A coal.

   B natural gas.

   C electricity.

   D petroleum.

6. Complete the following restricted-response questions using the appropriate word. *(1 mark for each part)*

   a) Heat, light and sound are examples of different forms of ....

   b) The law of .... of energy states that energy can neither be created nor destroyed.

   c) Kinetic energy depends on the mass and .... of an object.

   d) At every .... there will be energy losses.

   e) Most heat losses in a house occur through the ceiling and ....

7. Use the code letters to match the terms or phrases in each column. *(1 mark for each part)*

Column 1		Column 2	
A	motion	F	photovoltaic
B	energy input/output	G	restraint
C	seatbelt	H	efficiency
D	gravitational	I	potential energy
E	solar	J	kinetic energy

Part B: Skills

8. Table 4.9 shows the percentage of total energy sources used in Australia.

Table 4.9 Total energy sources used in Australia, %

Energy resource	% used
oil and oil products	37
black coal	29
natural gas	15
brown coal	12
wood/plant fibre	5
hydroelectricity/solar	2

a) What percentage of energy usage is derived from coal? *(1 mark)*

b) What percentage of energy is derived from renewable sources? *(1 mark)*

c) Construct a pie graph of this data. *(3 marks)*

9. The data in Table 4.10 represents the energy consumption per person per day in three countries.

Table 4.10 Energy consumption in three countries per person per day

Country	Energy usage (MJ/person/day)
United States	970
Australia	500
India	35

a) Calculate the yearly energy usage of an Australian family of four people. *(2 marks)*

b) Explain the differences in energy usage of these three countries. *(2 marks)*

10. In a technological society such as the United States, the energy usage per person per day can be broken down into contributions from various sectors. For example, agriculture and industry require energy to provide products and services to each person. Table 4.11 shows these contributing sectors.

Table 4.11 Energy usage per sector

Sector	Energy usage (MJ/person/day)
agriculture/industry	380
homes/offices	280
transport	265
food consumption	45

a) What percentage of energy usage is required for transportation? *(1 mark)*

b) Which of these sectors is strongly reliant on energy derived from the combustion of fuels derived from oil? *(1 mark)*

c) Plot the tabulated data as a bar graph. *(3 marks)*

11. Four objects, the same size and shape, are dropped from a given height. One of the objects is in a vacuum, the other three are not. The kinetic energy of the objects is shown in Figure 4.44.

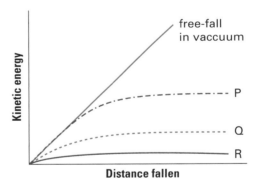

Figure 4.44 Kinetic energy versus time

a) Explain why the object that fell in a vacuum shows a straight line curve. *(2 marks)*

b) Why do graphs for objects P, Q and R flatten out? *(1 mark)*

c) Once these graphs for objects P, Q and R flatten out, explain why there is no increase in kinetic energy even though they are still falling through greater distances. *(2 marks)*

d) Which object, P, Q or R, has the greatest mass? Explain. *(2 marks)*

12. Figure 4.45 shows the path a ball follows as it is thrown through the air.

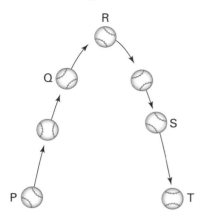

Figure 4.45 A ball tossed into the air

a) At what point is the potential energy the greatest? *(1 mark)*

b) At what two points is the potential energy the same? What can you say about the kinetic energy at these points? *(2 marks)*

c) Which has the greater kinetic energy: Q or S? *(1 mark)*

d) At what point is KE = 0? *(1 mark)*

13. Figure 4.46 shows a boy on a skateboard.

ground

Figure 4.46 Boy on a skateboard

Describe the changes in both kinetic and potential energies as the boy skates up the ramp. *(3 marks)*

14. A person claims that she has created a cup where water will flow around indefinitely (see Figure 4.47).

Figure 4.47 A perpetual motion device

Her theory is that the pressure of the water forces it out from a small opening at the bottom. The kinetic energy of the water then allows it to flow up and over the top of the cup where it can then fall back into the cup. This maintains the water level and keeps the pressure on the water coming out of the opening constant, so the water will continue to flow around.

Comment on this claim. *(4 marks)*

Go to pp. 247–249 to check your answers.

Summary

1. Various types of motion can be measured using equipment such as stopwatches, tape measures and electronic motion detectors.

2. Distance and displacement measure length. Distance has magnitude; displacement has both magnitude and direction.

3. Speed and velocity determine how fast an object is travelling. Speed has magnitude; velocity has both magnitude and direction.

4. If an object speeds up or slows down, it is accelerating. Deceleration is negative acceleration.

Summary cont.

5. Equal and opposite forces are balanced and the object does not move.

6. Newton's first law: an object at rest or moving uniformly in a straight line will continue to do so unless compelled to change by some external force.

7. Newton's second law: this effectively states that force equals mass times acceleration, with the direction of the force being in the same direction as acceleration.

8. Newton's third law: to every action there is an equal and opposite reaction.

9. Inertia is the resistance of a body to a change in its motion.

10. The law of conservation of energy states that energy can neither be created nor destroyed, though it can be changed from one form into another.

11. Kinetic energy is energy due to motion ($KE = \frac{1}{2}mv^2$)

12. Gravitational potential energy is energy due to position ($PE = mgh$)

13. A variety of processes can occur in energy transfer and transformation, so that the usable energy is reduced and the system is not 100% efficient.

14. In car crashes, kinetic energy changes into other forms of energy: heat, deformation and sound.

15. In an oscillating pendulum, kinetic energy is changed to potential energy and vice versa.

16. Buildings can incorporate various features to make them less reliant on outside energy sources for heating and cooling, and may also be able to generate their own electricity.

17. While non-renewable energy sources are convenient and energy rich, there is only a finite amount we can draw on. Renewable energy is virtually limitless and strides have recently been made to make them more convenient and less costly.

18. Alternative energy sources for transport and newer and smaller batteries for portable electronic devices have become essential for our modern methods of commerce, trade and communications.

Syllabus checklist

Are you able to answer every syllabus question in this chapter? Tick each question as you go through the list if you are able to answer it. If you cannot answer it, turn to the appropriate page in the guide as is listed in the column to find the answer.

	For a complete understanding of this topic	Page no.	✓
1	Can I name the equipment I will need to measure various types of motions?	143, 146, 162	
2	Can I distinguish between the terms distance and displacement?	138–140	
3	Can I distinguish between the terms speed and velocity?	138–140	
4	Can I recall why an object accelerates?	142	
5	Can I recall what happens to a body when the forces acting on it are balanced?	141–142	

	For a complete understanding of this topic	Page no.	✓
6	Can I recall Newton's three laws of motion?	145–147	
7	Can I explain the meaning of the word inertia?	145	
8	Can I explain the law of conservation of energy?	150	
9	Can I calculate kinetic energy?	150	
10	Can I calculate gravitational potential energy?	151	
11	Do I understand energy transfers and transformations?	152	

For a complete understanding of this topic		Page no.	✓
12	Do I understand what the efficiency of a machine is?	152–153	
13	Do I know what energy changes occur in a car crash?	154–155	
14	Do I know what energy changes occur in a simple pendulum?	156	
15	Can I recall some features of energy-efficient buildings?	156–158	

For a complete understanding of this topic		Page no.	✓
16	Can I compare renewable and non-renewable energy sources?	158–159	
17	Can I describe innovative energy transfer devices, especially in transport and communications?	160–162	

Chapter test

Go to **p.v** for *Tips for tests and examinations*   **80 min**

Part A: Multiple-choice questions

(1 mark for each)

1. Figure 4.48 shows the position of a car on a road, travelling east, at intervals of 5 seconds.

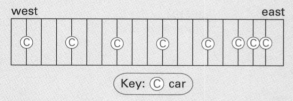

Key: Ⓒ car

Figure 4.48 Position of a car at regular time intervals

Select the correct statement about the record of motion.
   A The car accelerated during the period of observation.
   B The car initially travelled at constant speed and then decelerated.
   C The car was moving at constant speed for the first 15 seconds and then accelerated uniformly for 10 seconds before stopping.
   D The car slowed down and then moved with constant speed in an easterly direction.

2. Which of the following objects undergoes uniform acceleration?
   A a parachutist gliding down to the ground
   B a skydiver
   C a steel ball dropped from 3 m above the Moon's surface
   D a car speeding away from a traffic light

3. The person to first propose the laws of gravitation was
   A Aristotle.
   B Galileo.
   C Newton.
   D Einstein.

4. Compared to the mass and weight of a person on Earth, on the Moon
   A his mass remains the same but his weight is less.
   B his mass is less but his weight remains the same.
   C both his mass and weight are less.
   D both his mass and weight remain the same.

5. A vehicle drips oil onto the road at a constant rate. Figure 4.49 shows the pattern of drops.

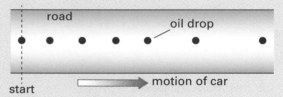

Figure 4.49 Oil drops on road

From this figure we could conclude that the car is
   A constantly decelerating.
   B travelling at constant speed.
   C stopped for half of the time.
   D moving at a constant speed and then accelerating.

6. Which of the following is *not* necessary to determine gravitational potential energy?
   A mass of the object
   B gravitational field the object is in
   C speed of the object
   D distance the object is above the ground

7. Which letter in Figure 4.50 represents the point where kinetic energy and potential energy are equal?

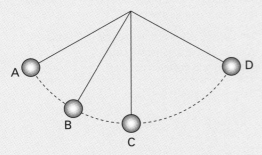

Figure 4.50 A swinging pendulum

8. A match is lit to start a fire. As the match burns, which of the following decreases?
   A kinetic energy
   B light energy
   C thermal energy (heat)
   D chemical energy

9. An electric hand drier is operating. Which of the following is *not* true?
   A Electrical energy is being completely destroyed.
   B Electrical energy is being completely conserved.
   C Electrical energy is being partly changed to heat energy.
   D Electrical energy is being partly changed to sound energy.

10. Which of the following is a renewable energy form?
    A coal seam gas
    B hydroelectric power
    C uranium
    D coal

Part B: Short-answer questions

11. Accelerating a 10-kg trolley to a certain speed takes a certain amount of force.
    a) What happens to this force as the mass of the trolley is increased? *(1 mark)*
    b) What happens to the force as the mass of the trolley is decreased? *(1 mark)*
    c) If the 10-kg trolley has a smaller force applied, what happens to its acceleration? *(1 mark)*

    d) Suppose the 10-kg trolley is sped up to the same speed in half the time. Explain how this new force compares to the original force. *(1 mark)*

12. What is the acceleration of a mass of 10 kg that is acted on by a 200-N force? *(1 mark)*

13. What force is needed to accelerate a 50-kg mass at 0.5 m/s²? *(1 mark)*

14. Moving oil tankers are very difficult to stop over short distances. Other boats must keep out of their way. If a tanker has a mass of 500 million kg, what force will achieve a deceleration of 0.01 m/s²? *(1 mark)*

15. Figure 4.51 shows a golf ball rolling from A to B down a smooth slope. The ball starts from rest. If the ball takes 10 seconds to roll from A to B and its speed at B is measured at 12 m/s, calculate the average acceleration during the motion. *(1 mark)*

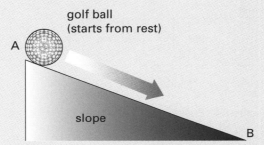

golf ball
(starts from rest)

A

slope

B

Figure 4.51 Golf ball accelerates down the slope

16. You are trying to convince an adult to wear her seatbelt. Using the words 'deceleration', 'force' and 'inertia', write a brief statement that will encourage the wearing of seatbelts. *(1 mark)*

17. When a person stands up in a stationary boat and moves forwards to tie it to its mooring, the boat moves backwards. Why does this happen? *(1 mark)*

18. After school finished, three students, Jenna, Ayshe and Jasmine, went home by walking, jogging or riding a bicycle (see Figure 4.52).
    a) How do you know each girl travelled at a constant speed? *(1 mark)*
    b) Who travelled at the fastest speed? Who travelled at the slowest speed? *(2 marks)*
    c) By which method did each of these girls go home? *(3 marks)*

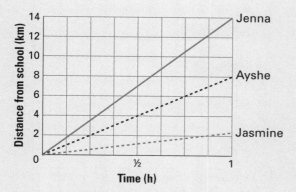

Figure 4.52 Distance-time graph

d) Use the graph to calculate the speed for each girl. *(3 marks)*

e) If Jasmine takes 1.5 hours to walk home, how far does she live from school? *(1 mark)*

19. Jim and Spiro went driving. The distance–time graph for part of their journeys is shown in Figure 4.53.

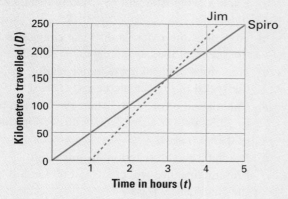

Figure 4.53 Distance travelled versus time

a) Who was travelling at the faster speed? How do you know? *(2 marks)*

b) Calculate the speed for each person. *(2 marks)*

c) What information is given on the graph to show Jim left 1 hour after Spiro? *(1 mark)*

d) At what time after Spiro started driving had they both covered the same distance? What distance was this? *(2 marks)*

20. The performance figures shown in Table 4.12 were obtained for two cars (X and Y) based on a standing start.

a) Why is attainment of specified speed measured from a standing start? *(1 mark)*

b) Which vehicle has the higher performance? Explain. *(2 marks)*

Table 4.12 Performance figures for two cars

Speed attained (km/h)	Time to reach specified speed (s)	
	Car X	Car Y
50	3.1	3.6
60	4.5	4.9
80	6.4	7.0
100	9.2	11.1

21. The data shown in Table 4.13 was collected for a car travelling along a straight road.

Table 4.13 Velocity and time of a car travelling on a straight road

Time elapsed (s)	Velocity (m/s)
0	0
1	3
2	6
3	9
4	12

What can be concluded from the data? *(1 mark)*

22. Table 4.14 shows the speeds of five objects (K, L, M, N and P) over a 5-second time interval.

Table 4.14 Speeds of five objects

Time (s)	Object's speed (m/s)				
	K	L	M	N	P
0	6	30	0	3	2
1	6	25	2	3	3
2	6	20	4	3	5
3	7	15	4	3	9
4	8	10	4	3	17
5	9	5	4	3	33

a) Which object has no net force acting on it throughout the 5 seconds? *(1 mark)*

b) Which object is decelerating? *(1 mark)*

c) Which object is initially moving with constant speed and then slowly accelerates? *(1 mark)*

d) Which object slowly accelerates to its desired speed and then maintains that speed for the rest of the time? *(1 mark)*

e) Calculate the average acceleration of object M in the first 2 seconds of its motion. *(1 mark)*

23. A student conducts an experiment to measure the motion of two unknown masses (M and N) along a smooth table. A constant force of 1 N was applied by means of a string connected to a falling weight as shown in Figure 4.54.

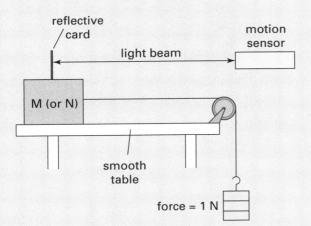

Figure 4.54 Motion experiment

A motion sensor recorded the position (measured from the starting line) of each mass at regular time intervals as they slid along the table. The results displayed by the data logger are shown in Table 4.15.

Table 4.15 Position of each mass at regular time intervals

Time elapsed	0	0.4	0.8	1.2	1.6	2.0
Position of M (cm)	0	8	32	72	128	200
Position of N (cm)	0	4	16	36	64	100

a) Describe the motion of each mass along the table. *(2 marks)*

b) Explain which body has the greater mass. *(2 marks)*

c) Calculate the average speed of M between 0.8 and 1.6 seconds. Give the answer in cm/s. *(1 mark)*

24. Figure 4.55 gives information on the stopping distance on dry bitumen roads for a typical driver with a reaction time of about 1 second.

The stopping distance is defined as:

$$\frac{\text{stopping}}{\text{distance}} = \frac{\text{reaction}}{\text{distance}} + \frac{\text{braking}}{\text{distance}}$$

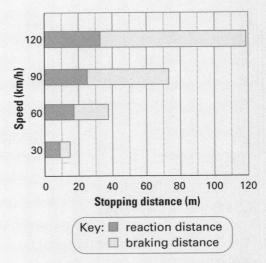

Figure 4.55 Stopping distance on a dry bitumen road

The reaction distance is the distance the car moves during the driver's reaction time. The reaction time varies between drivers but it is usually between 0.75 and 1 second.

a) Explain what is meant by braking distance. *(1 mark)*

b) How does the reaction distance change as the speed of the car increases? *(1 mark)*

c) How does the braking distance change as the speed of the car increases? *(1 mark)*

d) Calculate the reaction distance at 120 km/h (= 33.3 m/s) for a driver with a reaction time of 0.75 s. *(1 mark)*

e) Predict how the reaction distance and braking distance will change at 60 km/h if the road is wet. *(1 mark)*

25. The following statements were made by Isaac Newton, or about him.

a) Writing in 1664 Newton entered the slogan 'Amicus Plato amicus Aristoteles magis amica veritas' ('Plato is my friend, Aristotle is my friend, but my best friend is truth') into his book. What do you think he meant by this? *(1 mark)*

b) On 5 February 1676, Newton wrote to Robert Hooke: 'If I have seen further, it is by standing on ye shoulders of Giants'. Explain what he meant by this. *(1 mark)*

c) William Stukeley wrote the following recollection after dining with Newton in 1726: 'The weather being warm, we went into the garden and drank tea, under shade of some apple trees, only he and myself.

Amidst other discourses, he told me, he was just in the same situation, as when formerly, the notion of gravitation came into his mind. It was occasion'd by the fall of an apple, as he sat in contemplative mood. Why should that apple always descend perpendicularly to the ground, thought he to himself. Why should it not go sideways or upwards, but constantly to the Earth's centre'.

i) Who is 'he' referred to here? *(1 mark)*

ii) What is the significance of this recollection? *(1 mark)*

d) A similar story was recorded at the time by John Conduitt: '… whilst he was musing in the garden it came into his thought that the power of gravity (which brought an apple from the tree to the ground) was not limited to a certain distance from the Earth but that this power must extend much farther than was usually thought. Why not as high as the Moon said he to himself and if so that must influence her motion and perhaps retain her in her orbit'.

i) Who is 'her' referred to in this passage? *(1 mark)*

ii) What additional information is being related here which was not mentioned in Stukeley's quote? *(1 mark)*

26. In some parts of Australia hot rocks have been discovered several kilometres underground. Explain how this heat energy can be extracted for our use. *(2 marks)*

27. a) Examine Figure 4.56 and explain how a pendulum helps demonstrate that energy is conserved in an isolated system. *(3 marks)*

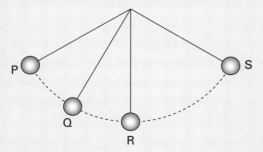

Figure 4.56 A swinging pendulum

b) In reality, the pendulum does not continue to swing indefinitely. Eventually it will stop. Why does the total energy seem to decrease? *(1 mark)*

28. Comment on each of these statements.

a) Some students incorrectly believe that energy is destroyed in energy transformations. *(2 marks)*

b) Some students incorrectly think that energy can be changed completely from one form to another without any additional energy transformations or loss from the system. *(2 marks)*

29. Figure 4.57 shows the path for a roller-coaster.

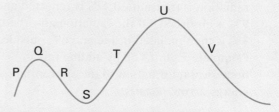

Figure 4.57 Path of roller-coaster

a) At what points in the journey is potential energy transformed into kinetic energy? *(2 marks)*

b) What happens to the speed of the roller-coaster as it passes through S? Explain this in terms of energy changes. *(3 marks)*

30. A 20-kg ball is raised 25 m off the ground.

a) Calculate its gravitational potential energy. *(2 marks)*

b) The ball is dropped. What happens to this potential energy? *(1 mark)*

c) When the ball finally hits the ground, has the energy the ball had been destroyed? Explain. *(2 marks)*

31. Use an example to explain whether this statement is correct or not.

'If you double the velocity of an object, its kinetic energy doubles.' *(3 marks)*

32. A 90-kg person climbs to the top of a 50-m cliff.

a) Calculate the gravitational potential energy he has gained. *(2 marks)*

b) If this same person climbed this hill on the Moon, the gravitational potential energy he would have gained would be 7290 J. Calculate the acceleration due to gravity on the Moon. *(2 marks)*

c) In which instance would more work need to be done to climb the cliff: on Earth or on the Moon? *(1 mark)*

33. a) Complete the following statements. When sunlight strikes a sheet of glass, some of the .... radiation is .... straight through, some is .... and some is absorbed by the glass. The heat energy absorbed by the glass is then .... to both the inside and outside as .... radiation. The sum of reflected, absorbed and transmitted heat always equals .... %. *(6 marks)*

b) In a 3-mm sheet of clear glass 83% of solar radiation is transmitted, 8% is reflected and 9% is absorbed. Of the radiation absorbed, 3% is then radiated inside and 6% outside. Complete Figure 4.58 by adding this numerical information to the appropriate energy arrow. *(5 marks)*

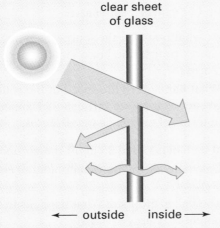

clear sheet
of glass

◄─── outside   inside ───►

Figure 4.58 How solar radiation moves through glass

c) Suggest reasons for why twice as much heat is radiated outside the glass as inside. *(2 marks)*

34. A 1200-kg vehicle is moving at 40 km/h.
a) Convert 40 km/h to m/s. *(2 marks)*
b) Calculate the kinetic energy of the vehicle. *(2 marks)*
c) What happens to this kinetic energy when the car comes to a stop? *(2 marks)*

35. A shopping cart is pushed up a ramp at a store. The cart and its contents have a mass of 45.0 kg. The ramp is 3.50 m long and rises 0.85 m. If the cart and ramp is 90% efficient, calculate the amount of energy needed to push it up the ramp? *(3 marks)*

36. State three things that can be done around your home to make it more energy efficient. *(3 marks)*

37. Measurements done with a simple lever show that when 250 J of energy is inputted, the output energy is 245 J.
a) Calculate the efficiency of this machine, as a percentage. *(2 marks)*
b) Explain the loss in energy. *(1 mark)*

38. A 10-kg object is dropped from the top of the Eiffel Tower (see Figure 4.59).

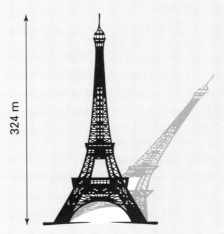

324 m

Figure 4.59 The Eiffel Tower in Paris

a) Calculate the object's gravitational potential energy:
   i) at the top of the tower *(2 marks)*
   ii) halfway down. *(2 marks)*
b) Calculate the object's kinetic energy:
   i) halfway down *(2 marks)*
   ii) at the bottom, just before impact. *(2 marks)*
c) What is the speed of the object when GPE = KE? What assumptions are you making here? *(4 marks)*

39. a) Explain the benefits of wearing a seatbelt in the car. *(3 marks)*
b) A mother complains that as her baby won't stop crying, so she will sit in the back as a passenger nursing the child. She claims this will be safe. Comment. *(3 marks)*

40. Around two centuries ago, the Englishman William Congreve drew a machine that worked by the capillary effects in sponges as shown in Figure 4.60. The sponges on the left-hand side fill with water and get heavier as the chain turns anticlockwise. This keeps a

downwards force on the chain, pulling more sponges into the water. As the sponges rise on the right-hand side the pressures of the heavy chain-plates squeezes out the water, making it lighter. And so the machine, and the wheel attached, should continue to turn anticlockwise. Congreve calculated considerable power could be generated by this machine to operate other devices.

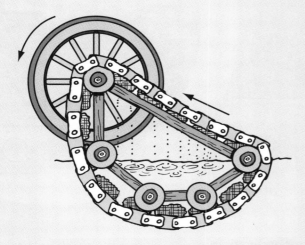

Figure 4.60 A perpetual motion machine

Explain whether or not Congreve's machine would work. *(3 marks)*

Go to **pp. 249–253** to check your answers.

CHAPTER 5

Investigations and problem solving

Overview

In this chapter you will learn about:

- ☑ first-hand investigations
- ☑ inferences, predictions and generalisations
- ☑ hypotheses and theories
- ☑ conducting background research
- ☑ working individually and in a team
- ☑ selecting equipment
- ☑ variables and fair testing
- ☑ experiments with animals
- ☑ making and testing a hypothesis
- ☑ designing an experimental procedure
- ☑ safety during a first-hand investigation
- ☑ accuracy and reliability
- ☑ writing scientific reports
- ☑ graphing and drawing diagrams
- ☑ random and systematic errors
- ☑ explanations and conclusions
- ☑ cause and effect relationships
- ☑ report presentation.

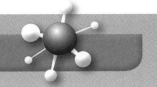

Glossary

Accuracy—the degree of closeness of measurements of a quantity to that quantity's actual (true) value

Continuous data—data that can take any of an infinite number of values between whole numbers, such as measuring

Controlled variable—a factor that is held constant during an investigation

Dependent variable—a factor that the investigator is observing or measuring in response to the independent variable

Discrete data—data where there is only a finite number of values possible, such as in counting

Extrapolation—extending a graph beyond the plotted values to an unknown situation by assuming that existing trends will continue or similar methods will apply

Generalisation—a statement that is true in the majority of cases

Hypothesis—a logical explanation of an observation or solution to an investigation that is made after all available evidence and information has been collected

Independent variable—a factor that the investigator selects to change or vary

Inference—a possible and reasonable explanation of an individual observation

Interpolation—constructing new data points within the range of a discrete set of known data points

Observation—something that can be seen, heard, felt, smelt or measured using a device

Placebo—a substance that does not contain the active material to be tested

Reliability—the consistency or repeatability of measurements

Validity—the extent to which a test or instrument measures what it claims to measure

5.1 First-hand investigations

The main objective of all scientists is to get the correct answer to the problem they are working on. Some would call this the pursuit of truth. And the very meaning of truth implies a way of checking and verifying the results. This checking needs to be exhaustive as the truth of a general proposition can be disproved by a single exception.

The first step of a scientific investigation takes place when an observation is made. This might be an observation of an event such as a pine cone falling from a tree. It might be an observation of some feature of an animal such as the presence of webbing between the toes of a bird. These observations may then lead you to think about the cause or reason behind the observation.

Louis Pasteur wrote, 'In the field of observation, chance favours only the prepared mind'. This means that you will only discover something new if your mind is prepared to understand what you observe. This is done by reading and planning.

The scientific method is generally described as a series of steps in which an observation or problem is investigated. These steps are:

> making observations (using your senses or with the aid of instruments)
> making inferences
> reviewing the known facts using data sources
> making predictions
> planning, designing and experimenting to test predictions
> formulating a hypothesis based on an analysis of collected data
> testing and modifying the hypothesis by further investigations
> discussing collected results
> making conclusions
> planning for further investigations about the problem.

Identifying data sources

In order to prepare for an investigation of some problem or observation you have made, you need to review what is currently known about this topic. This involves identifying:

▷ what information or data needs to be collected to help you understand the issues

▷ the possible sources of this information or data (e.g. library books, textbooks)

▷ dictionaries, encyclopaedias, periodicals and multimedia resources including the internet

▷ the relevant parts of the gathered information by doing some background reading, highlighting key ideas and summarising.

In this way you will develop an understanding of the problem to be investigated.

Inferences, predictions and generalisations

Some problems will be investigated by conducting research in the laboratory or in the field. Some problems will be investigated by second-hand data research. Second-hand data is work that has been published by others.

We will now look at examples of three of the steps of the scientific method.

Inferences

Following an observation, a scientist may make an inference (see Figure 5.1). This is one possible explanation of the observation.

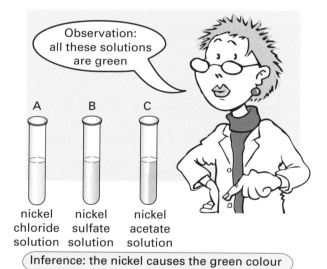

Figure 5.1 Scientists make inferences about the observations they make.

Predictions

The next step is to test the inference by making a prediction and performing an experiment to test the prediction. These experiments may support the inference or they may not. A new explanation may need to be sought.

Generalisations

As more supporting data is collected, the investigator may see a pattern emerging. At this point the investigator may be able to make a generalisation about the topic under investigation. Generalisations are statements that are true in the great majority of cases.

Examples

1. After the last lesson was over and the students had gone home, the teacher observed that the last sink in the laboratory had pencil shavings in it. She decided that the three boys sitting there had let their pencil shavings fall in the sink rather than the bin.
   This is an inference based on her observation. The inference may not be correct as boys from an earlier class may have let their shavings fall into the sink.

2. If the concentration of the acid is raised, the speed of the reaction will increase.
   This is a prediction and suggests that the student has done some preliminary experiment on the rate of the reaction and she is now predicting that using a more concentrated acid will make the reaction go even faster.

3. A senior student used a chemical data book to record the colours of a wide variety of different ionic compounds. In his report he wrote that all copper compounds were coloured but all potassium compounds were white.
   This is a useful generalisation about the compounds of copper and potassium.

Hypotheses and theories

The next step in the scientific method is to generate a hypothesis. What is a hypothesis? A hypothesis is a statement concerning the observation(s) or solution to a problem being investigated. A hypothesis is *not* a wild guess. Hypotheses are temporary statements that lead towards the development of scientific theories.

Hypotheses are only made after looking at *all* the available evidence and information that has been collected. This is why background reading of identified data sources is so important. The work of others may help you to produce a good hypothesis. Hypotheses are the result of a scientist making inferences, making predictions and developing generalisations.

The hypothesis must be able to:

- predict the results of future investigation about the problem
- suggest ways in which it can be tested to determine whether or not it is true.

Hypotheses are not always correct. If the data collected during the investigation does not support the hypothesis, a new hypothesis must be developed.

Examples

1. A student wrote in her notebook: 'Based on our bushwalk, this plant species appears to grow best in dry, sandy soils in a sunny environment rather than moist, rich soils and a sheltered, shady environment'.
   This is a hypothesis that can be tested. The student can now perform an experiment in which this plant species is grown under different conditions.
2. The student read the following comment on a social web site: 'Most Australians prefer rock music to jazz'.
   This is *not* a hypothesis as it involves a personal opinion and is not scientifically based. This opinion will vary from one group to another.
3. A student read on a blog that human ancestors were tree dwellers in the African plains and that earlier hominid species were exclusively cave dwellers.
   This is *not* a hypothesis. It does suggest an answer to a problem. It cannot, however, be tested directly as there are no living human ancestors or hominids. The finding of hominid bones in caves does not provide sufficient evidence that they exclusively lived in caves.

A scientific theory is the result of very extensive research that supports a hypothesis, or a group of related hypotheses. Over a longer period of time the theory may become so universally accepted that it becomes known as a scientific law. Sometimes old theories are replaced by new theories. The law of mass–energy conservation is an example of an old theory (the law of energy conservation) being replaced by a newer law when Albert Einstein showed the equivalence of mass and energy. No experiments have ever been able to disprove the conservation of mass–energy theory and so it has been elevated to the status of a law of science. Many scientists believe that the theory of evolution should now be called

the law of evolution as ongoing research has always supported the theory for well over a hundred years.

Background research and reliability of secondary data sources

The following points should be noted when gathering information from secondary sources.

- Use a wide range of resources to gather secondary information. Do not just rely on the internet. Not all the information on the internet is accurate or correct. Much of it is not peer reviewed. CD-ROMs, periodicals, library books and newspapers are also valuable sources of information. Ensure that you reference sources from which you have collected information in the appropriate manner (e.g. Author, Year, Title, Publisher, Place). For articles on the internet, record the title of the article, author (if known) and the URL.
- When using library books or textbooks to locate information, you should look for key words in the index. Look at the table of contents at the front of the book to locate relevant chapters. There may also be a glossary of terms to help you understand difficult technical words.
- Once you have gathered the second-hand data, you will need to collate and summarise it. You must not plagiarise the work collected. You must read and make notes from this collected information, placing your notes into a scaffold/table which you have constructed earlier. You can then use these note summaries to construct your own text.
- Information from secondary sources may contain various types of graphs (e.g. histograms, sector graphs, line graphs, divided bar graphs), flow charts and diagrams. You can use this type of information to extract data.
- As you gather second-hand data, you must decide whether the information is relevant or irrelevant. For example, if you are gathering information on water movement in flowering plants, any data on non-flowering plants would be irrelevant.
- Not all the gathered data will be reliable. You need to check its reliability by comparing it with other sources. Science articles that appear in respected journals and that have been peer reviewed are more likely to be reliable than an article that is self-published. Articles written by creation scientists are not reliable as they do not follow the scientific method.

> Your collected data needs to be organised for easy analysis. Tables, proformas, scaffolds and diagrams are commonly used to organise information. Computer databases and spreadsheets are becoming increasingly important ways of organising collected data.

Using science to make claims about commercial products and practices

Most companies that produce commercial products behave ethically but there are some companies which may be unethical in that they only keep data that is favourable to them. They may employ scientists to monitor quality control or to do research with the aim of producing new products. When these products are advertised, the advertising company may present only the positive data. It is only when independent tests are done that the consumer finds out the truth of the claims made about a product. For example, a company may produce a skin cream that contains stem cells that claims to reduce face wrinkles. Independent testing, however, may show that the reduction in wrinkles is minimal and that the product simply fills in the wrinkles and makes the skin look smoother. Such companies use vague terms such as 'reduce' to avoid litigation. Another example is the claim of 'no added sugar', which may be true and correct for some food items but the product may already contain more sugar than is deemed sufficient for daily intake. This can give the illusion that the item is healthy.

The labels of bottles contain information about the product as well as various claims about it (see Figure 5.2). All commercial products must be properly tested to meet government regulations before they can be sold.

Figure 5.2 Bottle labels contain information and claims about the product.

5.2 Working individually and in a team

Students need to be able to work individually on some occasions and in teams on others. There are advantages in both ways of working. There are also responsibilities that must be considered.

Working individually requires students to:

> appreciate the importance of taking personal responsibility in planning and performing a task
> work to realistic timelines and goals
> persevere with an activity to achieve a reasonable endpoint
> accept personal responsibility for a safe working environment for themselves and others in the laboratory
> evaluate the effectiveness of their work in completing the task.

Working in teams requires students to:

> identify the different roles of each team member
> negotiate and allocate responsibility as a team member
> accept and perform the roles decided by the team
> collaborate with others in setting and working to agreed timelines and goals
> accept personal responsibility for maintaining a safe working environment for all team members
> work cooperatively to monitor the progress of the investigation
> evaluate the process used by the team and the effectiveness of the team in completing the task.

5.3 Selecting equipment

The equipment chosen for a practical investigation must be appropriate for the task. You need to ensure that the experiment can be done safely using the correct equipment.

Examples

1. A digital temperature probe is often more accurate than a simple alcohol thermometer. A mercury thermometer is more accurate than an alcohol thermometer. A thermometer whose scale is divided into fifths or tenths of a degree is more suitable to determine the variation in

body temperature of a student over 2 hours than a thermometer marked in whole degrees.

2. A 100-mL measuring cylinder marked with 1-mL scale divisions is more suitable to measure exactly 73 mL of water than a 100-mL beaker with 10-mL divisions.

3. The reaction of solid potassium sulfide with dilute sulfuric acid should be performed in a beaker in a fume cupboard, as the evolved hydrogen sulfide is very poisonous. The student should also wear safety glasses to avoid the splashing of acid into the eyes.

4. An ammeter is used to measure the current flowing in a circuit. If the current is very small then a milliammeter or a microammeter (galvanometer) should be used.

5. Distillation of volatile, flammable liquids is best performed using an electric heater rather than a Bunsen burner. The absence of a flame makes it more likely that accidental fires will not occur.

6. Using an electronic balance which weighs to 2 or 3 decimal places is more accurate than using a sliding poise balance when measuring the weights of small quantities of materials.

7. Quantitative filter paper has finer pores than qualitative filter paper and so it is better to use when filtering very fine precipitates.

5.4 Fair testing and variables

Many factors can influence the results of an experiment. These factors are called variables. In order to investigate a problem experimentally, all the variables must be controlled so that only the variable being investigated can affect the result. This is known as fair testing.

Variables

During an investigation, the experimenter tests what happens when he or she alters one variable. The effect of a change in this factor (or independent variable) on another variable (the dependent variable) is investigated. All other variables are kept constant (i.e. controlled).

- The independent variable is the one that is systematically allowed to change by the researcher. It is the 'change' that you allow to happen when conducting an experiment.

- The dependent variable is affected by the change in the independent variable. It is the 'what happens' part of the investigation.

- The controlled variables are the other factors that can alter the result if they are not held constant.

Example 1: Apples

- **Hypothesis:** apples will remain fresher and have a longer storage life if kept in the refrigerator rather than at room temperature

- **Independent variable:** temperature

- **Dependent variable:** storage life

- **Controlled (constant) variables:** same types of apples; apples of the same age after picking; same refrigerator and temperature settings; same spacing between apples

Example 2: Rate of reaction

- **Hypothesis:** zinc metal dissolves faster in sulfuric acid if the acid is heated

- **Independent variable:** temperature of the sulfuric acid

- **Dependent variables:** rate at which the zinc dissolves

- **Controlled (constant) variables:** same mass and shape of zinc pieces; same volume of acid; same concentration of the acid; same vessel

Using a control

Measurements may only be reliable in some experiments if a control is used. This is particularly true in biological or biochemical systems where many factors can alter a result. A control is an experiment that is performed as a comparison with those in which the independent variable is allowed to change.

Examples

1. A new plant fertiliser made from seaweed is to be tested to see if it improves the growth rate of geraniums. Ten plants are tested. Five plants receive the dose of fertiliser recommended on the packet. Five plants are used as controls. They do not receive any fertiliser. The growth rate of the two groups is compared in order to determine whether the fertiliser makes any difference to the growth of the geraniums.

2. A new petrol additive claims to give improved distance travelled per litre of fuel. Using the same car in each run, the car is filled with normal petrol and driven 200 km and then the amount of fuel

required to refill the tank is determined. This is repeated five times and the results averaged. These results are the control group. The experiment is repeated five times over the same route with the same amount of fuel additive added to the tank. These results are averaged and compared with the average of the control group to determine whether there has been an improvement with the fuel additive.

Experiments with living things

Animals cannot be used in laboratory experiments unless permission is sought from the appropriate governmental authorities. Supporters of the use of laboratory animals in university research believe that such research is essential to discover the possible toxicity of drugs as they are developed. Mice, rats, fish and birds have commonly been used in such experiments. Many animal rights groups believe that animal testing of drugs and other medications should be banned altogether and that only human volunteers should be used. In schools, no live animal testing is allowed.

In many experiments involving human subjects, scientists adopt special methods to ensure that bias does not influence the result. In addition, all living things of the same species have such variability that it is difficult to control the variables. Two common methods used to overcome these problems are the blind and double-blind experiments.

Blind experiments

When testing whether a particular medication works on humans, it is important that the subjects do not know whether they are the test group or the control group. The control group receives a placebo. This is a tablet, capsule or other medication that looks the same but has no active or test ingredient. Only the test group receives the medication with the active agent being tested. This procedure overcomes problems in attitude and wishful thinking.

Double-blind experiments

This technique goes one step further than the blind experiment. In this case the possible bias of the scientist is removed because he/she does not know which medication samples contain the test ingredient. Only the person preparing the samples knows the code and that person does not communicate with the person administering the test. See Figure 5.3.

You can grow grass on a busy street.

Are you male pattern bald?
Then this tablet is for YOU!

It will:
- grow your existing hair faster
- grow new hair on your head
- grow your existing hair thicker
- give you positive proof within 6 months, provided you remain on the course.

Figure 5.3 This hair product makes claims that would need to be tested by a double-blind study.

5.5 Designing an experimental procedure

It is important when undertaking a practical first-hand investigation that the procedure adopted is safe and that modifications are made as problems arise. It is important to develop a planned procedure before undertaking experimentation. The planned procedure will:

- identify the variables that need to be kept the same
- specify the independent variable
- specify the dependent variable
- ensure that the selected procedure is valid
- ensure that the measurements are valid and accurate
- ensure that the measurements are reliable.

Example: Asthma drug tests

A drug company is trying to perfect better anti-asthma drugs.

Hypothesis: asthma attacks can be reduced by using a new anti-asthma drug called AsthmoZ

Experimental procedure:

1. Two thousand young asthma sufferers (aged between 20 and 22) are recruited as volunteers to test an asthma drug. In the 6 months before the trial, they record the number of asthma attacks they have.

2. The 2000 volunteers are divided into two groups: 1000 will receive AsthmoZ in 50 mL of blueberry

juice at 7 am each morning. The other 1000 volunteers will receive 50 mL of normal blueberry juice. These are the control group. Each volunteer is unaware if they are taking the drug or not.

3. The treatments continue for a further 6 months. The volunteers record the frequency of their asthma attacks in this next 6 months.

Independent variable: presence/absence of asthma drug

Dependent variable: frequency of asthma attacks

Constant variables: same amount of drug; same amount of juice; same time of administration; age range of volunteers

Procedure and measurements are safe, valid, accurate and reliable: The drug has been pretested on animals for a long time and found to be safe. The drug is then tested on several volunteer subjects and administered in increasing doses and side-effects noted. Eventually, if the drug has been found to be safe and it is approved by medical authorities for further testing.

The methods used are valid as these procedures are well documented and approved in the medical literature. The accuracy of the results depends on the volunteers correctly filling out their diary records and taking the juice at the same time each day.

Reliability of results: The results are reliable if a large number of volunteers are used.

Experimental results: See Table 5.1.

Conclusion: The results of the drug trial show that the AsthmoZ drug reduces the number of asthma attacks quite significantly (~40%).

5.6 Lab rules and safety in a first-hand investigation

A laboratory is a potentially dangerous place. In order to work safely in a laboratory, it is vital that you follow the safety rules. Now it is time to remind you of these important rules. Follow them and accidents will be minimised.

These rules are not in any order because they are all equally important.

Rule 1: Follow the instructions! Ask if you do not understand what to do.

You may be doing an experiment with many steps. Listen to the teacher's instructions. Follow the demonstration of how to use the equipment safely. Read the steps of the experiment. If you still do not understand, ASK!

Rule 2: Never run or fool around! You may damage yourself or someone else.

This rule is common sense. You should always stay with your work group. Don't wander off to visit friends. Keep your mind on the task. If you muck about, you may burn or spill chemicals on yourself or others.

Rule 3: If an accident occurs, stay calm and get help.

If you cut yourself, burn your skin or clothes or spill chemicals on your skin or clothes, it is important not to panic. Ask others to help you. Someone else in the group can alert the teacher. Remember the following:

> Always wear your safety glasses.
> If you cut yourself, wash the wound and stop the bleeding by wrapping a clean cloth around the wound. Seek help and follow the teacher's instructions.
> If you burn your skin, run cold water over the burn. If necessary, use the shower. Keep the cold water treatment up for 15 to 20 minutes. Follow the teacher's instructions.
> If your clothes catch fire, roll onto the floor and smother the flames. Your classmates should wrap you in the fire blanket. One member of the group should immediately fetch the teacher.
> If you spill chemicals on your skin or clothes, wash the chemicals off immediately and seek the teacher's advice.

Table 5.1 Results of AsthmoZ experiment

	Total asthma attacks in the 6-month period before the drug is tested	Total asthma attacks in the 6-month period when the drug is tested
juice only (control group)	300	318
juice + drug	315	190

> If you get chemicals in your eye (this probably means you aren't wearing the safety glasses!), wash your eye with large amounts of water. Keep doing this while others seek the teacher's assistance. See Figure 5.4.

These students are not wearing safety glasses.

Figure 5.4 Always wear safety glasses when doing experiments.

It is important that you know where emergency equipment, such as fire blankets or the first aid kit, is kept in the laboratory so that in an emergency you can access them immediately.

Rule 4: Never eat or drink in a laboratory.

Your food may become contaminated if left on the tables. Your hands will not be clean and so food should not be consumed.

Rule 5: Do not sit on the experimental benches.

When an experiment is being conducted, you might knock it over if you sit on the bench. You will also take longer to react and move away from any spills which may occur. And, of course, benches may not always be cleaned properly so there may be traces of chemicals left on them. These could stain or burn your clothes. See Figure 5.5.

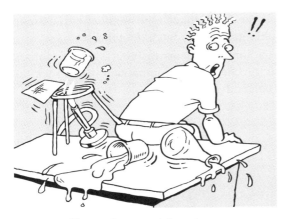

Figure 5.5 Never sit on work benches.

Assembling equipment

In a first-hand investigation, the selected equipment needs to be assembled to produce an apparatus that will perform the required task. Assembling pieces of equipment and using the apparatus requires good manipulation skills and attention to safety.

Example 1: Evaporation of a solution

The process of evaporation involves heating a solution in an evaporating basin using a Bunsen burner.

> Care must be taken not to touch any hot equipment until it is cooled down.
> You must wear safety glasses to ensure that your eyes are protected in case hot liquid is ejected from the flask.
> Heating should be done slowly to avoid possible ejection of hot liquids. Whenever you are heating anything, you should always monitor the situation. Don't leave apparatus to boil over while you leave the area to do something else.
> When a Bunsen burner is not in use, it should be turned off or adjusted to give a yellow safety flame, and removed from under any glassware.

Example 2: Reactions with acids

> Acids are corrosive and can damage the skin and eyes.
> Safety glasses must be worn at all times.
> Never use concentrated acids as their reactions can lead to excessive heat production.
> Use only small volumes of acids at any time.
> When pouring liquids from reagent bottles (e.g. acids), it is good practice for you to pick up the bottle with the label facing the palm of your hand. There are two important reasons for this. If any spills do occur, they will run down the side of the bottle away from where your fingers are. This will avoid damaging the label because if any spills do occur, they will consistently be away from it.
> Always put the lid back on the bottle of acid.

Example 3: Electrical circuits

> Ensure all electrical leads are free of corrosion.
> Make sure any leads and power cords do not trail over the edge of a bench or near the sink.
> Ensure the power is always turned off when not in use.

> Use a tapping key to turn on the current and collect your measurements rapidly. Do not leave the current on when no measurements are being made.

 Experiment 1

Viscosity of liquids

Aim

> To determine which of three liquids is more viscous

Materials

> liquids: water, sugar syrup, cooking oil
> beakers: 25 mL, 100 mL and 250 mL
> electronic balance
> measuring cylinders: 10 mL and 100 mL
> funnel
> ring clamp
> retort stand
> stopwatch

Method

1. Measure 100 mL of the liquid being tested into a funnel which has the stem stoppered by a finger as shown in Figure 5.6. These liquids are non-toxic.

2. Remove the finger and time the number of seconds taken for the 100 mL of substance to drain through.

3. Repeat five times. Average the results.

4. Repeat steps 1 to 3, using each substance in turn.

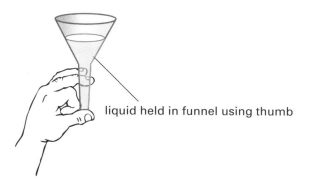

liquid held in funnel using thumb

Figure 5.6 Liquid in a funnel prior to testing

Results

The results of this experiment are shown in Table 5.2.

Table 5.2 Flow times

Trial number	Water	Syrup	Cooking oil
1	14.3	20.1	17.3
2	14.7	20.3	16.9
3	14.0	20.0	17.1
4	14.1	20.2	17.2
5	14.0	20.5	17.1

Analysis

1. Calculate the average flow time for each liquid.

2. Determine the order of viscosity of these liquids.

Go to p. 253 to check your answers.

Conclusion

 Write a suitable conclusion.

Go to p. 253 to check your answer.

In 1927, the pitch drop experiment was started at the University of Queensland, and is now the world's longest continuously running laboratory experiment (see Figure 5.7). This demonstrates that some solid-appearing substances are, in fact, very high viscosity fluids. A heated sample of pitch was poured into a sealed funnel and allowed to settle. In 1930 the seal at the neck of the funnel was cut allowing the pitch to start flowing. Large droplets form and fall over a period of about 8 to 9 years. The pitch has a viscosity around 230 times that of water and, to date, nine drops have fallen. There is enough pitch in the funnel to allow the experiment to continue for at least another century.

Figure 5.7 The pitch drop experiment

Experiment 2

Dissolving salt in water

Aim

⟩ To determine the effect of temperature on the rate of dissolving salt in water

Method

1. Measure out 0.50 g of salt onto a shiny square of paper. Repeat this to obtain seven samples.

2. Measure out 200 mL of water into a beaker, place this beaker in a water bath and allow it to come to the temperature of the bath.

3. At time zero, add the salt and stir at a fixed rate. Measure the time it takes for the salt to dissolve.

4. Repeat this procedure at different temperatures. Record your results in a table.

Results

See Table 5.3.

Table 5.3 Time to dissolve versus temperature

Temperature of water (°C)	Time to dissolve (s)
18	38
21	30
25	23
28	20
34	18
37	15
40	14

Analysis

Draw a line graph of this data.

Go to p. 253 to check your answer.

Conclusion

  Write a suitable conclusion.

Go to p. 253 to check your answer.

 Test yourself 1

Part A: Knowledge

1. Reliability in a first-hand school investigation can be improved by *(1 mark)*

   A repeating the experiment five or more times.

   B making different predictions.

   C using a larger team of students.

   D only doing valid experiments.

2. If you accidently spill acid on your skin and clothes while conducting an experiment, you should immediately *(1 mark)*

   A wrap your skin in cloth to exclude the air.

   B stand under the shower in the lab to wash your skin and clothes for 20 minutes.

   C ask the teacher what you should do.

   D ask your friends to tell the teacher.

3. Bert is required to heat a test tube containing an acid as part of an experiment. Identify the correct procedure he should use. *(1 mark)*

   A Hold the test tube base a few millimetres above the top of the Bunsen burner.

   B Hold the test tube with metal tongs when heating the acid.

   C Point the test tube being heated towards the wall or window and away from other students.

   D Fill the tube with acid and then heat the tube with a yellow Bunsen flame.

4. Sally's research project involved experiments to test whether the shoots of a plant always grow upwards. She filled glass test tubes with a nutrient aqua culture solution and then 1-week-old seedlings are placed into the tubes and held in place with cotton wool. She clamped the tubes at different angles from 10° to 90° from the horizontal. She observed the direction in which the shoots grew. Select the correct statement about the experiment. *(1 mark)*

   A The dependent variable is the angle of the tubes.

   B A mature plant should be used as a control.

   C The temperature of the nutrient solution should be controlled.

   D The independent variable is the direction in which the shoots grow.

5. Francis is asked to half-fill a test tube with salt water from the large 5-L container on the teacher's bench. Which of the following procedures would show good experimental technique? *(1 mark)*

   A Hold the test tube over the sink while another student pours from the large bottle.

B First pour some of the salt water into a beaker and then pour from the beaker into the test tube.

C Use a dropper to transfer the salt water from the large container to the test tube.

D Hold the test tube in a wooden test-tube holder while pouring out the salt water from the large bottle.

6. Complete the following restricted-response questions using the appropriate word.
(1 mark for each part)

a) When you reference articles on the internet, record the title of the article, ... (if known) and the URL.

b) When conducting chemical experiments, you should always wear safety ....

c) Measurements are .... if repeated experiments lead to consistent results.

d) If acid splashes onto your hand during an experiment, you should hold your hand under running .... to remove the acid quickly.

e) A student watched a video set in Australia. She noticed that the sky was blue and people were walking around with short-sleeved shirts and shorts. She .... that the video was shot in summer.

7. Use the code letters to match the terms or phrases in each column. *(1 mark for each part)*

Column 1		Column 2	
A	placebo	F	repeated experiments
B	accuracy	G	no active ingredient
C	manipulated variable	H	held constant
D	reliability	I	digital thermometer
E	controlled variables	J	independent variable

Part B: Skills

8. Four groups of pupils were asked to record the temperature of melting ice with a Celsius thermometer. The results they obtained are in Table 5.4. Suggest a possible reason for the results being different. *(1 mark)*

Table 5.4 Temperature of melting ice

Group	Temperature (°C)
1	0.5
2	0.0
3	0.5
4	1.0

9. Read the following account of a disastrous day in the laboratory.

Mollie has been heating a beaker of water using a Bunsen burner. She filled the beaker to the top and placed it on the gauze. She lit the Bunsen burner with a scrap of paper and turned the collar of the Bunsen burner until the hole was closed. While the water was boiling, she went over to speak to her friend. When she came back, she turned off the Bunsen burner and then tried to pull the hose off the tap. It seemed stuck, so she pulled harder. As it came off the tap, the end of the hose hit the leg of the tripod and the beaker fell off, crashed to the floor and broke. Hot water sprayed over the legs of her friends. Her friends ran around hysterically while Mollie cried.

List all the rules that are being broken and next to each rule write what Mollie or her friends should have done. *(8 marks)*

10. Describe the technique for each of the following laboratory procedures. Your answers should refer to ways of improving the accuracy of the procedure.

a) Martin wishes to pour a green solution from one beaker to another. *(1 mark)*

b) Cecilia is going to weigh 3 g of blue crystals onto a clean watch glass. *(1 mark)*

c) Melvin is asked to record the volume of methylated spirits in a measuring cylinder. *(1 mark)*

11. Edgar weighs a clean beaker. He adds some sugar to the beaker and reweighs it. He then removes some sugar and reweighs the beaker. Here are his results:

- mass of beaker = 23 g
- initial mass of beaker and sugar = 27 g
- final mass of beaker and sugar = 25 g

a) Calculate the mass of sugar originally added to the beaker. *(1 mark)*

b) What mass of sugar was removed from the beaker? *(1 mark)*

12. Mimi poured two cups of coffee. She covered one with a saucer. Using a thermometer, she measured the temperature of each cup over time. Table 5.5 shows her results.

Table 5.5 Covered and uncovered coffee

Time (minutes)					
0	2	4	6	8	10
Temperature (covered) (°C)					
85	76	68	62	57	54
Temperature (uncovered) (°C)					
85	74	65	58	52	48

a) Draw a line graph showing the information in this table. (5 marks)
b) How often did Mimi record the temperature? (1 mark)
c) Why do you think both cups had the same initial temperature? (1 mark)
d) What is the temperature of the coffee in both cups after 5 minutes? (2 marks)
e) When did the temperature in the uncovered cup cool to 55 °C? (1 mark)

13. Table 5.6 shows the nutrients found in milk from humans and cows.

Table 5.6 Human milk versus cow's milk

Nutrient	Human milk (100 ml)	Cow's milk (100 ml)
lactose (g)	7.50	4.50
fat (g)	3.50	4.00
protein (g)	1.10	3.50
calcium	33.00	125.00
phosphorus (mg)	15.00	96.00
total minerals (mg)	210.00	720.00
vitamin C (mg)	4.00	1.40
vitamin A (mg)	0.06	0.07
thiamin (mg)	0.02	0.04
riboflavin (mg)	0.03	0.19

a) How many grams of protein are found in 100 mL of human milk? (1 mark)
b) How many grams of protein are found in 100 mL of cow's milk? (1 mark)
c) Which milk contains more total minerals, human or cow? (1 mark)
d) About how many times more vitamin C is present in a volume of human milk

compared to cow's milk? Answer to nearest whole number. (1 mark)
e) How much fat would be in a litre of human milk? (1 mark)
f) How much fat would be in a litre of cow's milk? (1 mark)
g) A human baby fed on only cow's milk needs to have extra nutrients supplied to make sure all are present in enough quantities. From the table, which two nutrients should be added? (2 marks)

14. For centuries, lunar observers have wondered about the possibility of water on the Moon. Some said there was no water, or if there was it had long since evaporated out to space. In 1884, Samuel Peirpont Langley (astronomer and aircraft designer) wrote, 'That we never see clouds on the Moon, even with the telescope, is itself proof that none exists there'. By the late 1960s, scientists were suggesting that there were some observations pointing to the presence of water on the Moon. But some of these guesses or predictions over the centuries were just fanciful. The writer H. G. Wells stated in 1901, 'The Moon must be enormously cavernous with an atmosphere within, and at the centre of its caverns a sea'.

a) Langley gave the lack of clouds as 'proof' for no water on the Moon. Explain what was wrong with his reasoning. (1 mark)
b) What evidence did Wells have for his statement? (1 mark)

Go to pp. 254–255 to check your answers.

5.7 Improving accuracy and reliability

In science, data is obtained by taking measurements. This can lead to an explanation of why substances have different properties, or how objects behave. During an experiment other factors, which may affect the outcome, need to be controlled.

Accuracy and reliability are important in science, as they are in any research activity. If your results are not accurate or reliable, it will be difficult for anyone to take them seriously.

Accuracy of measurements depends on the quality of the measuring apparatus and how carefully the measurement is taken. Thus an electronic balance that measures mass to two decimal places is more accurate than another that only measures mass to whole grams. If the apparatus is not working properly, or the individual using it makes a mistake, any measurements may be inaccurate.

For reliable data, the variation within the measured values must be small. There will always be some variation in any set of measurements, regardless of what is being measured. This will be due to a number of factors, including the way the measuring apparatus is used. In a set of data, each measurement should closely approximate others made under similar conditions. That is, the results are repeatable; each time a measurement is taken it has approximately the same value. This makes the set of data reliable. Repeating experiments at least five times is a way of increasing reliability.

Random and systematic errors

All measurements are prone to random errors. Random errors in any measurement can lead to values being inconsistent when the experiment is repeated. Random errors, also called experimental errors, affect each measurement differently. Being random, they are inherently unpredictable and are usually scattered about the true value (see Figure 5.8). These errors are caused by unforeseen fluctuations in the readings of the instrument being used, or in how the experimenter interprets these readings.

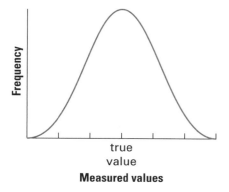

Figure 5.8 Random errors are randomly scattered around the true value.

On the other hand, systematic errors are predictable, and typically constant or proportional to the true value. One important source of this error, for example, may be the imperfect calibration of the measuring instrument (zero error). This is a constant systematic error. For example, if bathroom scales are not zeroed and show 2 kg before you step on them, then your mass will be measured 2 kg more than what it ought to be. Constant errors may be simply due to incorrect zeroing of the instrument. These errors can be very difficult to deal with because they will only be removed if their effects can be observed.

Systematic errors can also be related to the actual value of the measured quantity. For example, it could be proportional or a certain percentage of the measurement, such as a ruler that may show a length consistently greater or less than the true length (see Figure 5.9).

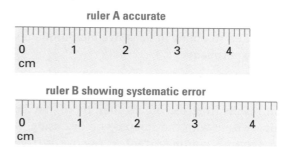

Figure 5.9 Ruler B will measure lengths a certain percentage less than the actual value.

A common way to remove systematic errors is through calibrating the measuring instrument. In voltmeters or ammeters, for example, the instrument error is very difficult to remove. These devices have built-in resistances, which can't be removed. But it can be minimised, such as providing a chart or graph to change the measured value to the true value (see Figure 5.10). On the other hand, removing the error of a thermometer is simpler. Just remove the old calibration and then carefully calibrate the thermometer again.

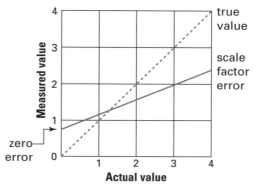

Figure 5.10 If the scale is out, the measured reading could be more or less than the actual value giving a systematic error.

Reliability in first- and second-hand investigations

Reliability is a measure of how much you can trust the conclusion drawn from your experimental results. If the results of some investigation can be repeated, then your conclusion may be considered reliable. Scientists constantly carry out similar, and sometimes even identical, investigations to check the reliability of someone else's experiments and see whether they can replicate the results. They aim to maximise the inherent repeatability or consistency of an experiment.

One way to check reliability is to compare your results with those of others. Reliability can be improved by carrying out repeat measurements; this is why you are often asked to obtain at least five measurements from your experiments.

If you repeat the experiment several times with different samples, and one generates completely different results from the others, then there may be something wrong with the sample you are using. If it is too extreme, you may want to remove it from the experiment and replace it with another. This data point is called an outlier. If you still keep getting wildly different results, then perhaps there is something wrong with the design of the experiment itself.

For many experiments, results will not be identical and there is always a chance that your sample group produces results clustering around the true value. Some very few may even be lying at one of the extremes. Using multiple sample groups will allow you to smooth out these extremes and generate a more accurate spread of results.

A first-hand investigation is one that you conduct yourself. A second-hand investigation is when you report on experimental results carried out by others. Researching on the internet or in the library is an example of a second-hand investigation. Even here you must check your sources to see that they are reliable.

For example, in 1989 a couple of research scientists announced that they had managed to generate heat from a process they called cold fusion at normal temperatures. These reports raised hopes of a cheap and abundant source of energy, and the announcement was widely reported in the media. Many researchers around the world tried to replicate the experiment, without success. Soon there were a number of reasons as to why it was unlikely to occur, experimental flaws were discovered in the original experiment and there were sources of experimental errors. Whether the researchers lied, or genuinely made a mistake, is uncertain but their results were clearly unreliable. So it is important to check your results with other, independent sources to see that your gathered information is correct.

The following points should be noted when gathering information from secondary sources.

> Use a wide range of resources. Do not just rely on the internet. Not all the information on the internet is accurate or correct. Much of it is not peer reviewed (checked by other experts). CD-ROMs, periodicals, library books and even newspapers are valuable sources of information. However, even information gleaned from newspapers should be checked. Remember, these are written by journalists, who may not know much science, and in their endeavour to simplify the information for a wider audience, and to make the newspaper's deadline, some errors may creep in.

> Not all the gathered second-hand data will be reliable. You need to check reliability by comparing it with other sources. Science articles that appear in respected journals and that have been peer reviewed are more likely to be reliable than an article that is self-published. Articles written by creation scientists are not reliable as they do not follow the scientific method. Some companies may be unethical in that they may publish data that is favourable to them.

Reliability simply describes the repeatability and consistency of an experiment or investigation. Are the measurements stable and consistent? Does the same measuring device yield results that are stable when the experiment is repeated many times?

Accuracy refers to how far the measurements are from the true answer. Figure 5.11 illustrates the difference between the terms accuracy and reliability. Each dot on the diagram represents an experimental result.

Validity refers to the extent that a study or research accurately reflects the specific thing that the researcher is trying to measure. Are we measuring what we intend to measure? If you choose the wrong measuring instrument to measure a quantity then the experiment cannot be valid.

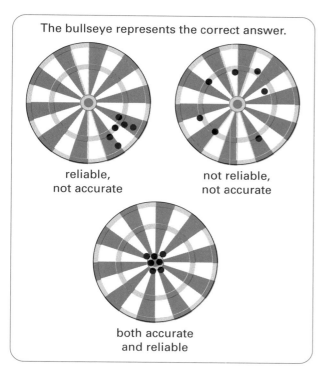

The bullseye represents the correct answer.

reliable,
not accurate

not reliable,
not accurate

both accurate
and reliable

Figure 5.11 Comparing accuracy and reliability using a model

5.8 Presentation of experimental data and analysis of trends in experimental results

Scientists and other researchers use a variety of methods to present experimental data and analyse trends in experimental results.

Constructing models

Figure 5.11 showed a model used to compare accuracy and reliability. Generally, a model is anything used in some way to represent something else. Some models are physical objects, such as a scale model of a building or fighter plane that can be assembled, and can even be made to work like the object it represents. Scientists use models as a way to extend human thought processes. All models are simplified views of reality but, even though they are not entirely correct, are nevertheless extremely useful. They are used to help us know and understand the subject matter they represent. Models are often used when it is either impractical or impossible to create appropriate experimental conditions where scientists can directly measure outcomes.

The following are some characteristics of good models.

- It is based on a given set of observations.
- It must be able to explain as many characteristics of these observations as possible.
- It should be as simple as possible.
- It should be able to explain phenomena other than the ones used to develop the model in the first place.
- It should enable predictions to be made, which can then be tested.

Centuries ago there was strong debate over whether the Earth was flat or round. This led to differences in predictions, depending on the model used. A spherical-Earth model, for example, would predict you could not fall off the end of the Earth. Like most educated people of the time, Christopher Columbus understood that the Earth was spherical and this allowed him to complete four voyages across the Atlantic Ocean.

The spherical-Earth model also explained the observation that a boat appears to 'sink' as it goes over the horizon. Over large distances the curvature of the Earth gives the illusion of a sinking boat as seen in Figure 5.12. The last part of a departing boat seen is the top of the mast. This happens regardless of the direction the boat is moving, and is downwards in all directions.

Figure 5.12 The sailboat in the distance appears to have dipped below the horizon.

But this model can also explain phenomena which appear to be different from the ones used to develop the model in the first place. For instance, a lunar eclipse occurs when the Earth passes between the Sun and the Moon. The spherical-Earth model predicts the shadow of Earth to be round as it passes across the face of Moon; it is.

No scientific model is ever totally complete. Sometimes new observations conflict with the model's predictions, so something must give as either the data or the model is incorrect. While Columbus picked the right model, he underestimated distances and how long it would take him to reach India. No ship in the 15th century could carry enough food and fresh water for such a long voyage, and the dangers in navigating through uncharted waters were formidable. Later, the model was refined with a better estimate of the Earth's radius, allowing for improved predictions about distances to locations on its surface.

All models have limitations; there is no model that can possibly explain every detail of scientific phenomena. For example, while we can use a globe (a model) to estimate the distance from one side of Australia to the other, this would not be exact. A globe is smooth (spherical) but crossing the Australian terrain is not. While these features could be added to make it more realistic, it would complicate the model.

Using diagrams to present data

Mathematical data can be presented graphically. A variety of different graphs are used to organise and represent information, allowing trends and patterns to be identified. Sometimes patterns are not immediately obvious when looking at a table of numbers until a graph is drawn.

A line graph is a very common method of plotting experimental data. This is generally used where the information presented is continuous. The following are rules you should remember when graphing (see also Figure 5.13).

1. Use grid paper to draw your graph. Alternatively, you can draw it on a computer using appropriate software, but include a feint grid in the background.
2. Your graph should occupy at least 80% of the available grid space.
3. The variable that you control (i.e. the independent variable) is placed on the horizontal axis. Number the grid lines along this axis. Label this axis and its units.
4. The variable being observed (i.e. the dependent variable) is placed on the vertical axis. Number the grid lines along this axis. Label this axis and its units.

5. Choose a suitable scale for each axis to ensure that the graph fills most of the grid space.
6. Plot the data points as small crosses (x) or dots (•) using a pencil.
7. Draw the 'line of best fit' through the data points. This line will not necessarily pass through all the points but should be as close as possible to them.
8. Write a title above the graph.
9. Once a line graph is drawn, new data can be extracted from the graph in two ways:
   a) Extrapolation. The line can be extended beyond the plotted points and new values of the dependent variable predicted from values of the independent variable that were not actually measured experimentally. This process assumes that the line shape does not change.
   b) Interpolation. New values of the dependent variable can be extracted from the graph for values of the independent variable between the measured data. This process is more accurate than extrapolation as it is within the range of measurements.

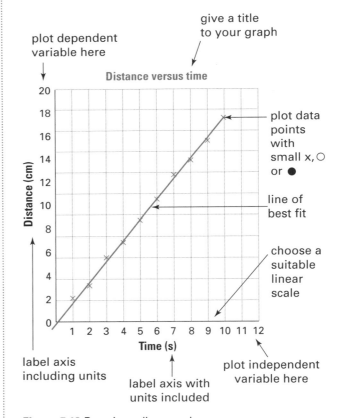

Figure 5.13 Drawing a line graph

When the data collected is discrete (i.e. not continuous), you should not represent the data as a line graph. Continuous data can take any of an infinite number of values between whole numbers. Discrete data is best represented using a column graph, pie chart or bar graphs.

Mathematical data may also be presented as a pie graph. For example, the percentage composition of a mixture can be presented this way. The following rules should be used to draw a pie (sector) graph (see also Figure 5.14).

1. Use a compass to draw a suitably sized circle that will fit on your page. A circle of radius 5 cm may be a good option.

2. Convert the percentage data to degrees. Thus, if one component is 30% then $\frac{30}{100} \times 360 = 108°$. (See the next section for more detail.) Repeat this with the remaining percentage data.

3. Draw a radius on the circle using a ruler and pencil.

4. Use your protractor to measure the first angle (e.g. 108°) and draw a second radius to produce the first sector of the pie graph.

5. Repeat this procedure to measure the remaining sectors.

6. Label each sector and give the graph a title.

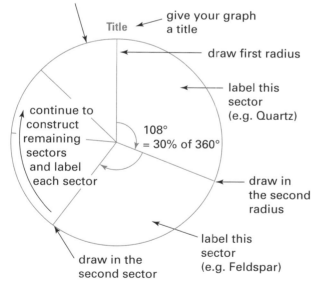

Figure 5.14 Drawing a pie graph

A radar chart is often used to graph information that varies periodically. This is really a line graph wrapped to form a circle or polygon. It displays values relative to a central point. For example, the average monthly temperatures for Sydney vary over a year, and these values repeat year after year. In Figure 5.15, for example, the maximum average day temperature is 26 °C and this occurs for both January and February. The minimum average night temperature of 8 °C occurs in July.

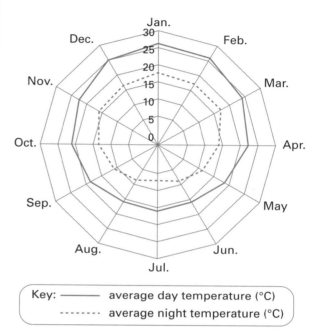

Key: ——— average day temperature (°C)
- - - - - average night temperature (°C)

Figure 5.15 A radar chart showing average monthly temperatures for Sydney over a year

Diagrams and maps often have different scales. The scale should be stated on the map or diagram as shown in Figure 5.16. The scale should be easy to use.

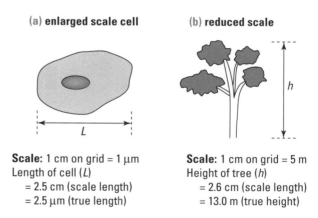

(a) enlarged scale cell

Scale: 1 cm on grid = 1 μm
Length of cell (L)
= 2.5 cm (scale length)
= 2.5 μm (true length)

(b) reduced scale

Scale: 1 cm on grid = 5 m
Height of tree (h)
= 2.6 cm (scale length)
= 13.0 m (true height)

Figure 5.16 Using scales on maps and diagrams

Computer software

Computer software can be used to generate graphs, tables, flow charts and diagrams. Graphing software often allows users to produce a variety of different graphs of the same data quickly and conveniently, such as those shown in Figure 5.17.

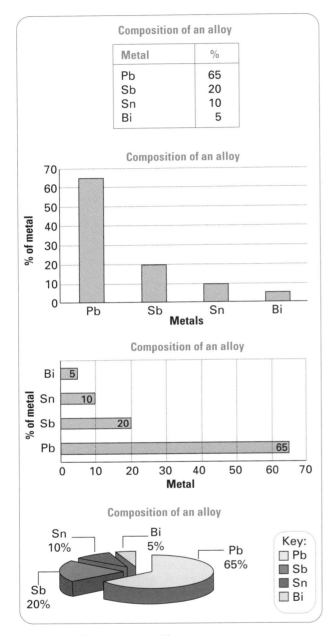

Figure 5.17 Computer graphing

Mathematical analysis of data

In many experiments you are asked to make several measurements, and then take an average. The reason for this was discussed earlier. For example, suppose you weighed four samples and their masses were 4.56 g, 4.40 g, 4.44 g, 4.51 g. The range of this data is *highest value – lowest value* = 4.56 – 4.40 = 0.16 g.

The mean (average) value is:

$$\frac{(4.56 + 4.40 + 4.44 + 4.51)}{4} = \frac{17.91}{4}$$
$$= 4.4775 \text{ g.}$$

However, notice that each measurement was made correct to two decimal places, so your average value cannot be more accurate than that. You should report your mean as 4.48 g. That is, round off your answer (in this case) correct to two decimal places.

Suppose your measurements were 4.56 g, 4.40 g, 4.44 g and 7.51 g. Can you see that the last measurement is not close to the other values? An outlier is an observation that is numerically distant (unusually large or small and out of place) from the rest of the data. If you were now to take an average:

$$\frac{(4.56 + 4.40 + 4.44 + 7.51)}{4} = \frac{20.91}{4}$$
$$= 5.2275$$
$$= 5.2 \text{ g}$$

By including this outlier, you get an average that doesn't represent (is not somewhere near the middle) of the other three values.

Outliers can occur by chance; some data points will be further away from the sample mean than what is considered reasonable. This can be due to incidental systematic error or poor experimental technique. The best thing you can do is to take another measurement and ignore the outlier. So, for example, 4.56 g, 4.40 g, 4.44 g, 7.51 g (deleted measurement) and 4.52 g (the new measurement) would lead you to ignore the outlier and work with the other four values. If you make careful measurements, you should not often come across outliers.

Graphical analysis using spreadsheet applications

Many of the graphs shown in this chapter can be drawn using spreadsheet applications such as Microsoft Excel. This can make your report look more appealing while still clearly presenting your information. There are other graphical programs, many of which are free and can be downloaded from the internet. Computer programs can present a variety of graphs and tables in many different and interesting orientations. This can save much time from manually drawing the graph, although you should still understand how to create one.

1. Open Microsoft Office Excel.
2. Enter the values you wish to draw (see Figure 5.18).
3. Click on one of the chart icons at the top, and then follow the instructions to create your graph. You may need to practice to obtain a graph that contains all the features you want.

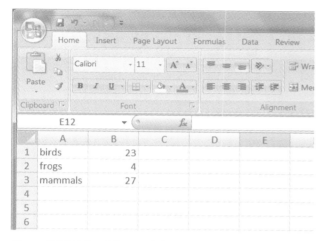

Figure 5.18 Using Microsoft Excel

Analysing trends

The following points should be noted when processing information that has been gathered from various first-hand and second-hand sources:

- Where applicable, use mathematical procedures to analyse the data. For example, if you have collected data on the velocity of a ball falling from rest as a function of time, then the formula $v = u + at$ can be used to determine the acceleration of the ball. (There is no need for you to remember this formula; the important idea is for you to follow the procedure used to obtain the acceleration of the ball.) When v is plotted as a function of t, then your data should fall on a straight line that passes through the origin. The slope of this line will be equal to the acceleration a.

- Data can also be determined from a graph by interpolation or extrapolation as shown in Figure 5.19. When extrapolating a graph, it is important to determine whether the extrapolation is valid.

- Reliability is improved by making repeated measurements (at least five). The collected measurements should then be averaged.

- When conducting a fair test, your data will either support or discount the hypothesis. If the hypothesis is supported, it does not mean that it

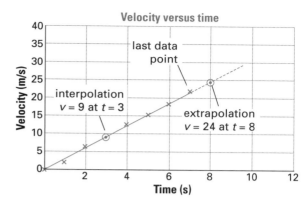

Figure 5.19 Obtaining data through interpolation and extrapolation of a graph

is necessarily correct, as further experiments may be contradictory and not support it.

- As you collect data during an investigation, you may notice trends or patterns starting to emerge. For example, if you are plotting a graph of the radii of atoms as a function of their atomic weight, you will begin to notice that there is a repeating pattern where the radius drops from Group 1 (I) to Group 18 (VIII) across any one period. This is shown in Figure 5.20.

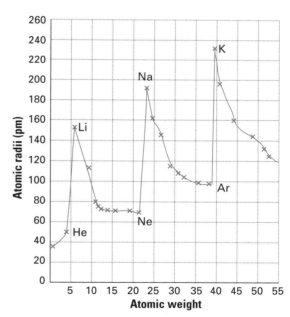

Figure 5.20 Patterns in data emerging when data is processed

- Once you have processed your results, you will need to draw valid conclusions. The conclusions must relate directly to the experimental results. You cannot make a conclusion about information that you have not gathered or measured.

There are 23 birds, 4 frogs and 27 mammal species which are believed to have become extinct since European settlement occurred in Australia. This information can be presented as a pie chart (sector graph) or divided bar graph. Both of these are useful for showing parts of a whole. Figure 5.21 is a pie chart of this data.

Vertebrate extinctions in Australia since 1788

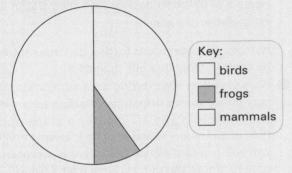

Figure 5.21 Pie chart of vertebrate extinctions

In order to calculate the central angle (the angle you measure at the centre of the circle) for each of these, you need to find:

$$\frac{\text{number in the category}}{\text{total number}} \times 360°$$

For example, 23 birds became extinct out of (23 + 4 + 27 =) 54 vertebrates. So the central angle for birds is $\frac{23}{54} \times 360° = 153°$ (to the nearest degree). Do the same for the other categories.

This information can also be shown as a divided bar graph, like those in Figure 5.22.

(a) **Vertebrate extinctions in Australia since 1788**

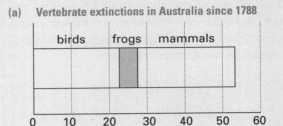

(b) **Vertebrate extinctions in Australia since 1788**

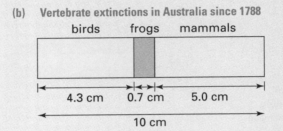

Figure 5.22 Two ways to show this information using divided bar graphs

In a divided bar graph, a scale can be drawn and each of the bars representing the category placed next to each other. For example, 4 frogs became extinct, so its bar begins at 23 (where the bird bar ends) and ends at 27.

Another way is to draw a bar, say, 10 cm long and determine what length each category occupies. This is similar to the sector graph:

$$\frac{\text{number in the category}}{\text{total number}} \times \text{length of whole bar}$$

For the birds this is $\frac{23}{54} \times 10 = 4.26 = 4.3$ cm.
Do the same for the other categories.

▷ As part of the scientific method, you will then provide plausible explanations of the phenomena being investigated. These possible explanations will be written in the discussion section of the report. There is also an opportunity at this point to justify any inferences you have made about the collected data. In the discussion, you may make some predictions that will lead to further experimentation.

▷ As more experiments are completed, you may be able to make some generalisations about your area of investigation.

5.9 Explanations and conclusions

On 17 July 1998 what was thought to be a 7.1-magnitude earthquake occurred in the sea 25 km off the coast of Papua New Guinea. Soon, a tsunami 10 to 15 m high pounded the shore killing over 2200 people and displacing around 10 000 people more.

Local people had different ideas on what caused it, as shown in Figure 5.23.

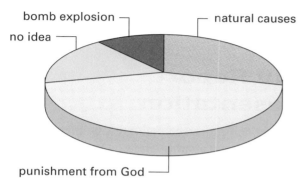

Figure 5.23 How local people interpreted the events

But there were inconsistencies.

- A 7.1 earthquake is not typically strong enough to create such a large tsunami.
- The tsunami took longer than usual (around 20 minutes) to reach the shore.
- A loud rumbling sound lasting over a minute heard by locals is not typical of earthquakes, or its after-shocks.

This led scientists to do more research and look for an alternate explanation. Besides interviewing people and looking at surface damage, they conducted surveys of the ocean floor around where this earthquake was thought to occur. A bowl-shaped depression in the sea floor slope and recent movements were observed. This confirmed their theory of an undersea landslide.

It is now generally accepted that the tsunami was caused by an undersea landslide and not by an earthquake. While the tsunami was originally thought to have been created by a 2-m vertical drop in the Pacific Plate, it is now known that the earthquake caused a huge underwater landslide. It was this that generated the tsunami.

And the implications? This event has changed scientists' ideas about small earthquakes producing undersea landslides, making them realise that landslides can be more hazardous. Undersea earthquakes near the shore are normally felt by people on land, and detected by seismic stations.

But undersea landslides give no warning and can generate 'surprise' tsunamis.

Alternative explanations

This example shows that scientists may interpret the same experimental data differently. Science advances through legitimate scepticism. Asking questions and querying other scientists' explanations is part of any scientific inquiry. Scientists evaluate the explanations proposed by other scientists by examining and comparing evidence, identifying faulty reasoning, pointing out statements that don't fit the facts, and suggesting alternative explanations for the same observations.

Different kinds of questions suggest different kinds of scientific investigations. So depending on what scientists are investigating, and what emphasis is placed on that investigation, will determine the kinds of questions that need to be asked and answered.

Scientific investigations sometimes result in new ideas and phenomena for study, and may generate new methods or procedures for an investigation. Applying new technologies to existing data can lead to new conclusions.

Cause and effect relationships

Cause and effect refers to an action or event that produces a certain response to the action in the form of another event. In other words, a cause is something that makes something else happen. Out of these two events, the cause happens first and the effect occurs afterwards.

Connecting words are often used to link the cause and effect. These include 'because', 'the reason for', 'therefore', 'consequently', 'since', 'as a result', 'due to' and 'thus'. Here are some examples.

- *Because* of the Moon's gravitational attraction, there are ocean tides.
- The Moon's gravitational attraction *affects* the ocean tides.
- *Since* the Moon has a gravitational attraction, so it follows that there are ocean tides.

There are several factors that cause and effect have in common.

- Cause and effect must be linked in space and time.
- The cause must be prior to the effect.

- There must be some constant relationship between the cause and effect.
- The same cause always produces the same effect.
- Where several different objects produce the same effect, there must be something common among them.

In science, especially physics and chemistry, it is reasonably easy to establish causality. A good experimental design neutralises any potentially confounding variables. The only difference between a control group and an experimental group is one variable with the aim being to determine whether that one variable produces different results.

But cause is not always obvious. For example, there is a high correlation between depression and alcohol consumption. It has been shown that people who suffer from higher levels of depression drink more. Does this mean that depression drives people to drink? Since alcohol is a depressant it is equally possible that heavy alcohol consumption makes people more depressed. That is, the same research leads to two different interpretations.

This is a 'chicken and egg' type of argument and makes establishing causality a difficult aspect of scientific research. As well, it allows interest groups to manipulate the results. For instance, alcoholic drink producers and sellers could claim that alcohol is not a factor in depression, and that depression is a problem that should be tackled by society. On the other hand, anti-drinking groups could claim that alcohol is harmful as it leads to depression and make a case for harsher drinking laws.

Critical thinking strategies

When you evaluate your work and draw conclusions, you will use critical thinking strategies. Here are some important points about these strategies.

- Evaluate which of a number of possible strategies is the best approach to solve a problem. For example, if you plan to study the ecology of a local swamp, will you use photographic records, physical and chemical measurements, statistical methods or recounts from personal observations? Some strategies may be more useful than others.
- Be flexible and willing to change your view when confronted with contradictory evidence. Your hypothesis is not necessarily correct and you need to be prepared to change it if collected evidence discounts it.

- Think creatively when solving a problem.
- Distinguish between facts and opinions. Facts are pieces of information that can be tested to check that they are correct. Opinions are personal attitudes and feelings that individuals have about an issue. In science, opinions carry no validity.
- Use logical reasoning when interpreting collected data. Poor reasoning is responsible for incorrect conclusions.

5.10 Report presentation

Collected and processed data must be presented to an audience in an appropriate way. The presentation of an experimental report is different to the way you would present an exposition. It is important to select the appropriate text type to present information. Note that the report on your investigation may be made up of several text types.

Different types of text

The following are some different types of text.

- Procedure. This type of text is used to describe how an experiment that has not yet been done is to be performed. Present tense is used. The steps of the procedure are usually numbered or presented as sequential bullet points.
- Procedural recount (experimental record). This type of text is used to record the procedure of the experiment that has already been performed. It is also used for the results and conclusion. Past tense is used in a recount.
- Report. This type of text is used to present information on a particular topic (e.g. the different types of frogs in Australia) that has been investigated using first-hand and/or second-hand data. Factual and descriptive information is presented.
- Discussion. This type of text identifies issues and presents points for and against. The report that you write for an investigation of a problem will have a discussion at the end. The discussion will often include explanations where causes and effects are discussed.

Including an abstract in a report

An abstract is an abbreviated version of a final report. Think of an abstract as a condensed summary of the entire paper. It is often limited to around 250 words, but there is no rule on this. An abstract appears at the beginning of the report. It lets people quickly decide if they want to read your entire report. In other words, it is like an advertisement for what you've done.

An effective abstract:

> uses one or several well-developed paragraphs that are well written, concise and able to stand alone
> contains an introduction, body and conclusion
> follows the time line of the report
> has a logical connection between the material
> simply summarises the report and adds no new information
> can be understood by a wide audience.

The following are some tips for writing an effective report abstract.

> Read the report, keeping the idea of abstracting in mind.
> Write a rough draft. Do not just copy key sentences from your report.
> Revise your rough draft. This is an opportunity to correct any weaknesses, remove irrelevant information, insert important information originally left out, cut down the number of words and correct grammatical and other errors.
> Carefully proofread the final copy.

When writing abstracts, it is important to be brief and state only what is relevant. A successful abstract is compact, accurate and self-contained. Writing a good abstract is hard work, but will repay you as it is easier to read and will entice other people to read your efforts.

Correct methods of referencing

Referencing is a standardised method of acknowledging the information sources you have used in your assignments or written work. Its two main purposes are to:

> acknowledge the source of the information if you are using the ideas of others
> allow the reader to trace the source, to verify your work and/or to obtain more information.

Referencing:

> shows that you are maintaining standards of writing

> acknowledges the work of other writers and gives them due respect
> shows that you have read and considered the relevant sources of information
> makes your work more credible.

At the end of your assignment, place a list of the references you have mentioned, used for information or quoted in the text. Arrange this in alphabetical order based on the author's surname. There are no absolute rules for referencing. However, the essential information that needs to be included is the author(s), the title and details concerning the imprint (date, publisher, date of publication).

The following are some examples of referencing.

> Book, 1 author:
Stamell, J, 2008, *Excel HSC Chemistry*, Pascal Press, Sydney.
> Book, 2 or more authors:
Thickett, G, Stamell J & Thickett, L, 2000, *Science Tracks 9*, MacMillan Education, Sydney.
> Journal article:
Stamell, J, 2000, 'Dependent vs independent variables', *Reflections*, 25(2), p. 26.
> Newspaper article:
Lennon, T, 2011, 'Early communication', *The Telegraph*, 16 August, pp. 28, 45.
> Web document:
Helmenstine, A M, 2011, *What is distillation?*, http://chemistry.about.com/cs/5/f/bldistillation.htm.

Often you don't need to use the whole book, only several pages from it. So it may be necessary to cite page numbers. Do this by writing the numbers as the final item of your referencing. For example, p. 34 for one page, pp. 34–55 for more than one page. If the author is unknown, start with the title of the work and place the year immediately after it.

Presentations using digital technologies

Digital technology is everywhere. What was once thought to be the realm of science fiction has now become science fact. Mobile phones, MP3 players and digital cameras are part of this digital revolution.

Digital technology allows for a variety of information, including images and sounds to be easily recorded and transmitted electronically. The technology is continually developing at a rapid rate. This is an improvement on the static presentation of paper alone.

As well, digital technology allows for a simple and seamless method of manipulating those digitised images and materials making it easy to rearrange, add to or subtract from them, and to organise them far more easily and efficiently. This provides you with a variety of ways to present information easily, but also makes it easier to plagiarise other people's works.

A digital presentation can take many forms. Microsoft PowerPoint, for example, has been a popular tool used for over two decades to help presenters provide image-rich and visually appealing multimedia presentations. Another form of presentation is using video clips from YouTube to demonstrate a process. In recent years, technology tools have become available online to make presentations even more engaging, interactive, or able to reach a diverse audience.

Presenting information using these technologies makes your presentation more appealing than just handing out sheets of paper. Consider the appropriate use of digital technologies when putting together your presentation.

 ## Experiment 3

Vehicle flow rate

Aim

> To determine the vehicle flow rate along a busy road

Method

1. Every hour between 8 am and 5 pm, count the number of vehicles passing a fixed location in one direction on a busy road for 10 minutes. Stand well back from the edge of the footpath.
2. Tabulate the results.

Analysis

1. Convert for vehicle flow rate from vehicles/10 minutes to vehicles/hour.
2. Table 5.7 shows the calculated data from one similar experiment.
   a) Draw a column graph of the vehicle flow rate versus the time of day.
   b) Suggest a hypothesis to account for the changing flow rate of traffic throughout the day.

Table 5.7 Vehicle flow rate data

Time	Flow rate (vehicles/h)
8.00–9.00	1500
9.00–10.00	1260
10.00–11.00	840
11.00–12.00	630
12.00–13.00	510
13.00–14.00	690
14.00–15.00	420
15.00–16.00	540
16.00–17.00	270

Go to p. 253 to check your answers.

Conclusion

 Write a suitable conclusion.

 Go to p. 253 to check your answer.

Test yourself 2

Part A: Knowledge

1. Which information is missing from the following reference? *(1 mark)*

   Thickett, GW, *Jacaranda HSC Chemistry*, Jacaranda Press, Sydney.

   A date of publication
   B country of publication
   C ISBN catalogue number
   D qualifications of the author

2. Pure ethanol has a boiling point of 78.1 °C. A student performed an experiment, as directed, to measure the boiling point of this alcohol and came up with the following values: 80.2 °C, 81.0 °C, 80.5 °C and 80.7 °C. He repeated the experiment using fresh samples of ethanol from another bottle and got similar results. From this information you would suspect that *(1 mark)*

   A the student is a poor experimenter.
   B the ethanol samples were not pure.
   C the temperature quoted in the literature is not correct.
   D there is an error in the thermometer he is using.

3. Which of the following is *not* a feature of a good model? *(1 mark)*

   A It is based on a given set of observations.

   B It explains many characteristics of these observations.

   C It should be as complex and detailed as possible.

   D It allows predictions to be made.

4. A common method to remove systematic error is through .... the measurement instrument. *(1 mark)*

   A replacing

   B calibrating

   C randomising

   D observing

5. The length of the dinosaur in Figure 5.24, from its nose to the tip of its tail, is closest to *(1 mark)*

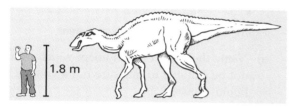

Figure 5.24 Comparing the height of a man with the length of a dinosaur

   A 5 m.

   B 6 m.

   C 7 m.

   D 8 m.

6. Complete the following restricted-response questions using the appropriate word.
   (1 mark for each part)

   a) Systematic errors are biases in measurement leading to a situation where the .... of many separate measurements differs significantly from the actual value of the measured attribute.

   b) There is a variety of different .... that can be used to organise and represent information, allowing trends and patterns to be identified.

   c) Data representing parts of a whole can be represented as either a divided bar graph or a .... graph.

   d) .... simply describes the repeatability and consistency of an experiment or investigation.

   e) To .... means to infer values of a variable in an unobserved interval from values within an already observed interval.

7. Use the code letters to match the terms or phrases in each column. *(1 mark for each part)*

Column 1		Column 2	
A	PowerPoint	F	effect
B	referencing	G	experimental record
C	rough draft	H	report
D	procedural recount	I	acknowledging
E	cause	J	multimedia presentation

Part B: Skills

8. Figure 5.25 shows two scales, allowing you to convert from one temperature scale to another.

   a) Water boils at 100 °C. What is this temperature in Fahrenheit? *(1 mark)*

   b) Water freezes at 32 °F. What is this temperature in Celsius? *(1 mark)*

   c) There are 100 degrees difference between the freezing and boiling points of water on the Celsius scale. How many degrees difference is this on the Fahrenheit scale? *(2 marks)*

   d) Strange as it seems, there is a temperature shown on this graph which is numerically the same on the Celsius scale as it is on the Fahrenheit scale. Can you find this temperature? *(2 marks)*

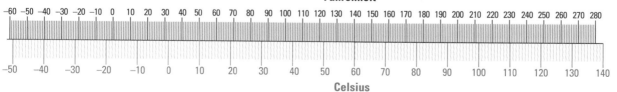

Figure 5.25 A way to convert from Fahrenheit to Celsius temperature

9. Figure 5.26 shows the blood concentration of a certain drug in a person's body. Use this graph to answer the following questions.

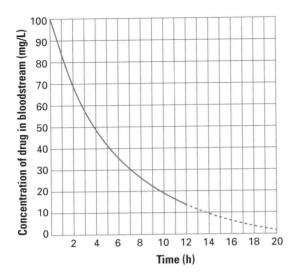

Figure 5.26 Concentration of a certain drug versus time

a) What is the initial concentration of the drug in a person's bloodstream? *(1 mark)*
b) An adult human male who weighs 70 kg has a blood volume of about 5 L. How many milligrams of this drug would be in his bloodstream after 7 hours? *(2 marks)*
c) The solid curve indicates measurements taken over the first 12 hours. The curve is shown dashed after that. What assumption was used to continue the curve up to 20 hours? *(1 mark)*
d) The half-life of a drug is the time that elapses for the concentration of the drug to halve. What is the half-life of this drug? *(1 mark)*
e) What is the concentration of the drug in the bloodstream after three half-lives? *(1 mark)*

10. Figure 5.27 shows the remaining volume of liquid in a long graduated glass vessel with a tap at the bottom.
a) Name the glassware she picked up. *(1 mark)*
b) The level of the surface of the liquid is not flat. Account for this. *(1 mark)*
c) What volume of liquid has been let out of the glassware via the tap? Assume the original water level was 0 mL. Include units.. *(2 marks)*

d) Why is it good practice to read the volume at eye level? *(1 mark)*

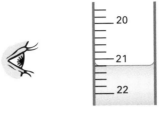

Figure 5.27 Measuring the volume of liquid released

11. Figure 5.28 shows some laboratory equipment.

Figure 5.28 Some laboratory equipment

a) Name the piece of equipment which would not be suitable to measure out a volume of liquid. *(1 mark)*
b) Which of these pieces would you use to measure out 100 mL of solution accurately? *(1 mark)*
c) Which of these pieces would be suitable to heat this solution? *(2 marks)*

12. Table 5.8 gives the typical composition, as percentages, of the igneous rock basalt.

Table 5.8 Mineral composition of basalt

SiO_2	TiO_2	Al_2O_3	FeO
48	3	15	11

MgO	CaO	Na_2O	Other
7	9	4	

a) Complete the percentage in the 'Other' cell. *(1 mark)*
b) Use the scaffold in Figure 5.29 to complete the divided bar graph for this information. *(3 marks)*

Figure 5.29 Grid for divided bar graph

13. A nomogram is a graph consisting of three curves, each graduated for a different variable. For example, the nomogram in Figure 5.30 shows how to find the magnitude of an earthquake. If the maximum amplitude on the seismogram is 2 mm, and the earthquake's epicentre occurred 400 km away, its magnitude is 4.7. This is shown by the line crossing the middle curve.

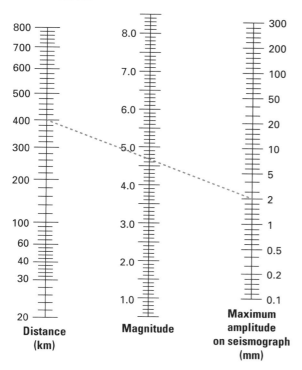

Figure 5.30 A nomogram to determine Earthquake magnitudes on the Richter scale

a) Suppose it is 380 km from the earthquake's epicentre and the seismogram showed a peak of 245 mm. What is the magnitude of the earthquake? *(1 mark)*

b) An earthquake, a distance of 100 km from the seismograph, has a magnitude of 3.0. What peak amplitude should it record at the seismic station? *(1 mark)*

c) An earthquake records a maximum amplitude of 2 cm. What is its minimum distance away if it is to have a magnitude of at least 6.0? *(1 mark)*

14. Table 5.9 gives the average day and night temperatures, in °C, for London.

Table 5.9 Day and night temperatures

Month	Jan.	Feb.	Mar.	Apr.	May	Jun.
Day	6	7	10	13	17	20
Night	2	2	3	5	8	11

Month	Jul.	Aug.	Sep.	Oct.	Nov.	Dec.
Day	22	21	19	14	10	7
Night	13	13	11	8	5	3

Using computer software such as Excel, draw a radar graph showing this information. *(4 marks)*

Go to   pp. 255–256   to check your answers.

Summary

1. The steps in a first-hand investigation are observation, inference, prediction, hypothesis, experimentation, analysis of results and making a conclusion.

2. Before conducting a first-hand investigation, background research is undertaken and secondary sources are checked for validity and reliability.

3. There are similarities and differences in the ways that experiments are performed individually and in a team.

4. Appropriate equipment must be selected for an experiment.

5. Fair testing involves controlling variables and allowing only one variable to change at a time.

6. Blind and double-blind controls are used to avoid bias in experiments involving human subjects.

7. A knowledge of laboratory safety rules is essential before first-hand investigations are conducted.

8. There are steps in science you can take to improve accuracy and reliability.

9. Two important types of errors are random and systematic errors.

Summary cont.

10. A first-hand experiment is one you do yourself; a second-hand investigation is where you report on work done by others.

11. There is a variety of methods to present experimental data and analyse trends in experimental results.

12. A scientific model is anything used in some way to represent something else.

13. Properly conducted experiments allow you to draw explanations and conclusions.

14. Experimental data may be interpreted differently, but over time one explanation will come to dominate.

15. Cause and effect refers to an action or event that produces a certain response to the action in the form of another event.

16. Collected and processed data must be presented to an audience in an appropriate way.

 ## Syllabus checklist

Are you able to answer every syllabus question in this chapter? Tick each question as you go through the list if you are able to answer it. If you cannot answer it, turn to the appropriate page in the guide as is listed in the column to find the answer.

	For a complete understanding of this topic	Page no.	✓
1	Can I remember the steps in a first-hand investigation?	175	
2	Can I explain why before conducting a first-hand investigation a background research is undertaken and secondary data sources are checked for validity and reliability?	177–178	
3	Can I recall the similarities and differences in the ways that experiments are performed individually and in a team?	178	
4	Can I explain why appropriate equipment must be selected for an experiment?	178–179	
5	Can I explain why fair testing involves controlling variables and allowing only one variable to change at a time?	179–180	
6	Can I explain why experiments involving human subjects use blind and double-blind controls?	180	
7	Can I explain why knowledge of laboratory safety rules is essential before first-hand investigations are conducted?	181–182	

	For a complete understanding of this topic	Page no.	✓
8	Do I understand what steps to take to improve accuracy and reliability?	186–189	
9	Can I explain the difference between random and systematic errors?	187	
10	Can I explain the difference between a first- and second-hand investigation?	188	
11	Do I know the variety of methods used to present experimental data and analyse trends in experimental results?	189–194	
12	Can I explain what a scientific model is?	189–190	
13	Can I draw explanations and conclusions from my experiments?	194–196	
14	Do I understand why experimental data may be interpreted differently?	195	
15	Can I explain cause and effect?	195–196	
16	Do I understand why collected and processed data must be presented to an audience in an appropriate way?	196–198	

Part A: Multiple-choice questions

(1 mark for each)

1. In experiments involving the testing of new drugs on humans, a placebo is a
   A   tablet containing the new drug to be tested.
   B   person who volunteers to take the drug.
   C   blind person who cannot see what is being done.
   D   control that is used for comparison.

2. In blind experiments involving testing drugs on humans
   A   the control group receives the drug.
   B   only the person preparing the drug samples knows the code and that person does not communicate with the scientist.
   C   the volunteers do not know if they are the test group or the control group.
   D   two scientists work together to prepare and administer the drug.

3. Repeating an experimental procedure five or more times increases the
   A   accuracy.
   B   validity.
   C   reliability.
   D   safety.

4. Which piece of equipment would be appropriate for measuring 5.6 mL of water?
   A   100-mL beaker
   B   500-mL beaker
   C   10-mL measuring cylinder
   D   5-mL measuring cylinder

5. Identify which second-hand source of scientific information is the most reliable?
   A   science reporters on TV
   B   *Nature* science journal
   C   science blogs on the internet
   D   creation science journals

6. Jenna measured the temperature at which a certain chemical melted and came up with the following values: 80.2 °C, 81.0 °C, 80.5 °C and 80.7 °C from four repetitions of the experiment. The differences in values are due to
   A   random errors.
   B   systematic errors.
   C   invalid measurements.
   D   unreliable data.

7. Which of the following is true?
   A   Cause and effect are not linked in time.
   B   The cause comes after the effect.
   C   The same cause always produces the same effect.
   D   There is a variable relationship between cause and effect.

8. All scientific knowledge comes from
   A   teachers and textbooks.
   B   teachers and experimentation.
   C   observation and textbooks.
   D   experimentation and observation.

9. A scientist was testing the effects of a certain chemical on the yield of fruit, so she sprayed an orchard with this chemical. A second similar orchard was left unsprayed. When the fruit was harvested, the numbers and sizes of each fruit were recorded. Which of the following is the independent variable in the experiment?
   A   the chemical
   B   the first orchard
   C   the second orchard
   D   the fruit yield

10. Which of the following is most likely to occur if a theory is challenged by new evidence?
    A   The evidence is discarded, modified or ignored.
    B   The theory could be altered.
    C   The theory is maintained as it has been around longer.
    D   Leading scientists in the field decide whether to keep the theory.

Part B: Short-answer questions

11. Here are some observations. Suggest one inference which might explain each observation.
    a) Snails always eat the leaves of the vegetables from the underside of the leaf. *(1 mark)*
    b) The plants growing along the coast are very stunted compared to those further inland. *(1 mark)*

c) The child sitting in that black car is sweating a lot. *(1 mark)*

12. Which of the following statements are generalisations? If the statement is not a generalisation, rewrite it so that it is a generalisation.
   a) All birds can fly. *(1 mark)*
   b) Most clocks do not tell the correct time. *(1 mark)*
   c) Very few metals are not shiny and silvery in colour. *(1 mark)*
   d) Various species of grass grow best in direct or indirect sunlight. *(1 mark)*
   e) All Australian beaches are sandy. *(1 mark)*

13. Soft water is water that allows soap to lather. The softer the water, the more bubbles that form. Hard water is water that does not allow soap to lather. This is caused by the presence of certain mineral salts in the water. Bath crystals and washing soda are known to affect the hardness of water. Given this information, design an experiment to test the hypothesis that bath crystals and washing soda soften hard water. Include:
   a) the aim of the experiment *(1 mark)*
   b) six variables that need to be controlled *(6 marks)*
   c) the method of the experiment *(7 marks)*
   d) the type of data you would collect that would support the hypothesis. *(2 marks)*

14. Table 5.10 shows the results of an experiment that Ashley performed on rubber bands (see Figure 5.31).

Table 5.10 Rubber band lengths

Weight added (kg)	Length (cm)
0.0	5.0
0.2	5.8
0.4	6.4
0.6	7.2
0.8	7.9
1.0	8.8

   a) What do you think was the aim of this experiment? *(1 mark)*
   b) Write a method for Ashley's report. *(6 marks)*
   c) What could Ashley conclude from her experiment? *(1 mark)*

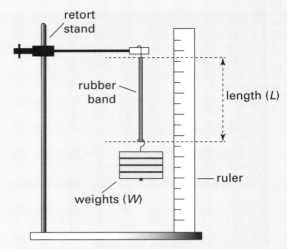

Figure 5.31 Ashley's apparatus

15. The acidity of a substance can be measured in two ways. One way is using a scale called a pH scale. On this scale, low numbers mean high acidity and high numbers mean lower acidity. Another way is to add a dye and observe a colour. The colours are related to the pH as well. Ewen selected a variety of liquids and tested their pH and their colour when the dye was added. With milk, he found the pH was 6.6 while with lemon juice it was 2.0. The dye turned yellow in the milk and red in the lemon juice. He repeated the test with rainwater and ammonia solution. The dye turned orange in the rainwater and blue in the ammonia. The pH of the ammonia was 11.0 and 5.6 for the rainwater.
   a) Present this information in the form of a table. Arrange your information in increasing order of pH. *(2 marks)*
   b) Which of the tested substances is the most acidic? *(1 mark)*
   c) Ewen tested some apple juice and found it had a pH of 3.0. Use this information and the other tests to predict the colour of the dye in apple juice. *(1 mark)*

16. Corey measured the volume (in millilitres) of a sample of air at different temperatures (°C). He collected the information in Table 5.11.
   a) State two problems with Corey's table of results. *(2 marks)*
   b) Sort out Corey's data and try to find a pattern in it.
      i) Redraw his table correctly. *(2 marks)*
      ii) Make a generalisation from this data. *(1 mark)*

iii) One of Corey's measurements is faulty. Which measurement is it? *(2 marks)*

Table 5.11 Volume of air versus temperature

Temperature of air sample (°C)	Volume of air sample
10	103.7
25	109.1
15	106.9
30	111.0
5	101.8
0	100.0
20	107.3

17. In 1662, Robert Boyle, an English scientist, conducted a simple experiment involving a sample of air trapped in a J-shaped tube by a column of liquid mercury (see Figure 5.32). The experiment began with the mercury levels equal. A line was drawn on the tube at this position and this became the reference line. As the heavy mercury was poured into the open arm of the glass tube, the mercury rose in the closed J-arm and compressed the air into a smaller volume. Boyle measured the height of mercury above the reference level in the open arm (h_1) and the height of the trapped air column (h_2) in the closed end of the tube.

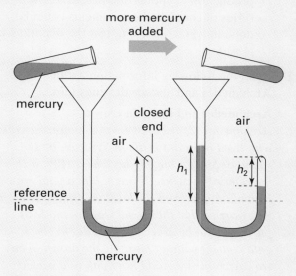

Figure 5.32 Boyle's experiment

Table 5.12 shows some typical results of Boyle's experiment.

Table 5.12 Boyle's law experiment

h_1 (mm)	h_2 (mm)	$h_1 \times h_2$ (mm^2)
190	400	
380	200	
760	100	
1520	50	

a) Complete the table by calculating the product of h_1 and h_2. *(1 mark)*

b) Suggest a mathematical relationship between h_1 and h_2. *(1 mark)*

c) h_2 is proportional to the volume of trapped air. h_1 is proportional to the pressure applied to the air by the weight of the column of mercury. What did Boyle conclude about the volume of air and the pressure applied to it? *(1 mark)*

18. The word *hypothesis* comes from the Greek word meaning 'foundation'.

The *Concise Oxford Dictionary* gives the following definitions for the term hypothesis:

Hypothesis:
1. Proposition made as basis for reasoning, without assumption of its truth;
2. Suggestion made as starting-point for further investigation of known facts;
3. Groundless assumption.

a) How does the Greek derivation relate to the scientific meaning of the word hypothesis? *(1 mark)*

b) One of the three dictionary definitions does not relate to the scientific meaning of the word hypothesis. Which definition is this? *(1 mark)*

19. Complete the following cloze sentences.

a) A hypothesis tries to explain many .... of instances related to a problem or question. *(1 mark)*

b) Very often during an investigation, there is more than one .... which can affect the results. *(1 mark)*

c) Discoveries occur when scientists notice a .... between observations. *(1 mark)*

d) Sometimes more than one .... can be made about a hypothesis. *(1 mark)*

20. Figure 5.33 shows a series of U-tubes containing different liquids balancing on mercury. The liquids do not mix with the mercury. Each liquid is added to the U-tube until the mercury levels in each are equal.

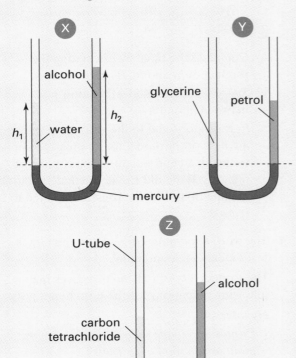

Figure 5.33 Balancing liquids in U tubes

a) The height of each liquid above the dotted reference line was measured and the results were:

X—h_1 = 30 mm, h_2 = 38 mm
Y—h_1 = 17 mm, h_2 = 26 mm
Z—h_1 = 14 mm, h_2 = 28 mm

   i) Work out the value of h_1/h_2 (height of liquid$_1$/height of liquid$_2$). *(3 marks)*
   ii) Use Table 5.13 to calculate the value of D_2/D_1 = density of liquid$_2$/density of liquid$_1$. *(3 marks)*

Table 5.13 Density of liquids

Liquid	Density (g/mL)
alcohol	0.8
petrol	0.9
water	1.0
glycerine	1.3
carbon tetrachloride	1.6

b) Use your calculations to suggest how the density of any liquid compared with water can be readily worked out by experiment. *(1 mark)*

21. For many years, scientists were interested in a fungal disease called blue mould. This fungus spore attacks the leaves of tobacco plants. The fungus threads grow in the leaf tissue and eventually produce spores that are released into the air. Outbreaks of this disease occurred at unpredictable times. After years of research, they realised that the production of spores and the spread of the fungus by these spores was related to the weather. The following observations were collected.

   • Spore cases only formed between 8 pm and midnight.
   • Spores were only released from the spore cases in the five hours before dawn.
   • The night-time temperature did not alter spore production rates.
   • Spores were not produced if the previous day was extremely hot or cold.
   • Spores were only produced under high night-time humidity (over 90%).

   a) When are tobacco plants at greatest risk of being infected by the blue mould? *(2 marks)*
   b) Select one of the factors that influence the production of spores and describe how a series of controlled experiments could be done in a greenhouse to test the hypothesis. *(5 marks)*

22. Read the following information about Archimedes and answer the questions.

Archimedes and the gold crown

Archimedes (287–212 BC) was a famous scientist who lived most of his life in Syracuse on the island of Sicily. One day his friend Hieron II, the ruler of Syracuse, brought him a gold crown he had bought from the local goldsmith. Hieron was worried that the crown was not made of pure gold. So he asked Archimedes to check the gold content without harming the crown in any way. Archimedes could not think of a way to solve this problem until one fateful afternoon. As he stepped into his bath, the water started to flow over the sides. Suddenly an idea came to Archimedes. He realised that the volume of water that overflowed must be equal to the volume of his own body as it submerged. He had found a way of checking the purity of the crown. Legend says that Archimedes was so excited that he jumped out of his bath and ran naked through the streets, yelling 'Eureka!' (I have discovered it!) Here are the steps of Archimedes' solution:

1. *First Archimedes weighed the crown.*
2. *Next he obtained (from Hieron) a lump of pure gold which was the same weight as the crown.*
3. *Placing the lump of gold on one side of a balance and the crown on the Archimedes reported his findings to Hieron and the ruler ordered the goldsmith to be put to death.*

a) Archimedes realised that the lump of gold and the impure crown had different volumes even though they weighed the same. If the lump of gold has a mass of 5000 g and a density of 19.3 g/cm^3, use the density formula ($D = m/V$) to calculate the volume of the lump of pure gold. *(1 mark)*

b) The crown is 75% gold and 25% silver. The mass of the crown is 5000 g. Use the density formula to answer the following questions.

   i) What mass of gold is present in the crown? *(1 mark)*

   ii) What is the volume of this gold? *(1 mark)*

   iii) What mass of silver is present in the crown? *(1 mark)*

   iv) What is the volume of this silver? (Density of silver = 10.5 g/cm^3.)*(1 mark)*

   v) What is the total volume of the crown? *(1 mark)*

   vi) Compare the volume of the crown to the volume of the lump of pure gold. *(1 mark)*

23. Read the following description of one type of grass tree (*Xanthorrhoea arborea*) and draw a labelled, scale diagram from this description. *(3 marks)*

In the Sydney area, about seven different species of grass trees are found. This description refers to one found in open heath and forests near Sydney. The grass tree consists of a sturdy trunk (about 50 cm in diameter and variable height from 50 cm to 200 cm) composed of a pithy material, which is surrounded by rings of old leaf stalks. Each year a new set of leaves grows and the old ones die off so that the outside of the lengthening trunk consists of dead leaf stalks.

The new leaves at the top are narrow and linear and up to 1 m long. A long flowering spike emerges from the top of the trunk and may grow up to 2 m in length. The top half of the spike consists of thousands of very tiny flowers which eventually die off and develop into seed cases.

Honeyeaters are attracted to the nectar present in the flowers.

24. Read the following text and answer the questions below.

In ancient Rome, the Roman baths were supplied with heated water. The water channels were lined with grooved black slate rock which absorbed solar energy. The heated slate then transferred this heat to the water. The first commercial solar water heaters were invented in the United States at the end of the 19th century. They were essentially metal water tanks painted black and placed inside wooden boxes with glass lids.

a) Why did the Romans select black slate? *(1 mark)*

b) Explain how the flat-plate solar hot water heater works. Set out your answer as a series of steps. *(4 marks)*

c) These flat-plate solar hot water heaters do not heat the water to very high temperatures. List all the factors in the design that need to be considered to make the water as hot as possible. *(4 marks)*

25. Read the following text and answer the question at the end.

To the ancient Greek philosopher Aristotle, it was impossible to have a space with no air in it. For over 2000 years since Aristotle, this view was strongly held. It was often quoted in Latin as horror vacui *which means 'nature abhors a vacuum'. Today we call this empty space a vacuum. A vacuum is simply a volume of space that contains no matter. Galileo Galilei established that a vacuum is possible (though many didn't believe him at the time), and that air has weight. Just before Galileo died in 1642, he found that a water pump could not raise water more than about 10 m, no matter how much he tried to get it to do so. Galileo's assistant, Evangelista Torricelli, took up the challenge of creating a vacuum. He experimented with water and other liquids. Eventually, in 1642, he had his assistant Vincenzo Viviani make a 1-m long glass tube. He filled it with mercury, plugged the end with his thumb and inverted it over a basin of mercury. When he took his thumb away, the mercury fell until the column was about 76 cm tall. This left a vacuum at the top as shown in Figure 5.34.*

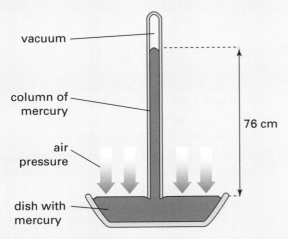

Figure 5.34 Torricelli's experiment

Torricelli reasoned that mercury was not being pulled up by the vacuum, as Galileo would have suggested. Instead, he said, it was pushed up by the weight of the atmosphere (air pressure). Air pressure pushed down on the mercury in the dish, forcing mercury up the tube.

Describe a way that Torricelli could prove that it was the air pressure that supported the column of mercury. *(4 marks)*

26. Many phenomena are better understood by describing their causes and effects. When scientists show a connection between one fact and another, they try to show a cause-and-effect relationship.

    a) Distinguish between cause and effect. *(2 marks)*

    b) Read the following paragraph and identify the cause and the effect. *(2 marks)*
    Scientists will make a detailed study of the damage done to the Great Barrier Reef. They fear the reef is at risk of disease from rising sea temperatures.

    c) P causes Q implies that P happens before Q does. For example, jumping into a swimming pool makes water splash. Is it always true that if Q follows P then P caused Q? Give examples as part of your answer. *(4 marks)*

27. A piece of zinc was dropped into an excess amount of acid and its loss in mass was measured every minute. Figure 5.35 shows the results.

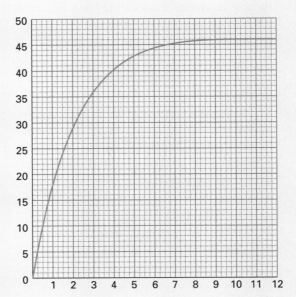

Figure 5.35 Graph of results reacting zinc with acid

    a) Write a suitable label for the horizontal (*x*) axis. Include units. *(1 mark)*

    b) Write a suitable label for the vertical (*y*) axis. Include units. *(1 mark)*

    c) Give the graph an appropriate title. *(1 mark)*

    d) When did the reaction cease? How do you know? *(2 marks)*

    e) What was the initial mass of zinc dropped into the acid? *(1 mark)*

28. The peppered moth (*Biston betularia*) is found in Europe, commonly on tree trunks. It is usually a dark grey colour with speckled markings to help camouflage it on tree trunks. Around 1850 some dark, almost black, moths were noticed alongside pale ones in a forest near the edge of a town. A century later around 90% of the moths in some areas where there was plenty of soot were dark. Figure 5.36 shows these two types of moth.

Figure 5.36 Light and dark forms of the peppered moth

The moth has a 1-year life cycle. The egg hatches into a caterpillar, which then feeds on leaves before pupating. In 1926 a scientist fed leaves impregnated with sooty chemicals to light-coloured moth caterpillars. He then allowed them to progress through their life cycles and produce offspring. He found that 8% of the offspring were dark coloured. He concluded that the soot caused mutations to produce dark-coloured moths.

a) Do you agree with the conclusion this scientist formed? *(2 marks)*

Later other scientists repeated the experiment where some light-coloured moths were fed leaves with soot and other light-coloured moths were fed leaves without soot. They found that dark-coloured moths were produced at the same rate from both groups.

b) What conclusion can you draw from this? *(1 mark)*

c) Explain why the later experiment is better scientifically. *(2 marks)*

d) Suggest a possible reason for dark-coloured moths being more prevalent in 1950 than they were in 1850. *(2 marks)*

e) In recent years evidence suggests that the proportions of dark-coloured moths in the natural population from this study area are falling. Suggest a likely explanation. *(2 marks)*

29. An area of tea-tree scrub on some coastal sand hills were completely burned out during a severe bushfire. Soon rain followed and a large number of tea-tree seedlings started growing. A botanist kept track of the number of tea-tree plants, calculating the average number in each square metre (see Table 5.14).

Table 5.14 Growth of seedlings after a fire

Time after bushfire	Average number of seedlings per square metre
1 month	1280
1 year	1090
5 years	580
10 years	241
20 years	42
30 years	9
40 years	2

There were no further bushfires, and consumer organisms were not noticed to any great extent over this time.

a) Describe what happened to the number of plants in the area over this time period. *(1 mark)*

b) Suggest a hypothesis to account for this change. *(1 mark)*

c) Would the number of seedlings per square metre ever reach zero? Explain. *(2 marks)*

30. a) Distinguish between random error and systematic error. *(4 marks)*

b) Consider Figure 5.37 and explain what it shows. *(4 marks)*

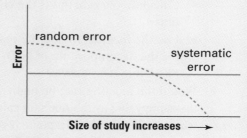

Figure 5.37 Systematic and random errors

c) In a science experiment, measurements are often repeated several times and an average taken. What is the purpose of this? *(1 mark)*

31. The change in the concentration of N_2O_5 (dinitrogen pentoxide) as it decomposes into NO_2 and O_2 was measured and gave the results shown in Table 5.15. The concentration is given in units called moles per litre.

Table 5.15 Concentration of dinitrogen pentoxide versus time

Time (minutes)	Concentration of N_2O_5 (mol/L)
0	10.0
1.5	8.6
3.0	7.7
4.5	7.0
9.0	5.3
14.0	4.1
20.0	3.1
30.0	2.2

a) Write a balanced equation for the decomposition. *(2 marks)*

b) Plot a graph of the concentration of N_2O_5 against time. Draw a curve of best fit through these points. *(5 marks)*

c) The reaction rate (how fast N_2O_5 is decomposing) is given by the slope of the curve at any point on it:

$$\text{reaction rate} = \frac{\text{change in concentration}}{\text{change in time}}$$

In this question you will calculate the rate of decomposition of N_2O_5 when $t = 10$ minutes.

- Draw a tangent to the curve, touching it when $t = 10$.
- Calculate the rise; this is the change in concentration.
- Calculate the run; this is the change in time.
- Use the formula to find the reaction rate for the decomposition of N_2O_5 when $t = 10$ minutes. *(4 marks)*

d) Would the reaction rate be higher, lower or the same value as the one you calculated when $t = 25$ minutes? Explain. *(2 marks)*

32. In an alkaline solution, hydrogen peroxide (H_2O_2) decomposes producing water and oxygen. Figure 5.38 shows this variation of the concentration with time.

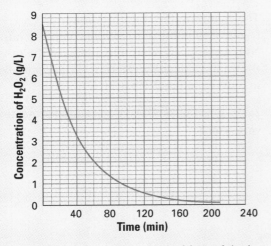

Figure 5.38 Rate of decomposition of hydrogen peroxide with time

a) Comment on the statement: 'It has been found by experiment that the rate of a chemical reaction depends on the concentration of the reactants'. *(2 marks)*

b) What was the initial concentration of the hydrogen peroxide? *(1 mark)*

c) What is its concentration after 80 minutes have elapsed? *(1 mark)*

d) Explain why the concentration of H_2O_2 is placed on the vertical axis, while time is placed on the horizontal axis. *(2 marks)*

33. Some books, and teachers, tell students that time always goes along the horizontal axis. Is this true? Can you think of an example where this might not be the case? *(3 marks)*

34. Bathythermographs have been used for many years by oceanographers to measure the temperature of the upper ocean. These are simple instruments designed to be deployed from moving ships.

a) Use a dictionary, or other source, to determine the origin of the word bathythermograph. *(2 marks)*

Figure 5.39 shows changing temperatures in the ocean.

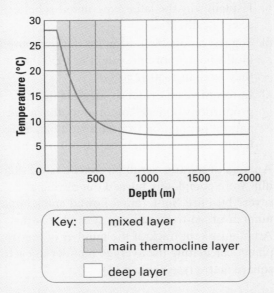

Key:
☐ mixed layer
▨ main thermocline layer
☐ deep layer

Figure 5.39 Changes in ocean temperatures in the tropics

b) Describe the temperature structure in the ocean in each of the three zones. *(3 marks)*

c) Approximately how deep does the mixed layer extend? *(1 mark)*

d) Suggest a reason why there is very little temperature variation in the mixed layer. *(2 marks)*

e) Given the temperature, can you use this graph to determine the depth? Explain. *(2 marks)*

35. Figure 5.40 shows the results of an experiment where two variables are plotted.

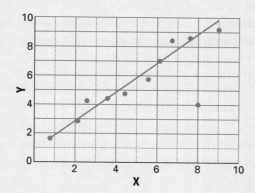

Figure 5.40 Experimental graph of two variables

a) The straight line drawn does not pass through all the points. Explain. *(2 marks)*

b) If the line is extended backwards to the *y*-axis, it cuts it at 1. What is this process called? *(1 mark)*

c) Is there an outlier shown on this graph? If so, identify it. *(1 mark)*

d) What should be done with any outliers? *(1 mark)*

36. After a bath, dogs and cats shake themselves dry. Recently, investigators determined the rate of shaking (the frequency of to-and-fro motions, measured in hertz or cycles/second) for a number of animals. Table 5.16 shows some typical results.

Table 5.16 Frequency of animal shakes

Animal	Average mass (kg)	Frequency of shake (Hz)
mouse	0.035	29
rat	0.35	18
guinea pig	0.9	14
domestic cat	4.5	9
poodle	7	6
labrador	30	5
giant panda	90	4
Sumatran tiger	150	4
brown bear	400	4

a) Use this information to draw a dot plot of shake frequency versus mass. *(4 marks)*

b) Describe what the graph shows. *(2 marks)*

c) Would it be true that all animals shake themselves dry? Explain. *(2 marks)*

37. Australia has the third-largest marine area of any nation in the world. This area is divided into six regions, as shown in Table 5.17.

Table 5.17 Australian marine regions

Marine region	Area (million km²)	Percentage of total area	Bar graph length	Sector graph angle
south-west	1.3	18.7	3.8 cm	67°
north-west	1			
north	0.625			
Coral Sea	0.972			
temperate east	1.47			
south east	1.6			
Total		100.0	20 cm	360°

a) Perform the following calculations and write them into a copy of the table.

- Calculate the total area of marine regions in Australia. Write this value into a copy of the table. *(1 mark)*

- In the third column, calculate the percentage that each marine region comprises of the total. The first one has been done for you:
$$\frac{1.3}{6.967} \times 100 = 18.7\ \%$$
(Round off correct to one decimal place.) *(3 marks)*

- This information will be used to draw a divided bar graph having a total length of 20 cm. Calculate the length of each bar in the bar graph. The first one has been done for you:
$$\frac{18.7}{100} \times 20 = 3.8\ \text{cm}$$
(Round off correct to one decimal place.) *(3 marks)*

- This information will also be used to draw a sector graph (pie diagram). Calculate the central angle for each sector. The first one has been done for you:
$$\frac{18.7}{100} \times 360° = 68°$$
(Round off correct to the nearest degree.) *(3 marks)*

b) Draw the divided bar graph with this information. *(4 marks)*

c) Draw the sector graph with this information. *(2 marks)*

38. Up until 150 years ago, many natural scientists believed in spontaneous generation. This was the view that some vital life force contained in, or given to, organic matter can create living organisms from inorganic (non-living) objects. After all, meat left out soon rotted and maggots were seen. Where did they come from? Milk or soup left out in the open for a few days, spoils. In the mid-1600s Anton van Leeuwenhoek used lenses to view bacteria and algae, but the knowledge that the world teemed with small organisms was regarded as an interesting but rather irrelevant fact.

Well, the maggot problem was solved by Francesco Redi in 1668 when he showed that maggots come from the eggs of flies. Naturalists generally soon came to reject spontaneous generation for organisms they could see without a microscope, but they held onto this notion for microscopic life, such as bacteria.

In 1745 John Needham carried out an experiment with chicken broth in narrow-neck flasks. Needham believed a life force was present in all inorganic matter, even air, and this could cause spontaneous generation to occur. He briefly boiled a flask with broth, sealed it and observed that bacteria still formed in the broth. This, he said, verified that bacteria arose by spontaneous generation.

In 1765 Lazaro Spallazani repeated the experiment but boiled his broth for a much longer period of time. No bacteria grew. He concluded that spontaneous generation does not occur.

This created a lot of controversy and argument, and it took Louis Pasteur to solve it. In 1864 Pasteur took two flasks; one with a straight narrow neck and the other with a narrow S-shaped neck. After the broth boiled, Pasteur left both flasks open to allow for the passage of air into the flask. The broth in the flask with the S-shaped neck did not spoil but the broth in the flask with the straight neck did. Later, Pasteur also broke the S-shaped necks of the flasks, and the broth then spoiled. These experiments are shown in Figure 5.41.

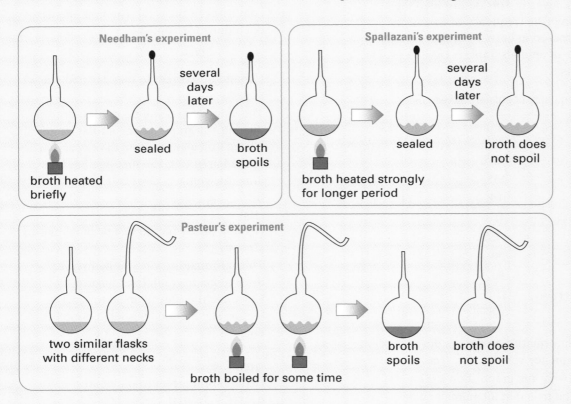

Figure 5.41 Experiments on spontaneous generation

a) In Needham's experiment, why was the broth heated before sealing? *(1 mark)*

b) Why did Needham seal the flask after boiling? *(2 marks)*

c) Did Needham's experiment prove that spontaneous generation occurred? Comment on his experiment. *(2 marks)*

d) Why didn't the broth spoil in Spallazani's experiment? *(1 mark)*

e) Needham criticised Spallazani's conclusion by saying that excessive heating had destroyed the life force necessary to enable life to arise from the broth. Did Spallazani's experiment refute Needham's criticism? Explain. *(3 marks)*

f) Why did Pasteur leave both flasks open to the air? *(2 marks)*

g) Account for why the broth in the straight-necked flask spoiled, but that in the S-necked flask didn't. *(2 marks)*

h) In 1864 Pasteur uttered his famous statement: 'The doctrine of spontaneous generation will never recover from the mortal blow inflicted by this experiment'. Comment on this statement. *(3 marks)*

39. Figure 5.42 shows the average daily sunshine each month for Perth.

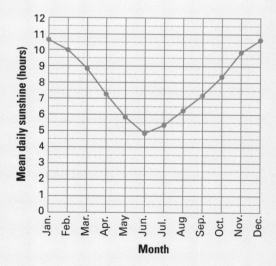

Figure 5.42 Mean daily sunshine for Perth

a) How else could this data have been presented? *(1 mark)*

Many flowering plants need a certain minimum amount of light each day, or a minimum amount of darkness, to flower. The ability to detect the length of the day or night or both makes it possible for the plant to synchronise its reproductive cycle to a particular time of year.

b) A certain plant needs at least 6½ hours of daylight for it to flower. In which months would this plant flower in Perth? *(2 marks)*

c) Another plant requires less than 8 hours of daily sunshine to flower. In which months would it flower in Perth? *(2 marks)*

d) Two plants are shown in Figure 5.43. P is a short-day plant. It must have sufficient hours of darkness to flower. Q is a long-day plant and must have sufficient hours of light to flower. When would these plants flower in Perth? *(4 marks)*

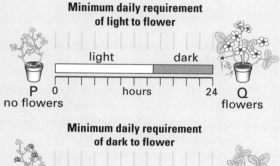

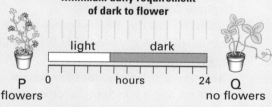

Figure 5.43 Light/dark requirements for plants to flower

40. The radar chart in Figure 5.44 shows the average daily amount of solar energy falling each month on three Australian cities. The energy is measured in kWh/m²/day. That is, the number of kilowatt-hours of energy falling on each square metre of land each day.

a) Which city overall receives the most solar energy? *(1 mark)*

b) For which month of the year does Darwin receive the greatest average solar energy? *(1 mark)*

c) Which city receives the most solar energy each day in January? What is this amount? *(2 marks)*

d) In which month of the year is the average solar energy falling on Sydney and Melbourne the same? *(1 mark)*

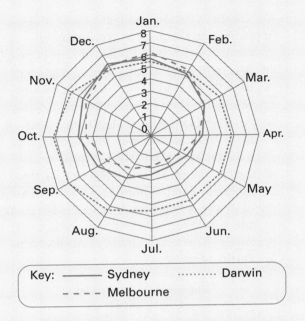

Key: —— Sydney   ⋯⋯⋯ Darwin
- - - - Melbourne

Figure 5.44 Solar energy falling on Sydney, Melbourne and Darwin

e) True or false: Darwin, being further north, consistently receives more solar energy each day than either Sydney or Melbourne. Explain. *(2 marks)*

f) Which city has the greatest range over a year in solar energy received? What is this range? *(4 marks)*

g) The average solar amount of radiation falling on Sydney in September is 4.32 kWh/m²/day. Can you determine this value from the graph? Explain. *(3 marks)*

h) Approximately how many kWh/m² of solar radiation fall on Darwin in May? *(2 marks)*

i) A hectare = 10 000 m². In February, Melbourne has approximately 14 hours of daylight each day and the solar energy radiation is 5.65 kWh/m²/day. Calculate the amount of energy, in kilowatt hours, falling on each hectare each hour. *(3 marks)*

Go to   pp. 256–263   to check your answers.

This test covers material from all the chapters in this book. It consists of the following.

- Section A: 25 multiple-choice questions *(1 mark for each)*
- Section B: 15 restricted-response questions *(1 mark for each)*
- Section C: 14 knowledge, skill and processing data questions *(total 60 marks)*

Total marks for this test: 100

Time: 2 hours

Part A: Multiple-choice questions

(25 marks—1 mark for each question)

1. What is the reading on the alcohol thermometer scale shown in Figure T1.1?

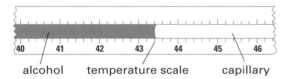

Figure T1.1 Alcohol thermometer scale

A 43.4 °C
B 42.4 °C
C 43.5 °C
D 43.6 °C

2. Figure T1.2 shows a line graph of velocity of a vehicle starting from rest, versus time. Use the graph to determine the velocity of the vehicle 5 seconds after it started its journey.

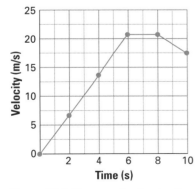

Figure T1.2 Line graph of velocity versus time

A 12.5 m/s
B 17.0 m/s
C 17.5 m/s
D 20.0 m/s

3. A falling body accelerates uniformly in the absence of air friction. Table T1.1 shows the velocity of a body that is dropped from rest in a vacuum. Determine the value of the downward velocity after 4 seconds.

Table T1.1 Falling body

Time (s)	Velocity (m/s)
0	0
1	9.8
2	19.6
3	29.4
4	
5	49.0
6	58.8

A 34.3 m/s
B 39.2 m/s
C 44.1 m/s
D 48.0 m/s

4. Newton's second law of motion states that the acceleration a of a body of mass m is directly proportional to the net force F applied. Which mathematical relationship is consistent with this information?

A $a = Fm$
B $m = Fa$
C $F = m/a$
D $F = ma$

5. Select the statement that is *not* used as evidence that present-day organisms have developed from different organisms in the distant past.

A Horse fossils show significant changes over the last 60 million years.
B The bones at the ends of the limbs of vertebrates are based on a common structure.
C Following extreme climate changes, fossil evidence shows the appearance of many new species.

D Breeding experiments with dogs show that new breeds can be developed.

6. The following information was gathered by a student.
   • The Palaeozoic era is older than the Mesozoic era.
   • Dinosaurs flourished in the Mesozoic era.
   • The Precambrian era came before the Palaeozoic era.
   • Mammal fossils are found in Mesozoic rocks but not in Palaeozoic rocks.

   Which of the following statements is true of the Palaeozoic era?
   A The Palaeozoic era is more recent than the Mesozoic era.
   B Fish and amphibians were the dominant vertebrate life forms during the Palaeozoic era.
   C Mammals first evolved during the Palaeozoic era.
   D The Palaeozoic era dates back to the formation of a solid crust on Earth.

7. As the Sun ages, it will evolve into a giant star. What colour is that giant star?
   A yellow
   B white
   C blue
   D red

8. The second most common element in the universe is
   A hydrogen.
   B carbon.
   C helium.
   D oxygen.

9. Figure T1.3 shows fossils in four different locations M, N, O and P.

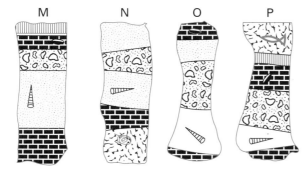

Figure T1.3 Fossils

In which location is the oldest fossil located?
   A M
   B N
   C O
   D P

10. Which of the following statements is *not* part of Charles Darwin's theory of natural selection?
    A Organisms with favourable variations survive to reproduce.
    B Within a species, there is a natural variation.
    C Over time, favourable characteristics are preserved in a population.
    D Characteristics acquired during an organism's life can be passed on to the next generation.

11. A 5-kg mass is placed on a sheet of paper on a table. If the paper is suddenly moved horizontally, the mass is left almost at the same position on the table. This observation is an example of the principle of
    A inertia.
    B mass conservation.
    C energy conservation.
    D action and reaction.

12. One of the worst mass extinctions on Earth occurred at the end of the Ordovician period 438 million years ago. One organism that was particularly affected was the marine trilobite. The extinction rate was higher for trilobites that lived in surface waters than for trilobites that were deep water dwellers. One theory put forward to explain these extinctions is that Earth at this time suffered periods of gamma ray bursts emitted from the collapse of a nearby giant star and the formation of a black hole. According to the theory, the gamma rays converted some gases in the atmosphere into toxic nitrogen oxides that temporarily destroyed the protective ozone layer. For over a year, life on Earth would have been exposed to dangerous radiation that was normally blocked by the ozone layer. This dangerous radiation that is normally absorbed by the ozone layer is
    A infrared.
    B microwave.
    C ultraviolet.
    D visible light.

13. The element most chemically similar to sulfur is
    A phosphorus.
    B chlorine.
    C carbon.
    D selenium.

14. Which of the following examples best illustrates Newton's third law of action and reaction?
    A Rockets move forwards by expelling gases produced in the combustion chamber.
    B A ball falls down to Earth because of the pull of gravity.
    C Heavy bodies tend to remain at rest.
    D A tennis ball has greater acceleration when it is struck by a greater force.

15. What is the correct symbol for the element indium?
    A I
    B In
    C Ir
    D Id

16. Figure T1.4 shows a family pedigree involving the inheritance of haemophilia, which is a sex-linked blood disease.

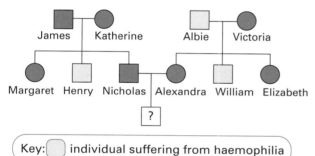

Key: ⬚ individual suffering from haemophilia

Figure T1.4 Family pedigree

If Nicholas marries Alexandra, what is the chance that any son born will be a haemophiliac?
    A 100%
    B 75%
    C 50%
    D 25%

17. A student was trying to determine how much light is absorbed by the chemical urea. She labelled six test tubes and introduced a measured amount of urea in solution into each test tube. She then placed each test tube in turn into a machine that measured how much light was absorbed by the solution. She compiled her results into Table T1.2. One of her measurements was entered incorrectly.

Table T1.2 Urea light absorption experiment results

Tube number	1	2	3	4	5	6
Volume of urea solution (mL)	0	0.18	0.75	1.50	3.30	5.20
Light absorbed	0	0.04	0.70	0.35	0.75	0.85

The incorrect entry was for test tube number
    A 2.
    B 3.
    C 4.
    D 5.

18. Which of the following statements is used as evidence to support the theory of evolution?
    A Reptiles, birds and mammals have a common ancestor because they all possess pentadactyl limbs.
    B Fossils become less complex in structure in more recent sedimentary strata.
    C Organisms pass on characteristics acquired during their lifetimes to their offspring.
    D Mutations of genes are always fatal and cannot contribute to evolutionary change.

19. Technology has increased the variety of materials available to our society. Which of the following materials was developed during the 20th century?
    A copper
    B steel
    C plastics
    D glass

20. According to the Big Bang theory of the universe
    A space and time did not exist before the Big Bang.
    B the universe consisted only of energy before the Big Bang.
    C atoms formed within the first second after the Big Bang.
    D a giant star exploded to produce all the matter and energy in the universe.

21. Table T1.3 shows the melting and boiling points of four elements.

Table T1.3 Melting and boiling points

	Fluorine	Chlorine	Bromine	Iodine
Melting point (°C)	−233	−102	−7	113
Boiling point (°C)	−188	−35	59	183

The element likely to be found as a liquid at room temperature is

A fluorine.

B chlorine.

C bromine.

D iodine.

22. A student mixed differing amounts of solutions P and Q in a test tube and noticed each produced a precipitate. Her results are shown in Table T1.4.

Table T1.4 Precipitate formed from mixing two solutions

Volume of solution P (mL)	Volume of solution Q (mL)	Precipitate (cm)
9	5	2.0
4	5	0.8
5	5	1.2
6	5	1.6
7	5	2.0
8	5	2.0
9	5	2.0

She could correctly conclude that

A when 2.0 cm of precipitate forms, then all of solution P is used.

B no precipitate forms when 3 mL of solution P is added to 5 mL of solution Q.

C when 7 mL of solution P is added then the 5 mL of solution Q is completely used up.

D varying the amount of solution Q will not change the amount of precipitate formed.

23. Mercury(II) oxide, a red powder, was used by Lavoisier in his famous work on combustion. He made it by heating mercury in air for a long time at temperatures just below its boiling point. He collected the red specks of mercury(II) oxide floating on the surface of the mercury:

mercury + oxygen → mercury(II) oxide

On being strongly heated, mercury(II) oxide yields oxygen and mercury:

mercury(II) oxide → mercury + oxygen

Which of the following statements is true?

A The amount of oxygen used in the first reaction is not equal to the amount liberated in the second reaction.

B The mass of oxygen used is greater than the mass of mercury obtained.

C The mass of mercury(II) oxide used in the second reaction is less than the mass of mercury used in the first reaction.

D The mass of mercury(II) oxide must equal the mass of mercury plus the mass of oxygen.

24. A car leaks oil onto the road at a constant drip rate. Figure T1.5 shows the pattern of oil drops on the road.

What can you conclude about the motion of this vehicle from this pattern of drops?

A The car is moving at constant speed.

B The car accelerated and then decelerated.

C The car decelerated and then accelerated.

D The car accelerated and then moved with constant speed before decelerating.

25. A scientist has at his disposal a small vineyard of 48 grapevines. He needs to test two new fungicides to see how effective they are against fungal disease. Which of the following procedures would be best?

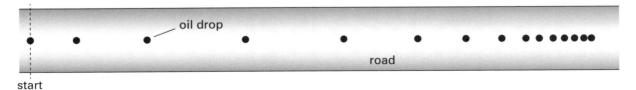

start

Figure T1.5 Oil drops on a road

A Select 24 vines at random for treatment with one fungicide, and the remainder with the other fungicide.

B Treat 16 vines at random with one fungicide, another 16 vines with the other fungicide and leave the remainder untreated.

C Select the 16 healthiest plants as control. Then randomly treat half the remainder with one fungicide and the other half with the second fungicide.

D Number all plants in order from 1 to 48. Treat the odd-numbered plants with one fungicide and the even-numbered plants with the other fungicide.

Part B: Restricted-response questions
(15 marks—1 mark for each question)

Complete the following restricted-response questions using the appropriate word.

26. The modern periodic table is arranged in order of increasing atomic .... of the elements.

27. Newton's .... law is known as the law of inertia.

28. Darwin found important evidence for his theory of natural selection on the .... islands.

29. Antibiotic resistance is an example of .... selection.

30. The mass extinctions of species throughout geological history seem to be related to worldwide ....

31. There is a natural .... in characteristics within the population of any species.

32. John Dalton stated that atoms are .... and they cannot be destroyed or created.

33. Dmitri Mendeleev's periodic table was based on increasing atomic ....

34. In the periodic table, metallic properties increase down a ....

35. Reactive metals such as potassium, sodium and calcium will react with cold water producing bubbles of .... gas.

36. When astronomers looked for various elements in distant stars and galaxies, they found the characteristic frequencies of key lines of the spectrum was shifted towards the .... end of the visible spectrum.

37. .... telescopes can show where clouds of cool hydrogen are located between stars.

38. When a car slows down it is said to be decelerating, but it can also be described as having .... acceleration.

39. .... is a force that causes objects to resist being moved across one another.

40. The acceleration of a body depends directly on the size of the net force and .... on the mass of the body.

Part C: Knowledge, skill and processing data questions
(60 marks)

41. The gene for a straight nose (S) is dominant over the gene for a turned-up nose (s). If two parents are heterozygous for straight noses, what is the chance that their first child will have a turned-up nose? *(2 marks)*

42. a) When did the Earth form? *(1 mark)*
    b) What evidence is there for the age of the Earth? *(1 mark)*
    c) What processes led to the internal heating of the Earth? *(1 mark)*
    d) Where inside the Earth is melted iron located? *(1 mark)*

43. In which era of Earth's history did the following life forms first appear?
    a) humans *(1 mark)*
    b) fish *(1 mark)*
    c) dinosaurs *(1 mark)*
    d) conifers *(1 mark)*
    e) amphibians *(1 mark)*

44. An isotope of element G (not its real symbol) has the following symbol: $^{64}_{29}$G.
    a) Use the periodic table to identify G. *(1 mark)*
    b) Calculate the number of neutrons in the nucleus of G. *(1 mark)*
    c) Discuss the reactivity of G in water and air. *(1 mark)*

45. Use the blank periodic table in Figure T1.6 and the periodic table published inside the front cover of this book to answer the questions.

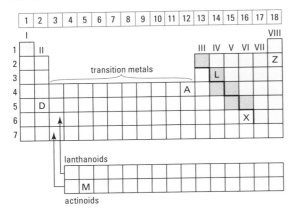

Figure T1.6 Blank periodic table

Six elements are shown using code letters.

a) Name these six elements. *(1 mark)*

b) Which of the six is a semi-metal? *(1 mark)*

c) Which of these six elements would have the lowest boiling point? *(1 mark)*

d) Write the electron configuration of the element labelled L. *(1 mark)*

e) Which elements are naturally radioactive? *(1 mark)*

f) Which element will react with water, releasing a colourless gas? *(1 mark)*

46. Use the periodic table to identify the following unknown elements.

a) Element Q: five valence electrons; member of Period 5. *(1 mark)*

b) Element D: member of Period 4; brown, fuming liquid. *(1 mark)*

c) Element X: member of Group 18 (VIII); radioactive. *(1 mark)*

47. Match each of the words in the following word list to its definition. Copy the matching pairs into your workbook. *(6 marks)*

Word list:

1. generalisation
2. scientific method
3. observation
4. experiment
5. inference
6. prediction

Definition:

A. a general procedure used to tackle scientific problems

B. another word for a test or trial

C. a possible explanation for an observation

D. the process of making a forecast of a future observation

E. the act of noticing things or watching closely

F. a statement that seems to be true in the majority of cases

48. The early stages of the Big Bang are shown in Table T1.5 but the events are jumbled. Use the code letters to match the numbers with the letters. *(5 marks)*

Table T1.5 Early stages of the Big Bang

Time after the Big Bang	Event
0	Big Bang: space and time form.
1. 10^{-12} to 10^{-6} seconds	A. The universe continues to cool and atomic nuclei form from protons and neutrons. The temperature is now 1 billion °C.
2. 10^{-6} to 1 second	B. Atoms (mainly hydrogen and helium) have formed as nuclei combine with electrons. Light waves have escaped to fill the expanding universe. The temperature of the universe has dropped to 3000 °C.
3. 1 to 10 seconds	C. Most of the matter and antimatter particles annihilate each other leaving an excess of protons, neutrons and electrons.
4. 3 to 10 minutes	D. The universe cools as it expands. Protons and neutrons form as well as their antimatter forms. The temperature is now 10 billion °C.
5. 377 000 years	E. Space inflates and becomes filled with radiation. Temperature equals 100 billion °C. Subatomic particles (e.g. quarks and electrons) and antimatter particles have formed.

49. Rebecca noticed that a piece of cork floated on water. She had seen this before. She knew that leaves and twigs of wood float on water. She became curious and suggested to her friend that the plant material floated on water because it was small and light. She forecast that all small pieces of wood would float, no matter what tree they came from. She started her investigation by obtaining eight different small pieces of timber. One at a time, she placed each in a bucket of water to see if they would float. All floated except two. One of these sank immediately, the other floated for a few seconds before slowly sinking. From the results of this investigation, she had to revise her original views.

   a) What observations had Rebecca made? *(1 mark)*

   b) What was her original inference? *(1 mark)*

   c) What prediction did she make from her inference? *(1 mark)*

   d) Describe the experiment she performed to test the prediction. *(2 marks)*

   e) Was her prediction correct? Explain. *(1 mark)*

   f) What do you think might be her revised explanation? *(1 mark)*

   g) What conclusion can you draw from this investigation? *(1 mark)*

   h) Describe another investigation she could perform to test her revised explanation. *(2 marks)*

50. One of the major features of Darwin's theory of evolution by natural selection was that in each population of organisms, there is natural variation. Darwin observed that chance variations could lead to evolutionary change. The evidence that was needed to explain why chance variation occurred was not known at that time. Identify two major areas of biology that helped to explain how chance variations arise. *(2 marks)*

51. When calcium salts, such as calcium chloride, are dissolved in water the water becomes hard. Hard water is water that will not lather (form bubbles) when shaken vigorously with soap solution. Propose an experimental investigation to test the following hypothesis:

   The hardness of water increases as the concentration of calcium salts increases. (5 marks)

52. Name the elements of Group 14 (IV) of the periodic table and classify them as metals, semi-metals or non-metals. *(5 marks)*

53. Describe what is meant by the term cosmic background radiation and explain the importance of this discovery to our understanding of the evolution of the universe. *(2 marks)*

54. Distinguish between nebulae and novae as examples of deep space objects. *(2 marks)*

Go to pp. 263–265 to check your answers.

Course test 2

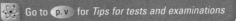

This test covers material from all the chapters in this book. It consists of the following.

⊜ Section A: 25 multiple-choice questions *(1 mark for each)*

⊜ Section B: 15 restricted-response questions *(1 mark for each)*

⊜ Section C: 13 knowledge, skill and processing data questions *(total 60 marks)*

Total marks for this test: 100

Time: 2 hours

Part A: Multiple-choice questions

(25 marks—1 mark for each question)

1. In science, theories are
   A known facts.
   B educated guesses.
   C absolute and unchangeable.
   D the best explanation for a set of data or observations.

2. In balancing a chemical equation you change the
   A subscripts.
   B superscripts.
   C coefficients.
   D chemical formula.

3. Which of the following is *not* a component of the theory of evolution by natural selection?
   A inheriting acquired characteristics
   B surviving and reproducing
   C competing for food, space and other resources
   D variations among species

4. As shown in this balanced chemical equation:
   $$Ca(C_2H_3O_2)_2 + Na_2CO_3 \rightarrow CaCO_3 + 2NaC_2H_3O_2$$
   the total number of oxygen atoms reacting is
   A 2.
   B 3.

C 5.
D 7.

5. An example of a genotype is
   A Dd.
   B pure-bred white fur.
   C recessive albinism.
   D hybrid brown eye colour.

6. The law of conservation of mass states that in a chemical reaction
   A the mass of reactants is greater than the mass of products.
   B the mass of reactants is equal to the mass of products.
   C the mass of reactants is less than the mass of products.
   D masses will vary depending on whether gases are formed.

7. The atomic number indicates the
   A number of protons in the atom.
   B number of electrons in the atom.
   C number of neutrons in the atom.
   D number of protons and neutrons in the atom.

8. An isotope of manganese has 25 protons and 30 neutrons. What is the mass number of this isotope?
   A 5
   B 25
   C 30
   D 55

9. The ions of the alkali (Group 1) metals have a charge of
   A −1.
   B 0.
   C +1.
   D +2.

10. In a chemical reaction, a hydrocarbon reacts with oxygen to form carbon dioxide and water. This type of reaction is an example of
    A neutralisation.
    B combustion.
    C displacement.
    D formation.

11. Water cycles around the water cycle over and over. This indicates that the total amount of water on Earth
    A increases.
    B decreases.
    C remains the same.
    D alternates.

12. Organisms that make their own food take which element from the air?
    A carbon
    B hydrogen
    C phosphorus
    D nitrogen

13. Humans impact the phosphorus cycle through
    A excessive pollution.
    B breeding animals.
    C clearing forests of plants.
    D using synthetic fertilisers.

14. There are many factors controlling permafrost distribution. The most important is
    A latitude.
    B climate.
    C geothermal heat.
    D ground cover material.

15. Figure T2.1 shows the reaction between hydrogen and nitrogen, forming ammonia.

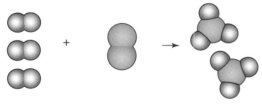

Figure T2.1 Reaction forming ammonia

Which is the correct formula for ammonia?
    A NH_3
    B $2NH_3$
    C N_2H_6
    D $(NH_3)_2$

16. In certain birds, black eye colour is dominant to blue eye colour. If a purebred black-eyed male bird mated with a purebred blue-eyed female bird, the most likely outcome for the offspring is
    A all black-eye.
    B all blue-eye.
    C 50% black-eye and 50% blue-eye.
    D 75% black-eye and 25% blue-eye.

17. Plants contribute to the carbon cycle
    A through plant respiration.
    B by photosynthesis.
    C when plant matter decays and becomes fossil fuels.
    D all of the above.

18. Consider the following reaction:
    $$2AgNO_3 + Ni \rightarrow Ni(NO_3)_2 + 2Ag$$
    Which of these statements is true?
    A Silver (Ag) is more reactive than nickel (Ni).
    B Nitrogen gas is liberated from the reaction.
    C Fine silver particles will be seen to settle out of the solution.
    D The nitrate ion (NO_3^-) decomposes and reforms.

19. How many genetically different kinds of gametes will an individual with genotype AAbb produce?
    A 1
    B 2
    C 3
    D 4

20. Ajit walks around the outside of a park, as shown in Figure T2.2.

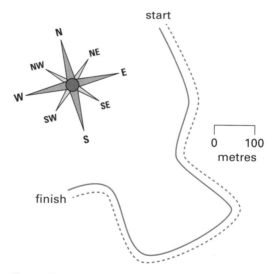

Figure T2.2 A walk around the park

Ajit's displacement is
    A 500 m SW
    B 500 m NE
    C 1200 m SW
    D 1200 m NE

21. In a chemical reaction, which in Figure T2.3 would be referred to as the supernatant?

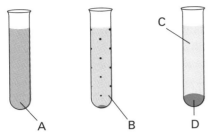

Figure T2.3 Possible results of a chemical reaction

22. Haemophilia is a disease caused by a recessive allele on the X chromosome. A carrier female marries a normal male. What is the probability a child born will display haemophilia?
    A 0%
    B 25%
    C 50%
    D 75%

23. Which one of the following reactions is an acid–base reaction?
    A $2Na + Cl_2 \rightarrow 2NaCl$
    B $CH_4 + 2O_2 \rightarrow CO_2 + 2H_2O$
    C $Mg(OH)_2 + 2HCl \rightarrow MgCl_2 + 2H_2O$
    D $2HgO \rightarrow 2Hg + O_2$

24. A game often played by Native Americans during winter is snow snake. This involves sliding a 2-m hardwood stick of diameter 2 cm the length of a long, straight trough in the snow (see Figure T2.4). The winner is the person who can make their snow snake travel the farthest. Throws have been recorded as travelling up to 2 km in less than 3 minutes with speeds clocked reaching over 150 km/h.

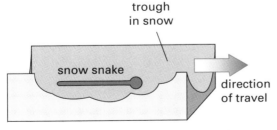

Figure T2.4 The Indian game of snow snake

Which of the following would have the *least* effect in making the snow snake travel the furthest?
    A smoothing and rounding the stick
    B compacting the snow in the trough
    C waxing or oiling the stick
    D making the stick heavier

25. A virus causing the deadly myxomatosis in rabbits was introduced into wild rabbit populations in the 1950s. This had a huge effect in reducing these plague numbers. However, the number of rabbits jumped again some decades later so calicivirus, causing rabbit haemorrhagic disease, was released in 1995. This was very effective at first but rabbit numbers are now surging, costing farmers and the nation in lost productivity. The comeback is forcing Australian scientists to globally search for new ways of destroying rabbits.

Which of the following would *not* be a reason for the calicivirus not being as effective as it once was?
    A There is a growing immunity in young rabbits to the once-deadly calicivirus.
    B The virus is becoming less active a killer because its strains are mutating and weakening in the wild.
    C Rabbit haemorrhagic disease and myxomatosis do not work well together.
    D Rabbits have learned to identify and avoid the calicivirus.

Part B: Restricted-response questions

(15 marks—1 mark for each question)

Complete the following restricted-response questions using the appropriate word.

26. Natural .... is the driving force behind evolutionary processes.

27. Any variation that can help an organism survive in its environment is called a(n) ....

28. Most .... in DNA are spontaneous and random, sometimes caused by exposure to radiation, or transcription errors during gene formation.

29. Sex cells, or ...., are different from other body cells in that they contain only half the number of chromosomes.

30. The visible outcome for a trait is known as the ....

31. In animals, male gametes are called ....

32. At any one time there may be several scientific .... that attempt to explain why the universe is the way it is.

33. Isotopes of an element have the same number of ....

34. The spontaneous disintegration of unstable nuclei by the emission of particles is called ....

35. The ion N^{3-} has three more .... than the neutral N atom.

36. Ground is termed permafrost if it remains at or below 0 °C for at least .... years.

37. A .... is any influence that causes an object to undergo a change in speed, a change in direction or a change in shape.

38. The .... energy of an object is the energy it possesses because of its motion.

39. In physics, ... is speed in a given direction.

40. Apart from water vapour, the three major atmospheric contributors to the greenhouse effect are nitrous oxide, carbon dioxide and ....

Part C: Knowledge, skill and processing data questions
(60 marks)

41. The dog breeds we have today were developed through artificial selection (selective breeding). Explain what is meant by this. *(3 marks)*

42. A group of mice becomes separated by the formation of a river. Over time, the northern mice became smaller and whiter, while the southern mice became larger and browner.
    a) What is this an example of? *(1 mark)*
    b) Suggest examples of how this might have occurred. *(6 marks)*

43. A person inherits two recessive genes for a given disorder. Will that person develop the disorder? Explain. *(2 marks)*

44. There are various effects of radiation on our DNA.
    a) Use examples to define background radiation. *(2 marks)*
    b) Use two examples to explain why high-energy radiation causes DNA damage. *(3 marks)*
    c) Describe one use in which high-energy radiation can be used beneficially in medicine. *(1 mark)*

45. Figure T2.5 shows an atom of an element.

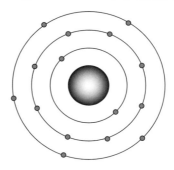

Figure T2.5 A model of an atom of an element

    a) Use the periodic table to identify the element. *(1 mark)*
    b) The figure is just a model representing an atom. State three differences between this model and a real atom. *(3 marks)*

46. Balance the following equations.
    a) $S + H_2SO_4 \rightarrow SO_2 + H_2O$ *(2 marks)*
    b) $ZnS + O_2 \rightarrow ZnO + SO_2$ *(2 marks)*
    c) $C_2H_2 + O_2 \rightarrow CO_2 + H_2O$ *(2 marks)*

47. There are two isotopes of copper. Cu-63 has an atomic weight of 62.9396 u and relative abundance of 69.50%. Cu-65 has an atomic weight of 64.9278 u and relative abundance of 30.50%. What is the weighted average atomic weight? *(2 marks)*

48. Explain what information can be extracted from Figure T2.6. *(3 marks)*

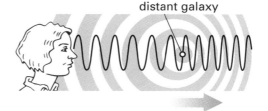

Figure T2.6 Observing a distant galaxy

49. a) A rifle can shoot a 4.5-g bullet at a speed of 950 m/s. Calculate the kinetic energy of the bullet. *(3 marks)*

b) Suppose the person is standing on a stationary skateboard as shown in Figure T2.7. Describe the motion of the skateboard as he fires two rounds from the rifle a few seconds apart. *(4 marks)*

Figure T2.7 Person firing a rifle standing on skateboard.

c) Which of Newton's laws is being obeyed by this example? *(1 mark)*

50. Vanadium is a hard, silvery grey, ductile and malleable metallic element with the symbol V. It has a number of different valencies.

a) What valencies are displayed by vanadium in the following equation? *(2 marks)*

$$V_2O_5 + 2SO_2 \rightarrow V_2O_3 + 2SO_3$$

b) The formula for calcium orthovanadate is $Ca(VO_4)_2$. What is the valency of the orthovanadate ion? Write the formula for the orthovanadate ion including its charge. *(2 marks)*

51. Figure T2.8 shows a pendulum in five different positions.

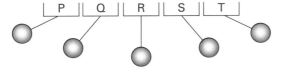

Figure T2.8 Pendulum in five different positions

a) In which position is the energy purely kinetic? *(1 mark)*

b) Describe the motion of the pendulum in moving from P to T. *(4 marks)*

c) With an ideal pendulum, the total energy of the pendulum never changes, and the pendulum will swing forever. Yet in reality such a pendulum slows down and stops. Explain. *(2 marks)*

52. A 3-kg projectile is launched straight up into the air with an initial launch speed allowing it to reach a height of 150 m (see Figure T2.9). (Take g, the acceleration due to gravity, as 10 m/s^2; ignore air resistance.)

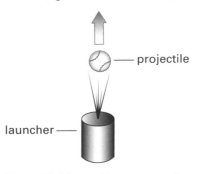

Figure T2.9 Launching a projectile

a) Determine the launch speed of the projectile. *(3 marks)*

b) If air resistance was not ignored, would the launch speed need to be greater, the same or less for the same height to be achieved? *(1 mark)*

53. In pea plants the allele for green pods is dominant to yellow pods. Two heterozygous (hybrid) green pod plants are crossed. Use G to represent the dominant allele and g for the recessive allele of this chromosome.

a) Draw a Punnett square to predict the outcome of this particular cross. *(2 marks)*

b) Suppose a total of 772 pods were obtained in this breeding experiment. How many would you expect to have:

   i) genotype Gg? *(1 mark)*

   ii) phenotype yellow seed pod? *(1 mark)*

Go to pp. 265–269 to check your answers.

ANSWERS

Chapter 1 answers

Experiment 1

Analysis: Individual results will vary, but you should expect that the dominant feature will occur in greater numbers. Repeat your analysis for your family members and compare these results to the analysis for the class.

Conclusion: Characteristics vary from individual to individual, but there is a relationship between related individuals.

Experiment 2

Analysis: Your experimental results will vary, but should be close to those calculated using the Punnett squares:

genotypes BB:Bb:bb = 1:2:1, also phenotypes black:white = 3:1

genotypes Bb:bb = 1:1, also phenotypes black:white = 1:1

genotypes BB:Bb = 1:1, also phenotypes all black.

Conclusion: Experimental results follow closely those predicted using the Punnet squares.

Experiment 3

Analysis:

1. Individual results will vary.
2. Your results should be close to 50%:50%.
3. The more results, the better the outcome and the more reliable it becomes. For example, a trial of 5 might yield 4 males and 1 female. But this is not representative of the population as a whole. If the number of trials was, say, 500 it would be very unlikely to yield 400 males and only 100 females.
4. Overall class results should indicate an approximately equal numbers of males and females.

Conclusion: The numbers of males and females are approximately equal in the population.

Test yourself 1

Part A: Knowledge

1. **B** ✓ A is wrong as the oldest rocks contain the simplest fossils. C is wrong as fossils cannot be found in all strata. D is wrong as not all animals that became extinct left fossils behind.

2. **A** ✓ They both have a pentadactyl limb and therefore share a common ancestor. B is wrong as a lizard is a reptile. C is wrong as this is not the point of the question. Even though lizards do appear in the fossil record before humans, it is not relevant to the pentadactyl limb similarity. D is wrong as humans did not evolve in the Palaeozoic.

3. **B** ✓ The Hadean eon lasted from 4600 Ma to 3800 Ma and thus A is wrong. C is wrong as the Proterozoic was from 2500 Ma to 545 Ma and D is wrong as the Phanerozoic is from 545 Ma to the present day.

4. **C** ✓ A is wrong as they have gene variations. B is wrong as physically fit is not correct ... it is reproductively fit. D is wrong as it is not a major factor

5. **C** ✓ Each island had different selecting agents. A is wrong as no interbreeding occurred due to geographical isolation. B is wrong as the ancestors were the same species. D is wrong as fitness has to do with reproductive fitness and not physical fitness.

6. **a)** extinction ✓; **b)** geographically ✓; **c)** even ✓; **d)** artificial ✓; **e)** varied ✓

7. A/H ✓; B/J ✓; C/I ✓; D/G ✓; E/F ✓

Part B: Skills

8. youngest = basalt ✓; oldest = limestone ✓

9. **a)** G ✓; **b)** C ✓; **c)** reptiles ✓

10. changes in environmental conditions including catastrophes which led to the extinction of various species ✓

11. When placed together, they should not be able to breed to form fertile offspring. ✓

12. a) i) lion = E ✓; ii) bat = A ✓; iii) whale = B ✓;
   iv) frog = C ✓; v) horse = D ✓

   b) These forelimbs are examples of the pentadactyl limb. Anatomical observations show that despite major size differences, the presence of a basic pattern of five fingers is present in each. ✓ This can be used to support the hypothesis that they all have arisen from a common ancestor with five fingers. ✓

13. a) i) 140 Ma ✓
    ii) monocotyledons = palms, orchids, pineapples, wheat, grass (any one) ✓; dicotyledons = eucalyptus, olives, primroses (any one) ✓

    b) i) 450 Ma ✓; ii) bryophyta (mosses) ✓

    c) seed ferns ✓

    d) i) gymnosperms ✓
       ii) conifers (pines), cycads and ginkgos (any two) ✓✓
       iii) false ✓

    e) palms and grasses as they are both monocotyledons ✓

14. a) E_3 = Palaeozoic era ✓; permian period ✓

    b) E_5 (65 Ma) ✓

    c) E_4 = 205 Ma ✓ ; the sea level was at its lowest point other than the E_3 event which produced the greatest level of extinction (96%).

Test yourself 2

Part A: Knowledge

1. D ✓ These are all reasons for producing insect-resistant crops. Friendly insects found around the cotton do not chew its leaves, roots or flowers, so are unaffected by the toxic chemical in the plant. D ultimately is the correct response as it includes all the others.

2. A ✓ The chromosome shown consists of two chromatids, hence B is incorrect. Chromosomes are made of DNA, and sections of chromosomes are called genes, so C and D are wrong.

3. D ✓ DNA is a polymer that has a double helix shape. This included both A and B. It is not a protein molecule, thus eliminating C.

4. A ✓ Gene therapy is the insertion, alteration or removal of genes within an individual's cells

and biological tissues to treat disease. Genome sequencing is figuring out the order of DNA nucleotides, or bases, in a genome that makes up an organism's DNA, so B is wrong. The human genome consists of over 3 billion of these bases. C is wrong as vaccination is the injection of a killed microbe to stimulate the immune system against the microbe, preventing disease. D is wrong as immunisation protects people against harmful infections before they come into contact with them in the community. Vaccination is now used to refer to all procedures for immunisation.

5. B ✓ Genes are the coding segments of the DNA. The gene is the unit of heredity occupying a fixed position on a chromosome. Genes achieve their effects by directing protein synthesis. They are composed of DNA, except in some viruses that contain RNA instead. The sequence of nitrogenous bases along a DNA strand determines the genetic code. A is wrong as a three-nucleotide codon in a nucleic acid sequence specifies a single amino acid. C is incorrect as this refers to an allele, which is one variant of that gene. The number of triplet codes determining a gene varies, so D is incorrect.

6. a) homologous ✓; b) karyotype ✓; c) meiosis ✓;
   d) fertilisation ✓; e) Watson, Crick ✓

7. A/I ✓; B/J ✓; C/G ✓; D/F ✓; E/H ✓

Part B: Skills

8. a) Sabina ✓
   b) Glenda ✓
   c) 2 (Kate and Lily) ✓
   d) short eyelashes ✓
   e) i) ee ✓; ii) Ee ✓; iii) Ee ✓

9. a) Only males (shown by squares) display the condition. ✓
   b) i) Helen ✓
      ii) Rupert ✓
      iii) 4 ✓
      iv) Waldemar ✓ and Henry ✓ (also known as Heinrich) (Remember, Irene is the daughter of Alice.)
      v) Leopold ✓ and Maurice ✓
      vi) Gonzalo ✓ (In family trees the order of children is given from left to right, from oldest to youngest.)

vii) Alexis ✓

c) While they didn't show the condition, their sons did. So they were carriers. ✓

d) It is likely that her carrier status resulted from a new mutation occurring in one of the gametes which led to her conception. ✓

e) i) Queen Victoria was Queen Elizabeth's great, great grandmother. ✓ The family line down to Elizabeth is: Victoria – Edward VII – George V – George VI – Elizabeth II.

ii) No ✓ Coming down this male line, none of whom showed haemophilia, the recessive gene was not present in the males and hence not in Queen Elizabeth.

10. Draw up a Punnett square (see Figure A.1). Now of their children, one out of two sons is expected to have red–green colour blindness. This makes it 50% of the male progeny. ✓✓ (Of course, this is only the theoretical probability. The couple may not have four children, but even if they did there is no guarantee there will be two sons and two daughters bearing the features shown in the Punnett square.)

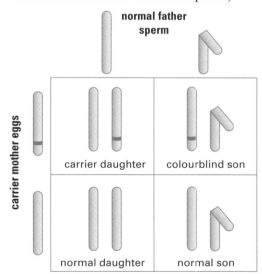

Figure A.1 Punnett square

A trait is a notable feature or quality in an individual passed on from individual to individual. There are physical traits (e.g. height, eye colour, blood type), behavioural traits (e.g. how one acts) and predispositions to medical conditions (e.g. haemophilia, cystic fibrosis, heart disease). A normal trait in a genetic context is a feature that occurs most commonly in a population. For example, about 8% of males, but only 0.5% of females, are colour-blind in some way or another, whether it is one colour or a colour combination. Hence, not being colourblind is the normal trait.

11. **a)** One comes from the female gamete and the other from the male gamete. ✓✓ (Fertilisation restores the chromosomes as homologous pairs.)

b) The instructions that a gene issues are the same irrespective of whether the gene is from the male or female parent. ✓

12. If red coat was dominant, then the F_1 generation would all be red-coat cattle. If white coat was dominant, then the F_1 generation would all be white-coat cattle. Surely some other factor is at play here so neither red nor white is dominant. ✓✓

13. **a)** WwEeNn ✓✓

b) There are $2^3 = 8$ possibilities: WEN, WEn, WeN, Wen, wEN, wEn, weN and wen. ✓✓

c) genotype: WWEeNn ✓✓; phenotype: wavy hair, unattached ear lobes, narrow nose ✓✓

14. **a)** The yellow pea seed allele is dominant to the green pea seed allele. ✓ When there is a genotype that consists of a dominant and a recessive allele, the F_1 phenotype generally looks like the dominant one. In this case, yellow is dominant.

b) One out of four offspring of heterozygous parents will be homozygous recessive. ✓ Since the recessive allele produces green pea seeds, only plants that are homozygous green for this trait will have a green phenotype. The homozygous yellow and the heterozygous ones will all be yellow.

Chapter test

Part A: Multiple-choice questions

1. **A** ✓ B is wrong as humans have not evolved from apes but a common ancestor of humans and apes. C is wrong as the genetic material has not changed and so no change will occur in the next generation. D is wrong as this statement was not part of the Darwin's theory.

2. **B** ✓ A is incorrect as many life forms had yet to evolve. C is wrong as the amphibians appeared in the Carboniferous period. D is wrong as mammals had not evolved.

3. **B** ✓ A, C and D are wrong as they branched away from the main trunk much later.

4. **A** ✓ Large size can be a feature that is passed onto the next generation. All the other features cannot be passed on and so B, C and D are wrong.

5. **C** ✓ A is wrong as Darwin did not observe any fossils of finches. B is wrong as Darwin did not know the age of each island. D is wrong as DNA was not discovered at that time.

6. **A** ✓ The only possibilities of this cross are Tt, which is heterozygous. So no offspring will be homozygous recessive. This makes B, C and D incorrect.

7. **D** ✓ Genes, and their interaction with the environment, decide the characteristics of an organism. This includes both A and B. C refers to the discredited Lamarckian idea that organisms pass on features they acquire during their lifetime.

8. **D** ✓ Look at the pattern for the child and compare it to the pattern of the parents. All 'bars' shown in the parents must be present in the same location in the child. So A, B and C are incorrect as there will be a 'bar' in the child's pattern that is not present in either parent.

9. **D** ✓ The correct order is D, A, C, B, so A, B or C do not make the first step.

10. **C** ✓ Hybrids are the offspring of genetically dissimilar parents or stock, especially the offspring produced by breeding plants or animals of different varieties, species or races. A, B and D are incorrect as none of these define a hybrid plant.

Part B: Short-answer questions

11. a) Palaeozoic ✓
    b) trilobites ✓
    c) trilobites, productids, goniatites ✓
    d) i) goniatites ✓
       ii) stromatoporoids, productids, goniatites ✓
    e) The Carboniferous would not have stromatoporoid fossils but would have trilobite, productid and goniatite fossils. ✓ The Cambrian would only have trilobite fossils. ✓

12. a) Marsupials evolved after Africa split away from the other continental masses of Gondwana, but before South America detached from the combined mass of Australia–Antarctica–South America. ✓
    b) Antarctica is the land bridge between Australia and South America. Thus, fossil marsupials should eventually be found there. ✓
    c) The environment of South America (including the presence of predators) may have led to the extinction of most South American marsupials. Australia was isolated and so marsupials survived in this environment. ✓

13. In nature, only a few breeds are reproductively fit to survive. Nature has eliminated the less fit. ✓ In domestic cats, many breeds survive as artificial selection is used to produce new types. Domesticated cats have few predators. ✓

14. A and B (according to the proposed evolutionary tree) evolved from their common ancestor before X evolved. Their sequences of nucleobases (nitrogen bases) should be different to the other three living frog species. ✓ Analysis of the DNA from the fossil remains of X (if DNA is available) will show more nitrogen base sequences in common with C, D and E. ✓

15. a) Geographic isolation ✓ due to the formation of the Nullarbor Plain caused the two isolated groups to evolve separately. New species formed as a result. ✓
    b) The gene pool was the same, as the frogs could interbreed. ✓
    c) Mutations can occur in these separated populations. Favourable mutations in one group will not be transmitted to the other group and so different species will eventually arise. ✓
    d) Frogs that can survive the dry conditions will be fitter to reproduce and pass these favourable characteristics onto their offspring. ✓ Over time the western frog population will be more dry-weather tolerant than the eastern frogs. ✓

16. Races develop when human populations are geographically isolated ✓ and mutations occur ✓, and the environment acts as a selecting agent ✓.

17. a) In the natural population there are some bacteria that have resistance to antibiotics but this ability does not give them any advantage in the absence of antibiotics. ✓

    b) In the presence of the antibiotic, the resistant bacteria are selected and they survive to reproduce. Their offspring are now more numerous in subsequent generations. ✓

18. a) about 330 million years ago ✓

    b) about 375 million years ago ✓

    c) mosses ✓

    d) about 445 million years ✓

    e) flowering plants ✓

19. a) false ✓; b) false ✓; c) true ✓; d) true ✓;

    e) false ✓; f) false ✓; g) true ✓; h) false ✓;

    i) true ✓; j) false ✓

20. A (Cenozoic) = H (recent life) ✓;
    B (Mesozoic) = G (middle life) ✓;
    C (Palaeozoic) = E (ancient life) ✓;
    D (Precambrian) = F (before the Cambrian) ✓

21. A (Phanerozoic) = G (appearance of life) ✓;
    B (Proterozoic) = H (early life) ✓;
    C (Archaen) = E (ancient) ✓;
    D (Hadean) = F (beneath the Earth) ✓

22. He promoted the idea that prominent people like the bishop should only argue about things they know and should not make comments on things they have no training in (i.e. evolutionary theory). ✓

23. A theory can only be found to be false by the processes of the scientific method whereas faith cannot be tested by the scientific method. ✓

24. During the lifetime of an individual, various environmental effects change their behaviour. For example, a person may decide to join a gym and build up muscle mass. Lamarck believed that some of these acquired characteristics could be passed onto future generations so over time there would be a distinct change in the appearance of these descendants. ✓

25. Darwin explained that due to environmental change, the leaves of the trees eaten by giraffes were only accessible for those members of the population that had slightly longer necks. These individuals then survived to reproduce and so passed these characteristics onto the next generation. Over long periods of time this process of natural selection always favoured those with longer necks and so the evolutionary process continued. ✓

26. It is used because it is easily obtained from the wild ✓, it is cheap ✓ to rear, each female produces hundreds of eggs ✓ and it has a short generation time ✓. (*Drosophila melanogaster* is a small, common fruit fly found near unripe and rotted fruit. It has been used for over a century to study genetics, lending itself well to behavioural studies. Thomas Hunt Morgan first studied *Drosophila* early in the 1900s. Geneticists have been using *Drosophila* ever since. It is one of the few organisms whose entire genome is known and many genes have been identified.)

27. a) i) 626 ✓; ii) 121 ✓; iii) 425 ✓; iv) 2.87:1 ✓;
       v) 3.16:1 ✓

    b) purple ✓

    c) Chance plays an important part. ✓ (The predicted or expected ratio does not indicate the actual ratio of purple to white grains in any particular corn cob. But it does indicate the most probable ratio. This is similar to tossing a coin. While you may expect a head to tails ratio of 1:1 in, say, 20 tosses you might get 12 heads and 8 tails. The millions of pollen grains producing a few hundred gametes that win the race to fertilise the ovules are totally independent of whether the gametes contain the dominant or recessive allele. Which gets to fertilise is determined purely by chance. If a sufficiently large number of flower heads are counted then the ratio will tend to be close to 3:1, but for one flower head it may deviate quite markedly from this value.)

28. GGACACTCGTTG ✓✓ The nucleobases in DNA are adenine (A), guanine (G), cytosine (C) and thymine (T). A binds with T; G binds with C.

29. deletion ✓ and substitution ✓ of bases

30. a) b genes ✓; b) Bb ✓

31. a) There is a decrease in mosquito mortality over time. ✓

    b) When first sprayed, the mosquito population goes into decline. But DDT quickly becomes ineffective; most mosquitoes become resistant in a matter of months.

DDT-resistant mosquitoes exist at low frequency in the global population. When this population is sprayed, selection favours the resistant mosquitoes and it is only a matter of time before resistant mosquitoes are present in the greater proportion. ✓✓

32. a) threonine–leucine–glycine–aspartic acid–phenylalanine–cysteine ✓✓

   b) i) substitution ✓
      ii) aspartic acid replaced by valine ✓

33. a) See Figure A.2. ✓✓✓

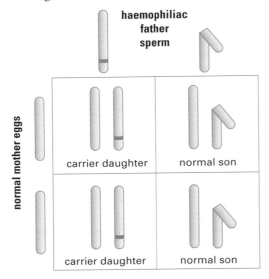

Figure A.2 Punnett square

   b) B ✓ Statements A, C, D and E are not true.

   c) No ✓ Only the carrier daughters carry the haemophilia gene but, as they also carry the dominant normal (non-carrier) gene, their phenotype will by normal and so won't display the condition. ✓

34. a) BbrrSS ✓

   b) 1 = brown eyes, round face, peaked hairline ✓
      2 = brown eyes, long face, straight hairline ✓

   c) blue eyes, long face, peaked hairline ✓

35. a) i) B ✓; ii) brown eyes ✓

   b) Gene pairs are at the same location (i.e. opposite) on each homologous chromosome. ✓

36. A/R ✓; B/P ✓; C/Q ✓

37. a) They are easily seen and are an easy meal for birds. ✓

   b) The dark moths will now not be easy to see when they are on the tree trunks. The

mottled moths, however, will be much easier to see and the birds will eat them. The population will change over time to favour the dark moths. ✓✓

38. a) higher plant/animal yields ✓, resistance to pests and diseases ✓, adaptation to particular environments ✓, and increased convenience in harvesting and storage

   b) Critics of gene technology suspect that we still know too little about the systems that we are tampering with. Could an inserted gene have effects of which we are currently unaware? Could it upset the balance of existing genes, causing the plant to produce greater quantities of natural toxins, or other side effects or to change its nutritional content? ✓✓ (Most researchers argue that there is no evidence of such unexpected changes. They point out that gene technology is much less likely to cause unwanted effects on plants than traditional selective breeding methods. These traditional methods, which have been carried out for thousands of years, involve moving thousands of genes from one organism to another. Modern gene technology, on the other hand, moves only a few targeted genes.)

39. a) X = deoxyribose sugar ✓; Y = nucleobases (or nitrogen bases) ✓

   b) nucleotide ✓

   c) It consists of many nucleotides (monomers) joined together to form very large molecules. ✓

40. a) The condition is shown by both males and females in approximately equal numbers. ✓

   b) Some of their children don't display the disease. This means they would have inherited a normal gene from each parent. But as both parents have the disease, they also carry the Darier's gene. Hence, both parents are heterozygous. ✓✓

   c) dd ✓

   d) Dd ✓

   e) Dd ✓

   f) No, since U did not inherit the Darier's gene from his father. ✓ Person U has genotype dd, while the person he marries also has this genotype ✓✓.

Experiment 1

Analysis: Calcium is the most reactive of the metals and copper is the least reactive. Magnesium is more reactive than zinc and zinc is more reactive than iron.

Conclusion: The activity of the five metals from most active to least active is: calcium; magnesium; zinc; iron; copper.

Experiment 2

Analysis: Your values will vary slightly but your averages should be similar to these.

A: 0 g	B: 0.65 g	C: 1.35 g	D: 2.0 g	E: 2.65 g	F: 3.4 g	G: 4.1 g

There should be no precipitate in A. After all, there was no KI present.

The average mass is shown in Figure A.3.

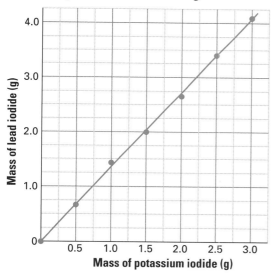

Figure A.3 Lead iodide graph

Conclusion: As the concentration of potassium iodide increased, there was a measurable change in the amount of lead iodide produced.

Experiment 3

Analysis
1. flasks 4 and 6
2. flasks 1 and 3
3. flask 1
4. Rust forms when iron combines with oxygen and water. The vinegar strips any protective coating off the steel wool and the oxygen in the bleach combines with the iron in the steel. This makes the wet steel wool go rusty very quickly.

Conclusion: Rust is caused by a combination of water and air and is accelerated by adding salt or acid to the water.

Test yourself 1

Part A: Knowledge

1. **B** ✓ We can calculate that $2 + 8 + 5 = 15$ electrons and therefore 15 protons are present in the nucleus. A is wrong as the element is a non-metal with five valence electrons. C is wrong as the atomic number is 15. D is wrong as this element is quite reactive with a five valence.

2. **B** ✓ A is wrong as germanium is a semi-metal. C is wrong as sulfur is a non-metal. D is wrong as all are non-metals.

3. **B** ✓ A is wrong as it belongs to Period 6. C is wrong as Te belongs to Period 5 and Po is incorrect as it belongs to Period 6.

4. **A** ✓ B is wrong as they are both metals. C is wrong as they are a semi-metal and a non-metal. D is wrong as these are a non-metal and a semi-metal.

5. **C** ✓ A is wrong as Np is an actinoid. B is wrong as No is an actinoid. D is wrong as W is a transition metal.

6. a) fluorine ✓; b) metals ✓; c) transition ✓;
   d) 4 ✓; e) potassium ✓

7. A/J ✓; B/F ✓; C/G ✓; D/H ✓; E/I ✓

Part B: Skills

8. a) metal ✓; b) non-metal ✓; c) metal ✓;
   d) semi-metal ✓; e) metal ✓

9. a) tellurium ✓; b) chlorine ✓

10. a) X = solid ✓; Y = solid ✓; Z = gas ✓
    b) X= phosphorus ✓; Y = sulfur ✓; Z = chlorine ✓ (they are three consecutive elements)

11. a) Period 2 ✓; b) metal ✓; c) gas ✓;
    d) antimony or bismuth ✓; e) synthetic ✓

12. a) chlorine ✓; b) oxygen ✓; c) argon ✓;
    d) bromine ✓

13. a) argon ✓
    b) neutrons = 40 − 18 = 22 ✓
    c) 2, 8, 8 ✓

d) eight electrons ✓

e) E is a noble gas and very unreactive. ✓

14. a) false ✓; b) false ✓; c) true ✓; d) true ✓;

e) true ✓

Test yourself 2

Part A: Knowledge

1. **B** ✓ Calcium has a valence of +2 and chlorine has a valence of −1; thus, the chemical formula of calcium chloride is $CaCl_2$. A is wrong because the correct formula for sodium chloride is NaCl (check valencies). C is wrong because the correct formula for nitrogen trioxide is NO_3 (notice tri- = 3). D is wrong because the correct formula for sulfuric acid is H_2SO_4 (the formula given is that for nitric acid).

2. **D** ✓ Sulfur burns or combusts in oxygen to produce sulfur dioxide. Sulfur dioxide is a gas that is soluble, so A is wrong. The reaction is not between an acid and a base, so B is wrong. The reaction is not decomposition but rather synthesis, so C is incorrect. It is possible for a reaction to be placed in more than one category. This reaction is both a combustion reaction and a synthesis reaction.

3. **A** ✓ Magnesium oxide is a base that is neutralised by sulfuric acid. As magnesium sulfate is soluble, this is not a precipitation, so B is incorrect. A more complex compound is not decomposed, so C is incorrect. The reaction does not burn in air, so D is incorrect.

4. **B** ✓ Acids attack carbonates and release carbon dioxide gas. The reaction is that of acid + carbonate → salt + water + carbon dioxide. So A, C and D are incorrect. While NO_2 and H_2 are gases at room temperature, H_2O is not.

5. **A** ✓ A compound breaks down or decomposes into two new compounds. B and C are incorrect as there is only one reactant, not two. D is incorrect as there is no evidence that what is formed is insoluble.

6. a) ionic ✓

b) covalent ✓

c) pentoxide ✓

d) effervescence (bubbling) ✓ (This is due to the release of H_2 gas.)

e) oxide ✓

7. A/G ✓; B/F ✓; C/J ✓; D/H ✓; E/I ✓

Part B: Skills

8. a) A = copper chloride ✓; B = nitrogen dioxide ✓; C = aluminium oxide ✓

b) $CuCl_2$ ✓; NO_2 ✓; Al_2O_3 ✓

c) A = ionic ✓; B = covalent ✓; C = ionic ✓

9. a) A/B/D ✓; b) D/F ✓; c) C/D ✓

10. a) A white precipitate would be observed to form when the colourless solutions are mixed. ✓

b) precipitation ✓

c) sodium chloride + silver nitrate → silver chloride + sodium nitrate ✓✓

d) $NaCl + AgNO_3 → AgCl + NaNO_3$ ✓✓ (the equation is balanced)

11. a) corrosion (rusting) or oxidation ✓

b) Both air and water are required for a nail to rust. Air or water alone do not cause rusting. ✓✓

12. a) Atoms and matter are conserved in a chemical change. ✓

b) Reactants are all diatomic molecules ✓; products are triatomic molecules ✓.

c) combustion reaction (H_2 burns in O_2) ✓

13. a) neutralisation ✓

b) to monitor the pH changes during the neutralisation ✓

c) The reactions are exothermic since heat is released. ✓

d) Y is magnesium carbonate because the neutralisation leads to the formation of a gas. Acids on carbonates release carbon dioxide gas. ✓✓

e) In X the final pH is high (> 10) whereas in Y the final pH is lower (between 8 and 9). ✓✓

14. a) sulfuric acid ✓ and hydrochloric acid ✓

b) H_2SO_4 ✓; HCl ✓

c) hydrogen ✓

d) carbon dioxide ✓

Chapter test

Part A: Multiple-choice questions

1. **D** ✓ A, B and C are wrong as these elements have lower activity than sodium.

2. **A** ✓ B is wrong as neon is inert. C and D are wrong as these non-metals are less active than fluorine.

3. **C** ✓ A, B and D are wrong as these are non-metals.

4. **A** ✓ B is wrong as lead is not a reactive metal and fluorine is a very active non-metal. C is wrong as silver is not very reactive and oxygen is reactive. D is wrong as sulfur is reactive.

5. **B** ✓ A and C are wrong as they developed the periodic table. D is wrong as Lavoisier investigated mass conservation in a chemical change.

6. **C** ✓ The complete balanced equation is: $C_2H_5OH + 3O_2 \rightarrow 2CO_2 + 3H_2O$ so the numbers in A, B and D are incorrect.

7. **B** ✓ The reaction is acid + base → salt + water, so options A, C and D are incorrect. While sodium chloride is a salt, in chemistry it is not the only salt that can be formed during neutralisation.

8. **D** ✓ The reaction is acid + metal → salt + hydrogen, so options A, B and C are incorrect.

9. **C** ✓ Covalent bonds form when atoms share electrons. A is incorrect as this describes ionic bonds. B is simply incorrect as in chemistry protons are not gained or lost. D is wrong as fusing does not describe covalent bonding.

10. **A** ✓ A molecule of pentane contains five carbon atoms and 12 hydrogen atoms chemically bonded together, so B and C are incorrect. D is also wrong as a penta-atomic molecule contains five atoms.

Part B: Short-answer questions

11. **a)** Group 15 (V) ✓
    b) non-metal ✓
    c) liquid ✓
    d) metal ✓
    e) F has a very high melting point. E is an active metal with a low melting point and G is a noble gas with a very low melting point. Thus the trend in melting point from left to right is that the melting point tends to rise and then decrease. ✓
    f) J ✓
    g) K ✓
    h) I ✓

12. **a)** He realised that not all elements had been discovered and so spaces should be left for them. ✓

b) The modern table is arranged according to increasing atomic number (Z) rather than increasing atomic weight. ✓

13. **a) i)** 2 (II) ✓; **ii)** 3 (III) ✓;
    iii) 16 (VI) ✓; **iv)** 14 (IV) ✓;
    v) 18 (VIII) ✓
    b) i) 4 ✓; **ii)** 3 ✓; **iii)** 1 ✓; **iv)** 6 ✓; **v)** 5 ✓

14. See Table A.1.

Table A.1 Atomic numbers and electrons

Element	Z	K shell	L shell	M shell	
Nitrogen	7	2	5		✓
Magnesium	12	2	8	2	✓
Sulfur	16	2	8	6	✓

15. **a)** 16 (or VI) ✓; **b)** non-metal ✓; **c)** –2 ✓;
    d) ionic ✓

16. mass of calcium oxide = 40.08 + 16.00
    = 56.08 g ✓

17. **a)** $Z = 37$ ✓
    b) rubidium ✓; Rb ✓
    c) metal ✓

18. **a)** actinoids or synthetic radioactive ✓
    b) noble gases ✓
    c) semi-metals ✓
    d) transition metals ✓

19. **a)** p = 20 ✓; n = 40 – 20 = 20 ✓;
    e = 20 – 2 = 18 ✓
    b) p = 13 ✓; n = 27 – 13 = 14 ✓;
    e = 13 – 3 = 10 ✓

20. **a)** p = 16 ✓; n = 32 – 16 = 16 ✓;
    e = 16 + 2 = 18 ✓; sulfur ✓
    b) p = 9 ✓; n = 19 – 9 = 10 ✓; e = 9 + 1 = 10 ✓;
    fluorine ✓

21. potassium, magnesium, aluminium, zinc, iron, lead, copper, gold ✓

22. **a) i)** reaction 3 ✓ (bubbles of CO_2 form)
    ii) reaction 1 ✓ (lead sulfate is insoluble)
    (reaction 2 = no reaction)
    b) reaction 3: calcium carbonate + nitric acid → calcium nitrate + water + carbon dioxide ✓
    reaction 1: lead nitrate + sodium sulfate → lead sulfate + sodium nitrate ✓

23. **a)** Group 1 (I) ✓
    b) These elements are a family of active metals. ✓ Their atomic weight increases down the group. Their melting and boiling

points decrease down the group. ✓ Their reactivity with water increases down the group. They all show a valency of +1 in their compounds with chlorine. ✓

24. See Table A.2.

Table A.2 Properties of some elements

Elem.	Z	K shell	L shell	M shell	N shell	O shell	Val.	
Co	27	2	8	15	2		+2	✓
K	19	2	8	8	1		+1	✓
O	8	2	6				–2	✓
Ca	20	2	8	8	2		+2	✓
N	7	2	5				–3	✓
F	9	2	7				–1	✓
Br	35	2	8	18	7		–1	✓
Zn	30	2	8	18	2		+2	✓
I	53	2	8	18	18	7	–1	✓
Ag	47	2	8	18	18	1	+1	✓
Fe	26	2	8	14	2		+2	✓

25. a) increase to Group 14 (IV) and then a decrease to Group 18 (VIII) ✓

   b) generally a decrease from left to right across the period ✓

   c) metals = Li, Be; semi-metal = B; non-metals = C, N, O, F, Ne ✓

26. a) calcium iodide (ionic) ✓

   b) sulfur dichloride (covalent) ✓

   c) hydrogen iodide (covalent) ✓

   d) mercury oxide (ionic) ✓

27. The correct order for the cards is as follows:
   - card 4: oxygen, Z = 8 ✓
   - card 7: fluorine, Z = 9 ✓
   - card 1: neon, Z = 10 ✓
   - card 5: sulfur, Z = 16 ✓
   - card 2: chlorine, Z = 17 ✓
   - card 8: argon, Z = 18 ✓
   - card 3: selenium, Z = 34 ✓
   - card 9: bromine, Z = 35 ✓
   - card 6: krypton, Z = 36. ✓

28. a) Ba^{2+}, Cl^-; barium chloride ✓ (as chlorine has a valency of –1, and 2 chloride ions are needed, barium must have a valency of +1)

   b) Ga^{3+}, NO_3^-; gallium nitrate ✓ (as the nitrate has a valency of –1, and 3 nitrate ions are needed, gallium must have a valency of +3)

   c) Rb^+, F^-; rubidium fluoride ✓ (as fluorine has a valency of –1, and 1 fluoride ion is needed, rubidium must have a valency of +1)

29. a) X = +3 ✓ (oxygen has a valency of –2, and 3 oxide ions are needed, total –6; so to balance each, X must have a valency of +3)

   b) Y = +5 ✓ (chlorine has a valency of –1, and 5 chloride ions are needed, total –5)

   c) Z = –2 ✓ (hydrogen has a valency of +1, and 2 hydrogen ions are needed, total +2)

30. a) heat released ✓; colour change ✓

   b) sulfur dioxide ✓

   c) sulfur + oxygen → sulfur dioxide ✓✓

   d) $S + O_2 \rightarrow SO_2$ ✓✓

   e) The gas is acidic, because the indicator turned red. ✓

31. a) 8 ✓ (there are two carbon atoms and six hydrogen atoms)

   b) ethane + oxygen → carbon dioxide + water ✓✓

   c) $2C_2H_6 + 7O_2 \rightarrow 4CO_2 + 6H_2O$ ✓✓

   d) Pass the gas through limewater, which will turn white if it is carbon dioxide. ✓✓

   e) The heat released from the combustion keeps the combustion process going. ✓

32. a) zinc sulfate ✓

   b) calcium nitrate ✓

   c) sodium chloride ✓

33. a) decomposition ✓

   b) carbon dioxide ✓

   c) magnesium carbonate → magnesium oxide + carbon dioxide ✓
   $MgCO_3 \rightarrow MgO + CO_2$ ✓

34. a) Y ✓ (slope of graph is greater)

   b) The acid was more concentrated in the reaction with Y. ✓

   c) sodium sulfide + nitric acid → sodium nitrate + hydrogen sulfide ✓

   d) $Na_2S + 2HNO_3 \rightarrow 2NaNO_3 + H_2S$ ✓

   e) The molecule in C has two atoms of hydrogen and one of sulfur; that is consistent with the equation. ✓

35. a) i) soluble ✓; ii) insoluble ✓; iii) soluble ✓; iv) soluble ✓

   b) i) yes ✓ silver chloride
   ii) yes ✓ barium sulfate

iii) no ✓

36. a) The volume of gas Y is twice that of gas X. ✓
    b) hydrogen gas ✓ (pop test)
    c) oxygen gas ✓ (glowing splint test)
    d) decomposition ✓ water → hydrogen + oxygen ✓
    e) $2H_2O → 2H_2 + O_2$ ✓
    f) The equation in e) shows twice as many molecules of hydrogen are formed compared with oxygen molecules. This is what the diagram shows. ✓

37. a) The Bunsen burner is on a heat-proof mat, preventing the bench from any heat damage. ✓ The student is using tongs to hold the test tube, so he doesn't burn himself as the test tube gets hot. ✓ The student is pointing the test tube away from himself, so if there is any emission it doesn't land on him. ✓
    b) decomposition ✓
    c) The only possibility is oxygen ✓ as lead nitrate consists of lead + nitrogen + oxygen.
    d) $2Pb(NO_3)_2 → 2PbO + 4NO_2 + O_2$ ✓

38. a) All factors, other than the one you are testing, need to be the same to be able to compare results.
    i)   It may be that more water will aid the dissolving process, and that would not be fair. ✓
    ii) As the temperature increases, dissolving occurs faster. ✓
    iii) The greater the mass, the longer it will take to dissolve. ✓
    b) Yes, as stirring moves the particles around and so dissolving should occur faster. ✓
    c) The crushed tablet presents a greater total surface area for the water to attack. So dissolving should occur faster. The solid tablet has a smaller surface area and the particles in the outer layer need to be dissolved and removed first before water can reach and begin dissolving the layer underneath. ✓✓
    d) icing sugar ✓

39. a) Painting the roof would give added protection to the iron sheeting. ✓ Near the seaside, salt spray along with water will attack and corrode the sheeting faster, as will acidic rainfall. ✓ Punching nails through the sheeting exposes the underlying mild steel to the weather, thus compromising the zinc coating. ✓
    b) $2Zn + O_2 → 2ZnO$ ✓
       $ZnO + H_2O → Zn(OH)_2$ ✓
       $Zn(OH)_2 + H_2CO_3 → ZnCO_3 + 2H_2O$ ✓

40. a) $2H_2O_2 → 2H_2O + O_2$ ✓
    b) When no catalyst is used, the decomposition is very slow. This is shown by the line marked 'no catalyst used', which has a very small slope. ✓
    c) A syringe with a scale can be set up and connected to the flask (see Figure A.4). ✓ The volume of oxygen in the syringe increases as the reaction proceeds. ✓ This volume can be noted, say, every 30 seconds, and a graph of volume against time can be plotted. ✓

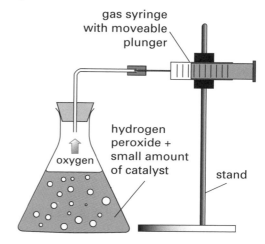

Figure A.4 Measuring the volume of oxygen produced

    d) P ✓
    e) No, the end point is still the same. Notice both curves plateau (flatten out) at the same volume of oxygen. It is just that curve P gets there faster. ✓✓
    f) The curve is steepest at the start (time = 0) meaning this is when oxygen is produced at the greatest rate. The reaction slows down as the curve flattens out. Eventually the reaction stops (no more oxygen produced) once the curve is completely flat. ✓✓
    g) X = MnO_2 ✓; Y = CuO ✓; Z = ZnO ✓
    h) As O_2 is formed, it leaves the flask and so the mass of the flask and its contents

decreases. The scale will show mass decreasing over time; the faster this dropped between time intervals, the more oxygen that was produced. How fast the oxygen evolves can be determined by taking mass measurements at regular intervals. ✓✓

Chapter 3 answers

Experiment 1

Analysis

1. See Figure A.5.

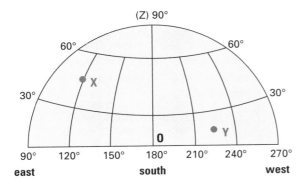

Figure A.5 Sky map

2. Achenar: azimuth = ~135°; elevation = 30°
   Canopus: azimuth = ~165°; elevation = ~10°
   Alpha Centauri: azimuth = ~255°; elevation = ~40°
   Crux : azimuth =~220°; elevation =~20°

Conclusion: Stars and constellations can be plotted on a two-dimensional star map to show their azimuth and elevation in the sky.

Experiment 2

Analysis

1. Both graphs will show temperature increases, but the one that is enclosed should show a greater rate of increase in temperature.

2. In the open container, heat is able to escape. In the enclosed container, heat is trapped and adds to other heat similarly trapped inside.

3. These results should be similar. Both materials allow light through but pose a barrier for escaping heat.

4. Light transmission under glass versus plastic is often a hotly debated subject among greenhouse owners and constructors. Each has their own viewpoint and to the grower, both

can be convincing. Light is only one factor in a number that the greenhouse operator needs to consider for their crop, although it is one of the more important fundamentals.

Conclusion: Enclosed containers are more efficient at trapping heat than containers with openings.

This experiment demonstrates an important fact that has led to tragedies. Never leave a child or pet unattended in a vehicle. Not even for a minute. Studies show that after 10 minutes in a closed vehicle, temperatures can rise by around 10 °C; after 20 minutes, by 15 °C; after 1 hour by 20 °C. A dark dashboard or seat can easily reach temperatures in the range of 80 °C to 90 °C. The thermoregulatory systems of small animals and children are not as efficient as those of an adult's and their body temperatures warm at a rate three to five times faster than an adult's.

Experiment 3

Analysis

1. Acid attacks and dissolves marbles. Bubbles of gas (which is CO_2) can be seen.

2. The more concentrated the acid, the faster is the reaction and less of the marble chip remains after the experiment.

3. The lower the pH (stronger the acid), the greater is the loss of mass.

4. Many buildings and statues are made from marble or limestone. Acid rain can wear them away. This is in addition to the damage it can do to animals and plants.

Conclusion: The stronger the acid, the faster it wears away marble chips.

Acid rain in polluted air reacts with the calcite in marble and limestone, dissolving exposed areas. In buildings and statues this causes roughened surfaces, removal of material and loss of carved details. Stone surface material may be lost all over or only in spots that are more reactive. Even marble benchtops in kitchens can react with food acids and dissolve. So it is important that a sealant layer is maintained to prevent the two from getting together. Sealers protect the porous stone against dirt, spills and stains.

Test yourself 1

Part A: Knowledge

1. **A** ✓ Helium is the next most abundant element after hydrogen. Thus B, C and D are wrong.

2. **A** ✓ There is no experimental evidence for B and C, and D is only one possibility but there is evidence that this might happen.

3. **D** ✓ A is wrong as planetary nebulae form from red giants and then its core will become a white dwarf. B is wrong as white dwarfs turn into black dwarfs as they cool. C is wrong as yellow stars like our Sun evolve into red giants and then white dwarfs and finally black dwarfs.

4. **B** ✓ A is wrong as cosmic background radiation supports the expansion of the universe but is not connected to red shifting. C is wrong as stellar evolution does not concern the red shift. D is wrong as this event does not concern the observed red shift of stars.

5. **A** ✓ Molecules in the atmosphere absorb ultraviolet and infra-red light. Scientists must use telescopes outside the atmosphere to observe these types of rays from distant sources. B is wrong as computing systems can be in many locations. C is wrong as mobile phones use microwaves. D is wrong as clear images can be obtained using advanced optics systems.

6. **a)** radio ✓; **b)** hydrogen ✓; **c)** supernova ✓; **d)** distance ✓; **e)** expand ✓

7. A/J ✓; B/I ✓; C/G ✓; D/F ✓; E/H ✓

Part B: Skills

8. **a)** See Figure A.6.
   b) Hottest stars: Sirius A (8000–11 000 °C); Alpha Centauri A (6000–8000 °C); Alpha Centauri B (~4800 °C). ✓
   Coolest stars: all the red dwarfs (< 3500 °C). ✓
   c) Rigel is whitish-blue and so its surface temperature is about 20 000 to 30 000 °C. ✓

9. **a)** the distance that light travels in a year ✓

b) 2 ly (see Figure A.7) ✓

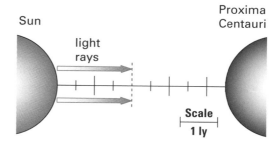

Figure A.7 Light travels 2 ly

c) 4.5 years (approximately) ✓

10. This star is undergoing a nova; it is shining much more brightly than normal. ✓

11. **a)** **i)** $\dfrac{83\,300\,000\,000\,000}{300\,000} = 27\,666\,667$ seconds ✓

   ii) $\dfrac{277\,666\,667}{60 \times 60 \times 24 \times 365.25} = 8.8$ years ✓

   b) 8.8 ly ✓
   c) $2 \times 8.8 = 17.6$ years ✓

12. d, e, b, a, c ✓

13. angle = 60° (= one-sixth of one complete revolution) ✓; time for one complete revolution = $6 \times 35 = 210$ million years ✓

14. F, H, C, B, ✓ D, G, A, E ✓

Test yourself 2

Part A: Knowledge

1. **B** ✓ Another name is rainfall. A is incorrect as this refers to gases becoming liquid. Similarly C is incorrect as this implies liquids becoming gases. D is wrong as this refers to solids becoming gases.

2. **A** ✓ B, C and D are all examples of greenhouse gases, and the question asked which is not.

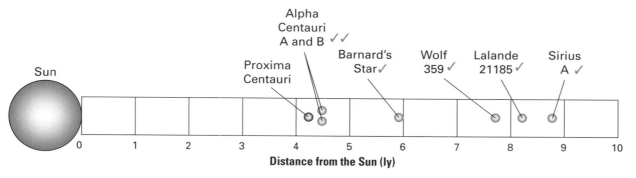

Figure A.6 Closest stars

3. C ✓ A is wrong as this refers to changing nitrates to nitrogen gas. B is incorrect as this refers to eliminating wastes from an animal's body. D is wrong as this refers to an association between organisms of two different species in which each member benefits. This describes the relationship between rhizobium and legumes. Rhizobia (from the Greek words *riza*, meaning 'root' and *bios*, meaning 'life') are soil bacteria that fix nitrogen after becoming established inside the root nodules of legumes.

4. D ✓ Around 80% of ocean pollution originates on land. A, B and C are incorrect as they only make up a small proportion of the pollution found in the oceans.

5. B ✓ This is shown in the figure. As for A, C and D, the opposite is shown for each of these.

6. a) heat ✓; b) chlorinated ✓;
   c) Molina or Rowland ✓ (either name will do);
   d) eutrophication ✓; e) stomata ✓ (also known as stomates)

7. A/G ✓; B/J ✓; C/I ✓; D/F ✓; E/H ✓

Part B: Skills

8. a) i) Z ✓; ii) X ✓
   b) W ✓
   c) from the grass ✓; in turn, the grass got it from the soil and so on, as part of the cycle of nitrogen

9. a) The concentration of carbon dioxide has increased with time; the increase has accelerated in the second half of the 20th century. ✓
   b) rise in carbon dioxide = 360 − 285
   $$= 75 \text{ ppm}$$
   % increase since 1900 $= \dfrac{75}{285} \times 100$
   $$= 26\% ✓✓$$

10. a) See Table A.3.

   Table A.3 Percentage of CO_2 emissions per type of transportation

Transportation sector	Percentage of CO_2 emissions
cars	58
buses and trucks	19
aeroplanes	12
shipping	6
rail transport	5	✓✓

   b) See Figure A.8.

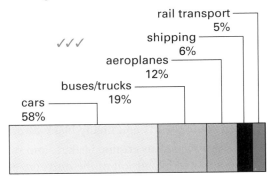

   ✓✓✓

   rail transport 5%
   shipping 6%
   aeroplanes 12%
   buses/trucks 19%
   cars 58%

   Figure A.8 Divided bar graph

11. a) Volatile organic compounds ✓ are compounds of carbon with other elements. They have low boiling points, which allow large numbers of molecules to evaporate ✓ (or sublimate) from the liquid (or solid) form of the compound and enter the surrounding air. They are emitted to the atmosphere from a wide variety of sources, both natural and man-made.
   b) i) 13% ✓ (the total adds to 100%)
      ii) non-road machinery ✓ ($\frac{1}{5} = 20\%$)
      iii) $\dfrac{28}{100} \times 360 = 101° ✓$
   c) total = 1150 + 142 = 1292 million t
      % from human sources $= \dfrac{142}{1292} \times 100$
      $$= 11\% ✓✓$$

12. a) 70 years ✓
   b) Most substances expand when they are heated. ✓ The ocean is no exception. While only increasing a few degrees, the huge volume of water will make distinct changes in the height at the surface. Increased CO_2 means more global warming. This heat is transferred to the ocean which then proceeds to warm up and expand. ✓
   c) No, the sea level rise does not stop. ✓ Thermal expansion is a slow process. Heating from the greenhouse effect in the atmosphere is quickly transferred into surface ocean waters. This then slowly penetrates deeper, causing more expansion at the ocean's depth. This results in further sea level rises. ✓ Even if greenhouse gas concentrations in the atmosphere were stabilised, sea level rise would continue for

hundreds of years, because of the time lags involved.

d) Sea level rises about 0.66 m in 600 years.

This is $\frac{660}{600} = 1.1$ mm/y. ✓✓

(With such a small annual increase, is it any wonder many people are not taking the problem seriously?)

13. a) Except for a slight increase after 1900, the trend has been downwards ✓ (less area covered) and at an increasing rate ✓.

b) Global warming has been thawing the permafrost. ✓ Less reflection off the surface means a further increase in melting, most likely increasing the rate. ✓

c) i) Extrapolation means extending the graph beyond the plotted points assuming the same trend continues. ✓ It is projected that permafrost will thaw at an increasing rate. ✓

ii) possibly just after 2000 ✓

d) Once the tundra starts to thaw, this gas can be released into the atmosphere. It is a potent greenhouse gas and this should accelerate the rate of warming and feeding into more permafrost thawing. ✓✓

14. P. Acidic gases, such as oxides of nitrogen and sulfur, are released into the atmosphere. ✓

Q. Winds carry these gases, along with CO_2, a long distance from where the industry is located. ✓

R. Acid rain produced when these oxides of carbon, nitrogen and sulfur dissolve in moisture and rain water. ✓

S. Acid rain is damaging to plant and animals, pollutes rivers and streams, and can erode stonework, especially marble statues and buildings. ✓

Chapter test

Part A: Multiple-choice questions

1. B ✓ A is wrong as dwarf stars can be the result of the evolution of Sun-like stars or they are stars like red dwarfs that were formed from the condensation of small amounts of stellar matter. C is wrong as a nebula is not hot and compact. D is wrong as protostars are not very dense.

2. B ✓ The order from hottest to coolest is: blue; white; yellow; red. Thus A, C and D are wrong.

3. C ✓ The Milky Way is a galaxy with a diameter of about 100 000 ly. A is wrong as it is spiral and not elliptical. B is wrong as it is not a supernova. D is wrong as these are deep space objects.

4. D ✓ Yellow stars become very large and red as they evolve. Thus A, B and C are wrong.

5. B ✓ A is wrong as Hubble discovered the red shifting of star light. C is wrong as they proposed the steady state theory. D is wrong as Sackett has been investigating exoplanets.

6. D ✓ The energy that drives this cycle comes from the Sun. While each of A, B and C have some energy, they too derive it from the Sun; hence, these alternatives are wrong.

7. D ✓ All of them aid the greenhouse effect. Deforestation means less CO_2 is taken out of the atmosphere, evaporation means more water is entering the atmosphere and more cows to feed a growing population means more methane in the atmosphere. So warming by the greenhouse effect will increase.

8. A ✓ The greenhouse effect on Earth makes this planet habitable. Without it, Earth would be a frozen wasteland. Don't confuse this with excessive warming through the enhanced greenhouse effect. So B and C are incorrect. Scientists have modelled scenarios that allow them to determine what the temperature would be like without this effect, so D is wrong.

9. C ✓ All the others do involve gaseous components as part of their cycles, so A, B and D are wrong.

10. D ✓ Animals needs to take in nitrogen through eating protein from plants or from other animals. Nitrogen fixation occurs in some plants, not animals, so A is wrong. B is wrong as animals cannot absorb nitrogen. C is wrong since, although air is some 80% nitrogen, we can't utilise it directly through breathing.

Part B: Short-answer questions

11. a) See Table A.4.

Table A.4 Azimuth and elevation of labelled stars

Star	Azimuth	Elevation	
A	210°	30°	✓
B	135°	15°	✓
C	180°	45–50°	✓

b) south ✓

c) Z means the zenith, the point directly above the observer. ✓

12. a) Milky Way ✓; b) galaxy ✓; c) star ✓;

d) Andromeda ✓; e) nebula ✓; f) nova ✓;

g) gamma rays ✓

13. a) 1000 °C ✓, +15 ✓

b) red dwarf ✓

c) D ✓

d) Z, Y, X ✓

e) +4.5 ✓

f) i) false ✓; ii) true ✓; iii) true ✓

14. a) distance = 7.7 × 9461
       = 72 849.7 billion km ✓

b) distance = 353 × 9461
       = 3 339 733 billion km ✓

15. a) No ✓ Cluster refers to the organisation of local galaxies. These stars are all in one galaxy (the Milky Way). They are a constellation, because they appear to be together in the sky. ✓

b) i) Alpha Crucis ✓

   ii) Although Beta Crucis is brighter in absolute terms, it appears dimmer, as it is further from Earth. ✓

16. a) $T = \dfrac{3\,000\,000}{510} = 5882$ K ✓

b) $T = 5882 - 273 = 5609$ °C ✓

c) wavelength $= \dfrac{3\,000\,000}{T} = \dfrac{3\,000\,000}{4300}$
       = 697.7 nm = 698 nm (red end of visible spectrum) ✓

17. a) X-rays, gamma rays and ultraviolet (some infra-red) ✓

b) visible near infra-red, microwaves, radio waves ✓

c) visible astronomy ✓, radio astronomy ✓

18. a) position 3, as the star is moving away from Earth ✓

b) Line X = position 3 ✓
   Line Y = position 2 ✓
   Line Z = position 1 ✓

c) position 1 ✓

d) They are moving away from us as the universe expands. ✓

19. a) Sun–Venus = 0.7 × 150
       = 105 million km ✓

b) Sun–Saturn = 9.5 × 150
       = 1425 million km ✓

20. X, Z, ✓ W, Y ✓

21. the local group ✓

22. a) radius = 6384 + 650 = 7034 km ✓

b) distance = $2\pi r = 2\pi(7034) = 44\,195$ km ✓

c) speed = $\dfrac{44\,195}{1.5} = 29\,463$ km/h ✓

d) distance = 29 463 × 8766 × 10
       = 2 582 726 580 km ✓

23. a) brightest at B and D; faintest at A and E ✓

b) 10 hours ✓

c) 70 hours ✓

24. a) Red shifting of starlight shows that all galaxies are moving away from one another. ✓ The discovery of the cosmic background radiation is consistent with the Big Bang theory. ✓

b) Expanding matter, which was thrown out, cooled to form quarks and electrons in the first one-millionth of a second. ✓ These particles clumped together to form protons and neutrons, in turn producing hydrogen and helium nuclei in the first 10 minutes. ✓

c) 13.7 billion years old ✓

25. a) quasar ✓; b) red giant star ✓;
   c) dark matter ✓; d) neutron star ✓;
   e) Big Bang ✓; f) asteroid ✓; g) infra-red ✓;
   h) pulsar ✓; i) black hole ✓

26. a) There has been a steady growth in the amount of emission of CO_2 into the atmosphere. This growth rate has increased since 1950 (slope of graph is steeper). ✓

b) perhaps the large number of domestic animals ✓ (methane producers) and humans ✓ (CO_2 producers) who have replaced forests ✓; more burning of fossil fuels ✓; natural sources such as volcanoes ✓ and oceans ✓; decay by fungi and bacteria ✓

c) Yes, there does not seem to be let-up in the amount of CO_2 released into the atmosphere. The rate may increase further. ✓

d) Your answer may vary, but will be greater than 7. ✓

27. a) This graph shows the concentration of CO_2 in the atmosphere. ✓ Figure 3.66 shows the amount of CO_2 released into the atmosphere on a yearly basis. ✓ The two graphs also

cover different time periods. ✓ This graph is from 1970 to 1998, ✓ while the previous graph is from 1850 to 1990. ✓

b) There are seasonal variations in the CO_2 concentration. ✓ CO_2 is greatest in the first quarter of the year, and least in the last quarter of the year. ✓

c) i) about 330 ppm ✓
   ii) about 358 ppm ✓

d) between 8% ✓ and 8.5% ✓

e) increased global warming ✓

28. a) A line of best fit is a straight line drawn through the centre of a group of data points plotted on a scatter plot, so that the data points are clustered very near to the line. ✓ It gives the best approximation to a given set of data. ✓

b) 1990 ✓ (as this is the point where 0 mm sea level occurs)

c) No. There needs to be some point from which rises (or falls) are measured. This was arbitrarily taken as 1990. Negative values before 1990 indicate a sea level lower than that in 1990. ✓✓ For example, suppose in 1988 the measurement was –6 mm. This just means that between 1988 and 1990 the sea level will rise by 6 mm.

d) Between 1990 and 2006 the sea level rose by 45 mm. Therefore slope = $\frac{\text{rise}}{\text{run}} = \frac{45}{16}$
   = 2.8 mm/y. ✓✓

e) Your values will vary, depending on the year. But at a rough estimate, 2012 should be 62 mm; 2015 should be 70 mm; 2018 should be 79 mm. ✓✓

f) Rising at some 2.8 mm/y, in 100 years the sea level should have risen 100 × 2.8 = 280 mm. ✓✓

29. No. In the greenhouse effect there are several gases that act as a blanket trapping heat inside the Earth's atmosphere. The main greenhouse gases in the Earth's atmosphere are water vapour, carbon dioxide, methane, nitrous oxide and ozone. ✓ With ozone depletion, there are certain gases (such as CFCs) that rise into the stratosphere and destroy ozone thereby causing 'holes'. ✓ Although CFCs are greenhouse gases, they are regulated because of their contribution to ozone depletion rather than

their contribution to global warming. The two processes are often confused in the media. ✓

30. a) The phosphorus cycle differs from the carbon, oxygen and nitrogen cycles as phosphorus is not found in the atmosphere. It is found primarily in sedimentary rock. ✓ Phosphorus is necessary in the formation of DNA and in the bones of vertebrate animals. Phosphorus can also be found in the bird droppings associated with nesting areas (guano). ✓

b) Erosion is the first mechanism that releases phosphorus from sedimentary rocks. At this point, it is available to all plants and animals to use. ✓ The plants are able to take in the phosphates and animals incorporate their phosphorus needs from plants. Phosphorus returns to the system when plants and animals decompose. ✓

31. Carbonic acid, from dissolving CO_2, leads to higher acidity in sea water. Near the surface where there are a number of animals with shells, this carbonic acid can inhibit shell growth. ✓ It is also suspected in causing reproductive disorders in some fish. ✓

32. P. Highly energetic ultraviolet radiation hits a CFC molecule. ✓
    Q. This breaks a C–Cl bond and a free chlorine atom forms. ✓
    R. The chlorine atom collides with an ozone molecule. ✓
    S. This removes an O atom from the ozone and chlorine combines with it to form ClO (chlorine monoxide). The remaining O_2 is oxygen gas. ✓
    T. A free oxygen atom is able to collide with ClO, breaking apart the bond. ✓
    U. O joins with an O to give O_2, and a free chlorine atom is available to destroy more ozone. ✓

33. a) CFC stands for chlorofluorocarbon, a class of chemical compounds. ✓ These are organic compounds containing carbon, chlorine and fluorine ✓, and are produced as volatile derivatives of methane and ethane. Many of them have been widely used as refrigerants, aerosol, propellants and solvents. ✓

b) Energetic ultraviolet rays are able to break apart the O=O bond to form two oxygen atoms. Some of these may react with O_2 to give O_3. But some are intercepted by the ClO molecule beforehand. ✓ See Figure A.9.

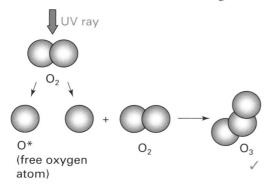

UV ray

O_2

O*
(free oxygen atom)

O_2

O_3
✓

Figure A.9 Forming a free oxygen atom

34. a) Since the bogs were formed they have been generating methane, mostly by the bacterial decomposition of organic matter. Most of this gas has been trapped within the permafrost itself. ✓✓

b) Methane is a powerful greenhouse gas, some 30 times more potent than carbon dioxide. Permafrost is an immense methane reservoir. While current emission levels are low, they are expected to substantially increase this century, accelerating warming in higher latitudes and globally. ✓✓ This is a major concern since it will produce growing feedback resulting in a gradual increase of the speed, depth and extent of permafrost thawing. This will further increase methane emissions, resulting in ongoing and more extensive land destabilisation, distortion of the surface and subsurface material, and development of swamplands. ✓

c) This can profoundly impact on flora and fauna, particularly species which have adapted to the cold tundra conditions. Because of the speed and extent of permafrost thawing, they may not have enough time to adapt to these changes and so face extinction. At the same time, warming and other changes to the environment are resulting in a northward movement of species. ✓✓

d) The loss of permafrost plus the retreating of sea ice causes rapid coastal erosion ✓ some five to six times faster than that due to rising sea level. Some coastal communities are forced to move to more stable land. ✓ There will be extensive damage to buildings and infrastructure ✓ now becoming evident as a result of land movement caused by loss of permafrost. This damage is expected to increase over the next 50 years, having substantial adverse effects on the Arctic population.

e) These adverse outcomes may be slowed by rapid reduction of enhanced greenhouse gas emissions ✓ but they cannot be stopped or reversed. Technology can be used to counter some of the effects of permafrost thawing on existing buildings and infrastructure ✓, otherwise damage to them cannot be prevented nor can an alarming increase in methane venting into the atmosphere.

35. P = percolation ✓; Q = surface runoff ✓; R = groundwater ✓; S = precipitation ✓; T = condensation ✓; U = transpiration ✓; V = evaporation ✓

36. a) the change in tides ✓, caused by the Moon; large and small waves ✓ caused by wind and the tides; high- and low-pressure areas in the atmosphere ✓, which change the surface level of the ocean; ocean temperature changes ✓, which alter the density and volume of the water; rainfall and rivers flowing into the ocean

b) The problem with measuring the sea level is that there are so many things that affect it. Sea level changes over the last century have been determined mainly from tide-gauge data, where the sea level is measured relative to some benchmark on land. Local and regional sea level variations do occur. Such influences can generally be compensated for to reveal trends in long-term records. ✓✓✓ Observed trends, however, can be complicated by the fact that the land can experience vertical movements as well.

37. a) $16 + 8 + 2 + 2 = 28$ mm ✓

b) $\dfrac{16}{28} \times 100 = 57\%$ ✓✓

c) $\dfrac{38}{100} \times 11 = 4.2$ mm ✓✓

38. Ozone is present in low concentrations throughout the Earth's atmosphere. Ozone in

the lower atmosphere is an air pollutant with harmful effects on the respiratory systems of animals and will burn sensitive plants. ✓ (Here it is formed by the reaction of sunlight on hydrocarbons and nitrogen oxides in the air, producing ozone directly at the source of the pollution or downwind from it. It can cause a reduction in agricultural yields as it interferes with photosynthesis and stunts overall growth of some plant species.) The ozone layer in the upper atmosphere is beneficial, preventing potentially damaging electromagnetic radiation from reaching the Earth's surface. ✓ (In the stratosphere it filters out ultraviolet rays that have shorter wavelengths, less than 320 nm.)

39. a) 6% ✓

b) See Figure A.10.

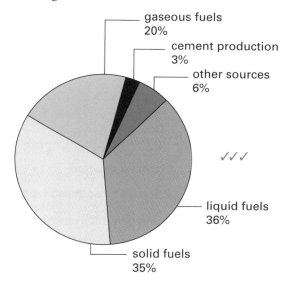

gaseous fuels
20%

cement production
3%

other sources
6%

✓✓✓

liquid fuels
36%

solid fuels
35%

Figure A.10 Pie chart

40. a) It is a system of surface and subsurface ocean currents, driven by temperature and salinity differences, which create density gradients between adjoining water masses. These currents are responsible for moving great amounts of thermal energy around the globe. ✓✓ This circulation moves water slowly, around 1/3 km/h, but it moves a lot of water.

b) At the poles the warm, salty water that has been transported north from tropical regions is rapidly cooled, forming a huge amount of cold water. When this seawater freezes, it does so with very little salt. This increases the salinity of the remaining unfrozen water.

The water becomes denser, and so drops to the ocean floor. The cooled water sinks to the deep ocean and travels around the globe, possibly not surfacing for hundreds of years. ✓✓

c) Near the equator, the current mixes with warmer water, warms and then rises as it is now less dense. ✓✓ Water heated near the equator travels at the surface of the ocean north into high latitudes where it loses some heat to the atmosphere. This keeps the temperatures in northern Europe and North America relatively mild.

d) Water becomes less salty if there is an increase of freshwater either from melting ice or precipitation and runoff from land. There is a worry that as the Arctic warms, through global warming, and more sea ice melts, this influx of freshwater will make the sea water at high latitudes less dense. Then it will not be able to sink and circulate around the globe. ✓✓ This could possibly stop the ocean conveyor and change the climate of the European and North American continents.

e) Yes. Besides salt, the circulation carries other substances. Dissolved oxygen in cold surface waters are carried deep down to the bottom of the ocean. This oxygenates the depths. Mineral and nutrient-rich warmer waters come to the surface allowing plankton to thrive. This provides a first step in the food chain. ✓✓

Chapter 4 answers

Experiment 1

Analysis: The dots in Part A are equidistant and so the student walked at constant speed. The dots in Part B are becoming further apart over time, which shows that the mass is accelerating as it falls under gravity.

Conclusion: Ticker tape timers can be used to demonstrate constant velocity motion as well as accelerated motion.

Experiment 2

Analysis

1. See Table A.5.

Table A.5 Friction and acceleration experiment

Time	Smooth surface	Rough surface
time to travel the first 30 cm (s)	3.16	3.87
time to travel the second 30 cm (s)	4.47 − 3.16 = 1.31	5.48 − 3.87 = 1.61
time to travel the third 30 cm (s)	5.48 − 4.47 = 1.01	6.71 − 5.48 = 1.23
time to travel the last 30 cm (s)	6.32 − 5.48 = 0.84	7.75 − 6.71 = 1.04

2. On each surface, the mass is accelerating as the time to travel each 30 cm is decreasing. The smooth surface has produced a greater acceleration of the mass than the rough surface. Greater frictional forces on the rough slope have decreased the net force acting on the mass.

Conclusion: The mass accelerates down a smooth and rough slope and the acceleration is less on the rough slope.

Experiment 3

Analysis

1. Noting the speed gives a good indication of the changes in kinetic energy. Noting the height gives a good indication of changes in potential energy. As the bob drops from the top of its swing, it speeds up (increasing kinetic energy; decreasing potential energy) until it reaches the bottom of the swing. Here it is travelling at maximum speed. As it climbs to the other end, it slows down (decreasing kinetic energy; increasing potential energy).

2. See Table A.6. (These are typical results; yours may vary.)

3. It is difficult to just time one complete swing. By timing 10 and averaging, errors are minimised and any small changes in the swing can be accounted for.

4. A typical plot is shown in Figure A.11. A straight line has been placed over the curve to show it is not a straight-line relationship.

5. As the length of line increases, the time for a complete oscillation increases although this is not a linear relationship.

Table A.6 Results for Experiment 3

Line length (cm)	Time for one oscillation (s)
10	1.0
15	1.2
20	1.4
25	1.6
30	1.7
35	1.9
40	2.0
45	2.1
50	2.2
55	2.3

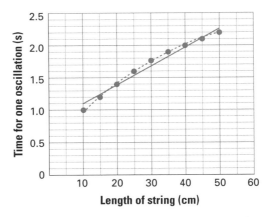

Figure A.11 Typical plot for oscillation experiment

Conclusion: A swinging pendulum shows changes in kinetic and potential energy. Accounting for small losses in energy, the total kinetic and potential energies remain the same. There is also a relationship between the length of the pendulum's string and the time for an oscillation.

Test yourself 1

Part A: Knowledge

1. A ✓ The same amount of steam is produced per second. B is wrong as more heat can boil more water per second and produce a greater thrust. C is wrong as reducing friction will increase the net force. D is wrong as the narrower the nozzle, the greater is the reaction force.

2. A ✓ After 15 seconds, there is no change in velocity. B is wrong as he was travelling quite slowly at the start. C is wrong as he will cover a greater distance when he is travelling at a higher speed. D is wrong as we have no information after 25 seconds.

3. **A** ✓ A body stays at constant speed unless acted upon by a net force. This is Newton's first law. B is wrong as it would accelerate if the force was unbalanced. C is wrong as the bicycle could not move forwards. D is wrong as the force of gravity is balanced by the reaction force of the ground on the bicycle.

4. **B** ✓ This is Newton's third law. A is wrong as no net force exists. C is wrong as the vertical weight force is not transmitted horizontally. D is wrong as the frictional force is 50 N.

5. **D** ✓ As there is no further motion then the forces are in balance. A is wrong as motion would result. B is wrong as the forces are balanced. C is wrong as no net force applies.

6. a) frictional ✓; b) field ✓; c) distance ✓; d) third ✓; e) decelerating ✓

7. A/I ✓; B/F ✓; C/J ✓; D/G ✓; E/H ✓

Part B: Skills

8. The effect of friction produced by the atmosphere must be considered. ✓ The larger the size of the object, the faster it can travel through air before air resistance becomes an issue in slowing it down. Eventually, a point is reached where the force due to air resistance balances the gravitational force and the object falls at a constant speed from then until it hits the Earth. ✓

9. Rhiannon's speed is twice that of Erin's. ✓

10. a) to measure the acceleration of the dynamics cart ✓

    b) The description should be concise enough for another student to be able to replicate the experiment. A possible description might be the following:
       1. Set up the apparatus as shown in the diagram. Adjust the moveable arm on the ticker timer so that the oscillations are distinct, making a single mark at each spot as a sample piece of tape is drawn through. ✓
       2. Masses should be attached to the mass holder so that a reasonable acceleration is achieved in moving the dynamics cart across the bench. ✓

    c) The cart accelerates slowly due to the falling mass (see Figure A.12).

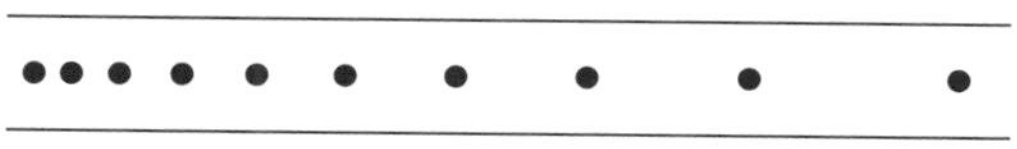

✓

Figure A.12 Ticker tape

11. a) C ✓
    b) D ✓
    c) B ✓
    d) In diagram A, the truck is accelerating. ✓

12. The strain on the line would be greater than the breaking strain. Bringing in the fish slowly does not put such strain on the line. ✓

13. Having a greater mass, a greater force is needed to slow the vehicle to a halt. A large moving object possesses a greater amount of inertia. ✓

14. a) the 50-kg child ✓
    b) the 30-kg child; for the same propelling force, the lighter child can achieve the greater acceleration ✓
    c) The head has considerable inertia and so continues to move forwards during sudden braking. The muscles of the neck then pull the head back as a reaction and damage can then be done to the spine during these sudden movements of the head. ✓

Test yourself 2

Part A: Knowledge

1. **A** ✓ Wood comes from trees that can be continually grown. B and C are incorrect as these were laid down millions of years ago and their rate of accumulation is too slow to be considered renewable. D is wrong as this energy source is not renewable.

2. **C** ✓ Chemical substances store energy in a battery. When connected in a circuit, a chemical reaction releases electrons that flow in an electric current. Thus A, B and D are incorrect.

3. **B** ✓ Water in a high dam has gravitational potential energy and when it falls down, the energy is converted to kinetic energy and then finally to electrical energy in the turbines. Thus A, C and D are incorrect.

4. **D** ✓ Australia relies on black and brown coal for most of its electricity production. While A and B are fossil fuels, they are not used to any great extent in Australia to generate electricity. C is not a fossil fuel.

5. C ✓ Electricity, whether through the power grid or through batteries, can power a whole range of appliances. A, B and D are all energy resources but do not have the same versatility as electricity, so these alternatives are incorrect. Coal, for example, is often burnt to provide electricity.

6. a) energy ✓; b) conservation ✓; c) velocity (speed) ✓; d) transformation ✓; e) walls ✓

7. A/J ✓; B/H ✓; C/G ✓; D/I ✓; E/F ✓

Part B: Skills

8. a) 29 + 12 = 41% ✓
   b) 5 + 2 = 7% ✓
   c) See Figure A.13.

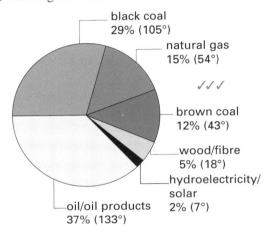

black coal
29% (105°)

natural gas
15% (54°)

✓✓✓

brown coal
12% (43°)

wood/fibre
5% (18°)

hydroelectricity/
solar
2% (7°)

oil/oil products
37% (133°)

Figure A.13 Pie graph

9. a) annual energy usage = 500 × 4 × 365
                         = 730 000 MJ ✓✓

   b) The United States has the greatest energy usage as it is the largest technological and industrialised society. People in the United States rely heavily on motor vehicles and electrical appliances. Australians are less dependent on energy and are less wasteful. In India many people live in rural and agricultural communities and do not drive cars. Their use of energy is much reduced. ✓✓

10. a) $\frac{265}{970} \times 100 = 27.3\%$ ✓
    b) Agriculture/industry and transport use oil-based products such as petrol and diesel. (Homes and offices obtain electrical energy from coal combustion.) ✓
    c) See Figure A.14.

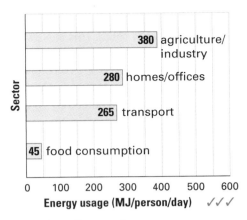

Figure A.14 Bar graph

11. a) As there is no air resistance, the object can increase its speed, and hence its kinetic energy, indefinitely. ✓✓
    b) Air resistance prevents the object from accelerating any further. ✓
    c) Once there is no further acceleration, the objects fall at a constant speed, so kinetic energy remains constant. That is, the objects have reached terminal velocity. ✓✓
    d) P ✓ Kinetic energy depends on both mass and velocity. Since the objects are of the same size (dimensions) and shape, the factor determining their terminal velocity must be mass. The greater the mass, the greater is the terminal velocity, and the greater is the kinetic energy. ✓

12. a) R ✓
    b) P and T. ✓ The kinetic energies are the same ✓ (though not necessarily the same as the potential energy).
    c) S ✓ The ball is travelling faster at this point.
    d) R ✓ The ball has momentarily come to a stop.

13. While the boy is on the ground, he has kinetic energy due to his motion. Assuming his speed here is constant, then so is his kinetic energy. ✓ His potential energy can be taken to be zero. As he climbs the ramp his velocity decreases, and so does his kinetic energy. His potential energy increases as kinetic energy is changed into potential energy. ✓ When he reaches the top he has maximum potential energy and, if he's still moving, there will be some kinetic energy left. ✓

14. This claim is definitely false. ✓ The water will flow out of the bottom but will not rise higher

than the level in the cup. ✓ To do so would mean that the water gains more potential energy than it originally had. This is a violation of the law of conservation of energy, which states that you can't create energy. ✓ While kinetic energy can be changed to PE and vice versa, the total of all energies must remain the same. ✓

Chapter test

Part A: Knowledge

1. **B** ✓ The distances between the first five points are equal and so the car is moving with constant velocity to the east. After that, it slows down as the distances between each car position become smaller. Thus A, C and D are wrong.

2. **C** ✓ There is no air on the Moon (no air resistance)—the ball falls under gravity and so is uniformly accelerated. A is wrong as the parachutist has frictional drag acting on him. B is wrong for the same reason. D is wrong as a car's acceleration can increase as the pedal is depressed further.

3. **C** ✓ Newton was the first person to propose the laws of gravitation. Therefore, A, B and D are wrong.

4. **A** ✓ B is wrong as the mass is constant and weight decreases. C is wrong as only the weight is less. D is wrong as the weight changes.

5. **D** ✓ The early drips are the same distance apart and then they get further apart. A is wrong as the drips would get closer together if this was true. B is wrong as the drips would be the same distance apart. C is wrong as there is no large puddle of oil.

6. **C** ✓ The formula for gravitational potential energy is GPE = mgh, so it depends on mass, gravity and height. Thus A, B and D are incorrect. It does not depend on the speed or velocity of the object.

7. **B** ✓ At A and D, PE is maximum and KE = 0; at C PE = 0 and KE is maximum. So A, C and D are incorrect. At B, PE is being changed into KE and, halfway down, PE = KE.

8. **D** ✓ The chemical energy in the match is being converted to other forms of energy. A, B and C are incorrect as each of the types of energy are increasing. From the heat, the kinetic energy of the particles increases.

9. **A** ✓ Electrical energy is not destroyed (conservation of energy). B, C and D are true, so they are not the response to the question.

10. **B** ✓ A, C and D are wrong as these are all non-renewable energy forms.

Part B: Short-answer questions

11. a) The force required increases. ✓
    b) Less force is required. ✓
    c) A smaller acceleration is achieved. ✓
    d) Twice the force was applied. ✓

12. $a = \dfrac{F}{m} = \dfrac{200}{10} = 20 \text{ m/s}^2$ ✓

13. $F = ma = (50)(0.5) = 25 \text{ N}$ ✓

14. $F = ma = 500\,000\,000 \times 0.01 = 5\,000\,000 \text{ N}$ ✓

15. $a = \dfrac{\text{change in velocity}}{\text{time}} = \dfrac{(12-0)}{10} = 1.2 \text{ m/s}^2$ ✓

16. There are various possible answers, such as the following.
    During an impact, the car comes to rest in a very short space of time and distance. That is, the deceleration is very high and, consequently, so is the force. An unrestrained person (or objects in the car) still move at such time due to their inertia. During a sudden stop, it is not uncommon for a person to be thrown through the window. Seatbelts prevent potentially catastrophic events and help save lives. ✓ (Sometimes a crying baby is nursed in the back seat by the mother. It is erroneously thought this is safe as a light child could be held during a mishap. It has been calculated that a 10-kg child can become as heavy as several bags of cement. And this is all in the space of a fraction of a second. The child could easily be hurtled against the windscreen.)

17. This is due to Newton's third law. A forward motion is obtained at the expense of a backwards push by the feet. In a boat, there is little friction between the boat and the water so the boat moves backwards. ✓

18. a) There was no indication of a change in speed; for example, the jog turning into a run, or the bicycle rider stopping to rest. ✓
    b) Jenna travelled fastest ✓, Jasmine travelled slowest ✓.
    c) Jenna rode the bicycle ✓, Ayshe jogged ✓ and Jasmine walked ✓.

d) Jenna's average speed = $\frac{14}{1}$ = 14 km/h ✓

Ayshe's average speed = $\frac{8}{1}$ = 8 km/h ✓

Jasmine's average speed = $\frac{2.5}{1}$ = 2.5 km/h ✓

e) 3.75 km ✓

19. a) Jim travelled faster ✓; the line is steeper ✓.

b) Jim's speed = $\frac{150}{2}$ = 75 km/h ✓;

Spiro's speed = $\frac{250}{5}$ = 50 km/h ✓.

c) The line for Jim starts at (1, 0). That is, after 1 hour the distance he had travelled was still 0 km. ✓

d) 3 hours ✓, 150 km ✓

20. a) There are a number of factors that will affect the initial acceleration result, including the mass of the car and the power of its engine. A standing start allows all these factors to be considered. ✓

b) Car X has the higher performance ✓ because it takes less time to reach the specified speeds. ✓

21. The speed increases uniformly. There is uniform acceleration. ✓

22. a) N: its speed does not change ✓

b) L: its speed is getting smaller ✓

c) K: constant for 2 seconds and then accelerates ✓

d) M: accelerates for 2 seconds and then has constant speed ✓

e) average acceleration = $\frac{(4-0)}{2}$

= 2 m/s² ✓

23. a) Mass M and Mass N both accelerate along the table ✓; M has the greater acceleration. ✓

b) N has the greater mass ✓ since its acceleration is less than that of M. ✓

c) average speed of M = $\frac{(128-32)}{(1.6-0.8)}$

= 120 cm/s ✓

24. a) the distance required to bring the car to a stop once the brakes are applied ✓

b) reaction distance increases ✓

c) braking distance increases ✓

d) $d = 33.3 \times 0.75 = 24.98 = 25$ m ✓

e) The reaction distance will not change but the braking distance will increase because the road has less friction. ✓

25. a) Plato and Aristotle lived long before Newton so 'friend' cannot be taken here as a contemporary buddy. Rather, he means he has respect for what Plato and Aristotle said and takes it seriously. However, beyond that, truth is even more important and he is willing to dismiss their arguments when he finds compelling evidence to the contrary. ✓

b) The Giants are the giants of science who laid the foundation work that Newton used to come up with his theories and laws. He was able to use this valuable information, collected by others, that allowed him to take a step forwards. ✓

c) i) Newton ✓

ii) This is the famous story of how Newton thought up his hypothesis of universal gravitation. (There is no indication the apple fell on his head, though.) ✓

d) i) the Moon ✓

ii) Gravity does not just cause objects to fall to the ground but, in addition, he suggested that it is the same gravity that influences the Moon and keeps it in orbit around the Earth. ✓

26. Bore a hole down to the hot rocks and pump cold water down to the rocks; the heat is transferred to the water and it is heated and boils. The water is then pumped out and passed through a heat exchanger, or the steam is used to drive turbines to produce electricity. ✓✓

27. a) Energy at P is completely potential. As the bob starts its journey down the slope, potential energy is being converted to kinetic energy, and this is actively occurring at Q. At R all potential energy has been changed to kinetic energy. Now the opposite begins to occur, that is, kinetic energy changes to potential energy as the bob moves up the slope so that when it gets to S all kinetic energy has been transformed into potential energy. ✓✓✓

b) Some energy is changed to heat and some is used in overcoming resistance as it moves through air. ✓ In reality the system is not completely isolated.

28. a) When watching a pendulum swing back and forth, for instance, it is easy for students to observe that the pendulum does not swing as high with each successive swing. Some assume that energy has been destroyed. ✓ This is also true with other devices where energy is changed from one form to another. Energy has not been annihilated; it has been simply changed into a form that is not useful to the system. ✓

    b) Machines are not 100% efficient. Some energy will be lost to the system due to these inefficiencies with every transformation. While the electricity in a light bulb is to generate light, some of that energy is also transformed to wasteful heat. ✓ Perpetual motion is a notion many believed in the past was possible. An imaginary perpetual motion machine operates where energy is transformed into another form and then transformed completely back into a useful form without putting any additional energy from outside the system into the machine. ✓

29. a) at R ✓ and V ✓

    b) The roller-coaster reaches its maximum speed at S then slows as it starts to climb on the other side. ✓ In terms of energy potential energy → kinetic energy before S (object losing height), so with more kinetic energy the roller-coaster speeds up. ✓ After S (object gaining height), kinetic energy → potential energy. This lessens kinetic energy and so the roller-coaster slows down. ✓

30. a) GPE $= mgh$
    $= 20 \times 9.8 \times 25$
    $= 4900$ J. ✓✓
    (In an examination you will be given $g = 9.8$ m/s². Sometimes, for convenience, g is taken as 10 m/s².)

    b) It is progressively converted into kinetic energy. ✓

    c) No ✓ The kinetic energy has been changed into heat and into deforming the ball and/or ground. ✓

31. The statement is incorrect. ✓ Assume a mass m is travelling at v m/s. Its KE = $\frac{1}{2}mv^2$. Now if you double the velocity (mass remaining the same), its KE = $\frac{1}{2}m(2v)^2 = \frac{1}{2}m \times 4v^2 = 2mv^2$. ✓

This kinetic energy is four times, not double, its original kinetic energy. ✓
(You could also use a numerical example to show the kinetic energy quadruples.)

32. a) GPE $= mgh$ ✓
    $= 90 \times 9.8 \times 50$
    $= 44\,100$ J ✓

    b) The acceleration due to gravity on the Moon is different. The person's mass does not alter. $90 \times g \times 50 = 7290$ (where g here represents the acceleration due to gravity on the Moon) ✓
    $$g = \frac{7290}{(90 \times 50)}$$
    $= 1.62$ m/s² ✓
    (This is approximately 1/6 that of the acceleration due to gravity on Earth.)

    c) More work would need to be done on Earth. ✓ (Of course, on the Moon he would also be wearing a space suit and carrying life-support equipment.)

33. a) solar ✓; transmitted ✓; reflected ✓; radiated ✓; infrared ✓; 100 ✓

    b) See Figure A.15.

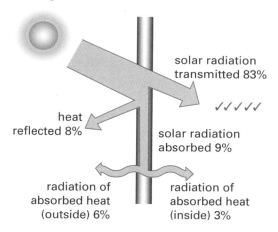

    Figure A.15 Solar radiation

    c) If things were equal on both sides then the same amount of heat should be radiated. Possible reasons might include that it is colder outside therefore more heat is lost ✓ or that the wind outside removes a layer of warmer air close to the glass, allowing more to be radiated ✓.

34. a) 40 km/h
    $$= \frac{40\ \cancel{km}}{\cancel{h}} \times \frac{1000\ m}{1\ \cancel{km}} \times \frac{1\ \cancel{h}}{60\ \cancel{min}} \times \frac{1\ \cancel{min}}{60\ s}$$
    $= 11.1$ m/s ✓✓

b) KE $= \frac{1}{2}mv^2$
$$= \frac{1}{2} \times 1200 \times 11.1^2$$
$$= 73\,926 \text{ J} \checkmark\checkmark \text{ (or approximately 74 kJ)}$$

c) The kinetic energy is dissipated as heat and in wearing out part of the brake linings. $\checkmark\checkmark$ (If you were to feel the brakes of a car, even after a short trip around the block they would be very hot, enough to burn you.)

35. The cart gains gravitational potential energy.
GPE $= mgh$
$$= 45 \times 9.8 \times 0.85$$
$$= 374.85 \text{ J} \checkmark$$

(Notice that the length of the ramp is immaterial. The longer ramp makes it more convenient so you are not lifting directly.) This 374.85 J represents the energy output.

$$\text{efficiency} = \frac{\text{energy output}}{\text{energy input}}$$

$$90\% = \frac{374.85}{\text{energy input}}$$

$$\therefore \text{ energy input} = \frac{374.85}{90\%}$$

$$= 374.85 \times \frac{100}{90}$$

$$= 416.5 \text{ J} \checkmark\checkmark$$

36. *One mark each for any three of these (there are more)*: cavity wall insulation; replacing incandescent globes with CFL globes; ceiling insulation; fit a hot water jacket around the hot water system; replace a conventional water heater with a solar-powered water heater; use draft excluders for doors and windows; keep blinds/shutters closed during hot days; replace less energy-efficient appliances $\checkmark\checkmark\checkmark$

37. a) efficiency $= \dfrac{\text{energy output}}{\text{energy input}} \times \dfrac{100}{1}$

$$= \frac{245}{250} \times \frac{100}{1}$$

$$= 98\% \checkmark\checkmark$$

b) A simple lever loses about 2% of the input energy to internal friction at its fulcrum, such that its efficiency is 98%. $\checkmark$ (Compare this to the efficiency of a motor vehicle being only around 15%. About 75% of the energy is lost through wasted heat from the engine brakes and suspension and another 10% is lost due to internal friction, including losses from tyre friction.)

38. a) i) At the top of the tower, $h = 324$ m, so
GPE $= mgh$
$$= 10 \times 9.8 \times 324$$
$$= 31\,752 \text{ J} \checkmark\checkmark$$

   ii) When $h = 162$ m,
GPE $= mgh$
$$= 10 \times 9.8 \times 162$$
$$= 15\,876 \text{ J} \checkmark\checkmark$$

b) i) Halfway down, half of the gravitational potential energy has been changed to kinetic energy, so KE $= 15\,876$ J $\checkmark\checkmark$

   ii) At the bottom the entire initial gravitational potential energy has been changed to kinetic energy, so KE $= 31\,752$ J. $\checkmark\checkmark$

c) GPE $=$ KE
$mgh = \frac{1}{2}mv^2$
So $v^2 = 2gh$
$$= 2 \times 9.8 \times 162$$
$$= 3175.2$$
$$\therefore v = \sqrt{3175.2} = 56.3 \text{ m/s} \checkmark\checkmark$$

You are assuming that all the gravitational potential energy has been converted into kinetic energy on the way down $\checkmark$ and you are ignoring air resistance $\checkmark$.

39. a) Most injuries to drivers and passengers are due to contact with hard surfaces such as the steering wheel, dashboard, windscreen and the sides and roof of the vehicle. $\checkmark$ Without restraint, the driver and passengers can be ejected like missiles through the car's window as they are still travelling at the speed of the car during a collision. Wearing a seatbelt doubles your chances of surviving a serious crash. $\checkmark$ Experiments using crash test dummies also indicated that wearing seatbelts should lead to reduced risk of death and injury in car crashes. $\checkmark$

b) Sitting in the back is not any safer than sitting in the front. During a collision, passengers have only a fraction of a second to react. The child will become a missile, even if the mother is restrained. $\checkmark$ It is not possible for a person to hold a child, or any reasonably sized object, with the strength needed to prevent it from being ripped from one's arms. $\checkmark$ Road safety researchers have calculated that an unrestrained child in a 50 km/h car crash suffers the same effects as being dropped onto concrete from a building's second floor. An unrestrained baby can weigh as much as a fridge during a crash; a box of tissues can become as heavy as a brick. ✓

(It is for these reasons that Australian laws state that the driver is responsible for ensuring that all people travelling in their vehicle are correctly restrained. If they or their passengers are not restrained correctly, they risk being fined.)

40. Ingenious as it sounds, this perpetual motion machine will not work. ✓ Frictional and other energy-sapping effects will take away from the kinetic energy and so the machine will slow and eventually stop. ✓ In addition, the law of energy conservation states that energy cannot be created, so where is the energy coming from if it is to be used to drive other devices? ✓

Chapter 5 answers

Experiment 1

Analysis

1. Average flow times:
   • water = 14.2 s
   • syrup = 20.2 s
   • oil = 17.1 s

2. The order of viscosity from low to high is: water, oil and then syrup.

Conclusion: Liquids vary in their viscosity and of the three liquids tested, the water was found to be least viscous and the syrup the most viscous.

Experiment 2

Analysis: See Figure A.16.

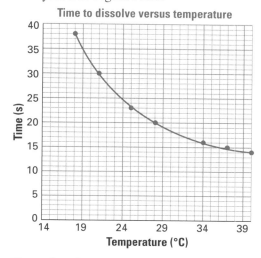

Time to dissolve versus temperature

Figure A.16 Solubility versus temperature

Conclusion: As the temperature of the water increases, the time for the salt to dissolves decreases.

Experiment 3

Analysis

1. You will need to convert your data to vehicles/hour. In order to do this, each measurement must be multiplied by 6.

2. a) A column graph of the supplied data is shown in Figure A.17.

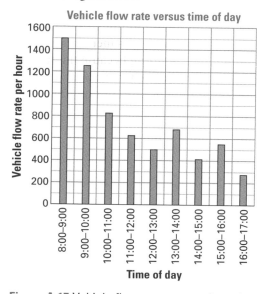

Vehicle flow rate versus time of day

Figure A.17 Vehicle flow rate versus time of day

b) Hypothesis: Peak periods have higher traffic flow rates than off-peak (e.g. 8–10 am: drivers going to work and students going to school; 1–2 pm: lunch-hour traffic).

Conclusion: Traffic flow varies at different times of the day, being especially heavy during the morning peak period.

(Remember, this experiment measured the traffic flow along the road in one direction only. From the experiment, it is reasonable to suggest that the direction measured flowed towards the main work centres, such as towards the city or town. This is because of a high traffic flow in the morning peak period. At this time of morning, traffic in the other direction should be low. In the afternoon peak, the opposite should be true: traffic on the road into town should be low, as observed in this experiment, while traffic out should be high. It is for these reasons traffic engineers often refer to 'traffic tidal flows'.)

Test yourself 1

Part A: Knowledge

1. **A** ✓ B is wrong as predictions are used to test inferences. C is wrong as having more students in the team will not make any difference. D is wrong as the experiment should have a valid method, otherwise it does not prove anything.

2. **B** ✓ A is wrong as the acid must be removed or diluted rapidly to minimise damage. C and D are wrong as this would take too long. Quick action is essential.

3. **C** ✓ A is incorrect as this will be too low to heat the tube. B is wrong as metal tongs will slip on the glass. D is wrong because the tube must be only partly filled otherwise acid will boil out, and because a blue flame is used for heating.

4. **C** ✓ A is wrong as the angle is the independent variable. B is incorrect as a plant of the same age should be used. D is wrong as the direction of growth is the dependent variable.

5. **B** ✓ Never pour from large containers into very small containers as splashing will probably occur. Thus A and D are wrong. C is wrong as it will take too long.

6. **a)** author ✓; **b)** glasses ✓; **c)** reliable ✓; **d)** water ✓; **e)** inferred ✓

7. A/G ✓; B/I ✓; C/J ✓; D/F ✓; E/H ✓

Part B: Skills

8. Each thermometer has an associated systematic instrumental error and must be calibrated to determine how accurate each scale is. ✓ (This answer assumes that all other variables, such as being near an open window, are controlled.)

9. See Table A.7.

10. **a)** Martin should use a stirring rod, pouring the liquid down the rod from one beaker to the other. ✓

    b) Weigh the watch glass; zero the reading; remove the watch glass; use a spatula to spoon blue crystals onto the watch glass; reweigh the glass. ✓

    c) Make sure his eyes are level with the surface of the liquid. ✓

11. **a)** 27 − 23 = 4 g ✓

    b) 27 − 25 = 2 g removed ✓

12. **a)** See Figure A.18.

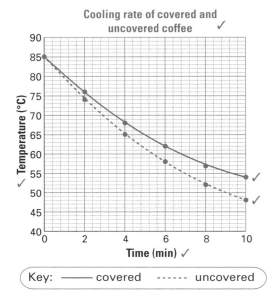

Figure A.18 Cooling rate graph

b) every 2 minutes ✓

c) in order to control a variable ✓

d) covered = 65 °C ✓; uncovered = 61 °C ✓

e) 7 minutes ✓

Table A.7 Mistakes and correct procedure

Mollie's mistakes	What she should have done
• overfilled the beaker	• beaker only one-half to one-third full ✓
• used paper to light Bunsen	• use only taper, match or lighter provided ✓
• used smoky flame: Bunsen air hole closed	• use blue flame: air hole open ✓
• left experiment to talk to friends	• always stay with your experiment/group ✓
• pulled tap hose and knocked over the equipment	• be very careful with hot objects, even in the clean-up ✓
• equipment too close to the edge of desk	• set up equipment away from desk edges ✓
• friends ran around after accident	• stay at desk or help injured friends—cold water on burns ✓
• cried	• tell the teacher immediately an accident happens ✓

13. a) 1.1 g ✓
    b) 3.5 g ✓
    c) cow's milk: it has 720 mg of total mineral ✓
    d) $\frac{4}{1.4}$ = ~3 times ✓
    e) 3.5 × 10 = 35 g ✓
    f) 4.0 × 10 = 40 g ✓
    g) lactose ✓, vitamin C ✓

14. a) Water may exist as invisible water vapour or as ice in hidden valleys and under the ground. Clouds do not have to be seen for water to exist. Langley had not considered this possibility. ✓
    b) He had no evidence for this statement. He assumed that air and water must exist as it existed on Earth and therefore it must be underground. An assumption is not evidence. ✓

Test yourself 2

Part A: Knowledge

1. **A** ✓ This is the most important information that should have been included as it gives an indication of how current the information is. B is incorrect as 'Sydney' identifies the country. C and D are incorrect as this information does not go in a reference.

2. **D** ✓ While the other alternatives are possible, a systematic error in the thermometer is most likely the cause. B is wrong because the student used two sources of ethanol, so it is unlikely the ethanol was tainted. C is wrong because the boiling point quoted in the literature could be checked against other sources for accuracy. A is wrong because it is unlikely there was poor experimental technique as his results are close to each other, and he repeated the experiment several times.

3. **C** ✓ A good model should be simple. A, B and D are incorrect as they are all features of a good model.

4. **B** ✓ Calibration removes systematic errors. A, C and D are incorrect. While replacing the instrument could fix the problem, it may not; this would be avoiding the problem in your instrument instead of fixing it.

5. **C** ✓ About 4 lengths of the scale give the length of the dinosaur. Therefore, A, B and D are incorrect.

6. a) mean ✓; b) graphs; ✓ c) sector (or pie) ✓;
   d) reliability ✓; e) extrapolate ✓;

7. A/J ✓; B/I ✓; C/H ✓; D/G ✓; E/F ✓

Part B: Skills

8. a) 212 °F ✓
   b) 0 °C ✓
   c) 212 − 32 = 180 °F ✓✓;
   d) −40 °F = −40 °C ✓✓

9. a) 100 mg/L ✓
   b) After 7 hours the concentration is 30 mg/L. ✓ So the mass is 5 × 30 = 150 mg. ✓
   c) that the decrease in concentration continues along at the same rate ✓
   d) 4 hours ✓
   e) around 12.5 mg/L ✓

10. a) burette ✓
    b) There is a strong attraction between the liquid and the surface of the glass, causing the ends to bend upwards. ✓
    c) volume of liquid let out = 21.2 mL ✓✓ *(one mark for the correct value and one mark for the correct units)*
    d) to avoid parallax error ✓

11. a) the wash bottle ✓
    b) the measuring cylinder ✓
    c) the flask ✓ and the beaker ✓

12. a) 3% ✓
    b) See Figure A.19. *(1 mark for correct labelling; 2 marks for correct length of each bar)*

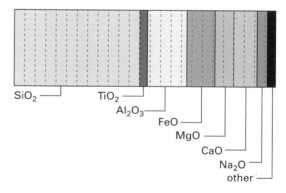

SiO₂ — TiO₂ — Al₂O₃ — FeO — MgO — CaO — Na₂O — other

Figure A.19 Divided bar graph

13. a) 6.8 ✓
    b) 1 mm ✓
    c) 500 km ✓

14. See Figure A.20 (next page). *(1 mark for correct grid; 1 mark for each correct graph; 1 mark for key)*

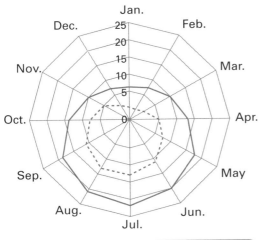

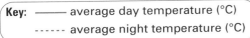

Figure A.20 Radar graph

Chapter test

Part A: Multiple-choice questions

1. **D** ✓ A placebo does not contain the new drug and is used to compare results. Thus A is wrong. B is wrong as a drug is not a person. C is wrong as the term 'blind' here refers to the fact that the volunteers do not know if they are receiving the drug or the placebo.

2. **C** ✓ This procedure eliminates any biases of the scientist. A is not correct as the control group receives a placebo. B is wrong as it applies to double-blind experiments. D is wrong as the number of scientists involved is irrelevant.

3. **C** ✓ A is wrong as accuracy depends on the equipment chosen and the skills of the experimentalist. B is wrong as no amount of repeating can improve an invalid experimental method. D is wrong as safety is not related to repetition.

4. **C** ✓ A and B are wrong as beakers are not used for accurate volume measurements. D is wrong as this measuring cylinder is too small.

5. **B** ✓ Articles in science journals such as *Nature* are peer reviewed and cannot be published without scrutiny from practicing scientists. A is wrong as science reporters are often journalists with an interest in science and may not be fully trained as a scientist. C is wrong as some bloggers may not fully understand the scientific principles. D is wrong as creation 'science' is not real science but only a matter of faith without scientific proof.

6. **A** ✓ In measuring there will always be slight differences due to random errors. B is incorrect as we have no way of knowing whether a different value was aimed for. C and D are incorrect as, given the experiment was performed properly, there is no evidence the measurements are invalid or the data is unreliable.

7. **C** ✓ Press the ON switch on the remote and the TV comes on. The same cause always produces the same effect. The next time you press it, the same result will occur; it doesn't cause the garage door to open or the doorbell to ring. A is incorrect as cause and effect are linked in time, with the cause coming before the effect (so B is wrong). D is wrong as it implies different things will occur with the same cause.

8. **D** ✓ These are the ultimate sources of all scientific knowledge. A, B and C are all incorrect as teachers and textbooks aim to pass this accumulated knowledge onto the next generation, but do not generate it. Both textbooks and teachers aim to make the knowledge and explanations logical and clear and to make learning science more efficient so that each generation does not need to reinvent this knowledge.

9. **A** ✓ B and C are incorrect as these are part of the controlled variables; that is, they must be identical in all other respects. D is wrong as this is the dependent variable: fruit yield depends on the effects of the chemical used.

10. **B** ✓ All theories are tentative and could be challenged if new evidence comes to hand. Of course, it may be a while before the theory is altered as other scientists will want to run their own experiments and to review the evidence first. A is wrong as this is not a legitimate scientific process. C is incorrect as theories are not kept because of their historical value. D is incorrect as, while leading scientists will also express their views, they do not own science and cannot ultimately dictate scientific progress. In any event, scientists being human have their own biases and some may like particular theories and be reluctant to give them up.

Part B: Short-answer questions

11. **a)** There are many possible suggestions; for example, the underside of the leaf is softer than the top or the top of the leaf is not as tasty. ✓

b) Many answers are possible; for example, plants are stunted by salt from the sea. ✓

c) There are a few different possibilities; for example, the black car is parked in the sun. ✓

12. a) Most birds can fly. ✓

b) This generalisation is correct. ✓

c) Most metals are shiny and silvery in colour. ✓

d) This generalisation is correct. ✓

e) Most Australian beaches are sandy. ✓

13. a) Aim: To see if (a) bath crystals and (b) washing soda added to hard water will make soap lather ✓

b) Variables controlled: *(any 6)* ✓✓✓✓✓✓
- constant concentration of hard water (made by adding the same amount of calcium chloride or magnesium sulfate to a given amount of water)
- type of bath crystals used
- type of washing soda used
- water temperature
- type of soap used to create bubbles
- demineralised water used as the control
- number of drops of soap used
- amount of water used in the test
- number of shakes used to create bubbles.

c) Method:
1. Place 5 mL of demineralised water in a large test tube, add three drops of detergent, stopper the test tube and shake it 50 times. ✓
2. Record the height of the foam formed. ✓
3. Place 5 mL of the hard water in a test tube with three drops of detergent, stopper the test tube and shake it 50 times. ✓
4. Record the height of the foam formed. ✓
5. Repeat each experiment five times. ✓
6. Repeat steps 1 to 4 with the addition of a rice-grain-size quantity of bath crystals. ✓
7. Repeat step 5 using washing soda. ✓

d) Data: Use a table to enter results; the hypothesis is supported if the height of foam in the demineralised water is the greatest and in the hard water it is the least, ✓ and that the presence of bath crystals or washing soda causes the foam height to be similar to the demineralised water ✓.

14. a) Aim: To discover any relationship between the mass added and the stretch of the rubber band ✓

b) Method:
1. Attached a boss head and clamp it to a retort stand. ✓
2. Tie an elastic band to the clamp. ✓
3. Measure the length of the rubber band. ✓
4. Add 200 g to the rubber band and measure the new stretched length of the band. ✓
5. Repeat step 4 with more 200-g weights until 1000 g has been added to the rubber band. ✓
6. Record the results in a table as you complete each step. ✓

c) A rubber band stretches as more weights are added. ✓

15. a) See Table A.8. *(1 mark for column with increasing pH values, 1 mark for correct colours shown)*

Table A.8 pH values and colours for various substances

Substance	pH	Colour
lemon juice	2.0	red
rainwater	5.6	orange
milk	6.6	yellow
ammonia	11.0	blue

b) lemon juice ✓

c) orange-red ✓

16. a) It is difficult to see any trend because there is no order to the readings. ✓ There are no units in the volume column (mL). ✓

b) i) See Table A.9. *(1 mark for placing the temperatures in increasing order in the table; 1 mark for units in the volume column)*

Table A.9 Volume of air versus temperature

Temperature of air sample (°C)	Volume of air sample (mL)
0	100.0
5	101.8
10	103.7
15	106.9
20	107.3
25	109.1
30	111.0

ii) As the temperature increases, the volume of the sample increases. ✓

iii) The value for 20 °C seems to include an error ✓; all other volumes increase by more than 1 mL, whereas this volume increases by only 0.4 units. ✓

17. a) See Table A.10. *(1 mark for all calculations correct)* ✓

Table A.10 Boyle's law experiment

h_1 (mm)	h_2 (mm)	$h_1 \times h_2$ (mm^2)
190	400	76 000
380	200	76 000
760	100	76 000
1 520	50	76 000

b) $h_1 \times h_2$ = constant ✓

c) The volume of air is inversely proportional to the pressure applied to it. ✓

18. a) Hypothesis in science is a proposal (based on accumulated observations) made as a starting point for further investigations of known facts. ✓

b) Groundless assumption is not a definition of scientific hypothesis. ✓

19. a) observations ✓; b) variable ✓;
c) relationship ✓; d) prediction ✓

20. a) i) X (0.79) ✓; Y (0.65) ✓; Z (0.50) ✓

ii) alcohol/water = 0.80 ✓
petrol/glycerine = 0.69 ✓
(Note: a more accurate value for the density of petrol will give closer results to the calculations from tube Y.)
alcohol/carbon tetrachloride = 0.50 ✓

b) Use a U-tube with the base filled with mercury. Place the liquid to be tested in the right arm (h_2 in Figure 5.33) and balance with water in the left arm (h_1). Calculate h_1/h_2. This ratio is the same as the ratios of the densities D_2/D_1. As the density of water (D_1) is 1.0 g/cm^3, then the height ratio gives the density of the liquid. ✓

21. a) when the night-time humidity, after midnight, is above 90% ✓ and temperature during the day before is moderate ✓

b) selected variable = temperature during preceding day ✓
Controls: *(any two)* ✓✓

- humidity levels in greenhouse held constant at 95%
- constant temperature during the night
- constant number of tobacco plants of the same age in pots
- control plants not exposed to blue mould spores.

Change the daytime temperature in the greenhouse through a range of temperatures from very high to very low. ✓ Record the number of spore cases which open at each temperature and the number of plants that become infected compared with control plants that are not exposed. ✓

22. a) $V = \dfrac{m}{D} = 259$ cm^3 ✓

b) i) $\dfrac{75}{100} \times 5000 = 3750$ g ✓

ii) $V = \dfrac{m}{D} = \dfrac{3750}{19.3} = 194$ cm^3 ✓

iii) $5000 - 3750 = 1250$ g ✓

iv) $\dfrac{1250}{10.5} = 119$ cm^3 ✓

v) total volume = $194 + 119 = 313$ cm^3 ✓

vi) volume of crown = 313 cm^3, volume of gold lump = 259 cm^3; the crown has a larger volume by 54 cm^3 (313 − 259) ✓

23. See Figure A.21.

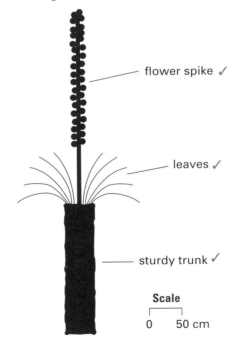

Figure A.21 Xanthorrhoea

24. a) The black slate absorbed the Sun's heat which was then transferred to the water as it ran over it. Black materials are the best heat absorbers. ✓

b) 1. Sunlight is absorbed by the dark material. ✓
2. Cold water is pumped into the coiled pipe below the black material but above the silver foil. ✓
3. Cold water absorbs the heat from the black material and any reflected heat from the silver foil. ✓
4. Hot water flows into the storage tank. ✓

c) Design factors to be considered:
- insulated base to prevent any heat loss ✓
- silvered aluminium foil to reflect light back onto the black material ✓
- glass is used; it's a good insulator ✓
- narrow-diameter pipes to ensure good contact with heated air. ✓

25. 1. Make another tube with a large hollow bulb at the end. ✓
2. If Galileo was right, then the larger vacuum should have an even stronger pulling effect. The mercury should move further up the tube. ✓
3. Perform the experiment with this larger bulb and compare the results with the first tube. ✓
4. If the height of the mercury column did not change when the larger bulb was used (which experiments showed that it did not), then this was evidence that the force did not come from the vacuum and supported the hypothesis that air pressure that supported the mercury column. ✓

26. a) The cause explains why something happens. ✓ The effect describes what happens. ✓

b) Cause: increasing water temperatures in ocean waters ✓; effect: coral on the Great Barrier Reef is at risk of disease ✓.

c) Just because Q follows P does not mean that P caused Q. ✓ For example, night follows day (or vice versa) but you can't say that night causes day any more than day causes night. ✓ They may be unrelated (e.g. I looked out the window and saw a possum) ✓ or they may have a common cause (many swimmers at the beach and many ice creams

sold have a common cause: a hot day) ✓. It is a common mistake to assume that of two related events, the earlier one caused the other.

27. a) time (minutes) ✓

b) loss in mass of zinc (grams) ✓ (While the units weren't specifically mentioned in the question, commonsense should prevail that it is neither milligrams—too small—nor kilograms—too large.)

c) change in mass when zinc reacts with acid ✓

d) after around 7 minutes ✓ as the curve becomes flat ✓ (no more loss in the mass of zinc)

e) 46 g ✓ (when all the zinc reacted, the reaction ceased)

28. a) No, he had no evidence that the soot caused a mutation. ✓ The gene for dark colouration could be recessive and present in the population to a small extent. This can exhibit itself in a small percentage of cases. ✓

b) Since production of dark-coloured moths occurred at the same rate, regardless of the leaves they were fed, it is not the soot which led to dark moths being born. ✓ There must be some other cause, such as the one mentioned in the answer to a).

c) This latter experiment had a control, a group against which to compare the results. ✓ The first scientist did not use a control, so he ended up jumping to the wrong conclusion. ✓ (It also shows the importance of experiments being repeatable by other scientists, and not just taking the word of one researcher.)

d) From the information supplied in the question, as the tree trunks become darker (sootier) the darker moths have a better chance of surviving being eaten as they are better camouflaged. ✓ As to what caused the trunks to become darker? Perhaps a polluting factory set up nearby pumped out soot and particulates that settled on nearby trees. ✓

e) The factory could have closed down. Alternatively, with more stringent regulations in recent years, the factory (or other enterprise) would have cleaned up its act thereby producing less soot, and less soot settling on tree trunks. ✓ This gives the lighter-coloured moths the advantage. ✓ (This question shows natural selection at work.)

29. a) As time progressed, the number of plants in the area decreased. ✓ This is shown by the average number in each square metre.

b) Discounting consumers and bushfires, a possible hypothesis is that there was competition within the species. ✓ Tea-trees can grow reasonably large and obviously thousands, or even hundreds, of seedlings within each square metre are not going to all survive. Weaker ones will give way to the stronger, or better nourished, plants.

c) No ✓ While the table seems to be trending that way, eventually a comfortable number will be reached where the remaining tea-trees have enough room to grow. ✓

30. a) Random errors in measurements are due to unknown and unpredictable changes in the experiment. ✓ These changes may be in the measuring instruments or in the environmental conditions. ✓ Random errors often have a normal distribution (spread symmetrically) around the true value. Systematic errors in observations are usually due to the measuring instruments. ✓ They may occur because there is something wrong with the instrument or how it handles data, or because the instrument is not being used correctly. ✓

b) The size of the study, or taking more measurements, does not affect systematic error. ✓ That bias will remain relatively constant. ✓ On the other hand, random errors due to chance events reduce significantly ✓ and in very large studies may be reduced altogether ✓.

c) This is done to reduce or nullify random errors. ✓ For example, if four measurements of the boiling point of pure water are 101.2 °C, 99.4 °C, 100.5 °C and 98.7 °C, random errors give slightly different readings each time. The average of these is (101.2 + 99.4 + 100.5 + 98.7)/4 = 99.95 °C which virtually eliminates these errors due to chance.

31. a) $2N_2O_5 \rightarrow 4NO_2 + O_2$ ✓✓

b) See Figure A.22. (*The straight line is for the next question.*)

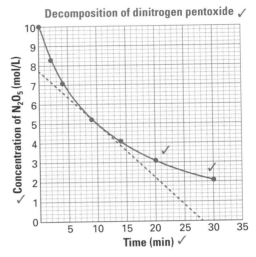

Figure A.22 Decomposition of nitrogen pentoxide

c) (*1 mark for correct tangent*); rise = 7.7 − 0 = 7.7 ✓; run = 28 − 0 = 28 ✓ (the rise and run were calculated where the line crosses each of the axes; other values are possible);

reaction rate = $\dfrac{7.7}{28}$ = 0.275 mol L per minute ✓ (Your values may be slightly different, but should be close.)

d) lower ✓ as the curve flattens out and is not as steep, so the rate is less ✓

32. a) The greater the concentration of the hydrogen peroxide, the greater is the slope of the curve. This indicates a fast reaction rate. ✓ As the concentration decreases, the steepness decreases and so the reaction rate also decreases. ✓

b) 8.5 g/L ✓

c) around 1.25 g/L ✓

d) Time is the independent variable, and this is placed on the horizontal axis. ✓ The concentration of H_2O_2 is placed on the vertical axis as this is the dependent variable. ✓ The concentration of H_2O_2 at any instant depends on time, not the other way around.

33. No, not always. ✓ Often time is the independent variable and therefore this generalisation would hold true most of the time. But it is not a blanket rule. There can be instances where time is the dependent variable. ✓ For example, the

cooking time for a chicken depends on its mass. Its mass does not depend on cooking time. ✓ As a general rule in roasting a chicken, calculate a cooking time of 45 minutes per kilogram of meat plus an additional 10 to 20 minutes at a temperature of 190 °C. Therefore, a 2.2-kg chicken will need to be roasting in the oven for at least 1 hour and 50 mins.

34. **a)** Bathythermograph is a melding of three Greek words: *bathos* meaning 'deep' + *therme* meaning 'heat' + *grapho* meaning 'write'. ✓✓ In science, when a new instrument, concept or object needs to be named, scientists often turn to Greek or Latin to cobble together borrowed words.

b) The upper mixed layer has a fairly uniform temperature similar to that at the sea surface. ✓ The thermocline is the zone below the mixed layer where the rate of change of temperature with depth is the greatest. ✓ Temperature decreases with increasing depth. Below the thermocline is a deep zone where temperature changes slowly, if at all. ✓

c) around 100 m ✓

d) Water at or near the sea surface is well mixed by wind and wave action, ✓ so heat is transferred downwards to the deeper layers by the action of this turbulence ✓. Therefore, a high degree of vertical uniformity showing little variation in temperature (also true of salinity and density, but this was not part of the question) is noted in the upper layer.

e) No, not really. ✓ While temperature decreases with increasing depths, there are places where it remains fairly uniform. ✓ For example, the temperature at the surface or 50 m down would be about the same. Similarly for 1000 m and 2000 m. And there may be seasonal effects that influence the temperature in the mixed layer.

35. **a)** This is a line of best fit. ✓ It is a line on a scatter plot which can be drawn near the points to more clearly show the trend between two sets of data. ✓

b) extrapolation ✓

c) yes, at (8, 4) ✓

d) It is often best to discard outliers before computing the line of best fit. ✓

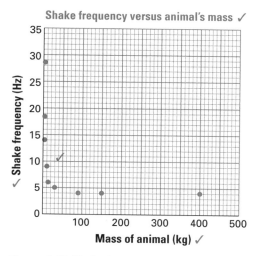

Figure A.23 Shake frequency versus animal mass

36. **a)** See Figure A.23.

b) The larger the animal, the lower is the shake frequency. ✓ But, it seems, that a minimum value is reached of around 4 Hz regardless of the mass of the animal. ✓

c) No ✓ Some animals may not have the ability to initiate to-and-fro motions ✓, so this graph should not be taken as applying to all organisms. Humans, for example, use towels.

37. **a)** 6.967 million km² ✓ (add the values in the first numerical column)
See Table A.11.
(3 marks if all correct; ½ mark for each correct in third column)
(3 marks if all correct; ½ mark for each correct in fourth column)
(3 marks if all correct; ½ mark for each correct in fifth column)

Table A.11 Australian marine regions

Marine region	Area (million km²)	% of total area	Bar graph length	Sector graph angle
south-west	1.3	18.7	3.8 cm	67°
north-west	1	14.4	2.9 cm	52°
north	0.625	9.0	1.8 cm	32°
Coral Sea	0.972	14.0	2.8 cm	50°
temperate east	1.47	21.1	4.2 cm	76°
south east	1.6	23.0	4.6 cm	83°
Total	6.967	100.0	20 cm	360°

b) See Figure A.24 (next page).

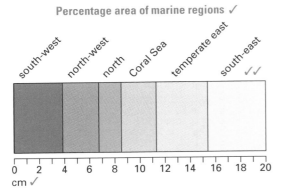

Figure A.24 Divided bar graph

c) See Figure A.25.

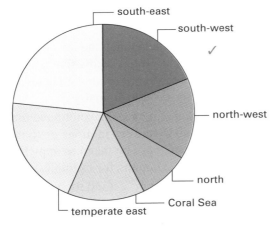

Figure A.25 Pie graph

38. a) to kill any bacteria or other life present in the broth ✓

b) He wanted to show that the life force was present in the broth and this created the bacteria. ✓ By sealing the opening, there was no chance of bacteria (or other organisms) entering the flask from the air. ✓

c) No ✓ He held the view that it did, so was biased to the outcome. He assumed that he had killed any living things in the broth (which heating gently does not), so that any re-appearance of life must be due to the vital force. ✓ He should have examined the broth to see whether all living things were killed before leaving it for several days. (Today, we know that the boiling time was insufficient to kill any of the microbe spores and that cooling the flasks left open to the air could cause microbial contamination. It can also be assumed that Needham did not use proper sterile techniques.)

d) He had heated it sufficiently to kill any life or spores present in the broth. ✓

e) There was no evidence for Needham's criticism. ✓ He erroneously concluded that, as he believed, a life force is necessary to spontaneously generate new life, then by overheating and destroying this life force Spallazani had prevented spontaneous generation. ✓ On the other hand, while Spallazani argued to the contrary, he did not have the evidence either. ✓

f) This was to refute Needham's criticism. ✓ If the argument hinges on how much heating will destroy the supposed life force, then leaving the flasks open will allow this life force to enter from the air, if it had been destroyed. ✓ So no argument could be made about how much heat was too much.

g) Both flasks were heated to the same extent, but only the flask with the straight neck had its contents spoil. While air could enter both, the heavier bacteria in the air (or travelling on dust particles) were trapped in the bottom of the ∪ of the S-neck and could not travel up and into the flask. ✓ So bacteria could only enter the flask with the straight neck. ✓ (If spontaneous generation had been a real phenomenon, the broth in the S-necked flask would have eventually spoiled because the microbes would have spontaneously generated.)

h) Pasteur had used a control in his experiment. ✓ He showed that microorganisms are not created spontaneously but come from other microorganisms. ✓ He also showed that a truly sterile solution remains lifeless indefinitely unless contaminated by living things. ✓

39. a) as a radar chart ✓

b) January, February, March, April, ✓ September, October, November, December ✓

c) April to September ✓✓

d) Plant P needs short days to flower. ✓ This occurs in Perth in winter (May to July). ✓ Plant Q needs long days to flower. ✓ This occurs in Perth in the summer (November to February). ✓

40. a) Darwin ✓

b) October ✓

c) Melbourne ✓, 6.1 to 6.2 kWh/m²/day ✓

d) March ✓ (Its value is around 4.3 to 4.4 kWh/m²/day.) Also, December is acceptable given there is very little difference (hardly discernible on the graph) between these two cities then.

e) This is false ✓, although this is true for most of the year, but not the whole year. Melbourne and Sydney beat it in December and January, and Melbourne also in February. It is not only the latitude that has an effect on the concentration of solar radiation; weather also plays a part. Bad weather can prevent radiation from coming through. ✓ Darwin has its monsoon season during the summer months.

f) Melbourne ✓ Max: 6.2 kWh/m²/day ✓ (Jan.), min: 1.7 kWh/m²/day ✓ (June) giving a range of 6.2 − 1.7 = 4.5 kWh/m²/day ✓.

g) No ✓, the closest you can estimate would be somewhere around 4.3 or 4.4 kWh/m²/day. Graphs are designed to give you a visual indication of the data and to show trends. ✓ For an accurate value you would need to consult a table of values. ✓

h) May has 31 days. Read about 5.75 kWh/m²/day ✓ from the table. So the radiation is 5.75 × 31 = 178.25 kWh/m². ✓ (Your value should be close to this.)

i) 5.65 kWh of energy falls on each m² each day ✓, so for a hectare 10 000 × 5.65 = 56 500 kWh falls each day ✓. So in each hour, 56 500 ÷ 14 = 4036 kWh ✓.

Test 1 answers

Part A: Multiple-choice questions

1. **A** ✓ With an alcohol thermometer, you read the base of the meniscus. Each scale division is 0.2 degrees and so the base of the alcohol meniscus is at 43.4 degrees. Thus B, C and D are wrong.

2. **C** ✓ Read the vertical axis when time is 5 s. Thus A, B and D are incorrect.

3. **B** ✓ Each row increases by 9.8 so A, C and D are incorrect.

4. **D** ✓ $F = ma$ is the mathematical form of Newton's second law. Thus A, B and C are incorrect.

5. **D** ✓ Modern-day experiments with dog breeding cannot prove what happened in nature in the past. A, B and C all provide evidence for evolution.

6. **B** ✓ Use the clues to determine that the Palaeozoic was dominated by fish and amphibians; reptiles evolved after amphibians. Thus A is wrong as the Palaeozoic is older than the Mesozoic. C is wrong as mammals did not appear until the end of the Mesozoic. D is wrong as the Precambrian era predates the Palaeozoic.

7. **D** ✓ Yellow stars become very large and red as they evolve. Thus A, B and C are wrong. Red stars are not as hot as yellow stars. Eventually our Sun will 'cool' to a red star.

8. **C** ✓ After the Big Bang, hydrogen was first formed and then helium. Thus, A, B and D are incorrect.

9. **B** ✓ Correlate similar fossils in different layers; layers containing the same indicator fossil are of the same age. Thus, the lowest layer in B is the oldest. A, C and D are wrong because their lowest layers are much younger.

10. **D** ✓ D is the Lamarck theory that suggests that characteristics acquired in life can be passed on. A, B and C are all statements from Darwin's theory.

11. **A** ✓ Inertia is the tendency of a body to remain at rest or to continue with its constant motion. B and C are wrong as this experiment is not relevant to these laws. D is Newton's third law.

12. **C** ✓ Ultraviolet radiation is absorbed by the ozone layer. A, B and D are wrong as these rays are not blocked by the ozone layer.

13. **D** ✓ Sulfur and selenium are in the same group of the periodic table. A, B and C are wrong as they do not belong to Group 16 (VI).

14. **A** ✓ The force on the gases is equal to the force acting on the rocket. B, C and D are incorrect as there is no reaction force described.

15. **B** ✓ A is wrong as this is iodine; C is wrong as this is iridium. D is wrong as this is not a symbol used in the periodic table.

16. **C** ✓ Alexandra is a carrier as her father had haemophilia. This faulty gene is on one of her X sex chromosomes. Thus, there is a 50% chance that any son will have the disease, meaning that A, B and D are wrong.

17. **B** ✓ The amount of light absorbed does not fit the pattern of the other data. Thus, A, C and D are wrong.

18. **A** ✓ B is wrong as fossils become more complex in more recent strata. C is wrong as acquired characteristics cannot be inherited. D is wrong as some mutations are good and lead to evolutionary change. The word *pentadactyl* is the joining of two Greek words: *penta*, meaning '5' + *dactyl*, meaning 'finger'; so a pentadactyl limb is an arm or leg with five fingers at the end of it.

19. **C** ✓ A is wrong as copper was discovered thousands of years ago. B is wrong as steel was first produced in the Iron Age several thousand years ago. D is wrong as glass has been used for about 1000 years.

20. **A** ✓ B is wrong as nothing existed before the Big Bang. C is wrong as atoms took much longer to form. D is wrong as one giant star could not do this.

21. **C** ✓ A and B are wrong as they are gases. D is wrong as iodine is a solid.

22. **C** ✓ At 7 mL of P and after there is no more precipitate forming, so C is correct. A is wrong as not all of P has been used because Q is the chemical that has been all used up. B is wrong as some precipitate will have formed. D is wrong as the amount of Q will affect the amount of precipitate.

23. **D** ✓ This is the law of mass conservation. A is wrong as the amounts must be equal. B is wrong as mercury has a much greater atomic weight. C is wrong as the mass of the mercury(II) oxide has to be more.

24. **B** ✓ A is wrong as the drips are not equally spaced. C is wrong as the car did the opposite. D is wrong as the car never moved at constant speed.

25. **B** ✓ A is wrong as it has no control. C is wrong as you should not select the healthiest plants for a control. D is wrong as there is no control.

Part B: Restricted-response questions

26. number ✓
27. first ✓
28. Galapagos ✓
29. artificial ✓
30. catastrophes ✓
31. variation ✓
32. indivisible ✓
33. weight ✓
34. group ✓
35. hydrogen ✓
36. red ✓
37. radio ✓
38. negative ✓
39. friction ✓
40. inversely ✓

Part C: Knowledge, skill and processing data questions

41. See Figure A.26.

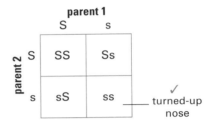

Figure A.26 Punnet square for nose shape

turned-up nose = 25% (one in four) ✓

42. a) about 4.6 million years ago ✓

b) Radiometric dating allows the ages of rocks to be determined. Some granites have been dated to 4.2 million years. ✓

c) the decay of radioactive elements; gravitational compression ✓

d) the outer core of the Earth ✓

43. a) Cainozoic (Cenozoic) ✓; b) Palaeozoic ✓; c) Mesozoic ✓; d) Mesozoic ✓; e) Palaeozoic ✓

44. a) copper ✓, symbol Cu

b) 64 − 29 = 35 ✓

c) Copper is quite unreactive in water and in air. Its surface slowly oxidises over time. ✓

45. a) Z = neon; L = silicon; A = zinc; D = strontium; X = polonium; M = thorium ✓

b) silicon ✓

c) neon ✓

d) 2,8,4 ✓

e) polonium and thorium ✓

f) strontium ✓

46. a) antimony ✓; b) bromine ✓; c) radon ✓

47. 1/F ✓; 2/A ✓; 3/E ✓; 4/B ✓; 5/C ✓; 6/D ✓

48. 1 = E ✓; 2 = D ✓; 3 = C ✓; 4 = A ✓; 5 = B ✓

49. a) Cork, leaves and twigs of wood float on top of the water. ✓

 b) Plant material floats on water because it is small and light. ✓

 c) All small pieces of wood would float no matter what tree they came from. ✓

 d) Eight pieces of wood of the same size from different trees were placed one at a time in a bucket of water. ✓ She observed whether they floated or sank. ✓

 e) No, two pieces of wood sank. ✓

 f) Some wood will absorb water and therefore sink. ✓

 g) Not all wood will float, even if it is small or light. ✓

 h) Weigh pieces of wood before and after being placed in water for the same length of time ✓ to see if they increased in mass and therefore absorbed water ✓.

50. genetic inheritance ✓; the structure of DNA ✓

51. Method:
 1. Prepare 5-mL samples of pure water and solutions of calcium chloride of increasing concentration (e.g. 0.5%, 1%, 2%, 4%) (independent variable). Place the samples in stoppered test tubes. ✓
 2. Prepare a standard soap solution by dissolving a known mass of soap flakes or liquid soap in a known volume of water. ✓
 3. Place 2 mL of soap solution in each test tube of calcium chloride solution and the pure water control. Keep the tubes at the same constant temperature. Stopper the tubes and shake each vigorously for the same time (say, 1 minute). ✓
 4. Compare the height of soap bubbles (dependent variable) formed in each test tube. ✓
 If the hypothesis is supported, there will be less soap foam produced as the hardness (i.e. calcium concentration) of the water increases. ✓

52. carbon (non-metal) ✓; silicon (semi-metal) ✓; germanium (semi-metal) ✓; tin (metal) ✓; lead (metal) ✓

53. Cosmic background radiation is microwave radiation that emanates from intergalactic space. This radiation is equivalent to a background temperature of –270 °C (or 3 degrees above absolute zero). ✓ These observations were consistent with the expansion and cooling of space following the formation of space and time billions of years ago. ✓

54. Nebulae are clouds of gas and stellar dust. Some glow brightly and others are dark. ✓ Novae are formed by explosions that shear off the outer layers of stars. This causes the star to shine more brightly than normal. Eventually, a nebula is left behind. ✓

Test 2 answers

Part A: Multiple-choice questions

1. **D** ✓ Theories are tentative explanations that fit the current facts and observations. They are not inviolate facts of themselves, so A is wrong; and they may change as more data and information come to hand, so C is wrong. A hypothesis is an educated guess, so B is incorrect.

2. **C** ✓ Only the coefficients in front of formulae can be changed. You can neither change the superscripts or subscripts within formulae (so A and B are incorrect) as this is tantamount to altering the chemical formula (so D is wrong). For example, to balance:
 $SnO_2 + H_2 \rightarrow Sn + H_2O$ only write numbers in front of formulae, like this:
 $SnO_2 + 2H_2 \rightarrow Sn + 2H_2O$

3. **A** ✓ Some earlier scientists believed that characteristics acquired during one's lifetime could be passed onto their offspring. Not so! A pirate with a wooden leg and a patch over one eye does not pass these characteristics onto his children. B, C and D are incorrect as these are all components of the theory of evolution.

4. **D** ✓ The reactants are on the left-hand side of the arrow. In the first reactant there are 2×2 = 4 oxygen atoms. In the second reactant there are 3 oxygen atoms. Total = 7 oxygen atoms. Hence A, B and C are incorrect.

5. **A** ✓ Genotype is the genetic makeup of a cell, an organism or an individual. This is shown using capital and lower-case lettering. B and D are statements about phenotype, while C is a comment that albinism is a recessive condition in humans, so B, C and D are wrong.

6. **B ✓** The notion of conservation shows that masses before and after reactions do not change. Hence A, C and D are incorrect. If gases are formed, they usually bubble from solution leaving the remaining substances to have less mass than the reactants. This confuses some students. But if the mass of gases produced is added to the remaining substances, then it equals the total mass of reactants.

7. **A ✓** On the periodic table, the atomic number gives the number of protons in the nucleus. In a neutral atom, this also equals the number of electrons. Electrons can be added to, or removed from, atoms forming ions; however, the number of protons does not alter so B is incorrect. C is incorrect as this does not have a specific name, although a different number of neutrons determines isotopes. The number of protons and neutrons is the mass number, so D is wrong.

8. **D ✓** Mass number = number of protons + number of neutrons = 25 + 30 = 55. So A, B and C are incorrect.

9. **C ✓** Alkali metals are found in the first group on the periodic table. There are Li, Na, K, Rb and Cs, and are very reactive metals that do not occur freely in nature. These can all lose one electron each to give a +1 positive ion. Hence, the other alternatives are incorrect.

10. **B ✓** A combustion reaction is when all substances in a compound combine with oxygen, producing carbon dioxide and water. A is incorrect as this is the reaction between an acid and base. C is incorrect as a displacement reaction is where a less reactive element is replaced in a compound by a more reactive one. D is incorrect as a formation describes two elements or simple compounds joining together to produce a more complex compound than the reactants.

11. **C ✓** Except for very small changes (negligible), the amount of water on the Earth (over time) remains the same. So A, B and D are incorrect. This does not mean that the amount of water locked up in ice sheets, or in oceans, has not altered over millions of years.

12. **A ✓** Green plants make their own food and take in carbon, as CO_2, from the air. B, C and D are incorrect as these are taken in through the roots.

13. **D ✓** Excessive use of synthetic fertilisers, containing phosphorus, impacts greatly on the phosphorus cycle. A, B and C have very little effect, so are incorrect.

14. **B ✓** All the factors listed affect the distribution of permafrost, but climate is the most important. Hence A, C and D are incorrect.

15. **A ✓** The reaction shown is $3H_2 + N_2 \rightarrow 2NH_3$. The correct formula for ammonia is NH_3 so B, C and D are incorrect.

16. **A ✓** Let B represent the allele for the dominant black eye and b represent the allele for the recessive blue eye. Pure breeding means the genotype is homozygous, so BB × bb. All the offspring would be Bb. That is, they would all be black eye. So B, C and D are incorrect.

17. **D ✓** Plants contribute to the carbon cycle in various ways. So while A, B and C are true, D is the alternative that is most correct.

18. **C ✓** Ni has displaced Ag ions from solution, as Ni is more reactive (so A is wrong). As Ag comes out of the solution, it will precipitate as a fine metal. The nitrate ion does not alter, so D is incorrect, and certainly no nitrogen is formed, so B is wrong.

19. **A ✓** The diploid organism AAbb can only produce Ab gametes. (Take one of each pair.) Hence B, C and D are incorrect.

20. **A ✓** Displacement is the shortest, or straight-line, distance from the initial to the final position. B is incorrect as the direction is opposite to that indicated from start to finish. Both C and D are wrong as 900 m is the total distance walked, not displacement.

21. **C ✓** The liquid lying above a solid residue after crystallisation, precipitation, centrifugation or other process is the supernatant. A is wrong as this is solution; B is wrong as this is suspension; C is wrong as this is precipitate.

22. **B ✓** The faulty, recessive allele is carried on the X chromosome; that is, haemophilia is a sex-linked gene. Let X^H represent the normal allele and X^h the recessive allele for haemophilia. A Punnett square generated for this is shown in Figure A.27.

From this Punnett square there is a ¼ chance (25%) a child (actually a male) will be born with haemophilia. So A, C and D are incorrect. 'Normal' in genetics refers to the most common or prevailing condition. In this case, since

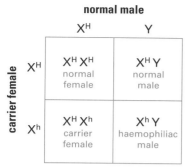

normal male

Figure A.27 Punnet square

most people in a population do not have haemophilia, then absence of this condition is normal.

23. C ✓ The acid is HCl, the base is Mg(OH)$_2$. A is a formation reaction, B is a combustion reaction and D is a decomposition reaction.

24. D ✓ The heavier the stick, the greater is the force required to achieve a given distance. A, B and C are incorrect as these would make a positive effect in allowing the snake to travel further. They all involve lessening the friction between the stick and the snow.

25. D ✓ Students can confuse this with animals recognising and avoiding poisonous plants or distasteful insects. Viruses are microscopic and rabbits, or any other creature for that matter, would not be able to identify or avoid them. How often have you tried to avoid a cold or a sore throat only to end up getting one? And this is with humans being more intelligent than rabbits! A and B are incorrect as these are the reasons for the virus becoming less virulent. C is wrong as the calicivirus worked well for over 15 years in an environment where the myxoma virus is also present. Now there are not as many deaths from either RHD or myxomatosis so scientists are searching for a new disease, bacterium, virus or other biological agent to introduce into Australia to kill rabbits now that calicivirus has outlived its usefulness.

Part B: Restricted-response questions

26. selection ✓
27. adaptation ✓
28. mutations ✓
29. gametes ✓
30. phenotype ✓

31. sperm ✓
32. models ✓
33. protons ✓
34. radioactivity ✓
35. electrons ✓
36. two ✓
37. force ✓
38. kinetic ✓
39. velocity ✓
40. methane ✓

Part C: Knowledge, skill and processing data questions

41. All dogs today descended from a common ancestor. ✓ Wild dogs were originally tamed and domesticated. Over the years, people developed different breeds of dogs by breeding preferred characteristics (selective breeding). ✓ This could be for hunting prowess, temperament, size, intelligence, colouration, length of tail or body or ears, and so on. In other words, humans had an end goal in sight and aimed for that. It is artificial in that the breeds did not occur naturally in the wild, but were directed in that way. ✓ It is difficult to imagine that a Great Dane and a chihuahua are the same species, *Canis familiaris*. Dogs are the only animal with such a wide variation in appearance without forming a new species.

42. a) divergence ✓

    b) The original gene pool (the variety of genes available to a population) was divided into two when the river formed. ✓ While the two environments might have been similar, they were not identical. Selective pressures favoured certain characteristics being passed on. ✓ For example, if on one side of the river it snowed more than the other side (perhaps being the upper side of a mountain) then white colouration would have a survival advantage. ✓ On the other side of the river, where there was little snow, mice could blend into their surrounding by being browner matching earthy colours. ✓ Size might have been favoured in that small size allows them to dart in-between rock crevasses to hunt prey and to avoid predators. ✓ Larger size might be due to stronger mice able to burrow into soil. ✓

43. Yes ✓, since genes work in pairs: one copy from each parent. If you inherit two normal copies of a gene, of course you won't develop the disorder. If you inherit one normal copy and one defective copy, you will be a carrier but not develop the disorder as the normal, dominant, gene masks the effects of the faulty gene. But if you inherit both recessive copies, you have no normal working copies to hide the effect of the defective genes ✓ and so will develop the disorder.

44. a) Background radiation is the ionising radiation constantly present in the natural environment of the Earth. ✓ This comes from natural and artificial sources. Our bodies, and chromosomes, are being continually bombarded by different forms of background radiation. This includes solar radiation, cosmic radiation and radiation from small amounts of radioactive elements in the ground or bricks in our homes and schools. ✓ Over millions of years our bodies have developed strategies to cope with this kind of low-level radiation. Organisms have evolved sophisticated DNA damage detection and repair mechanisms to deal with minor damage.

b) Injury to living tissue results from the transfer of energy from this very energetic radiation to atoms and molecules in the cell's structure. This ionising radiation causes atoms and molecules to become ionised or excited. ✓ Radiation can produce a variety of damage to DNA. It can rupture the DNA strand, alter the bases, destroy sugars, and break or form crosslinks. With increased exposure to ionising radiation comes the increased possibility of our genes mutating or developing cancers. ✓ (Skin cancer is the obvious example where too much UV radiation can produce faults in our genes.) Unsafe and uncontrolled exposure to radiation may lead to mutations in the DNA of our body cells or reproductive cells. ✓ If the damage is in our sex cells, this may be passed on to the next generation.

c) We also routinely come into contact with medical radiation (e.g. X-rays, radioactive tracers injected into our bodies). Radiation is also used to treat cancers; just as radiation can damage the DNA in our normal cells, it can be targeted to destroy the DNA in cancerous cells. ✓

45. a) Phosphorus ✓; there are 15 electrons, so there are 15 protons in its nucleus, giving it an atomic number of 15.

b) Figure T2.5 is two-dimensional (flat), whereas real atoms are three-dimensional. ✓ This figure gives the erroneous impression that electrons are in fixed positions instead of moving around the nucleus. ✓ The nucleus in a real atom is much smaller than that shown in the model (the nucleus is about 10 000 times smaller than the atom diameter). ✓

46. *(1 mark for balancing reactants and 1 mark for balancing products)*

a) $S + 2H_2SO_4 \rightarrow 3SO_2 + 2H_2O$ ✓✓

b) $2ZnS + 3O_2 \rightarrow 2ZnO + 2SO_2$ ✓✓

c) $2C_2H_2 + 5O_2 \rightarrow 4CO_2 + 2H_2O$ ✓✓

47. $\dfrac{69.5}{100} \times 62.9396 + \dfrac{30.5}{100} \times 64.9278$
$= 63.5460$ u ✓✓

48. The figure shows an example of the red shift ✓ as distant objects move away from us. In astronomy a red shift occurs when light seen coming from an object, such as a distant galaxy, is proportionally increased in wavelength. ✓ That is, the emission or absorption lines of elements in the spectrum of an astronomical object are shifted ✓ to the red end (lower frequency, longer wavelength). The faster the distant galaxy is receding, relative to us, the greater is the shift of these spectral lines to the red end of the electromagnetic spectrum.

49. a) $KE = \frac{1}{2}mv^2$ ✓ where $m = \dfrac{4.5}{1000} = 0.0045$ kg ✓ and $v = 950$ m/s
$KE = \frac{1}{2} \times 0.0045 \times 950^2 = 2030.625$ kJ ✓

b) When he fires the first round, the skateboard moves off quickly in the opposite direction. ✓ If no further rounds are fired (and assuming he hasn't fallen off), the skateboard will slow down due to friction. ✓ Firing the second round will speed up the skateboard to a greater speed ✓ but as there are no further rounds to fire, the skateboard will slow and eventually stop ✓.

c) Newton's third law ✓: to every action there is an equal and opposite reaction.

50. a) In V_2O_5 the valency of O is 2–,
so $5 \times 2– = 10–$. So each vanadium ion
has $10+ \div 2 = 5+$ charge. ✓ This makes the
compound electrically neutral:
$2 \times (+5) + 5 \times (–2) = 0$.
In V_2O_3 the valency of O is 2–, so $3 \times 2– = 6–$. So each vanadium ion has $6+ \div 2 = 3+$ charge. ✓ This makes the compound
electrically neutral:
$2 \times (+3) + 3 \times (–2) = 0$.

b) The Ca ion has a charge and valency of
2+. This means the total valency of two
orthovanadate ions must balance the
2+ valency of the calcium ion. So each
orthovanadate ion has a valency of 1– ✓.
That is, VO_4^- ✓.

51. a) R ✓

b) The pendulum is momentarily stationary at
P, having maximum gravitational potential
energy. ✓ As the pendulum moves to Q, it
increases speed as PE is changed to KE. ✓
At R all of the PE has changed to KE, with
KE now being maximum and PE = 0. The
opposite now occurs as the pendulum moves
to S where speed decreases and KE changes
into PE. ✓ Eventually, at T the pendulum
becomes momentarily stationary with PE
maximum and KE = 0. ✓

c) In ideal pendulums, energy is constantly
transferred between potential and kinetic
energies. In the real world, a swinging
pendulum eventually stops due to friction. ✓
The friction is shown as a form of heat
energy which includes air resistance and
sound energy. ✓ There are slight energy
losses with each swing, so the pendulum
does not return to its original height.

52. a) The gravitational potential energy gained by
the projectile is
$GPE = mgh$
$= 3 \times 10 \times 150$
$= 4500$ J. ✓
This was the initial kinetic energy it had just
as it left the launch pad.
So KE = $\frac{1}{2}mv^2 = 4500$ ✓
$\frac{1}{2} \times 3 \times v^2 = 4500$
$v^2 = \frac{4500}{1.5} = 3000$
$\therefore v = \sqrt{3000} = 54.8$ m/s ✓

b) The launch speed would need to be
greater ✓ as it requires this extra KE to
overcome air resistance.

53. a) See Figure A.28. (The pea pod is shown
only to indicate the phenotype, for use in
later questions. It is not necessary for you to
include it in your diagram.)

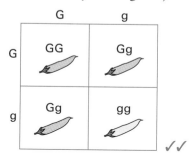

Figure A.28 Punnet square

b) i) $\frac{1}{2} \times 772 = 386$ ✓
ii) $\frac{1}{4} \times 772 = 193$ ✓

Index

Page numbers in **bold** are definitions of terms.

Notes